THE CENTER
IS JESUS CHRIST
HIMSELF

THE CENTER
IS JESUS CHRIST
HIMSELF

Essays on Revelation,
Salvation & Evangelization
in Honor of
ROBERT P. IMBELLI

Edited by Andrew Meszaros
Foreword by Cardinal Timothy M. Dolan
Preface by Bishop James Massa

THE CATHOLIC UNIVERSITY OF AMERICA PRESS
Washington, D.C.

The paper used in this publication meets the minimum requirements of American National
Standards for Information Science — Permanence
of Paper for Printed Library Materials, ANSI Z39.48–1984.

∞

Design and composition by Kachergis Book Design

Library of Congress Cataloging-in-Publication Data

Names: Imbelli, Robert P., honoree. | Meszaros, Andrew, editor.
Title: The center is Jesus Christ himself : essays on revelation, salvation, and
evangelization in honor of Robert P. Imbelli / edited by Andrew Meszaros ;
foreword by Cardinal Timothy M. Dolan ; preface by Bishop James Massa.
Description: Washington, D.C. : The Catholic University of America Press, 2021. |
Includes bibliographical references and index.
Identifiers: LCCN 2021001950 | ISBN 9780813234106 (cloth)
Subjects: LCSH: Catholic Church — Doctrines.
Classification: LCC BX1751.3 .C39 2021
LC record available at https://lccn.loc.gov/2021001950

CONTENTS

Foreword   vii

CARDINAL TIMOTHY DOLAN

Preface   xi

BISHOP JAMES MASSA

Introduction and Acknowledgments   xv

ANDREW MESZAROS

1. Christocentrism in Theology and Evangelization in the Thought of Robert P. Imbelli   1

ANDREW MESZAROS

PART 1. THE CENTER OF REVELATION

2. Joseph Ratzinger Warming the Christic Imagination, October 1962   29

JARED WICKS, SJ

3. Salvation and the Holy Trinity: Interpersonal Relations with Jesus Christ and the Holy Spirit   52

FREDERICK LAWRENCE

4. Faith, Reason, and Incarnation in Irenaeus of Lyon   77

KHALED ANATOLIOS

5. Analogy and the *Analogatum Princeps* at Vatican II   95

THOMAS G. GUARINO

PART 2. THE CENTER OF THE ECONOMY OF SALVATION

6. Was Christ "Beautiful in Laying Down His Life" on the Cross?   111

GERALD O'COLLINS, SJ

7. Trinitarian Christology in the Gospel of Matthew   130
MATTHEW LEVERING

8. The Trinitarian Shape of the Mystical Body of Christ   153
in the Theology of Isaac of Stella
NATHANIEL PETERS

PART 3. THE CENTER OF THE CHRISTIAN LIFE

9. *Deus adorans, Homo adorans*: Joseph Ratzinger's   173
Liturgical Christology and Anthropology
CHRISTOPHER RUDDY

10. The Incarnate Word in Catholic Moral Theology: The   189
Christocentric Visions of Pope John Paul II and Robert Imbelli
RYAN CONNORS

11. "To weep with those who weep and to rejoice with those   205
who rejoice": Signature Divine Affectivity Humanly
Expressed in Hugh of St. Victor
BOYD TAYLOR COOLMAN

PART 4. THE CENTER OF EVANGELIZATION

12. Augustine the Preacher: Practicing the Rhetoric of Love   231
BRIAN E. DALEY, SJ

13. Spirit of Christ, Spirit of the Kingdom: Christocentrism   252
and a Pneumatology for Mission
ANDREW SALZMANN

14. The Mission and Person of Christ and the Christian   272
in Hans Urs von Balthasar
ANGELA FRANKS

15. The Creed of the Council of Chalcedon and the   300
New Evangelization
THOMAS WEINANDY, OFM, CAP

Bibliography   313
Contributors   331
Index   335

FOREWORD

CARDINAL TIMOTHY DOLAN
Archbishop of New York

Mihi vivere Christus est. For to me life is Christ (Phil 1:21). St. Paul's words to the Philippians serve as the motto of St. Joseph's Seminary, Dunwoodie, which has bookended Fr. Robert Imbelli's distinguished academic career. Fr. Imbelli first taught at Dunwoodie as a young priest and professor and has returned there now, in his retirement, to continue to educate future priests by his words and example.

I highlight this Philippians verse for two reasons. In the first place, Dunwoodie's motto could serve very much as Fr. Imbelli's own. He has devoted his academic life to the field of Christology, but even more significantly, he has devoted his priestly life to the person of Christ.

The Philippians verse, and its association with Dunwoodie, also calls to mind Father's lifelong connection to the Archdiocese of New York. Throughout his many years at Boston College, Fr. Imbelli remained a New Yorker at heart and always called the archdiocese home. Indeed, his many decades serving outside the archdiocese have made him something of an ambassador. Through his numerous writings, public lectures, university courses, and his service to the Church in the United States, Rome, and around the world, Fr. Imbelli has represented the archdiocese very well indeed. New York is honored to have been able to share such a fine priest with so many for so long.

That "ambassadorial service" includes, of course, the many students that Fr. Imbelli has taught and mentored over the past five decades, as well as the many scholars with whom Fr. Imbelli pursued theological wisdom. We all know those rare professors who stand out for their teaching excellence and personal warmth, and whose gift for friendship has forged bonds that long ago transcended the walls of a lecture hall. Fr. Imbelli certainly has that gift, and no surer proof is needed than the essays that follow. These authors, each of whom has now distinguished himself in his own field, demonstrate their admiration for their professor, their priest, their colleague, and their friend.

A festschrift such as this offers the opportunity to glimpse a legacy in tangible form, as former students who take wing and produce scholarship in their own right, and academic peers who worked with and even studied with Fr. Imbelli, pay tribute to a man who has played such a pivotal role in their own education. Festschrifts are quite rare, requiring the combination of a long and influential career and students sufficiently numerous, accomplished, and grateful. It is the mark of the very finest educators, and it is most fitting that Fr. Imbelli now joins that lofty company.

Among that company stands Pope Benedict XVI, who recently received the latest in a long series of festschrifts. Some observers have noted similarities in the academic trajectory of Joseph Ratzinger and Robert Imbelli. Both men began their teaching careers surrounding Vatican II, either in its preparation or immediate wake. Their work reflected the hope and promise of those exciting years. Always a man of the Church, Fr. Imbelli took up the Council's challenge to search for new ways of communicating the faith to the modern world.

Then-Cardinal Ratzinger and Fr. Imbelli also grounded those same promises in a healthy realism, especially amidst the confusion that reigned in the postconciliar years. Father welcomed the magisterium of Pope John Paul II, which did so much to clarify and confirm the Council's lasting impact. Despite easy caricatures of shifts and swings, however, Fr. Imbelli has stressed a papal continuum, writing, for example, that both Paul VI's *Evangelii nuntiandi* and Pope Francis' *Evangelii gaudium* speak to the "Christic heart" of Vatican II. That common thread, so needed in our own time of ecclesial division and polemics, can be traced in the career of Fr. Imbelli as well. His entire academic output, in words spoken and printed, has remained steadfastly fixed on the person of Jesus Christ who is, as Hebrew 13:9 tells us, "the same yesterday, today, and forever."

Such "Christocentricity" has at times made Father a voice crying in the wilderness of academia. When the name of Jesus has caused many theological faculties not to bow but to blush, and to devote more energy to apologies than apologetics, Fr. Imbelli has courageously challenged Catholic universities and publications to reject the lure of secular acclaim and instead to embrace their Catholic identity with fresh brio. He has taken seriously Our Lord's words about the salt that loses its flavor. In that mission, Father has stood among his own peers as a witness to the Good News. He has called them to a renewed discipleship that flows, quite simply, from being in love with Jesus Christ.

Fr. Imbelli, however, never confined his discipleship to the ivory tower. I mentioned earlier that Father has always remained a New Yorker at heart. He has also, and even more importantly, remained a parish priest at heart. Throughout his long years at Boston College, Father resided not in faculty housing but in a parish: celebrating Mass, preaching homilies, giving retreats, and showing his pastoral zeal. Father knows that all knowledge is rooted in the One who is the Truth (Jn 14:16) and who comes to us in the sacraments of his Church. Even in his well-earned "retirement," he continues to assist at a local parish in the Bronx every weekend. Fr. Imbelli has always seen only harmony between his priestly and professorial calling, and, whether from the pulpit or the lectern, he has desired to proclaim nothing "except Jesus Christ, and him crucified" (1 Cor 2:2).

Some years ago, in an address at Father's alma mater, the Gregorian University in Rome, Pope Francis reminded the students that theology must be done "on one's knees." The Holy Father's point, borrowing the famous phrase of Hans Urs von Balthasar, is that theology must always have prayer as its life source, rooted in a living faith, and seeking knowledge not for its own sake but in order to love Jesus Christ more perfectly. This present volume stands as a fitting tribute to a man who has toiled with great love in many parts of the Lord's vineyard. On the occasion of this festschrift, I offer my warm congratulations to this priest of New York, Fr. Robert Imbelli, to whom life is Christ.

PREFACE

BISHOP JAMES MASSA

Auxiliary Bishop and Rector, St. Joseph's Seminary

My friendship with Father Robert Imbelli began in the early 1990s at a conference devoted to assessing the experience of Catholics who had studied at theological schools founded or sponsored by other Christian denominations. Yale Divinity School hosted the gathering of ecclesial ministers and scholars who had all earned degrees from universities with historic divinity schools or large doctoral programs in religious studies like Yale, Chicago, and Duke. I had earned a Master of Divinity degree from Yale right out of college in the mid-1980s, roughly a decade and a half after Father Imbelli completed his PhD through the university's Department of Religious Studies. The conference presentations focused on whether theological education in a multiconfessional setting was adequate to the task of equipping Catholics with the necessary philosophical and theological resources necessary for being well-formed in their own ecclesial tradition.

Robert's experience at Yale was quite different from mine. He entered doctoral studies after having earned two prior degrees in theology while a seminarian in Rome during Vatican II (1962–1965). The Department of Religious Studies that he encountered in the late 1960s appeared divided and uncertain of its direction. Robert eventually wrote a dissertation on the religious philosopher Josiah Royce, a rather laborious exercise for him that served mainly to orient his thinking about the relationship between Christology and pneumatology. What proved to be of lasting influence, however, were the providential encounters with one of his dissertation readers who helped him edit, and ultimately complete the thesis, namely, the Lutheran theologian George Lindbeck (1923–2018).

Professor Lindbeck, who had served as an ecumenical observer at Vatican II, later became the chief spokesman for what would be called the "Yale School." His 1984 book, *The Nature of Doctrine: Religion and Theology in a Postliberal Age*, largely defined the postliberal approach to theology, which could be said to privilege the word of God (the biblical story) and the "work of God" (liturgy and other communal practices) in shaping the identity and life of the Christian community. The influence of Lindbeck and his colleague Hans Frei (d. 1988) on the Catholics of Yale—and those who would later become Catholic—is difficult to overestimate. For Father Imbelli and his contemporaries, Lindbeck's mature proposals would be digested, and critically so, long after they had completed graduate studies. Yet already in the period when Father Imbelli was completing his doctoral thesis, the post-liberal architect was pointing in a direction beyond the reductions of faith to subjective experience—so common in Liberal Protestant theology—and the fragmentation of theology overall into various ideological camps.

I locate the Yale period of Father Imbelli's career as an important marker in the genesis of his Christocentric theology. My reasons for doing so are twofold. For one, his own scholarship reflects postliberalism's commitment to ressourcement (the return to scripture and patristic and medieval texts) and its critique of liberal theologies that eclipse the primacy of God's revelation in Christ. The second reason has to do with the yet to be fully realized ecumenical potential of Robert's project for re-reading the history of inter-confessional conflict and doctrinal disputes through a Christocentric lens.

Nearly all the essays in this volume are penned by Catholic scholars who have been either students or colleagues of Father Imbelli. Together, they are a heartfelt summons to the Catholic theological world to restore the pre-eminence of the Church's faith in the Incarnate Word as the essential starting point for the theological craft. But the treatments of the broad range of themes contained herein are also, even if not explicitly stated, a demonstration to our sisters and brothers of other confessions of how scholarship in a Christological key can be a means of healing the wounds of the past and identifying new ground for professing the faith in common. This festschrift, after all, is dedicated to someone who has been engaged ecumenically since the days of his doctoral studies. He has served on the Anglican Roman

Catholic Dialogue in the United States and has been a regular contributor to journals, magazines, and blogs that engage Christians from varied ecclesial and cultural backgrounds.

"God was in Christ reconciling the world to himself," St. Paul tells the Church of Corinth (2 Cor 5:19). A return to the Christological center logically leads the theologian to engage in efforts to heal the rifts within, as well as between ecclesial communities. In that spirit, Father Imbelli became a leading member of the Catholic Common Ground Initiative in the 1990s, when relations in the United States among theologians of differing schools and between theologians and bishops had become particularly quarrelsome. The late Cardinal Joseph Bernardin of Chicago (1928–1996) enlisted Father Imbelli as his theological advisor for the project, as Robert was well known for engaging both sides of theological debates and for his fairmindedness when assessing positions differing from his own. Following the publication of the Common Ground mission statement, "Called to Be Catholic," Robert reminded both the initiative's supporters and critics of its second core principle that aimed at Christologically focusing all efforts at theological and inner-Church reconciliation: "Jesus Christ, present in Scripture and sacrament, is central to all that we do; he must always be the measure and not what is measured."

Whenever Father Imbelli enters into theological or ecclesial controversy, he does so with an irenic spirit that seeks to overcome false dichotomies. Yet it is a matter not merely of his style of expression but also of his way of doing theology that refers everything back to the mystery of Christ. The disjunction between exegesis and dogma begins to find a resolution for him when one sees the Incarnate Word in both his historical and ongoing ecclesial dimensions. The sharp distinction between a doctrinal paradigm and a pastoral paradigm in recent discourse, sometimes employed to contrast Vatican II with prior tradition or to compare recent pontificates, begins to be overcome when we realize that in the person of Christ, truth and love are one. Likewise, the service of worship and the task of theology, the episcopal office and the role of theologians should not be played off one another but rather understood in a relationship of mutual conditioning and support. Theology can be a reconciling work, and for theologians who envision their ministry Christologically, it is about the business of healing and building communion.

I hope this volume of Christologically inspired essays finds a broad readership among members of the guild, but also among pastors, seminarians, and lay women and men who are still finding their bearings in the theological world. The authors who write from their expertise in the various disciplines benefit from enjoying a shared faith in Christ as universal Redeemer and a communion of friendship with Father Imbelli. But like Pope Emeritus Benedict XVI's paradigm for the Church and her liturgy, the latter is an "open circle" that includes many great and holy participants from the recent past and distant ages. It is a wonderful book for acquiring a taste for theology at its ecclesial best.

As a bishop and fellow believer, I owe so much to Father Robert Imbelli. He has rekindled my "Christic imagination," enabling me to relish in surprisingly new ways the musical, artistic, and literary treasures of Catholic culture. He has introduced me to wonderful red wines in Italian restaurants in the Bronx and seafood pastas that I would never have contemplated eating. He has reined me in when I have veered away from the Christological center when grappling with the crises in today's Catholic Church, or when indulging in theological polemics that generate more heat than light. He has also helped me cultivate the practice of recalling the liturgical readings of the day so that they might shed some light on whatever might be the topic of conversation at hand. We have dined together hundreds of times since that Yale conference thirty years ago, when we first discovered our common experience of being educated in a multiconfessional setting and of our indebtedness to many of the same teachers. Every one of those meals has been a "little Emmaus," with bread broken and wine poured and the unmistakable presence of him who—in one of Robert's favorite quotes—brings "all newness by bringing himself" (St. Irenaeus).

INTRODUCTION

ANDREW MESZAROS

This book arose out of a desire to honor and thank a colleague of some, a teacher of many, and a priest for all. And for those who know Robert P. Imbelli, associate professor emeritus of Systematic Theology at Boston College, one sure way to do so is to collect essays that, together, confess the name that is above every name: the Lord Jesus.

Among his many contributions to the Church, two stand out. The first is his incisive diagnosis of the ecclesial crisis we have been experiencing for decades now; the second is the Christian demeanor with which he addresses that crisis. With respect to the crisis, Fr. Imbelli has suggested that the current polarization and partisanship within the Church, while complex in their genesis, are ultimately "symptoms of a more severe crisis: an eclipse of the enlivening and unifying center of the faith. That center is Jesus Christ himself."[1]

In living through and addressing this crisis, however, Fr. Imbelli has exhibited a serenity and charity that transcend *la controverse du jour*. One of his many counsels—written to me, a frustrated graduate student, years ago—is indicative: "I always find it important to go beyond positions that people may espouse in order to discern their underlying concerns. Hence one should read sympathetically, but also discerningly." Fr. Imbelli's patience,

---

1. Robert P. Imbelli, *Rekindling the Christic Imagination* (Collegeville, Minn.: Liturgical Press, 2014), xv.

joy, and humor in the midst of crisis reveal his deep faith in the Church, his profound respect for her tradition, and, ultimately, his love for her cofounders, Jesus Christ and his Holy Spirit.

Fr. Imbelli's virtue is what has allowed him to confront a very real crisis with sobriety and clear-sightedness. The theological eclipse of Christ manifests itself in an all-too-prevalent aversion to affirming Christ as unique and universal savior; it is also noticeable when theologians tacitly succumb to the demands of the culture rather than the Gospel, or when they acquiesce too easily to the rationalist and historicist criticisms of Christianity. According to Imbelli, the Church and her missionary efforts ail because Christ is eclipsed. In order to let Christ shine, theologians, for their part, have to bring him back to the center of their theology. Theology that relativizes the revelation of Christ and the salvation wrought in him becomes vulnerable to many pitfalls and ultimately weakens the pillars of ecclesial life, which support not only the Christian pursuit of a life in Christ but also the Christian duty to proclaim the Gospel.

In this respect, then, the year 2020 is significant, for we celebrate the 55th and 20th anniversaries of *Ad Gentes* and *Dominus Iesus*, respectively—documents in which the relationship between soteriology and missiology is brought to the fore. After having narrated the story of salvation in the missions of the Son and Spirit, *Ad Gentes* proclaims, "God, by means of mission, manifestly works out the history of salvation."[2] It is no accident that *Dominus Iesus* cites its elder ecumenical *auctoritas* seven times. Sensing that this evangelizing mission had become endangered by a host of erroneous philosophical and theological presuppositions, *Dominus Iesus* set out to confirm basic Christological and soteriological truths that *Ad Gentes* took for granted, such as (i) "the definitive and complete character of the revelation of Jesus Christ," (ii) "the unity of the economy of the Incarnate Word and the Holy Spirit," (iii) "universal salvific mediation of the Church," and (iv) "the unicity of the redemptive sacrifice of Christ, eternal high priest."[3] According to *Dominus Iesus,* then, the aspect of the Christian faith most vulnerable at this moment is Christological.

Such a commemorative year as 2020 offers itself to us as a fitting occasion to honor Robert P. Imbelli with essays that uphold, shore up, and penetrate

---

2. Vatican Council II, *Ad Gentes*, December 7, 1965, no. 9.

3. Congregation for the Doctrine of the Faith, *Dominus Iesus*, August 6, 2000, nos. 4 and 11.

great truths of our faith. All the essays in this volume are "Christocentric" to the extent that their authors, in their pursuit of a deeper understanding of one or another aspect of the faith, make privileged and indispensable reference to Christ, who "came as a light" to dispel darkness.

Christocentric theology is at its best when, as Fr. Imbelli exhorts so often, it is animated by appeals to the imagination (Meszaros). According to Joseph Ratzinger, Christ is the epiphany of God (Wicks) and the perfect worship of the Father (Ruddy). His sacrifice on the cross is beautiful (O'Collins), and through our encounter with Christ, the love of the Spirit is poured into our hearts (Lawrence). The volume unpacks the relationship between Christ and the Trinity in the Gospel of Matthew (Levering), on the one hand, and that between the Trinity and Christ's Body in the thought of Isaac of Stella (Peters), on the other. For Irenaeus of Lyons, faith and reason are synthesized in the Incarnation of Christ (Anatolios). The volume draws attention to the Christocentricity of Vatican II's texts, with Christ as the "source" in which we all participate in analogous ways (Guarino). The volume also highlights the transformative power of infused virtues (Connors) and draws attention to those virtues—*compassio* and *congratulatio*—often forgotten or underappreciated (Coolman), as elements of the Christian life that result not from our own merits but from God's grace mediated to us by Christ. The catechist and preacher receive counsel from St. Augustine on how to use wisely and effectively the Scriptures (Daley). The volume upholds the unity of the missions of the Son and Spirit (Salzmann), and elaborates on the transformative consequence of the Son's mission on our personhood (Franks). The volume also affirms the great Christological confession of Chalcedon, and examines its significance for evangelization (Weinandy).

This collection of essays, then, is a specimen of the major contours of a Christocentric theology. Together, the essays exhibit—more by example than by metareflections on method—how Christocentric theology anchors theological subdisciplines (e.g., dogmatic, moral, biblical, historical, etc.) in the Center that alone is capable of holding them together. Further, the essays tighten the theological coherence between various avenues of theological inquiry, such as Trinitarian theology, Christology, pneumatology, and missiology.

As these essays will confirm, Christocentric theology is not the same as reducing all theological disciplines to Christology, nor is it to be judged according to how many times the name of Christ appears (although any absence of *the* Name usually indicates a problem). Rather, Christocentric theology is determined by the position occupied by Jesus Christ. What is it, or better, Who is it, who "holds all things together" (Col 1:17) in one's theology? Is a given theology shot through with the conviction that in Christ shines forth "the deepest truth about God and the salvation of man"?[4]

We give thanks to Fr. Imbelli for his teaching, mentorship, feedback, and prayers over many years. Since I first met Fr. Imbelli during my undergraduate years at Boston College, I have become acquainted with his penchant for either photocopying or emailing texts of interest. In this way, colleagues, friends, and students have received hundreds of texts from him to read. With this festschrift of fifteen essays, we begin to return the favor.

Thank you, Fr. I.

4. Vatican Council II, *Dei Verbum*, November 18, 1965, no. 2.

ACKNOWLEDGMENTS

I would like to thank the Scholastic Trust at St. Patrick's College, Maynooth, as well as Fr. William Leahy, SJ, at Boston College for their generous support of this project. I am also grateful to the staff at the Catholic University of America Press for all their help. Finally, warm thanks go out to all the contributors to this volume and to the inspiration behind it: Fr. Robert P. Imbelli.

He must increase, but I must decrease.
—*John 3:30*

Man can vary and perfect his culture without end. He can discover and exploit new potentialities in it. The very Universe can grow immeasurably, and distant stars can one day reveal a humanity more numerous, more civilized — more miserable — than our own: the Deed of Christ would still take it in. It embraces all worlds, just as it shines above time. For all equally, for each one of us and at all times, for those who believe in man and for those who despair of him, its rays are those of Eternal Life.

— Henri de Lubac, SJ

Praise to the Holiest in the height
And in the depth be praise:
In all His words most wonderful;
Most sure in all His ways!

O loving wisdom of our God!
When all was sin and shame,
A second Adam to the fight
And to the rescue came.

O wisest love! that flesh and blood,
which did in Adam fail,
should strive afresh against the foe,
should strive and should prevail

And that a higher gift than grace
should flesh and blood refine,
God's presence and his very self,
and essence all-divine.

O generous love! That He who smote
In man for man the foe,
The double agony in man
For man should undergo;

And in the garden secretly,
And on the cross on high,
Should teach His brethren and inspire
To suffer and to die.

— St. John Henry Newman

I

Christocentrism in Theology and Evangelization in the Thought of Robert P. Imbelli

ANDREW MESZAROS

One can only lament the fact that more than fifty years after what was meant to be a "new Pentecost," the Church finds herself in a quagmire of intraecclesial debates rather than throwing all of her energy behind mission and evangelization. The hope expressed in this paper is that a Christocentric theology—and more generally, an ecclesial life with Christ at its center—will help convert us away from the "self-referentiality" repeatedly deployed by postconciliar theologians and, especially, Pope Francis, and refocus us toward the main tasks given to us by Christ and reiterated authoritatively at Vatican II: sanctity and evangelization.

Over the years, what has been characteristic of Robert P. Imbelli's theological writings is his laser beam–like focus on Christ-centered teaching, preaching, and writing. For anyone who knows Fr. Imbelli, his theological interests are many, and his cultivated appreciation for the Catholic tradition as a whole—including music and the fine arts—is conspicuous and, especially for the younger generation of theologians, commendable. Perhaps the priority on his theological agenda, however, is to reawaken in us a sense of the radical novelty, uniqueness, and life-altering event of the Incarnation. His defense and elaboration of the salvific universality of Christ is one component of his struggle against a certain kind of "Christological amnesia," an amnesia that

for years now seems to have afflicted some Catholic colleges, organizations, and journals. It manifests itself in vapid mission statements and generic-brand editorial exhortations. It is as though one blushed to mention the Name, lest one be considered crassly triumphalist or lacking in ecumenical sensibility.[1]

Of course, Imbelli is not after rhetorical lip service to the savior. Christocentricity is not a quantitative category, but the conspicuous absence of the Name above all other names is indicative of a theological trend that is impoverished and, indeed, failing to serve the proclamation of the Gospel. All Catholics, but especially those charged with educating and ministering, have to ask themselves seriously: To what extent have we indeed "fallen from our first love" (Rev 2:4).[2]

In the three sections of this paper, I use the writings of Imbelli to lay out the rationale, contours, and promises of Christocentric theology.[3] I will first provide some examples of the Christological amnesia that has beset Catholic theology since Vatican II. Next, I will discuss the salient characteristics of a Christocentric theology and how it can help carry forward the missionary and evangelical vision of Vatican II. Finally, I appeal to the thought of John Henry Newman to help unpack some of the major entailments of the "Christic imagination," which Imbelli shows to be a *sine qua non* for the new evangelization.[4]

1. Robert P. Imbelli, "At the Name of Jesus," *The Catholic Thing,* January 21, 2018, https://www.thecatholicthing.org/2018/01/21/at-the-name-of-jesus/, accessed September 10, 2018.

2. Imbelli, "At the Name of Jesus."

3. I warmly recommend Imbelli's award-winning and eminently readable *Rekindling the Christic Imagination: Theological Meditations for the New Evangelization* (Collegeville, Minn.: Liturgical Press, 2014). My essay is no substitute for it. I have, therefore, purposefully focused on and drawn from Imbelli's other writings, before and since this gem of a book.

4. Imbelli himself appeals to Newman in his reflections on the imagination. I simply carry these reflections further here. See "Refashioning Catholic Imagination: Newman's writings offer a framework for a new way of thinking," *America* 203, no. 7 September 27, 2010, https://www.americamagazine.org/issue/748/article/refashioning-catholic-imagination, accessed September 17, 2018.

What Happened after Vatican II?

Having had the privilege of completing his theological studies in Rome during Vatican II, Imbelli was and remains a defender of the Council, its texts, and the Church's ongoing appropriation of them. His enthusiasm for the conciliar documents, however, is due, not to their historical novelty, but to their kerygmatic strength. The kerygma, of course, is the proclamation of Jesus Christ. Imbelli's interpretation of the Council, then, clearly follows a Lubacian line.[5]

The Christocentricity of Vatican II

The *raison d'etre* behind any *aggiornamento* was ultimately evangelization:

> In September 1963, Paul summed up the goal of the Council in these words: "to proclaim to the whole world ... that Christ is our beginning and guide, our way, our hope, and our goal." Each of the documents that the Council laboriously produced ... bears this clear Christological imprint.[6]

In so many of his writings, Imbelli highlights this "imprint." Here is just a taste of what all the council fathers and theologians both assumed and wished to communicate:

> *Dei Verbum* 2: The deepest truth about God and the salvation of man shines out for our sake in Christ, who is both the mediator and the fullness of all revelation.[7]
>
> *Lumen Gentium* 1: Christ is the Light of nations.[8]
>
> *Sacrosanctum Concilium* 9: Therefore the Church announces the good tidings of salvation to those who do not believe, so that all men may know the

5. Henri de Lubac's Christocentric influence on both the council and the thought of Imbelli is evident. De Lubac is, in a sense, a privileged interpreter of the council for Imbelli. For a study on the Christocentricity of de Lubac's thought, see Donath Hercsik, *Jesus Christus als Mitte der Theologie von Henri de Lubac*, Frankfurter Theologische Studien 61 (Frankfurt: Knecht, 2001).

6. Robert P. Imbelli, "The Transfiguration of Humanity (Homage to Paul VI)," *The Catholic Thing*, August 6, 2017, https://www.thecatholicthing.org/2017/08/06/the-transfiguration-of-humanity-homage-to-paul-vi/, accessed September 10, 2018.

7. Vatican Council II, *Dei Verbum*, November 18, 1965, no. 2; all Vatican II documents are available at vatican.va.

8. Vatican Council II, *Lumen Gentium*, November 21, 1964, no. 1.

true God and Jesus Christ whom He has sent, and may be converted from their ways, doing penance.[9]

Gaudium et Spes 10: The Church firmly believes that Christ, who died and was raised up for all, can through His Spirit offer man the light and the strength to measure up to his supreme destiny. Nor has any other name under the heaven been given to man by which it is fitting for him to be saved. She likewise holds that in her most benign Lord and Master can be found the key, the focal point and the goal of man, as well as of all human history. The Church also maintains that beneath all changes there are many realities which do not change and which have their ulti-mate foundation in Christ, Who is the same yesterday and today, yes and forever. Hence under the light of Christ, the image of the unseen God, the firstborn of every creature, the council wishes to speak to all men in order to shed light on the mystery of man and to cooperate in finding the solution to the outstanding problems of our time.[10]

These passages are indicative. Similar passages are ubiquitous through-out the conciliar corpus.[11] Their didactic mode and declaratory voice are at the service of evangelization. But in declaring the object of this evangeliza-tion, the documents are expressing a revealed *datum* that all the council fa-thers believed and, indeed, accepted as *given*: namely, the Christological sub-stance of the faith that God became man to save us from our sins and death.

Among the constitutions, Imbelli advocates giving hermeneutical pri-ority to *Dei Verbum*. This means that theologians, taking into account the virtues of 'inter-textual' reading of the texts, ought to view *Dei Verbum* as foundational because any theological assertion has to be rooted in God's revelation, whose pinnacle and goal is Jesus Christ. *Dei Verbum* merits the position *primus inter pares* because "it establishes the *revelatory given* which is foundational to all else that the council says, the Word from which all else derives. And that foundation is Christological: Jesus Christ is the foundation upon which all is built."[12]

---

9. Vatican Council II, *Sacrosanctum Concilium*, December 4, 1963, no. 9.

10. Vatican Council II, *Gaudium et Spes*, December 7, 1965, no. 10.

11. Another example is the entire first chapter of *Lumen Gentium*, "The Mystery of the Church." See also *Gaudium et Spes*, nos. 22, 45.

12. Robert P. Imbelli, "Receiving Vatican II: Renewing the Christic Center," *Lonergan Workshop* 26 (2012): 190. Elsewhere, Imbelli puts it slightly differently: *Dei Verbum* has priority, "for if God has not revealed Himself, all else — liturgy, Church order, mission — is mere human construct. And

If this "Christological imprint" throughout the conciliar documents is ubiquitous, why have significant portions of postconciliar theological reflection failed to produce the same kerygmatic thrust? At best, Catholics have lost a sense of urgency; at worst, we are witnessing a "silent apostasy."

Christological Amnesia

One self-inflicted problem the Catholic Church faces is an amnesia or eclipse of Christ, most problematically among Catholic academics. In a word, elements of liberal Protestantism have crept into Catholic theological discourse. H. Richard Niebuhr summed up this liberalism well: "a God without wrath brought men without sin into a Kingdom without judgment through the ministrations of a Christ without a cross."[13]

In a column more than twenty-five years ago, Imbelli summed up the problem as one of Christological doubt:

Before the Christological question, "who do you say I am?" some stand mute, while others confess other ultimate loyalties, thereby eroding the one foundation upon which all baptized Christians, whether professional theologians or not, can stand securely. In many and varied guises a Christological "de-centering" is abroad in the guild of academic theologians: whether in the name of ecumenical openness, feminist suspicion, or deconstructive ambiguity and pluralism. But the outcome of this massive assault is to evacuate the gospel of its distinctive content: the proclamation and celebration that Jesus Christ is Lord.[14]

Such "Christological minimalism" often manifests itself in selective omissions of Jesus or his more controversial claims (or both). As just one example, the Jesuit motto "Men for others," instilled in students as a motivation toward service, is rarely if ever communicated with the Christological sub-

---

if God's fullness does not truly shine forth in Jesus Christ, the eternal Word who has become one of us, even unto death, death on a cross, then there is no distinctive originality to Christian revelation." Robert P. Imbelli, "Eucharist and New Creation," *The Catholic Thing*, March 29, 2018, https://www .thecatholicthing.org/2018/03/29/eucharist-and-new-creation/, accessed September 13, 2018.

13. H. Richard Niebuhr, *The Kingdom of God in America* (1937), quoted in Robert P. Imbelli, "A Pure Distillation of 1970's Catholicism," *The Catholic Thing*, August 28, 2016, https://www .thecatholicthing.org/2016/08/28/a-pure-distillation-of-1970s-catholicism/. C. S. Lewis called it "Christianity-and-water" in *Mere Christianity*, originally in his *Broadcast Talks* (London: Geoffrey Bles, 1942), 41.

14. Robert P. Imbelli, "'Dual Loyalties in Catholic Theology': An Exchange of Views," *Commonweal*, April 24, 1992, 21–22.

stance that Pedro Arrupe SJ originally attached to it: the "Man-for-others."[15] The horizontal thrust, however important, usually comes at the expense of the vertical.

For his part, Imbelli identifies three popular theological tendencies that run the risk of Christological eclipse: portraying Jesus as a prophet (and often reducing him to one in the process); highlighting the ethical program of Christianity (and often reducing Christianity to the ethical program); and, following from the first two, a theology of the "consequential cross."[16] That is, some contemporary theology—even Catholic theology!—holds that salvation was completed by Christ during his earthly ministry, through his teaching, healing, and radical challenge to authorities for which, of course, he was crucified; but the cross was a consequence of the salvation he had already wrought and which had made him so unpopular.[17] One hears a variation of this in the claim—in itself legitimate but often distorted—"Jesus preached the coming of the kingdom of God, not himself."[18]

No wonder, Imbelli reflects, that despite all the exhortations for a "new evangelization," we are making little progress, especially if "Jesus is just another voice, hawking his wares in the secular wilderness."[19] The question

---

15. Robert P. Imbelli, "Commentary: At the Name of Jesus," *First Things*, September 19, 2018, https://www.firstthings.com/web-exclusives/2018/10/letters-from-the-synod-2018-13, accessed October 19, 2018. The full text of Arrupe's can be found at https://jesuitportal.bc.edu/research/documents / 1973 _arrupemenforothers/, accessed October 31, 2018.

The relevant text of Arrupe reads: "Today our prime educational objective must be to form men-for-others; men who will live not for themselves but for God and his Christ—for the God-man who lived and died for all the world; men who cannot even conceive of love of God which does not include love for the least of their neighbors; men completely convinced that love of God which does not issue in justice for men is a farce."

Arrupe continues: The man for others *"is the man filled with the Spirit; and we know whose Spirit that is: the Spirit of Christ, who gave his life for the salvation of the world; the God who, by becoming Man, became, beyond all others, a Man-for-others."* For a similar example of reductionism with respect to Irenaeus's great dictum, see Robert Imbelli, "Christ Brings All Newness," *The Catholic Thing*, December 13, 2015, https://www.thecatholicthing.org/2015/12/13/christ-brings-all-newness/, accessed September 7, 2018.

16. The phrase belongs to William Frazier in "The Incredible Christian Capacity for Missing the Christian Point," *America* 167, no. 16, November 21, 1992.

17. Imbelli, "Receiving Vatican II," 193–97.

18. Jim Purcell, "Focus on Preaching the Kingdom Is Key to Ending Clericalism," *National Catholic Reporter*, August 20, 2016, https://www.ncronline.org/news/spirituality/focus-preaching-kingdom-key-ending-clericalism, accessed September 10, 2018. For Imbelli's take on this, see Imbelli, "A Pure Distillation of 1970's Catholicism."

19. Imbelli, "A Pure Distillation of 1970's Catholicism."

put forward by John Courtney Murray, "What think ye of the *homoousion?*" situated as it was in an ecumenical context, is now just as relevant for Catholic theologians themselves. In other words, it is increasingly necessary to engage in a kind of quasi intra-Catholic ecumenism between those who would either maintain and defend, on the one hand, or diminish and relativize, on the other, the major Christological dogmas and soteriological claims attached to them. The reactions to *Dominus Iesus* were indicative of this intraecclesial tension.

On *Dominus Iesus*

In 2000, a theological firestorm ensued when the Congregation for the Doctrine of the Faith issued a declaration, "On the Unicity and Salvific Universality of Jesus Christ and the Church," with the incipit, *Dominus Iesus*. The negative reactions to *Dominus Iesus* ranged from taking offense to, to dismissal of, and derision at the CDF. The reaction in *Commonweal* was indicative. One Protestant and two Catholics responded to the document. According to the Protestant reaction, *Dominus Iesus,* far from bringing clarity about the faith, offered instead "few clues as to how to reason about the truth" and "its claims have to do with authority." It was a "missed opportunity." "Instead of having an intellectually vibrant encounter among Catholic thinkers and with others, many see a reversion to pre–Vatican II declarations."[20]

From a Catholic perspective, Philip Kennedy opined that *Dominus Iesus* was a "rhetorically somber though theologically questionable document," "a forceful text" yet "far from convincing." It constituted a "setback in Catholic teaching rather than an advance," and the dogmatic reasoning behind this is that

Because God is illimitable, no historical reality can manifest the full richness of God. Jesus Christ is not the complete revelation of God in history, but a partial manifestation of what God may be like. Since Jesus is not the unveiling of the fullness of God in the world, other religions may have their say about God's salvific nature. Even according to classical dogmatic theology, Jesus Christ is the enfleshment in history of the Second Person of the Trinity. The fullness of the Trinity is not incarnate in Jesus. Consequently, there is more to God, so to speak, than has been shown in Jesus Christ.[21]

20. Martin E. Marty in Martin E. Marty, Robert P. Imbelli, and Philip Kennedy, "Rome and Relativism: '*Dominus Iesus*' and the CDF," *Commonweal*, October 20, 2000, 12–15, 12–13.

21. Philip Kennedy in Marty, Imbelli, and Kennedy, "Rome and Relativism," 14–15.

Whether Kennedy's passage here amounts to an unqualified denial of *Dei Verbum* 2 is a question that would require more space to ascertain.[22] But what is indisputable is that for Kennedy, the Incarnation's revelatory, and therefore salvific, import has limits, and these limits are attributable to something other than our finitude and God's infinite mystery. It is further attributable to the fact that the *second* person of the Trinity became incarnate and not, say, all three.[23] The question arises, however: Is it up to us to determine *how and through whom* a Trinitarian God, in his own wisdom, would choose to *reveal himself to humans*? Either way, the upshot is that, for Kennedy, with respect to what we know about God and salvation, the case is still open, the jury still out.

Imbelli's reaction, in contrast to those of the other two contributors, could not have been more different. While he understands the unease over the document's tone or the discomfiture at certain omissions, the document amounts to nothing more than a reaffirmation of the Christic center of the faith at a time when this central doctrinal content is no longer taken for granted in the way it had been. This is a time, rather, of "Christological drift and ambiguity" in which

> some are suggesting "multiple incarnations" of the Christ, or that Jesus is Savior only for Christians, or that the salvific role of the Spirit is more universal than that of Jesus Christ, or that the Trinity is but one "model" for speaking of the incomprehensible mystery of God. Such "unitarianism of the Spirit" is no figment of some over-heated Roman imagination. It appears in print, both at a popular and a more sophisticated theological level. If the Church's magisterium cannot authoritatively declare that such is not "the faith delivered once and for all to the saints" (Jude 3), then there is no legitimate role for the magisterium. It is simply otiose.[24]

---

22. According to *Dei Verbum* 2, Christ is the "mediator simul et plentitudo totius revelationis." Colossians 2:9 is another text that must be reckoned with: "For in him the whole fullness of deity dwells bodily."

23. The revelation of the *Trinity* happens precisely *through* the sending of the Son and Spirit. Suggesting — even if only obliquely — that the fullness of revelation could only be accomplished if all three persons were to be incarnate seems to ignore the role of the pneumatological mission as that which reveals the Son. How else is a *Trinitarian* God meant to reveal himself?

24. Robert P. Imbelli, "The Reaffirmation of the Christic Center," in *Sic et Non: Encountering "Dominus Iesus,"* ed. Stephen J. Pope and Charles Hefling (Maryknoll, N.Y.: Orbis, 2002), 99–100.

The allergic and at times even rancorous reactions to the document stem, according to Imbelli, from a decades-long selective reading of Vatican II texts that missed the forest for the trees. The uniqueness and universal salvific significance of Christ was "professed and presumed by Vatican II." Indeed, it guaranteed the legitimacy of the council and its continuity with tradition. Setting aside this Christological substance for too long caused the shock. "There is abroad a measure of innocent and sometimes quite intentional apostasy."[25]

Of course, other salient issues in *Dominus Iesus* emerge that have always merited and indeed garnered for themselves theological reflection, such as the precise role that the Church plays in the salvation of the non-Christian, or the precise relationship between the work of the Son and the Spirit. The document itself exhorts theological reflection in these areas, including, for example, "if and in what way the historical figures and positive elements of these religions may fall within the divine plan of salvation."[26] But these questions acquire importance and, in fact, can only be asked precisely, indeed only, because, "we have seen and testify that the Father has sent his Son to be the Savior of the world" (1 Jn 4:14). Any qualification or relativization of the unique and universal salvific efficacy of Christ alters the doctrine of the Incarnation and hence curbs the revelation of God to humankind.

Christocentric Vision for Theology

Unpacking the relationship between theology, on the one hand, and the person of Jesus Christ, on the other, is a delicate task. In examining Imbelli's Christocentrism, one observes that he is not dipping into a debate over the specific organizing principle of theology akin to those in the first half of the twentieth century. Nor is Christocentrism in competition with pneumatology, or to be pitted against "Theocentrism."[27] Rather, Imbelli is promoting Christocentrism as a response to a certain Christological amnesia that

25. Robert Imbelli in Marty, Imbelli, and Kennedy, "Rome and Relativism," 13. This essay forms part of the larger reflection published as "The Reaffirmation of the Christic Center."

26. *Dominus Iesus*, 14. The entire text is published in Pope and Hefling, *Sic et Non*, 3–23.

27. Jacques Dupuis and Joseph Ratzinger are, in this respect, in accord. Dupuis: "Christian theology is not faced with the dilemma of being either Christocentric or theocentric; it is theocentric by being Christocentric and *vice-versa*. Ratzinger: "Christocentrism presupposes the event of God becoming man and is, therefore, at bottom nothing other than Theocentrism."

See Jacques Dupuis, *Toward a Christian Theology of Religious Pluralism* (Maryknoll, N.Y.: Orbis,

is a betrayal of the Council. It is not so much a theological methodology as a set of priorities to be recovered that would be at the service of the new evangelization.

Theology and Evangelization

Imbelli's writings express a profound theological instinct concerning theology and mission. It is an instinct that senses the profound connection between a Christ-centered theology, on the one hand, and salvation, on the other. John Paul II expressed it thusly when he addressed the Augustinian Patristics Institute:

Placing oneself, therefore, in the school of the fathers means learning to know Christ better and to know the human person better. This knowledge ... will enormously help the church in the mission of preaching to all, as she does tirelessly, that Christ alone is our salvation.[28]

The soteriological end dictates the program. If one does not believe that in Christ alone we are saved, then one will not preach it or teach it. And if one will not preach or teach salvation in Christ, the theological formation and study that is geared toward that preaching and teaching need not prioritize, in the Pope's words, "learning to know Christ better."

In commenting on *Dominus Iesus*, Imbelli notes the link between soteriology and the discipline of theology:

Christological normativity, the uniqueness and salvific universality of Jesus Christ, was not invented by the current [2000] CDF. It is simply the doctrine of the faith. *Dominus Iesus'* reaffirmation of this faith does not preclude further theological investigation. Indeed, the declaration several times encourages precisely such reflection. . . . But such theological exploration must be faithful to the dogmatic content of revelation, if it is truly to be theology: faith seeking understanding.[29]

1997), 191; Joseph Ratzinger, "Toward a Theory of Preaching," in *Dogma and Preaching: Applying Christian Doctrine to Daily Life* (San Francisco: Ignatius Press, 2011), 45.

28. John Paul II, "Address to Professors and Students of the Augustinian Patristics Institute (*Sono Lieto*)," May 8, 1982, *AAS* 74 (1982): 798, quoted in Congregation for Catholic Education, "Instruction on the Study of the Fathers of the Church in the Formation of Priests," *Origins* 19, no. 34 (1990): 560, n.13.

29. Imbelli in Marty, Imbelli, and Kennedy, "Rome and Relativism," 14.

Here, Imbelli makes the critical observation that the Christological substance of the faith does not preclude, and in fact calls for further, theological investigation. In doing so, however, he is tacitly asking every theologian the question: Of which faith, exactly, am I seeking understanding? Is it the Catholic faith according to which, besides Christ, "there is no other name under heaven" (Acts 4:12)? Or is it some other?

What Is Christocentric Theology?

With Imbelli, we can look to the Congregation for Catholic Education's 1989 "Instruction" on Patristic studies to identify the characteristics of a Christocentric theology. That document describes the theology of the Fathers as "Christ centered." The Congregation writes that their theology "is entirely *centered* on the mystery of Christ, to whom all the individual truths are referred in a wonderful synthesis." The question naturally arises about what it means "to center" something on someone else. The document continues:

Rather than getting lost in numerous marginal problems, the fathers seek to embrace the totality of the Christian mystery by following the basic movement of revelation and of the economy of salvation that goes from God through Christ to the church, sacrament of union with God and dispenser of divine grace, in order to return to God.[30]

In this tripartite schema—God, Christ, and Church—Christ is in the middle; he is at the center. God reveals through Christ, and humankind returns to God through Christ. This is not only the heart of the Christian faith but also precisely what makes the Christian faith unique.

The virtues of Patristic theology need not be limited to that era. Nor does Christocentric theology imply that all theology must become patrology. In the Fathers we have exemplars of doing theology well, and we would do well to imitate them, and, in continuity with Catholic tradition, imitate the way in which subsequent generations of theologians, such as the great medievals, faithfully received them. In other words, a robust Christocentricity is not only characteristic of Patristic thought but perennially valid.

In addition to naming the unique substance of the Christian faith, Christocentric theology also involves *referring* all things under theological consideration to Christ. Study of the Church and sacraments, for example,

---

30. Congregation for Catholic Education, "Instruction on the Study of the Fathers," 555.

must find reference to Christ; even the study of God and the Trinity must have reference (at least eventually) to God's revelation in Christ.

The same is the case with moral doctrine and concern to address contemporary needs in the world. With respect to morals, a Christocentric theology's prime pastoral-theological task would be "to admonish and teach so as to 'present everyone perfect [*teleion*] in Christ' (Col 1:27–28)."[31] Similarly, pastoral action, outreach, and social doctrine must be "brought back to charity, and charity to Christ, the universal way of salvation."[32] Christocentric theology has as its center Christ because the deification or even "Christification" as expressed in, say, Galatians 2:20, is the end of all preaching and teaching, and therefore, by implication, of theology.[33]

I have been crucified with Christ; it is no longer I who live, but Christ who lives in me; and the life I now live in the flesh I live by faith in the Son of God, who loved me and gave himself for me (Gal 2:20).

Commenting on this passage, Imbelli observes, "Christic conversion entails this radical de-centering of self and re-centering in Christ: a transformed subjectivity."[34] With respect to our theology and preaching, this means that if we want Christ at the center of our lives, he needs to be at the center of our ecclesial discourse.

Christocentric theology, then, means, for a start, stating boldly the Christological substance of the faith: Incarnation, redemption, and transformation. Secondly, it means that all of the questions considered in theological discourse—whether morals or ecclesiastical structures, or whatever—should be "centered" on, or given reference to, Jesus Christ, lest a distorted vision of the Christian faith is promoted, whether intentionally or not.[35]

This reference to Christ is crucial for the New Evangelization because

---

31. Robert P. Imbelli, "'Mercy and 'Metanoia,'" *The Catholic Thing*, September 11, 2016, https://www.thecatholicthing.org/2016/09/11/mercy-and-metanoia/, accessed September 10, 2018.

32. Congregation for Catholic Education, "Instruction on the Study of the Fathers," 558, quoted by Imbelli in "Mercy and 'Metanoia.'"

33. Imbelli, "Eucharist and New Creation."

34. Imbelli, "Receiving Vatican II," 204.

35. It seems to me that this "centering" of realities on Jesus Christ is but a more proximate and intermediate theological step before relating Christ to God the Son, and thereby to God the Trinity, and then to God considered in his unity. Again, admitting that no such position is being staked out by Imbelli, a robustly Christocentric theology seems compatible with a theology that proceeds to examine all things *sub ratione Dei*.

the person of Christ is, among all the realities contained in the one mystery of the Christian faith, the reality that is closest to us, most accessible, most *personal*: God in the flesh. Of course, this person of Christ is mediated to us through word, sacrament, and sacramentals, but this same person, his voice, his teaching, and his deeds and example, are capable of impressing the imagination and touching the heart more than other realities. Other mysteries of the faith, no less real, include, for example, grace and the capacity for heroic virtue, the indissoluble bond of matrimony, the indefectibility of the Church, the human's image and likeness to God, Mary's Immaculate Conception and Assumption into heaven, and God's providence and human suffering, to name only a few. To be sure, these realities can only ever be partially understood, but how much more impoverished would our understanding of them be without reference to Christ? Christocentric theology refers these realities to Christ, in whom we find "the love which moves the Sun and the other stars."[36] If we can relate these realities to Christ—realities which may very well seem distant, extraneous, or inconsequential at first sight—then we can better see their relevance, their consequence, and their beauty.

Next to embracing the theological approach itself, schools and departments of Catholic theology can foster Christocentric theology with two undertakings. The first would be to prioritize a shared liturgical context for doing theology, especially at modern research universities where so much of contemporary theology is now practiced.[37] As Imbelli has consistently pointed out, a doxological starting point is key to Christocentric theology:

The Christological center of Christian faith is manifest in the church's worship "through Jesus Christ our Lord," but it also permeates and "informs" all Christian reflection and action. As [Franz Jozef] van Beeck forthrightly avers: " the Catholic church and her members can make no real sense, either of their identity or of their mission, unless they go back to their abiding foundation: the risen Lord."[38]

36. Dante Alighieri, *The Divine Comedy*, trans. C. H. Sisson (Oxford: Oxford University Press, 2008, orig. 1980), *Paradiso* XXXIII, 145; cf. Imbelli, *Rekindling the Christic Imagination*, 21–43.

37. That the seminary is no longer the privileged locus of Catholic theology necessitates some adjustments. See Robert P. Imbelli, "Continue the Conversation: Suggestions for theologians and bishops in search of common ground," *America*, May 30, 2011, https://www.americamagazine.org/issue/778/article/continue-conversation, accessed September 17, 2018.

38. Robert P. Imbelli, "Catholic Identity after Vatican II: The Theology of Frans Jozef van Beeck," *Commonweal*, March 11, 1994, 14. Imbelli continues: "Such emphasis upon the centrality of Christ for Christian vision and mission might appear tautological were it not that the

Imbelli, following van Beeck, identifies the link between "Christian reflection" (i.e., theology) and soteriology as the commission of the risen and ascending Lord: "Go teach!"

Another undertaking for faculties of theology is to resist a retrenchment of their kerygmatic obligations. Academic theology's laudable inclination toward "advancing the field of research" or "contributing to global challenges" are too often shored up with refrains such as "We do theology, not (advanced) catechetics." Such refrains express the desire to maintain a legitimate sphere for creativity but are invoked all too often in support of a scholarly sovereignty. A Christocentric theology, however — where Christ stands as a mediator between God and the Church, and the Church between Christ and the world — cannot but be an ecclesial theology at the service of the Church's mission.[39] In sum, to cultivate Christocentric theology, especially at research universities, will require a liturgical context and a willingness to assist in the Church's proclamation.

Ad fontes! Common Sources for Catholic Theology

Christocentric theology can help dissolve a seemingly insurmountable polarization among Catholic theologians. For Imbelli, dissolving this polarization is indeed about finding the center, but this center has nothing to do with a compromise between two extremes. Healing polarization involves refinding the Center who is Jesus. Everything else stems from this.

Discussions and debates about the Church's self-organization, its moral exhortations, its doctrines, its sacramental and liturgical rituals and disciplines will bear fruit only if these discussions are Christocentric. That is, for the debates to make any progress, they must appeal to the center of God's revelation and the witnesses thereto. The tension, for example, stemming from selective attention to certain texts between those whose preferred chapter of *Lumen Gentium* is chapter 3, "On the Hierarchy," versus those who prefer chapter 2, "On the People of God," can only begin to be addressed if we refocus our gaze on chapter 1, "On the Mystery of the

---

Christological center (which Vatican II took as a given) needs today to be recovered in a way that is creative and compelling, in the face of and (one dares hope) as a reconciliation of the polarizations that have plagued the post–Vatican II period. Certainly, one of the main attractions of van Beeck's synthesis is *the centrality of the person of Jesus Christ in his theology and the clearly Christic form of his spirituality*" (my emphasis).

39. Imbelli, "Continue the Conversation."

Church," — the Church whose beginning and end is Christ.[40] The profoundest "re-Sourcement" is a return to the "Christian faith's enlivening Source, Jesus Christ."[41]

This is not a truism or a platitude. It has concrete consequences for Catholic theological methodology. Today, it is too often the case that different theological "camps" do not even speak the same language. They appeal to different authorities and place heavy argumentative burdens on individual theologians, usually from the twentieth century. Some, through a defective understanding of "development," see little — if any — need to demonstrate continuity with the past. The clearest manifestation of this is both sides' appealing predominantly to particular texts by their preferred pontiff — whether recently deceased, emeritus, or currently in office — rather than arguing from the scriptures and their traditional glosses to a given conclusion. For all the tension and differences among the "majority" and "minority" at Vatican II, they all agreed on their fundamental Catholic theological principles, and that *texts* were crucial to showing, not imposing, a conclusion to an argument.

A Christocentric theology helps retrieve common theological principles and authoritative sources and texts to which interlocutors on all "sides," as it were, buy into. In other words, it might be time for Catholics to retrieve common Catholic authoritative words and texts akin to the classical *loci theologici*, as well as a related custom of weighing theological propositions with "notes." Such a retrieval is necessarily implied in putting Christ back in the center. For the Christocentric theologian, the Gospel is normative, but its normativity presupposes an identifiable and enduring content, a content that was communicated through Christ's deeds and words, and which was promulgated "with his lips."[42] The Apostles and other "apostolic men" who were witnesses to these deeds and words "committed the message of salvation to writing." And witnessing to the tradition are the "words of the Holy Fathers."[43] Words — whether those of the scriptures, or those of tradition that interpret them — matter. The validity of theologians' claims should be evaluated according to the extent to which they are rooted in and supported by the Gospel and its authoritative interpretations from tradition. Appealing

40. Imbelli, "Catholic Identity after Vatican II," 16.
41. Imbelli, *Rekindling the Christic Imagination*, xxiv.
42. *Dei Verbum*, no. 7.
43. *Dei Verbum*, no. 8.

to scripture, tradition, and authoritative doctrine is not proof-texting but merely taking seriously the Gospel-content, which is given and accessible to all.

Going back to the Source and the sources entails an assent to those authoritative interpretations of the Gospel we call doctrine and in some cases dogma. Adhering to doctrine is crucial not only for theologians in their pursuit of truth but also in their service of the New Evangelization. A Christocentric vision for theology and evangelization does not see dogma as a problem or a hindrance. Rather, dogmas and doctrines generally *facilitate* our coming to know and follow Christ. We throw obstacles in front of ourselves only when we present those teachings without the regular appeal to the person about whom those teachings tell us something. What is needed is dogma rightly understood—dogma that is understood not in a flat, intellectualist sense, but as theological propositions that are firmly embedded in a Christic imagination, or truth claims that "come alive," as it were, in the person of Jesus Christ.

"Many a man will live and die upon a dogma," Newman rightly reminds us. But "no man will be a martyr for a conclusion."[44] Dogmas are not conclusions but rather articles of faith and expressions of the truth, of that which *is*. For the theologian, they are to be probed, not debated. And for the evangelist, they are to be imbued with Christ, for we are more than certain about dogmas because we know personally—we have experienced in some mediated way—the one who has uttered them to us through the Church. In other words, dogma is subject to a certain "realization," as it were, in the Christian, for which the imagination is key.

"Realizing" the Gospel for the New Evangelization

For the new evangelization, naturally, it is not sufficient to reiterate constantly the Christological substance of the faith, although that reaffirmation is necessary. In a secular age, one can only hope to transmit the faith if individuals can encounter and thereby develop a personal relationship with Jesus Christ

44. John Henry Newman, *An Essay in Aid of a Grammar of Assent* (London: Longmans, Green, and Co., 1903), 92. This passage of Newman's is originally from his "Tamworth Reading Room," published in the *Times* (1841), nearly thirty years before he quotes it in his *Grammar of Assent* (1870).

It is for this reason that Imbelli underlines in different ways the distinctly personal character of revelation, especially as it is taught to us in *Dei Verbum*. The relevant question is not so much "*What* is the Good News?" but rather "*Who* is the Good News?" Catholicism is not so much a "religion of the Book" but rather the "religion of the one to whom the Book points."[45] Perhaps Imbelli's favorite appeal is to St. Irenaeus, who, when asked by Marcionites what the novelty of Christ is if the Old Testament is from the same God, responded: "Christ brought all newness by bringing himself" (*Omnem novitatem attulit, semetipsum afferens*).[46]

In short, "the New Evangelization is not about a program, but about a Person and about participation in the new life he enables."[47] Preachers, teachers, and parents, by ways in accordance with each vocation, must first make possible and then foster a personal relationship with the Lord by, to use the title of Imbelli's book, "rekindling the Christic imagination."

Doctrine and Practice

Rekindling this imagination, or awakening in us a vision for friendship with Christ and the transformation that this requires, begins with an encounter with the person of Jesus, who is both "truth and life." Teaching doctrine(s) without fostering personal encounters with Christ is usually a nonstarter. Without this encounter, whether through liturgy, devotion, or serving our neighbor, doctrinal propositions will leave us cold.[48]

The reverse tendency, however, consists in exhorting one to Christian discipleship without the Christological and moral doctrines that define the terms of this discipleship. Such a tendency is happy to preach Christ and the good news but reticent to unpack the content and demands of the new covenant, satisfying itself with undefined or unelaborated terms, such as "Gospel." This tendency misleads by suggesting that once Christ is in some undefined way affirmed, one's "journey" and its "accompaniment" can bear fruit

---

45. Robert P. Imbelli, "The Heart Has Its Reasons," *C21 Resource, Exploring the Catholic Intellectual Tradition* (Spring 2013): 6.

46. Robert P. Imbelli, "Christ Brings All Newness." The quotation by Irenaeus is from *Adversus Haereses* IV, c. 34. It is also cited by Pope Francis in *Evangelii gaudium*, 11.

47. Imbelli, *Rekindling the Christic Imagination*, 84.

48. De Lubac says it best: "if the articles of faith are numbered, the Object of Faith is marvellously one." See Henri de Lubac, "The Light of Christ," *Theology in History* (San Francisco: Ignatius Press, 1996), 217.

without laying out the rationale behind the journey and its goal (i.e., holiness and friendship with God). Avoiding the hard and demanding truths about Christian discipleship—namely sin, the demands of the moral law, and the necessity of conversion—is tantamount to suggesting that one can live a good, happy, fulfilled, Christian life without radical abandonment to Christ.[49]

Imbelli's vision is different. And this is where the Christological concentration in the thought of Henri de Lubac (and Vatican II!) is crucial. All doctrine, even the most technical, is but an elaboration of the person of Christ, who reveals the Father in the Spirit.[50] Doctrine emanates from Christ, who reveals himself; and it ushers us back to Christ by showing us the Way of discipleship. Doctrine, then, reveals both Christ and what it means to be a Christian. Truth and life, doctrine and discipline are rooted in a Person, "in the *novum* of the living Christ." To support this integration of the two, Imbelli appeals to de Lubac: "in this Person of Christ … the reality of charity and the truth of dogma are indissolubly united."[51] It is, then, in the encounter with this living Person that one's discipleship takes root, which entails, indeed, confessing and therefore assenting to truth, and uniting oneself to God in holiness. Such an integration between doctrine and practice is *not* "an ideal to be pursued" but "a reality to be experienced and embraced."[52]

Rooting doctrine and practice in the Person of Christ means that our progress toward knowing and loving God entails an ever-deeper encounter with him. This intentional "schooling" in Christ is mystagogic, a process which, for Imbelli, must extend beyond its very particular place at the end of the Rite of Christian Initiation of Adults. All Christians who have others in their care—not just the ordained pastor but also the catechist, the youth

---

49. Cf. Robert P. Imbelli, "Second Peter: From Periphery to Center," *The Catholic Thing,* June 10, 2018, https://www.thecatholicthing.org/2018/06/10/second-peter-from-periphery-to-center/, accessed September 13, 2018: "A salient conviction of the author [of Second Peter] is that conduct derives from doctrine. Change the doctrine and wayward conduct, both adulterous and covetous (2:14) will follow in its wake."

50. In terms of Christocentric focus, one of the best commentaries on *Dei verbum* has to be Henri de Lubac's "Commentaire du préambule et du chapitre I," in *La Révélation divine, Unam Sanctam 70,* ed. B.-D. Dupuy (Paris: Cerf, 1968), 157–302.

51. Robert P. Imbelli, "On Being Truly Dogmatic," *First Things,* January 9, 2018, https://www.firstthings.com/web-exclusives/2018/01/on-being-truly-dogmatic, accessed September 7, 2018. The quotation is in de Lubac, "The Light of Christ," in *Theology in History,* 216.

52. Robert P. Imbelli, "The Principled Ambivalence of Pope Francis," *First Things,* November 7, 2017, https://www.firstthings.com/web-exclusives/2017/11/the-principled-ambivalence-of-pope-francis, accessed September 7, 2018.

minister, the educational instructor, the spiritual director, and the parent—are called to be "mystagogues"; they are "to probe wisely and reverently the Mystery of the faith."[53] They are responsible for facilitating a penetration of the Christian mystery, of humbly sharing "something of what we have seen and what we are striving to become."[54]

A vivid religious imagination makes possible the mystagogical process, for oneself and for others. Before we continue our consideration of how, according to Imbelli, we are to "realize" the Gospel, we turn to John Henry Newman in order to delve more deeply into what is meant by this religious imagination.

John Henry Newman and the Christic Imagination

One of Newman's perennial contributions to modern Catholic thought is his recognition of the role played by the imagination in the shaping of one's worldview and religious development. Newman understood that the transmission of the faith required a *living* faith on the part of those transmitting it.[55] Following from this, he also perceived the persuasive limits of rational argument. That is not to say that Newman did not value the power of argument. His writings testify to its efficacy! Newman never denied that arguments persuade or convince; he denied that they dependably stir us toward action. Yes, you might be convinced that something is true, but that is it: you are convinced. Then what?

Being merely convinced of the truth of something is tantamount to what Newman calls "notional assent." Notional assents are assents to propositions when the subject has little if any experience of the object of assent. With experience comes real apprehension and, hence, real assents based on those apprehensions. It is one thing for a cartophile to assent to the proposition, "An island is a landmass surrounded by water"; it is quite another for the sailor who sails around them to assent to the same. For the latter, it is more *real*; drawing from his experience and memory, he can, through his imagination,

---

53. Robert P. Imbelli, "Faith, Belief, and the Trinity," *The Catholic Thing*, June 11, 2017, https://www.thecatholicthing.org/2017/06/11/faith-belief-and-the-trinity/, accessed September 10, 2018.

54. Imbelli, "On Being Truly Dogmatic."

55. Cf. Joseph Ratzinger, *Salt of the Earth: The Church at the End of the Millennium*, trans. Adrian Walker (San Francisco: Ignatius Press, 1997), 267: "Christianity will be doomed to suffocation if we don't learn something of interiorization, in which faith sinks personally into the depth of one's own life and in that depth sustains and illuminates."

make present a synthetic "image" or "impression" of islands. And even others to whom he testifies about islands can also, through their own imaginations, make present to themselves this image, more or less vividly.[56] It is no wonder, then, that before Newman settled on the distinction between notional assent and real assent, his original distinction in previous drafts of the *Grammar of Assent* was between the notional and the *imaginative*.

The imagination, for it to do its work, must be provided with the raw material of experience, whether immediate or mediated. Unlike a prophet, for example, the ordinary Christian, according to Newman, goes about receiving impressions of divine truth by regularly reading the scriptures, by devotions such as the rosary, by studying theology or receiving instruction, and by talking to those who are further down the road of discipleship.[57] In other words, "the stuff out of which the (Christian or religious) imagination forges its object is the church's tradition of faith."[58]

The imagination, however, does not stop at placing an image before the mind to contemplate. The imagination, for Newman, goes further and vivifies this image in a way that evokes a response on the part of the subject contemplating it. In short, it "realizes" it. "Realizing" something, in Newmanian terms, is to make it one's own—to appropriate it. If something is realized, it stirs us to action. For Imbelli, our redemption and the price paid for it needs to be "realized" by us; it has to "permeate our imagination" in order for it to drive our dispositions, actions, and lives.[59] Newman clarifies:

Strictly speaking, it is not imagination that causes action; but hope and fear, likes and dislikes, appetite, passion, affection, the stirrings of selfishness and self-love. What imagination does for us is to find a means of stimulating those motive powers; and it does so by providing a supply of objects strong enough to stimulate them.[60]

56. For a thorough study of Newman and the imagination, see Terrence Merrigan, "The Imagination in the Life and Thought of John Henry Newman," *Cahiers victoriens et édouardiens* 70 (2009): 187–217. There, Merrigan distinguishes between the "prehending imagination" and the "realizing imagination." My essay assumes and is indebted to these categories without spelling them out here.

57. John Henry Newman, *Fifteen Sermons Preached before the University of Oxford* (London: Longmans, Green, and Co., 1909), 333.

58. Merrigan, "The Imagination," 196.

59. Robert P. Imbelli, "The King Whom God Gives," *The Catholic Thing*, November 26, 2017, https://www.thecatholicthing.org/2017/11/26/the-king-whom-god-gives/, accessed October 25, 2019.

60. Newman, *Grammar of Assent*, 82 (my emphasis).

A vivid religious imagination makes present images or impressions that stimulate our desires. To existentially appropriate the Christian faith, one has to feed not only the head, as it were, but also the heart. And the heart, as Newman writes, "is commonly reached, not through the reason, but through the imagination, by means of direct impressions, by the testimony of facts and events, by history, by description."[61]

Rekindling the Christic imagination amounts to preachers, teachers, and parents providing these direct impressions and describing vividly, whether by word, music, or art, the history of which Newman speaks. Argument is necessary but insufficient. According to Newman, "Persons influence us, voices melt us, looks subdue us, actions inflame us."[62] While Newman, here in context, is refuting the idea that, with "useful knowledge" we can educate people into religiosity and moral improvement, his words apply just as much to elucidating a "Christic imagination."

Persons influence us:
Immediately they left their nets and followed him. (Mt 4:20)
And Zacchaeus stood and said to the Lord, "Behold, Lord, the half of my goods I give to the poor; and if I have defrauded any one of anything, I restore it fourfold." (Lk 19:8)
Voices melt us:
The sheep hear his voice, and he calls his own sheep by name ... and the sheep follow him, for they know his voice. (Lk 10:3–4)
They said to each other, "Did not our hearts burn within us while he talked to us on the road, while he opened to us the scriptures?" (Lk 24:32)
Looks subdue us:
And the Lord turned and looked at Peter.... And Peter went out and wept bitterly." (Lk 22:61–62)
And whenever the unclean spirits beheld him, they fell down before him and cried out, "You are the Son of God." (Mk 3:11).
Deeds inflame us:
Then he poured water into a basin, and began to wash the disciples' feet, and to wipe them with the towel with which he was girded. (Jn 13:5)
And when the centurion, who stood facing him, saw that he thus breathed his last, he said, "Truly this man was the Son of God!" (Mk 15:39)
When he was at table with them, he took the bread and blessed, and broke it,

61. Newman, *Grammar of Assent*, 92. (Also from the "Tamworth Reading Room.")
62. Newman, *Grammar of Assent*, 93.

and gave it to them. And their eyes were opened and they recognized him.
(Lk 24:30–31)

"Persons influence us, voices melt us, looks subdue us, actions inflame us." Rekindling the Christic imagination amounts to making Jesus Christ's voice audible; his looks visible; his actions tangible. That is why we cannot restrict instruction to the conceptual, however essential it is. Imbelli exhorts us to "embrace the *via pulchritudinis*—the way of beauty."[63] Art, music, literature, and poetry are all gifts for the new evangelization. Giotto, Hopkins, Dante, and Bach can impress upon the imaginations the living form of Christ, as can beautiful liturgical space and a dynamic liturgical orientation.[64] Most important, however, are the sacraments, especially the Eucharist, and the liturgy more generally. Therein lies the genius of the Catholic spirit: making visible that which is invisible.

Developing a Christic imagination is not only essential for transmitting the faith but is also crucial for navigating the moral maze in contemporary secular culture. At a time when *discernment* is in vogue, a Christic imagination is the prerequisite for its proper exercise.

Christocentric Discernment

Before the idea of "discernment" garnered for itself the attention it enjoys today, Imbelli registered its crucial importance and the urgency of shoring up what could be a slippery concept. In 1992, for example, he already cautioned:

How do we discern whether the tunes we are humming to our high-pitched guitars are the Lord's songs in an alien land or alien songs in the house of the Lord? Such discernment should not simply be remanded to the magisterium, but should profoundly engage the entire Catholic theological community. I, for one, believe that the ultimate test must be a Christological one. So it has been from the beginning: "Beloved, not every spirit is to be trusted; test the spirits to see whether they are of God.... Every spirit that confesses that Jesus Christ has come in the flesh is of God" (1 John 4:1–2). But precisely there lies the heart of the matter.[65]

---

63. Imbelli, "Faith, Belief, and the Trinity."

64. Imbelli, "The Reaffirmation of the Christic Center," 106.

65. Imbelli, "Dual Loyalties in Catholic Theology," 21. See also Imbelli's column, "History, Hope and iPhones. Continuing the Conversation," *Commonweal,* October 7, 2011, 8.

Imbelli's appeal to the Johannine confession is pointful. According to the Johannine rule, some pastoral proposals or provisions are not worthy of pursuit because their protagonists find it difficult to declare Christ's salvific unicity and primacy. But they might also be questionable because the proposals themselves do not take seriously the transformation that is possible in one to whom "Jesus Christ has come in the flesh." An arid imagination has not tasted what it is that we are called to, and what all is possible with God's grace.

An adequate understanding of discernment, then, must be able to integrate the category of experience and imagination with care. With so many appeals to contemporary "experience" in our theological discourse, Imbelli reminds us that a properly theological appeal to experience must be a "Christic experience" or "the experience of the converted subject who is being transformed in the image of Christ, crucified and risen."[66] This experience is the "stuff" out of which the imagination constructs a vision of discipleship. In other words, theological appeals to "experience" in Catholic dogmatic and moral discourse are legitimate for Imbelli but miss the mark, or even lead astray when the appeals seek anything other than insight gained from conversion to Christ. In Christian discernment, Christ "must always be the measure and not what is measured."[67]

More recently, we witness Imbelli's own Christocentric theology in action when we see reflections on the spiritual life, the moral life, and ultimately discernment and accompaniment, constantly being referred back to Jesus Christ. In the aftermath of the two synods on the family (2014–2015) and the release of *Amoris laetitia,* Imbelli wrote a piece replete with characteristic Christological depth. His brief comments on "pastoral accompaniment" at the end are preceded by reflections on the meaning of "obedience" and transformation, ruminating on multiple passages in Paul's letters, especially from Romans and Galatians. As Imbelli guides his readers through

66. Imbelli, "Receiving Vatican II," 208.

67. National Pastoral Life Center, "Called to Be Catholic: Church in a Time of Peril," quoted by Imbelli in "Introduction. Discernment, Newness, Transformation: Musings Inspired by a Conference," in *Handing on the Faith: The Church's Mission and Challenge,* ed. Robert P. Imbelli (New York: Herder and Herder, 2006), 4. Elsewhere, Christ is referred to by Imbelli as "the measure of all discernment." Robert P. Imbelli, "Model of the Church: Cardinal Avery Dulles (1918–2008)," *Commonweal,* January 12, 2009, https://www.commonwealmagazine.org/model-church, accessed November 26, 2018.

the major themes of St. Paul, he observes that the obedience of faith is our response to what God has done for us in Jesus Christ (cf. Rom 1:3–4). We obey because we belong to Christ and were branded as His own at baptism (cf. Rom 6:4, 16; 14:7–9; cf. Phil 3:12). Living a *new* life in Christ, we are to be transformed in him (Rom 12:1–2; cf. Gal 2:19–20). It is only after unpacking this Pauline vision of transformation in Christ that Imbelli finally comments:

The Apostle's call to transformation can be easily muffled by the dismal din of our contemporary therapeutic culture. And the widespread appeal to "my experience" risks canonizing an individual's present condition and foreclosing authentic change. In this context, the increasingly rote rhetoric about "pastoral accompaniment" can reinforce, rather than counter, this cultural declension. Pastoral accompaniment needs clearly to incorporate and be governed by the challenge to conversion, an imperative that lies at the very heart of the Gospel: "metanoeite!" i.e., repent. (Mk 1:15). For the telos of pastoral accompaniment is not a gradual approximation to an "ideal," however sublime. It is the entrance into a new life, defined by a new, life-altering relationship with Jesus Christ.[68]

We see in this passage how Christ is at the center: he lies "ahead" of us in his call to conversion, and lies "behind" us as the cause of all things new. More remote theological concepts such as "accompaniment" and "discernment" require the mooring of this synthetic vision of Christian discipleship based on the New Testament.[69] Without this anchor, such categories easily slip into the Zeitgeist. The Zeitgeist is nothing other than the *signa temporum* when read without the "the defining stipulation: *in light of the Gospel*."[70]

---

68. Robert P. Imbelli, "The Obedience of Faith," *The Catholic Thing,* December 18, 2016, https://www.thecatholicthing.org/2016/12/18/the-obedience-of-faith/, accessed September 10, 2018.

69. For comments on relating discernment with conversion and transformation, see also Imbelli, "Refashioning Catholic Imagination."

70. Imbelli, "The King Whom God Gives." In the same piece, Imbelli also claims, rightly, that for John Henry Newman, "the norm of discernment is always Jesus Christ crucified." That is to say, one component part of discernment is conversion: the dying of the old self and the putting on of the new.

Conclusion

The conciliar vision for the Church, her spiritual and intellectual life, is unflinchingly Christocentric. Robert Imbelli reminds us that fidelity to the Council entails recentering our theology accordingly, so that our evangelization and intraecclesial disputes be oriented toward the transformation to which Christ calls us.

A Christocentric theology is a theology that, among the many other aspects of its method, can relate the different dimensions of the Christian life and the various mysteries of the faith to the one Mystery incarnate. In doing so, it can provide an invaluable service to preachers, teachers, and parents who are responsible for fostering relationships with the Lord. A New Evangelization that is led by a Christocentric theology fashions imaginations with a Christic imprint and consciences with a Christic compass.

While what is ultimately at stake in evangelization is in no way comparable to victory or loss in a baseball game, the process by which one fails in evangelization is analogous to how one loses in America's pastime: any treatise, article, homily, address, or "statement" that has a Christological reference point is a pitch inside the strike zone; silence on Christ is not a ball, it's a wild pitch. And with too many wild pitches, you not only walk batters but you end up giving up runs and losing the game.

Part 1

THE CENTER OF
REVELATION

2

Joseph Ratzinger Warming the Christic Imagination, October 1962

JARED WICKS, SJ

In 2008, I published six texts composed by Professor Joseph Ratzinger while he was a peritus of Vatican II.[1] Given how the honoree of this volume esteems the thought and teaching of Ratzinger as both professor and as Pope Benedict XVI, it is a pleasure to present here a newly available seventh Ratzinger text from the time of his service at the Council. This text, *De voluntate Dei erga hominem* (The Will of God Regarding Human Beings), composed of only 753 words in five numbered paragraphs, rested in an archive from 1962 to 2012, but has now become accessible.

I offer here a small gem from the early days of Vatican II, a brief theological statement that rewards our pondering with enrichments of faith and life. This Ratzinger text can affect one's sense of the human vocation under God's address all through history. It presents Christ as the epiphany of God and of our humanity in the true contours of both, and as the one in whom and by whom God is leading us back (*reducendo*) from misery through redemption to communion with God and the great wedding feast of salvation. The text

---

1. "Six Texts by Prof. Joseph Ratzinger as *peritus* before and during Vatican Council II," *Gregorianum* 89 (2008): 233–311.

affirms that in all divine speaking the theme is Christ, who in the incarnation is God's expressed truth calling and forming us. To this, the apostolic writings testify and this the Church proclaims, but the several revealed truths lead back to the one truth, Jesus Christ, who brings us to union with God. This modest account can add a warm glow to one's "Christic imagination" by its account of how Christ comes, as the *Verbum vocans nos*, and of his mission to lead humankind and the cosmos to their place in that final kingdom and nuptial supper that God intends as the completion of creation and history.

The Context at Vatican II

Ratzinger composed *De voluntate Dei erga hominem* at Vatican II in October 1962, shortly after he gave a critical lecture on the first of the prepared Council schemas, *De fontibus revelationis,* to the German-speaking bishops whom Cardinal Joseph Frings, president of the German bishops' conference, had convened at the Anima College in Rome on October 10, the day before Vatican II's formal inauguration.[2]

On October 15, Ratzinger brought a typed copy of his *De voluntate Dei* to a meeting at the Pontifical German-Hungarian College with Bishop Hermann Volk of Mainz and the Jesuit theologians Karl Rahner and Otto Semmelroth, who resided in the College. The group found the Ratzinger draft to be a fine foundational part of the proposed larger schema that Rahner had conceived of as a replacement for the four doctrinal drafts presented for the first Council period. Rahner also brought to the meeting his own ideas for this new schema, which he still had to prepare in multiple copies so the group could examine his draft as well, with a view to combining it with Ratzinger's *De voluntate Dei erga hominem.*[3]

---

2. That text is in Wicks, "Six Texts," 241–43 (introduction), 269–85 (in English), 295–309 (original German). It is now in Ratzinger's *Gesammelte Schriften*, ed. Gerhard Ludwig Müller, vol. 7, 1–2, *Zur Lehre des Zweiten Vatikanischen Konzils* (Freiburg: Herder, 2012), 1:157–74. A week later, Karl Rahner spoke in the same venue, incisively criticizing the second schema for the Council, *De deposito fidei pure custodiendo.* In a conclusion agreed to by Frings, Rahner argued that *De deposito* should be eliminated from the Council agenda. Rahner related this in his October 19 letter to Herbert Vorgrimler, cited by Günther Wassilowsky in *Universales Heilssakrament Kirche: Karl Rahners Beitrag zur Ekklesiologie des II. Vatikanums* (Innsbruck-Vienna: Tyrolia-Verlag, 2001), 182–83, n. 45.

3. Otto Semmelroth tells in his Vatican II diary how Rahner arrived in Rome already planning an alternative schema to replace the four doctrinal drafts distributed earlier to the Council

The collaboration between Rahner and Ratzinger on melding their texts gained a larger context on October 19 at a meeting convened by Volk of nine bishops and fifteen theologians, mostly French and German, to discuss coordinating the emerging responses to, and possibly replacing, the four official doctrinal schemas.[4] At the meeting, Rahner spoke against merely giving the existing schemas a new orientation by composing introductory passages and then revising parts of them, as Volk and Jean Daniélou were proposing. Speakers in the Council Hall should instead call on the fathers to vote them down so that new schemas of positive and uplifting themes from contemporary theology could come on the agenda. Bishop Alfred Bengsch of Berlin, who had been on the Central Preparatory Commission from mid-1961 to June 1962, agreed with Rahner, because that commission's many proposed revisions of the doctrinal schemas had been stubbornly ignored by the Theological Commission headed by Cardinal Alfredo Ottaviani and guided by its Secretary, Fr. Sebastian Tromp. It was agreed that the theologians Rahner, Ratzinger, Jean Daniélou, Yves Congar, and Michel Labourdette, OP, would become redactors of possible replacement texts to then be reviewed by the larger group at a subsequent meeting.

The small German-French redaction group met on October 21 with Volk. They decided to first work further with an introductory orientation text, a *proemium*, being drafted by Congar; and following that, to have Rahner and Ratzinger further collaborate in preparing for the Council an alternative text of attractive and uplifting biblical-theological content. This would show the Council members the potential of contemporary Catholic thought to express the Gospel of Christ with a freshness lacking in the official texts, *De fontibus* and *De deposito*, which bore marks of their creation under the influence of detail-minded and censorious officials of the Congregation of the Holy Office.[5]

---

fathers. Semmelroth then described the October 15 meeting, at which the other three found the Ratzinger text "sehr gut. . . . Man sollte es als ersten Teil unbedingt benutzen." I thank Prof. Günther Wassilowsky for a copy of his transcription of Semmelroth's diary for 1962.The dates given in future references indicate the date of the diary entry by Semmelroth.

4. This meeting's deliberations are related by Yves Congar in his diary entry of October 19, 1962, related in Congar's *My Journal of the Council* (Collegeville, Minn.: Liturgical Press, 2012), 98–100, and by Semmelroth in his diary entry for that day. Brendan Cahill also relates these deliberations in *The Renewal of Revelation Theology (1960–1962)*, Tesi Gregoriana: Serie Teologia, 51 (Rome: Gregorian and Biblical Press, 1999): 172–80.

5. Congar, *My Journal*, 107; Semmelroth (whom Rahner asked to join the group), in his diary entry of October 21.

One of the ten Council presidents, Cardinal Frings, for whom Ratzinger had already ghost-written three Council-related texts before Vatican II opened,[6] gave another context to Ratzinger's *De voluntate Dei erga hominem*. At the Council, Ratzinger resided with Frings at the Anima College, to which Frings invited six leading cardinals to meet on October 25, with the aim of bringing them together in a joint action against the preparatory doctrinal schemas.

Frings's guests were Cardinals Bernard Alfrink (Utrecht), Franz König (Vienna), Achille Liénart (Lille), Leo-Josef Suenens (Malines-Brussels), Giovanni Batista Montini (Milan), and Giuseppe Siri (Genoa).[7] Frings urged upon them that in order to correspond better with Pope John's opening address of the Council, the fathers must have working documents of a positive style and spirit that could bring them together as teachers of the Gospel to the world. The doctrinal schemas placed first in the official booklet distributed in late summer constituted a serious problem for the Council because they were, according to Frings, so heavily laced with censures and admonitions, so minimally enriched by biblical themes, and so textbookish in style that they were sure to be strongly opposed by many Council members. To illustrate what Frings believed they needed, he invited his guests to hear a short proposal that could serve in a replacement schema, one that Frings's peritus, Ratzinger, had drafted. Ratzinger then proceeded to read to the seven cardinals his *De voluntate Dei erga hominem*.[8]

After the reading by Ratzinger, the gathered cardinals did not agree on a course of action, but four of them, Alfrink, König, Suenens, and Liénart, joined Frings two weeks later to circulate the longer text then being prepared by Rahner and Ratzinger to the Vatican II participants.

---

6. See my "Six Texts," 253–68, giving these compositions by Ratzinger: (1) Frings's lecture in Genoa on November 20, 1961, contrasting the Church-world relationships in the eras of the two Vatican Councils, 1869–1870 and 1960–1961; (2) a draft "introductory constitution" of June 1962 to illustrate Frings's conviction that the Central Preparatory Commission needed to state clearly the aim and goal of the Council; (3) the September 17, 1962, letter of Frings to the Cardinal Secretary of State in evaluation of the seven initial schemas recently distributed to the future Council fathers.

7. The first four cardinals were, like Frings, presidents of their episcopal conferences, while Siri and Montini were members of the Council's Secretariat for Extraordinary Matters.

8. Cardinal Joseph Ratzinger told about this meeting both in "Kardinal Frings und das II. Vatikansiche Konzil," in *Kardinal Frings: Leben und Werk*, ed. Dieter Froitzheim (Cologne: Wienand Verlag, 1979), 198–99, and in *Milestones: Memoirs 1927–1977* (San Francisco: Ignatius Press, 1998), 128.

Three days after the seven cardinals met at Frings' residence, the German-French redaction group of five theologians met again, this time at Volk's residence, to review their progress, which was considerable. They studied and approved Congar's completed *proemium*, which had the form of a creed offered as an introductory, tone-setting, text for all of Vatican II's teaching.[9] Then, as Congar recorded, "Rahner read the text he had prepared with Ratzinger to replace the four unsatisfactory doctrinal schemas. It is very good, especially on Church-Scripture-Tradition, which are well linked together."[10] Thus, in less than two weeks, Ratzinger and Rahner had combined their October 15 texts and further developed them into a longer Latin text, which, in its circulated form, had 2,844 words in three chapters divided into eleven numbered paragraphs, under the title *De revelatione Dei et hominis in Jesu Christo facta*.[11]

The title of the joint product came from Ratzinger's first text, in which the third paragraph had the title, "Jesus Christ the Revelation of God and Man," which it articulated in seven dense sentences. In *De revelatione Dei et hominis*, these sentences, slightly revised and expanded, make up the second part of chapter I, no. 3.

On November 8, after the announcement that *De fontibus revelationis* would be the next schema for Council treatment, Rahner and Ratzinger worked together, with help from Semmelroth, for nearly seven hours on polishing their combined text for publication in the informal manner, common at Vatican II, of mimeographing.[12] Cardinal Frings sponsored this,

9. Congar described the meeting in *My Journal*, 125, entry for October 28. He later called his *proemium* "an ample, kerygmatic confession of faith," adding that Frings had it duplicated in two hundred copies. Yves Congar, "Erinnerungen an eine Episode auf dem II. VatikanischenKonzil," in *Glaube im Prozess*, Festschrift K. Rahner, eds. Elmar Klinger and Klaus Wittstadt (Freiburg: Herder, 1984), 28, to which the *Proemium* was added in Latin and German on pp. 51–64. It deserves study, especially in comparison with the *Nova Professio Fidei*, drafted earlier by the Preparatory Theological Commission but not given to the Council.

10. Congar, *My Journal*, 125, still on October 28. Semmelroth's entry of the day speaks of the new text as "Fr. Rahner's schema that Ratzinger had worked through." But Congar added that some sections would probably not be approved, such as chapter II, no. 3, on the world's religions and philosophies being a phase of the Gospel's preparation.

11. This is now found in Karl Rahner's *Sämtliche Werke*, vol. 21, *Das Zweite Vatikanum. Beiträge zum Konzil und seiner Interpretation* (Freiburg: Herder, 2013), 1: 217–36, and in Ratzinger's *Gesämmelte Schriften*, vol. 7, no. 1, 183–209. Both editions give the Latin original and a German translation. Cahill gives it in Latin and English in *The Renewal of Revelation Theology*, 300–317. I introduce it in *Investigating Vatican II: Its Theologians, Ecumenical Turn, and Biblical Commitment* (Washington, D.C.: The Catholic University of America Press, 2018), 91–93.

12. Semmelroth told of the November 8 session and called the end product "a very beautiful

along with the four other episcopal conference presidents. Copies of *De revelatione Dei et hominis in Jesu Christo facta* began to circulate on November 12.[13] The next day, the conciliar Doctrinal Commission held its first meeting, and two days later, the momentous debate began in St. Peter's on *De fontibus revelationis.*

At the Doctrinal Commission meeting, the commission's president, Cardinal Ottaviani, and the secretary, Sebastian Tromp, both rebuffed all criticisms of *De fontibus*, with Ottaviani urging the duty of the members to give their backing to it in the debate about to begin—against which some members protested. One Commission member, Archbishop Pietro Parente, had a copy of *De revelatione Dei et hominis*, which he attacked because he said it contained doctrinal errors and its circulation was irregular, being that it was an alternative to schemas approved for distribution by the Pope.[14]

In the debate on *De fontibus*, which took place from November 14 to 20, some speakers showed substantive agreements with *De revelatione Dei et hominis*, especially by insisting on Jesus Christ as the central reality in God's revelation to humankind.[15]

Several theological studies have analyzed the Rahner-Ratzinger schema of 1962, but without having access to Ratzinger's initial contribution, which went into the combined text almost completely.[16] Here, we take up Ratzing-

---

draft," but he had reservations because it was more complex than what the large assembly of fathers would likely agree to and treated only fleetingly some topics of *De fontibus*.

13. Congar said in *My Journal*, 166, that there were three thousand copies (entry of November 14). Semmelroth said Frings, the main promoter, planned for 2,500 copies so that every Council father could have a copy (entry of November 8), but Semmelroth thought that was dangerous, as the alternative text might well not fit with the expectations of many bishops and they would drop back to favor *De fontibus*. Perhaps with this danger in mind, Rahner composed a frontal attack, *Disquisitio brevis de Schemate* "De fontibus revelationis," run off by mimeograph at the German-Hungarian college the morning of November 11 for distribution to the Council fathers. That text came out in Hanjo Sauer, *Erfahrung und Glaube:Die Begründung des pastoralen Prinzips durch die Offenbarungskonstitution des II,Vatikanischen Konzils* (Frankfurt/Main: Peter Lang, 1993), 657–68; Rahner, *Das Zweite Vatikanum*, 1:237–61.

14. Congar had information on the November 13 meeting from two participants, Archbishop Gabriel Garrone and Bishop Marcos McGrath, which he then related in *My Journal*, 164–67.

15. See Sauer, *Erfahrung und Glaube*, 137–200, for example, 161 (Archbishop Emile M. Guerry, Cambrai, France), 165–67 (Bishop Paul Schmitt, Metz, France), and 178 (Apostolic Vicar Pierre Martin, New Caledonia, Oceania); Cahill, *Renewal of Revelation Theology*, 183–204.

16. Sauer, "Von den 'Quellen der Offenbarung' zur 'Offenbarungselbst,'" in *Glaube im Prozess*, 522–37; Sauer, *Erfahrung und Glaube*, 121–36 and 484–507; Cahill, *Renewal of Revelation Theology*, 176–80; Francesco Testaferri, "Lo 'Schema Rahner-Ratzinger': *De revelatione Dei et hominis*

er's earlier schema, which anticipates Vatican II's remarkable turn to a fresh account of God's revelation. After the text, I will review its contents to show the valuable themes of Ratzinger's text in its own right as a contribution to the Christological refocusing of Catholic revelation doctrine.

Background in Ratzinger's Work of
De voluntate Dei erga hominem

Joseph Ratzinger had begun teaching Fundamental Theology in the Catholic Theology Faculty of the University of Bonn in spring 1959. In the first semester of 1959–1960, he lectured on "the nature and reality of divine revelation." Cardinal Frings of Cologne was soon in contact with Bonn's new theology professor. In mid-1961, Ratzinger wrote for Frings a lecture-text on the contrasting cultural-historical conditions surrounding Vatican I (1869–1870) and the conditions of the new council in the early 1960s.[17]

In June 1962, again at Frings's request, Ratzinger composed in Latin a three-page draft of an "Introductory Constitution," a text that Frings wanted the Vatican II Central Preparatory Commission to see as implicitly giving criteria for selecting truly relevant texts from the many schemas presented by the particular preparatory commissions.[18] The "Introductory Constitution," posits as basic for the Council that, even amid modern forgetfulness of him, God is not absent from the depths of the human person, for "there still remains in the hearts of those created in God's image (Gen 1:27) an outcry for God, for the God who alone can fill human hearts which are made with a capacity for the infinite."[19] This Augustinian formulation will return lightly adapted in the opening passage of the text presented below.

From September 9 to 11, 1962, Ratzinger took part in a meeting in

---

in Jesu Christo facta e la discussione sul De fontibus all'inizio del Concilio Vaticano II," Lateranum 80 (2012): 29–60, which gives the text in Latin and Italian on 40–52, with comments on 52–59.

17. I presented the lecture in "Six Texts," 234–36 (introduction) and 253–61 (summary with selected passages in English). Before the Genoa address that he had a friend give in Italian, Frings had the German original duplicated for the German bishops' meeting of August 29–31, 1961. That text came out in Herderkorrespondenz 16 (1961/62): 135–38, and Geist und Leben 34 (1961): 448–60, from which French and Italian versions were published in early 1962. Pope John XXIII read the Italian version later and told Frings that he agreed heartily with the lecture.

18. Wicks, "Six Texts," 237–39 (introduction), 261–64 (English version), and 293–95 (original Latin).

19. Wicks, "Six Texts," 262 (in English) and 293–94 (original Latin), that is, "Attamen in

Mainz, convened by Bishop Hermann Volk, at which ten German theologians discussed the seven draft schemas just sent to the Council fathers as possible agenda items of the Council's first working period.[20]

After the theologians met, Ratzinger responded to another request by Cardinal Frings by sending him a concise evaluation in Latin of the first seven schemas. This became the third early ghost-written text, when the Cardinal used it as his letter of response to the Cardinal Secretary of State on the initial schemas, specifically on which of the schemas should enter the Council's agenda and in what order they should be treated. On September 17, Ratzinger's evaluative text went into the mail to Rome over Frings own signature.[21] As the theologians had concluded at Mainz, this letter said that *De fontibus revelationis* needed to start with a new chapter on revelation itself, which could draw on chapter 4 of *De deposito*. To this, Ratzinger added that chapter V of *De fontibus*, about scripture in the Church, should be transformed by taking over all or part of the pastoral schema *De verbo Dei*, prepared for the Council by the Secretariat for Promoting Christian Unity, by a group chaired by the Secretariat member, Bishop Hermann Volk of Mainz.

The theologians formulated at Mainz a list of recommended changes and amendments of the schemas in eight pages, of which Ratzinger sent a copy to Cardinal Frings on September 28. Ratzinger's reflections led to further elaborations on why the changes were needed, in fifteen pages, sent to Cardinal Frings on October 3.[22] These reasons included (1) that when the

---

corde hominis ad Dei imaginem conditi (cf. Gen 1:27), clamor quidam manet, qui Deum quaerit, Deum, qui solus implet hoc cor capax infiniti et nonnisi in infinito amore quiescens."

20. Along with the four doctrinal schemas, there were draft decrees on the mass media and ecumenical relations between Catholic eastern churches and Orthodox churches, along with the draft constitution on liturgical renewal. Rahner reported on the meeting to Cardinal Franz König of Vienna in a September 19 letter, now in Rahner, *Sämtliche Werke*, vol. 21, 208–14. On *De fontibus,* the view prevailed in the September meeting that after changing its title to *De revelatione* or *De Verbo Dei* and adding a new first chapter, it could be revised to serve in the Council. But both Rahner and Ratzinger became more critical of *De fontibus* in Rome a few weeks later.

21. Ratzinger, *Gesammelte Schriften*, vol. 7, no. 1, 33–41, in Latin and German, while an English translation is in Wicks, "Six Texts," 239–41 (introduction) and 264–68 (English version). I also treated the Ratzinger-Frings letter among the initial comments by future Council fathers on the first schemas in "Peter Smulders and Dei Verbum: 1. A Consultation on the Eve of Vatican II," *Gregorianum* 82 (2001): 251–55, and again in *Investigating Vatican II*, 85–88.

22. Norbert Trippen, *Joseph Kardinal Frings (1887–1978)*, 2 vols. (Paderborn: Ferdinand Schoningh, 2003–2005), 2:313–14. The text of the reasons is in Ratzinger, *Gesammelte Schriften*, vol. 7, no. 1, 142–56. The reasons would be essential if Frings or another Council father were to advocate the changes while speaking in St. Peter's or submitting a request in writing.

first schema calls scripture and tradition "sources of revelation," this is seriously wrong because God's revelation is the originating source—which led to eight amendments of the text, (2) that changes were needed to chapter IV of *De deposito fidei*, on "revelation and faith," to overcome the text's "intellectualizing" of revelation as instruction in truth—to the detriment of the history of revelation and of God's action in and upon humans as he reveals himself, and (3) that *De deposito* as a whole was quite unsatisfactory, lacking a clear order and being in style more liable to repel than to attract people to the Church's faith.[23]

Thus, before Vatican II began, Ratzinger was reflecting in different contexts and with others on God's revelation and its communication in tradition and scripture. Some of his ideas entered the October 10 lecture to the German-speaking bishops on *De fontibus*. He argued there that the title was misleading, because in reality there is one main source, namely God acting to manifest himself and his salvation, for which then the "sources" meant by the title, scripture and tradition, are subsequent communications and "material attestations." But revelation as God's action and as it enters the persons addressed is always more than the attesting formulations. Where the schema aims to define a material plus of revealed truths given by the Apostles beyond scripture's content, it is taking tradition as a set of statements, which is to depart from the fathers, who saw such hidden lore as gnostic. For them, tradition came from the vital appropriation of scripture by the living, praying, and witnessing Church animated by the Holy Spirit. Bonaventure and Aquinas saw God's saving truth either in scripture or as flowing from it, while not being only a material content. For the great doctors revelation is "always more than its material principle, the Scripture, ... it is life living on in the church in a way that makes Scripture a living reality and illumines its hidden depths."[24]

Against this background, I now present Joseph Ratzinger's *De voluntate Dei erga hominem*, first by a summary of its five paragraphs, then by the full text in my translation, and lastly by drawing attention to some of its theological highlights.

23. Ratzinger, *Gesammelte Schriften*, vol. 7, no. 1, 141, 147, 150.
24. Citing "Six Texts," 276, which translates the German given on p. 301.

Introductory Summary

(1) The eschatological kingdom of God is the final goal of the world and of all God's speaking to and dealing with human beings, whose make-up gives them receptivity to God's call to union with himself, which is central in God's bringing all creation to be his kingdom. (2) God leads the world to its goal through human beings whom he addresses (*alloquitur*), by attracting them in ways hidden throughout their history to the good, to the beautiful, and to lasting love. God addresses humans also manifestly first in Israel and then in Christ, who is God's own word calling humans—a word now become man. (3) Christ is the living divine word seeking us, to bring about the final summing up of all creation in himself. He leads us back (*reducens*) from the misery of our wandering and attempted self-sufficiency to true life in God who is revealed as creating and loving us. Christ makes clear who God is, as Father, Word, and Love, from whom comes the gratuitous gift of life in God, while Christ imparts the benefit of the victory he won over our sin by his super-abounding love. (4) In Christ's union of God and a human nature, the final kingdom of God has begun. All divine speaking concerns Christ and leads toward him for its completion. When one submits to God's hidden address, there Christ and his salvation are at hand, while in the other direction, for those who adhere to Christ made manifest no human truth ever given them is lost, but instead becomes fully meaningful. This is especially true of the Old Testament on God's spousal calling of a people, as a step preparing for the perfect union of God and humanity in Christ, God's word made man. (5) Christ the Lord and Word is present in the Church as truth forming us and as life showing itself, in Christ's body that lives by God's Spirit. Church teaching does not bring new truths but shows forth faithfully the one truth made manifest in Christ, attested by the Apostles and their writings, and adhered to as a wellspring of water welling up to eternal life. The particular truths given in the Old and New Testaments and explained in the Church's teaching and proclamation—all of these lead back to the one truth that is Jesus Christ, God and man, in whom human beings are called to the nuptial banquet of intimate union with God.

Joseph Ratzinger's Text of October 1962

The Will of God Regarding Human Beings

1.[The Kingdom of God as the End of the World] Human beings are from the origin of their nature made in God's image (Gen 1:26f) and, thereby being open to God, are destined to hear God's voice and receive the love of God who loved us first (1 John 4:19), by which they become united to God and through them the world is led back to God [in Deum reducatur] and so "God may be all in all" (1 Cor 15:28). This is the aim of all divine speaking, that all creatures become the kingdom of God, a kingdom of peace, love, and happiness.

2. [The Way in Which the World Is Led to this End] To attain this end, God addresses human beings "in many and various ways"(Heb 1:1) throughout the whole course of human history, thereby attracting them by hidden ways to desire infinite goodness, eternal beauty, and never-failing love. To attain this end, God also assembled a people for himself from Abraham and over time manifested ever more clearly his word calling human beings. Finally, in the man Christ Jesus born of the Virgin Mary, God's own internal Word, by which he eternally expresses himself and eternally knows and loves all his works, became an external word: God's word calling human beings became man (John 1:14).

3. [Jesus Christ as the Revelation of God and of Human Beings] In this man, Jesus Christ, who is the living word of God seeking us out, all created reality is to be recapitulated. He is the revelation revealing God and humans, leading us back [reducens] from our desertions into our true life by leading us back [reducendo] to God. In him is revealed the truth both of God and of humanity. He reveals who human beings are, that is, that we come from God's word creating us and we go toward God's word loving us. For we became a lie in wanting to suffice unto ourselves and in denying God, which was to live contrary to our own truth and live miserably.

Christ reveals who God is, that is, the Father who made us, the Word who seeks us, and the Love who loves us even though we flee to ourselves in wanting to be like God (Gen 3:5–10). Revealing this, the Lord Jesus Christ is an efficacious revelation, because what he says, that he truly is, the truth rescuing us from a lie and love redeeming us from the solitude into which we flee, just as Adam fled from God's voice, when he tried to be equal to God, even though he knew he was not God (Gen 3:8). The same Christ, who is revelation, is as well the grace of God for us, and this in two ways. He is grace, because he manifests the love by which God loved us first (1 John 4:19), going ahead of us from eternity, and giving to us, in a way above all nature, the gift that he himself is, because ultimately God gives in revelation nothing other than himself. He is grace, as well, because he loves humankind even when in Adam we fled from him as sinners. Indeed, by a love than which none is greater (John 15:13), Christ handed himself over for us, vanquishing our sin by his own greater love (see Rom 5:8–11; John 3:16).

4. [Jesus Christ Comprehending All Reality] In this man, Christ Jesus, the end toward which human history tends has already begun, for he is himself the kingdom of God, because in him "God is all in all" (1 Cor 15:28), as he is true God and true man. Therefore, all of God's speaking, as it occurs throughout history, arises in a hidden way from what is Christ's (see John 16:14), it regards him, tends toward him, and is fulfilled in him. Wherever therefore a person obeys the voice of God speaking however hiddenly, there Christ is present with the salvation he imparts. And vice versa where he is and one believes in him and lives from him, no part of all the truth ever given to humanity is lost, but instead it is led into in full light. But above all, the economy of the Old Testament, in which God calls a people to spousal union, tends toward the perfect union between God and humankind, in which through Christ, the Word of God made man, the wedding feast is prepared, which is God's union with human beings (see Luke 13:29; Rev 19:9).

5. [The Lord Jesus Present in the Church] Jesus the Lord is therefore God's word (see John 1:1–18; Rev 19:13), as truth teaching us and life revealing life to us (see John 14:6). This living truth, which he is, remains present in the church, the body of Christ living by the Spirit of God. The church therefore does not reveal new truths but offers this one truth that appeared in the Lord Jesus. To this the Apostles and their writings give witness, this the church protects faithfully, and to this truth it is bound and from this source it draws water welling up to eternal life (see John 4:14). But the several revealed truths which are found in the Old and New Testaments and developed in Holy Mother Church's teaching and preaching, all lead back [reducuntur] to the one truth that is Jesus Christ, God and man, in whom, as was said, all humankind is called to the wedding feast, that is, to intimate union with God.[25]

---

25. "De voluntate Dei erga hominem," in Ratzinger, *Gesammelte Schriften*, vol. 7, no. 1, 177–82 (original Latin, with a German translation). The Herder volume published for the first time the Latin text from the Ratzinger archive, which is now in the Institut Papst Benedikt XVI, Regensburg, Germany. The copyright holder, Libreria Editrice Vaticana, gave permission for this publication of the text and of the author's English translation.

Theological Highlights

Joseph Ratzinger's alternative Vatican II schema unfolds its theme from human beings' creation in God's image, with their capacity to hear the word of God and be loved by him. God's speaking and loving arise within the divine action of bringing the world, which went out from God in creation's *exitus*, to return to himself in the *reditus*, which will fulfill the kingdom announced by Jesus. The text will show how God addresses human beings, in his word and his love, interiorly all through history and then audibly and visibly in Israel and in Christ, as the central nos. 3 and 4 will develop in depth.

This short work on the will of God in regard to human beings has a generic title, which indicates only indirectly the main topic, God's revelation in Christ. But the title harkens back to Vatican I's basic statement, "that it pleased God's wisdom and goodness ... to reveal himself and the eternal *decrees of his will* to the human race."[26] Ratzinger's title contrasts with that of the official schema *De fontibus revelationis* by its naming "God's will," from which arise God's address to and graced attraction of humans to union with himself. Ratzinger places first not the "sources" in which *we seek and come to know* God's word but instead God's will, the source of his benevolent *actions regarding us,* in prevenient speaking and offering of grace, which culminate in Christ, who comes to us as the fullness of God's saving word and grace.

In no. 1, Ratzinger states the main topic, what God wills regarding human beings in the broad framework of the "the Kingdom of God," proclaimed by Jesus, as in Mark 1:15, but which is here characterized in Pauline terms as the final goal to which God is leading the world and all creation, namely, "that God may be all in all," from First Corinthians 15:28.[27] The Kingdom will recur in no. 4, regarding its anticipation in the incarnation,

---

26. Vatican Council I, *Dei Filius*, April 24, 1870, Ch. 2., "De revelatione," available in *Decrees of the Ecumenical Councils*, ed. Norman P. Tanner (London and Washington, D.C.: Sheed and Ward and Georgetown University Press, 1990), 2:806.

27. Ratzinger could well be drawing here on Rudolph Schnackenburg's biblical theology of the Kingdom of God in *Gottes Herrschaft und Reich* (Freiburg: Herder, 1958), in which section 22 treats First Corinthians 15 on the final handing over of the Kingdom by Christ to the Father and God being "all in all." Rudolph Schnackenburg, *God's Rule and Kingdom*, trans. John Murray (New York: Herder & Herder, 1965), 292–95. Yves Congar concluded his *Proemium*, near the time of Ratzinger's text, also by citing First Corinthians 15:28. See Congar, "Erinnerungen an eine Episode," in Klinger and Wittstadt, *Glaube im Prozess*, 64. Ratzinger's 1964 Advent sermons

even before any proclamation, for in Christ as God and man, the Kingdom is present, and God is inchoately "all in all."

The world "coming out" by God's creative act will arrive at its intended end in God by God's own "bringing back" (*reducatur*). It is by human beings who are united with God, that the cosmos is brought back to God and so attains its end. In no. 3, the "bringing back" will be Christ's action in his revealing of both God and man, by which he leads humans from sin into true life in God.[28]

The human return to God, realized by God's speaking and loving his human creatures, is possible because of our creation in God's image by which we are *Dei capax*, as Augustine affirmed about the human mind created in God's image, "in this, . . . it is capable of Him, and can be partaker of Him."[29] Made in the image of God, we humans are destined to receive God's speaking, by "hearing God's voice," which combines with our receiving God's prevenient love. This is the way to our union with God and to our service of bringing the world back to God and his being "all in all." Thus, the end of all God's speaking is the final kingdom, characterized by "peace, love, and happiness."[30]

Paragraph no. 2 of the Ratzinger schema introduces the ways by which God draws human beings to union with himself and brings them into his Kingdom, that is, by "speaking in many and various ways" to them across history, as said in the opening of the Letter to Hebrews, which was for Vatican I in 1870 the central New Testament witness to God's revelation.[31]

---

in Münster also placed the Kingdom theme at a central place. Joseph Ratzinger, *What It Means to Be a Christian* (San Francisco: Ignatius Press, 2006), 27–29.

28. See the comments on no. 3, below, on the Bonaventurian source of the *reductio* theme. Congar also speaks in his *Proemium* of the God of grace attracting and leading human beings back (*reducendo*) to himself." "Erinnerungen an eine Episode," 54.

29. *De Trinitate*, XIV, 8, 11. The later alternative schema, *De revelatione Dei et hominis in Jesu Christo facta,* the product of collaboration between Ratzinger and Karl Rahner, incorporates much of Ratzinger's no. 1 into its chapter I, no. 1, but moves the *capax Dei* theme to the following paragraph, in which three "articles" profess the ecclesial faith in human personhood.

30. The combined Rahner-Ratzinger schema revised and lengthened the final sentence of no. 1 by (1) saying the Kingdom is the end of "all divine *action and* speaking," (2) changing the earlier final four words on the kingdom to become a thirteen-word citation of the Preface of Christ the King from the *Missale Romanum*, and (3) adding at the end that in the Kingdom, "God is glorified by the gifts he imparts to his creatures," which includes a phrase from Vatican Council I, *Dei Filius*, April 24, 1870, Ch. 1, "De Deo rerum omnium creatore," available in *Decrees of the Ecumenical Councils*, 2:805.

31. See Vatican I's *Dei Filius*, which in chapter 2 cites Hebrews 1:1–2a on divine speaking,

Paragraph 2 treats first the whole course of human history, in which God is addressing human beings in ways that are hidden, being interior and spiritual, to attract them back to himself. This is a universal divine action, which the text characterizes as influencing persons to have desires of yearning and longing for more-than-human, transcendent objects, namely, "infinite goodness, eternal beauty, and never-failing love." Thereby, in humans and through their moving beyond imperfect goods, beauties, and loves, the world is on its way under God's influence toward its end in God's Kingdom. Below, no. 4 will return briefly to God's hidden ways of address, to add that in responding to them persons are obeying God's voice and there Christ is present to impart salvation.

Linked with this universal and interior spiritual drama, there are as well, in the history of peoples and events, particular divine manifestations that promote the movement of humans and their world to God's Kingdom and are essential for our understanding of all revelation. Thus, a complete account must affirm and combine the *two realms* of divine "speaking" in which God addresses and calls humans to himself, that is, both the hidden but universal realm of spiritual attraction and the historical, particular realm of action among people, amid human social realities, in God's voiced speaking by persons whom God selects and moves to serve his Kingdom in the world.

Amid the historical particulars of God's calling us, the assembled people of God, Abraham and his descendants, are first, because in them the forms and contents of God's word calling humans became over time gradually clearer.[32]

An advance in the text comes in no. 2, when it specifies that which becomes gradually clearer and more manifest in history, namely, God's word

---

contrasting it with reason's knowledge of God from his creatures, indicated by Romans 1:20. In *De voluntate Dei*, the verbal forms in Hebrews 1:1–2a, *loquens* and *locutus est*, lie behind the verb of the first sentence of no. 2, *alloquitur*. In the second of the late summer 1962 schemas distributed to the Council fathers, this line of Hebrews gave to chapter 4 of *De deposito fidei pure custodiendo* a central point of critical emphasis, namely, that God's actions in history and the human experience of God are in revelation subordinate to his speaking by prophets and in Christ. For *De deposito*, history and experience are polyvalent in their meaning, while the spoken component of revelation gives precision to their content and meaning for humankind.

32. The movement to more clarity could well be seen in Israelite experiences under directives of the law, which over time lead to the clarity of Deuteronomy 6.The many warnings and promises of prophets develop toward inner transformation, as in Jeremiah 31 and Ezekiel 36. Israel's prayer of individuals culminates in Psalm 73:21–28.

calling human beings (*verbum suum, vocans hominem*). This call or vocation has been implied in no. 1, on all humans being destined to hear God's voice, and is present with growing clarity in the assembly of Abraham's offspring. Yet further, the word-of-call becomes supremely specific in the particularity of the incarnation in the womb of the Virgin Mary of God's own internal word of eternal, immanent Trinitarian knowing and loving. The interior word of God's own life becomes God's external word to humankind, which is the divine word made man at a particular time and place by the conception of Christ from Mary.

Ratzinger's schema on the revelation of "the will of God regarding human beings" has moved from the anthropology of its opening words, through indicators of salvation history, to become Christological, with dogmatic Trinitarian roots. If the opening account in no. 1 suggested a controlling "anthropological turn," the development of no. 2 corrects this by moving resolutely to God's Word-calling-man become Mary's child and so dwelling on earth.[33]

In no. 3, and continuing in no. 4, Ratzinger makes the main contribution of his schema, by giving a Christological account of God's revelation of himself and of human beings.[34] The schema identifies Christ in its characteristic way with the accent on his activity, as "the living word of God seeking us out." It indicates again the final goal, already stated in no. 1, speaking here in cosmic terms about the universal "recapitulation" of all created reality in Christ, as in Ephesians 1:10.[35]

A precious contribution of no. 3 is the dual content of Christ's revelation, that is, its communication of the truth both of God and of human beings,

---

33. In the later Rahner-Ratzinger schema, no. 2 of Ratzinger's earlier schema became chapter I, no. 3. A new text, inserted as no. 2 in this chapter of *De revelatione Dei et hominis*, is a paragraph of 232 words, giving in three articles the Church's professed faith regarding human beings and their call from God (*Confitetur ergo Ecclesia . . . , Quapropter credit . . . , Ecclesia profitetur*), as appropriate in a schema proposed to a council. This may well have been inspired by Congar's parallel work at the time on a *symbolum*, with articles of revealed doctrine, offered as a *proemium* introducing all the Vatican II teaching and decrees.

34. As noted above, no. 3 of *De voluntate Dei erga hominem* makes up in *De revelatione Dei et hominis in Jesu Christo facta* the second part of chapter I, no. 3.

35. See Schnackenburg, *God's Rule and Kingdom*, 308–10, on the difference between First Corinthians 15, on God's ultimate triumph over death, and Ephesians, which attends to Christ's victory over the destructive powers of this world and to his rule that brings the perfect order of God into the cosmos under Christ's headship.

which then entered the title of the longer collaborative Rahner-Ratzinger schema, *De revelatione Dei et hominis in Jesu Christo facta*. The dual content of God's revelation became a standard doctrine of Vatican II, appearing in the revised text of *De revelatione* from the Joint Commission in April 1963, which was enriched in the 1964 revision in phrasing that passed with a slight amendment into *Dei Verbum* itself.[36] Well known is how *Gaudium et Spes* made the same point, on Christ who "by the revelation of the mystery of the Father fully reveals man to man himself and makes clear his supreme calling."[37]

The periti at work in the early days of Vatican II were emphatic on God's revelation being the illumination of the truth of God *and of* human beings. This came, perhaps first, in Ratzinger's schema of October 1962, but it was also important for Congar, who affirmed, before giving the creedal articles of his *Proemium*, that God's revelation of truths about himself *always* illumines as well the human vocation to live in saving communion with God. He added that theology makes a tragic error whenever it separates the revealed doctrine of God from insight into human existence under God's care.[38] This also entered Daniélou's draft chapter, *De revelatione et verbo Dei*, which Archbishop Gabriel Garrone (Toulouse) presented on November 27, 1962, to the newly formed Joint Commission for revising *De fontibus*, as a new opening passage for the revision. This states in its no. 1 God's dual revelation of his own triune life and of the human vocation to share in God by grace and glory.[39]

No. 3 of *De voluntate Dei erga hominem* characterizes Christ's mission and work of revealing God and humans as central to his "leading humans back" from their sinful wanderings into their authentic life (*hominemque*

---

36. On the revelation of the mysteries in 1963: "Qua revelatione veritas tam de Deo quam de homine in Christo illuscescit." Cited from Sauer, *Erfahrung und Glaube*, 701–2. The July 1964 revision developed the assertion almost to its final form: "Intima ergo per hanc revelationem tam de Deo quam de hominis salute veritas nobis in Christo illuscescit, qui non solum mediator, sed et plenitudo totius revelationis existit." *Dei Verbum* 2 has in the last clause, "mediator simul et plenitudo" (Sauer, 741).

37. Vatican Council II, *Gaudium et Spes*, December 7, 1965, no. 22.

38. Congar, "Erinnerungen an eine Episode," 51–52.

39. Sauer gives the text in *Erfahrung und Glaube*, 686–87. On Daniélou's work at this time, with several texts offered from the Garrone archive, see Pietro Pizzutto, *La teologia della rivelazione di Jean Daniélou. Influsso su Dei Verbum e valore attuale* (Rome: Gregorian University Press, 2003). I treated the first Joint Commission text in *Investigating Vatican II*, 93–96.

reducens ... in veram vitam suam), which is a "leading back" to God (*reducendo eum in Deum*). Here Ratzinger adopted a theme of St. Bonaventure's, known well to him from his habilitation thesis of 1955. The Bonaventurian classic text, *De reductione atrium in theologiam*, speaks (1) of our human minds being "led back" to God (*reducuntur ad Deum*), by God's eternal Likeness-Image-Offspring, who in the fullness of time (Gal 4:4) assumed human form (n. 8). *De reductione* tells (2) of him who assumed flesh "to lead us back" (*ut nos ... reduceret*) to the Father (no. 12). Bonaventure said further (3) that the Word and Mediator, through whom creatures came out (*exierunt*) from God, then completed reality's return (*reditus*) by becoming human "in order to lead humans back to God" (*ut homines reducat ad Deum*) (n. 23).[40]

Ratzinger's *De voluntate Dei*, no. 3, states Christ's revelation of our human reality in insistent terms that move beyond the foregoing accounts of our creation (no. 1) and of God's hidden and manifest ways of addressing us (no. 2). No. 3 posits as a central revealed content that Christ leads us back *from our fall* into sin, for once we came out from God, in our freedom we tragically chose paths of desertion from true life, of becoming untruthful (*mendax*), and of denying God to seek self-sufficiency. This dark side then becomes in the rest of no. 3 a decisive truth about human beings and the presupposition of the revelation in Christ of God's *salvific* will and work of leading back to himself his fallen human creatures.

The text had adverted briefly, late in no. 2, to the immanent divine and Trinitarian life of God, in eternal address, knowledge, and love of the divine works, by the internal Word who then became human to call humans. Then no. 3 gives the revelation of who God is *for us*, on the "economic" Trinity, as the Father relating to us in creation, as the Word seeking and searching for us, and as Love still longing for us in spite of our fleeing to ourselves in wanting to be like God, as did the first couple in Genesis 3:5–10. This brac-

---

40. St. Bonaventure, *The Reduction of the Arts to Theology*, Latin-English edition, ed. Zachary Hayes (St. Bonaventure, N.Y.: Franciscan Institute, 1996), 46–47, 50–51, and 58–59. Near the end of the account of Bonaventure's revelation doctrine in his 1955 habilitation thesis, Ratzinger explained Bonaventure's use of *reductio* in both logic and theology, with an offering of five texts on the notion regarding Christ and grace, for example, "regnum ecclesiae per Spiritum et Filium traditur Deo et Patri, dum ad ipsam supremam et paternam unitatem *reducitur*, ultra quam non est cogitare assensum" (*In IV Sent.*, Dist. 1, ad 2, q. 2, ad 3). Ratzinger, *Offenbarungsverständnis und Geschichtstheologie Bonaventuras* (Freiburg: Herder, 2009), 409–13, esp. n. 40.

ing revelation of our human identity comes from Christ in history, who not only speaks to reveal all this, but as well is "God who acts," soteriologically and effectively, in his revelation.[41]

The final lines of no. 3, on Christ being not only revelation but also the grace of God for us, affirm the dual gratuity, not of nature and supernatural grace but of the way in which God's action and gifts unfold in our regard. The text might remind readers of how Henri de Lubac's *Surnaturel* (1946) stirred many in the postwar era of the 1950s, especially Thomists, to discuss nature and grace, while Joseph Ratzinger was studying theology in Munich. But here the duality is different and is spiritually and pastorally of the highest importance.

Jesus Christ is unmerited grace to and for us in two manners or on two levels. First, Christ brings God's love for us that is prior to and prevenient of any and every loving response on our part to God (as in 1 Jn 4:19). This initiating divine love is both benevolent and beneficent in the astounding way of a giving in the superior order of God's *self*-gift, which is the deepest truth of God's communication in revelation. Revelation, thus, is much more than the I-Thou dialogue of divine word and human response, for it completes its coming by granting to human beings a *participation* in God and in his truth, dignity, and life.

The further gratuity of God's giving lies in its directing itself in love to those who flee from their divine origin and elevation to God. Essential to the truth of the human reality is that we became from the start sinful "refusniks" who do not cherish God's amazing gift, but freely reject it and the relation to God that it brings. Here enters "the love than which none is greater," as said in John 15:13, which in Christ's deed is even more startling than in the cited discourse, because God's redemptive and rescuing love, made actual in Jesus' sacrifice, does not extend itself to obedient friends who cherish what they have learned. Instead, it goes out to humans whose sinful refusal of this love it overcomes by the transforming love of Jesus' self-offering on our behalf, carried out in the midst of those attempting to escape from his many-sided gift.

---

41. One thinks of G. Ernest Wright's *God Who Acts: Biblical Theology as Recital* (London: SCM, 1952), and of the polarity of Catholic and Protestant revelation theologies that Ratzinger stated at the beginning of his 1955 habilitation thesis. While Catholics feature the revealed *sacra doctrina*, Protestants emphasize that revelation is *actio divina* and never exists independently of God acting. Ratzinger, *Offenbarungsverständnis und Geschichtstheologie Bonaventuras*, 59–65.

In the final line of no. 3, Christ "vanquished" our sin by his greater love.[42] Christ incarnated God's so great love (Jn 3:16), as he gave himself to death *pro nobis*, on our behalf and for our benefit, while we were still sinners and enemies, but now have been justified, reconciled, and are headed toward salvation (Rom 5:8–11).

No. 4 of Ratzinger's alternative schema continues the Christological development of no. 3 by affirming that even in its particularity of beginnings amid the progeny of Abraham and in the womb of Mary, Jesus Christ's revelation of God and the human has universal outreach and significance—it is *complectens omnia*. No. 4 first completes no. 1's broad statement that the Kingdom of God is the final goal of the world, for Christ realizes the kingdom in himself, where everything is "brought back" to God, as Christ effects this, and in him God is "all in all." Christ's coming is the eschatological event that anticipates the final end and goal of human history, for in Christ there is present a union of God and human nature.

Paragraph no. 4 echoes no. 2 as well on God's speaking both an internal hidden address to humans in history and external words of localized revelation in Christ to engender faith in him and life from him. The two modes of speaking are interrelated, because what the Spirit of truth offers to humans in hidden ways, as we know from John 16:14, is really derived from what is Christ's, concerns him, leads to him, and in him finds its completion. The eschatological horizon of the end of no. 4 seems operative already in its middle section, because the affirmed relations from and to Christ will be clear only at the end.

In the vast world beyond the scriptures and Christianity, God speaks in hidden ways to humans, to relate them to Christ, who, although unknown to them, brings them his saving grace and benefits. Connecting and explaining this duality of Christ who is both well-known and incognito could pose a major challenge to one's theology—*if* one ambitioned having a complete account. But around the time of the Council, Ratzinger at times eschewed saying much about how God's saving grace enters lives outside the sphere of the preached Gospel and sacraments of Christ. Instead, he insists

---

42. Regarding the last phrase, "vincens peccatum nostrum," it can be noted that the motif of battle and victory gained ground in soteriology in the 1950s through Gustave Aulén's *Christus Victor* (as in the title of both the 1931 English and 1949 French translations from the Swedish original). This current of thought drew on Irenaeus and Luther to offer an alternative to Anselm and to the Latin juridical account of Christ's redemptive deed.

on Christians being called to a representative service that, in ways God knows and actualizes, does benefit all of humankind.[43]

No. 4, in a manner correlative to the move from wider humankind to Christ, moves from Christ to all reality, about which scripture enlightens us in a basic manner. For Jesus Christ is the one Lord through whom all reality exists.[44] This indicates that knowing Christ as revealed is connatural with the whole expanse of truth gained by human investigation, for all other truths have their ultimate meaning when they are related to, or "led back to," Christ, from whom the realities concerned have their being.[45]

The final end toward which human history moves has begun proleptically in Christ, whom the Church confesses as being true God and true man in the union of the incarnation, a mystery of union that anticipates and prepares the end. No. 4 moves toward affirming the end as the "perfect union between God and humankind," which is expressed biblically in God's spousal union with his people and celebrated at the nuptial banquet of the Lamb as told in Revelation 19:9 — a theme that Ratzinger valued so much that he brought it back to conclude the whole schema in no. 5.

But Christ's historical reality and gifts were prepared in Israel, in the economy made known by Israel's scriptures. Central here is God's call of his people to a spousal relation of communion of life, which begins to realize what God intends for all humanity, namely, that those from East and West, and North and South, will by the grace of Christ, the word of God made flesh, come to share in the nuptial banquet described in Luke 13:29, which shows, in an attractive image, humankind celebrating its arrival at its final end and goal of union with God.

---

43. See "Stellvertretung," in *Handbuch theologischer Grundbegriffe*, ed. Heinrich Fries (Munich: Kösel, 1962), in English; "Vicarious Representation," trans. J. Wicks, in *Letter and Spirit* 7 (2011): 217–19; *What It Means to Be a Christian*, 45–46 (On what basis God saves the others: "That is his business, not ours.") and 62, where he moves deftly from God's mercy "sufficiently abundant for everyone" to that abundance extending even to calling for "our participation as instruments of his mercy and his loving-kindness." On this theme, see Christopher Ruddy, "'For the Many': The Vicarious-Representative Heart of Joseph Ratzinger's Theology," *Theological Studies* 75 (2014): 564–84.

44. See 1 Corinthians 8:6; John 1:3; and Colossians 1:15–17.

45. In the collaborative *De revelatione Dei et hominis*, the first four sentences of Ratzinger's *De voluntate Dei erga hominem*, no. 4, have their place in chapter II, no. 1, on God's hidden presence in humanity's history, where they make up, after modest revision, the first four sentences of the longer paragraph.

Finally, no. 5 of *De voluntate Dei* speaks to Christ's active presence in the church. The context given in October 1962 demanded that a fresh account of God's revelation to humankind had to at least sketch an ecclesial dimension.[46] So no. 5 extends further the Christology of nos. 3 and 4 by affirming the ongoing presence of the living, saving Christ in his church. In the body he assembles, he lives on, actively giving out of his fullness a revealing word that is for church members both formative of them in truth and full of vital guidance of their living, according to John 1:16–18 and 14:6, respectively.

Under Christ's influence, the church communicates revealed truths in its proclamation and doctrines, but these truths are not new inventions, for they make present in different contexts the one ample truth of the epiphany of God the Savior in Christ. Christ's apostles witness amply by their lives and writings to this truth, to which the church is bound and which it guards intact, while its members derive from its abundance "water welling up to eternal life" (Jn 4:14).[47]

Ratzinger's 1962 alternative schema concludes with another Bonaventurian affirmation, this time on the expansion and contraction of the word of God, which first moves outward into multiple doctrines, namely, the particular revealed truths brought to us by our reading the Old and New Testaments, which the church explains in preaching and doctrine. But all authentic teachings have as well the innate tendency toward returning from dispersion into unity, as they are brought back to the one master truth that is Jesus Christ. He is the one who is God and man, in whom all humans are called by him, ever the *Verbum vocans hominem*, to the nuptial banquet celebrating their salvation in intimate union with God.

46. While Vatican II's initial seven schemas did not include a *De Ecclesia*, many bishops and theologians knew when the Council opened that the preparatory commissions, both theological and central, had worked on this major topic. In October, a schema *De Ecclesia* with eleven chapters was almost ready for printing and distribution to the fathers, which occurred on November 23. I treat *De Ecclesia*'s preparation and the December discussion of it in St. Peter's in *Investigating Vatican II*, 120–33.

47. No. 5 of *De voluntate Dei* constitutes the first part of chapter II, no. 1 (*De revelata praesentia Dei in praedicatione Ecclesiae*) in the Rahner-Ratzinger text, expanded by thirty words. That chapter goes on to treat scripture theologically in accounts of appropriate biblical interpretation, of biblical inspiration, and of the significant mutual relations between the Church and scripture.

Concluding Remarks

Two details of rhetoric and language can bring out elements of particular value in this brief text of early Vatican II theological labor by peritus Joseph Ratzinger. His final affirmation in no. 5, on the call of "all humans" (*omnis genus humanum*) to union with God, forms an elegant *inclusio* with the final clause of no. 1 on "all creatures" (*omnis creatura*), who have the Kingdom of God as their end. Between these, God carries out his will regarding human beings by a manifold speaking to his human creatures and especially by the actions of Christ—which the schema repeatedly indicates in present participles (*vocans, quaerens, revelans, reducens, eripiens, vincens, complectens, erudiens*).

The author's choice of language thereby gives this brief Latin schema of October 1962 a characteristic potential for enriching our thinking by its main content, that is, by its Christologically developed understanding of God's word in its depths and range—as the call, issued and made effective in Jesus Christ, of our human family to union with himself.[48]

48. A shorter version of this presentation appeared in no. 2 of the 2020 volume of *Gregorianum*, under the title, "Another Text by Joseph Ratzinger as *peritus* at Vatican II," to conclude the report that the author made in "Six Texts," in 2008. I describe the context of this drafting by peritus Joseph Ratzinger in *Investigating Vatican II*, 80–97, on the behind-the-scenes work on God's revelation by several theologians early in Vatican II.

3

Salvation and the Holy Trinity

Interpersonal Relations with Jesus Christ and the Holy Spirit

FREDERICK LAWRENCE

In many, if not all, of the lectures I attended by my former colleague in Boston College's Theology Department, my esteemed and beloved friend, Robert Imbelli, he never failed to emphasize the Christ-centeredness ("Christic") of Catholic theology. To be sure, he was quite right to do so in light of the many currents in Catholic Christian culture both in the United States and abroad. Indeed, he frequently wondered whether Bernard Lonergan—either in his Latin works *ad usum auditorium* for his students at the Gregorian University in Rome, or perhaps even more so in *Method in Theology*, which saw the light of day during the post-Roman period of his life—had not somehow lost that Christ-centered focus that was so crucial for him. Moreover, there arose a wider concern that when Lonergan, late in his career, distinguished between "faith as the eye of being in love with God," which transvalues human values, and "belief," as assenting to truths revealed by God that go beyond our immanently generated acts of understanding and judging, he was no longer doing justice to the expressed content of divine revelation. This paper is intended to be a response to that concern.

I begin by with a definition by the late, English-born, Irish Dominican theologian, Herbert McCabe, in his *Exploring the Catholic Faith*: "Faith is a divinely given disposition of the mind by which we begin to share in God's understanding of himself. In faith, we think of the history of humanity and our own life story as centered on the love of God for us as revealed in the Son of God, Jesus Christ, the Word of God made flesh."[1] Indeed, Aquinas's treatment of *caritas* as friendship encompasses both the fact that the recognition that "God is faithful, by whom you were called into the fellowship [*koinonia, conversatio*] of his Son, Jesus Christ our Lord" (1 Cor 1:9), and that the God of our Lord Jesus Christ "wills all men to be saved" (1 Tim 2:4). Thus, out of unbounded love for his Triune nature as *love* (1 John 4:8), God draws all creatures according to their own dignity back to himself as end[2] in a movement responding to this original event of love, so that by creation, election, incarnation the Triune God enters into intimate companionship and communication with human beings: *societas, convivere, conversatio*.[3] That is what revelation is all about.

Beyond both Extrinsicism and Reductionism: Hans Urs von Balthasar and Karl Barth on the Gift of Salvation

In the pre–Vatican II era, such leading theologians as Hans Urs von Balthasar and Karl Barth advocated, albeit in very different ways, the Christocentric notion of salvation precisely as framed by the doctrine of the Triune God. Balthasar saw the affinity between Catholic teaching and the later Barth's insight into the relationship between the Word of God and the Word of Man.[4] He saw that once Barth had solidly overcome the *Kulturprotestantis-*

1. Herbert McCabe, *Exploring the Catholic Faith. A Guide through the Basics* (Boston: Pauline Books and Media, 2008), 56–57.

2. Thomas Aquinas, *Summa Theologica* II-II, q. 23, art 1: "cum ... sit aliqua communicatio hominis ad Deum secundum quod nobis suam beatitudinem communicat." See Eberhard Schockenhoff, "The Theological Virtue of Charity (IIa-IIae, qq. 17–22)," in *The Ethics of Thomas Aquinas*, ed. Stephen Pope (Washington, D.C.: Georgetown University Press, 2002), 246–48.

3. See the article by Joseph Bobik, "Aquinas on *Communicatio*, the Foundation of Friendship and *Caritas*," *The Modern Schoolman* 64 (November 1986): 1–18.

4. See Karl Barth, *The Word of God and the Word of Man*, trans. Douglas Horton (New York: Harper Torchbook, 1957), and *The Humanity of God* (Richmond, Va.: John Knox Press, 1960).

mus without the polemical interpretation of God's being *totaliter aliter* of his *Epistle to the Romans*, he was acknowledging that Christ Jesus is the ground of the natural revelation,[5] and that nature is both open to, even though not intrinsically demanding, earning, or deserving of, the gracious bestowal of God's personal love, and is indispensable to precisely the *gift* character of God's sharing of Godself. This is true both of God's kenotic readiness to become man and to empty himself even to death on the Cross (Phil 2:7), and of the eschatological realization of the Kingdom of God.

As regards the eschatological dimension of salvation, the *anakephalaiosis* of all things in heaven and on earth described in Ephesians 1:10, according to Balthasar and Barth—especially human existence and the realization of the image of God in us—centers on and culminates in the unity of divinity and humanity in Christ who grounds a universal communion with the Triune God and constitutes the ultimate communication to human beings of God's absolute and unconditional love for every one of us. Christian believers have come to realize that Christ Jesus is God's concrete command, which is always personal. Commenting on Karl Barth, Balthasar wrote that discipleship of Christ corresponds to life in Christ; as we have to respond to the existence of Christ Jesus, we are imitators of God (Eph 5:1). Such imitation and discipleship of Christ do not follow from an ethical demand but rather flow from the reality already fulfilled in the person of Jesus and his utterly foolish, even seemingly absurd (*amour fou*), love on the Cross. We owe our obedience to Jesus and his command of love.[6]

The point of stressing this harmony between Barth and Balthasar is that the latter's grasp of the *analogia entis* is fully compatible with Karl Barth's *analogia fidei*, inasmuch as it rejects the extrinsicist position that Reginald Garrigou-Lagrange defended against Maurice Blondel by overstressing the difference between correct use of the *analogia entis* in theology from the *analogia fidei*. When correctly understood, the theoretical distinction between created nature and God's self-communication in history does not place God's unmerited favor upon a finite Procrustean bed; instead, it highlights the

---

5. In Hans Urs von Balthasar, *Karl Barth: Darstellung und Deutung seiner Theologie* (Köln: Jakob Hegner, 1962), Balthasar argued that even Barth's *analogia fidei* presupposes the distinction between nature and supernature, not least in holding the Chalcedonian doctrine of "two natures united in one and the same," by which the Incarnation exists as the pure instance of grace as God's unmerited favor.

6. Balthasar, *Karl Barth*, 246.

gift-character of God's sharing with humankind his infinite love "poured out in our hearts by the Holy Spirit" (Rom 5:5) as mediated by his Son, Christ Jesus, true God and true man. Unsurprisingly, Barth acknowledged that theologically, "Hänsli" (as one Swiss theologian liked to refer to the other) and he agreed much more than they disagreed. Indeed, in one of his final seminars on Vatican II's *Dei Verbum*, while the elderly Barth joked about the Council's language of "adhering to the vestiges" of previous authoritative Church teachings, his reception of the document was extremely positive.

The Light of Glory and the Mediating Role of Christ Jesus

Thomas Aquinas's analogy of light helps us to make sense of Herbert McCabe's apparently exorbitant phrase, "we begin to share in God's understanding of himself." The light of glory is the final piece of Aquinas's analogy of light. It is the condition of the possibility of the eschatological revelation, the beatific vision. But here we also make a shift from the link between the reception of revelation to the quintessential revelation communicated in the dramatic story lived by God incarnate in Christ Jesus.[7] If, following Aristotle's definition of a plot, a story is a set of actions and passions heading toward a point, Lonergan's "*Existenz* and *Aggiornamento*" provides a significant clue to the meaning of Jesus' story: "Christ in his humanity did not will means to reach an end, but possessed the end, the vision of God, and overflowed in love to loving us."[8] Lonergan spoke more at length on this in his course on Christology, the English translation of whose Latin text *ad usum auditorum* is *The Incarnate Word*:

---

7. Rowan Williams. "Postmodern Theology and the Judgment of the World," in *Postmodern Theology: Christian Faith in a Pluralist World*, ed. Frederick P. Burnham (New York: Harper and Row, San Francisco, 1989), 96. In his contribution to this book, Williams makes a statement, the implication of which will be taken up later in this paper: "The words and work of Jesus demand choice for or against him; they force to the light hidden directions and dispositions that would otherwise never come to view, and thus make the conflicts of goals and interests between people a *public* affair. The inner rejection of one's own identity as God's creature and the object of God's love, the violence done to human truth *within* the self, becomes visible and utterable in the form of complicity and rejecting of Jesus."

8. Bernard Lonergan, "*Existenz* and *Aggiornamento*," in *Collected Works of Bernard Lonergan*, vol. 4, *Collection*, ed. Frederick E. Crowe and Robert M. Doran (Toronto: University of Toronto Press, 1993), 230.

Living on this earth, Christ had human knowledge both effable and ineffable, besides his divine knowledge. As a **beholder** [i.e., one who "possessed the end, the vision of God"], he immediately knew God by that ineffable knowledge which is also called beatific, and in the same act, though mediately, he also knew everything else that pertained to his work. As a **pilgrim** [i.e., one "who overflowed in love to loving us"], however, he elicited those natural and supernatural cognitional acts which constituted his human and historical life.[9]

Lonergan's claim that "Christ as God exercises divine knowledge" is related to the fact that as "the one undivided Christ had two natures without confusion, so also he exercised without confusion two natural operations divine and human." The claim that Jesus is a pilgrim is based on the belief that "Christ is perfect in humanity, true man [composed] of rational soul and body, consubstantial with us as regards his humanity, like us in all things apart from sin."[10] Possessing the end, then, Christ as beholder living on this earth "knows God immediately." This phrase contrasts our need to gain knowledge through our senses and imagination with the fact that all Jesus knows by the light of glory and the vision of God or beatific vision he is able to know through the mediation of the divine essence. Hence, the highpoint of God's self-communication occurs in and through the drama of Jesus' existence translated into the human terms of a first-century Palestinian Jewish idiom, and in this way constitutes the *effable* knowledge drawn from his Jewish tradition both written and oral.

Through the many things Jesus suffered and did in all his interpersonal encounters and situations, he needed to ask and answer questions for intelligibility, truth, and value, and to exercise the self-correcting process of learning (just as the rest of us do) in order to figure out gradually the appropriate words and deeds, speeches and actions needed to communicate the *mysteries* of divine revelation. According to his friend and former colleague Charles Hefling, appropriating the Trinitarian presuppositions of Jesus' mission of communication entails reaching the kinds of understanding at stake in the epitome of God's self-communication that occurs in Christ Jesus, insofar as the man Jesus, by his words and deeds, by his death and resurrection, has

9. Bernard Lonergan, *Collected Works of Bernard Lonergan*, vol. 8, *The Incarnate Word*, trans. Charles C. Hefling, ed. Robert M. Doran and Jeremy D. Wilkins (Toronto: University of Toronto Press, 2016), 573.

10. Lonergan, *Collected Works of Bernard Lonergan*, vol. 8, 663.

made effable or expressed in fully human terms the ineffable mystery of God's absolute and unconditional character as Love. To understand the mystery of the act of creation, one would have to *be* God; to understand the mystery of the gift of charity as "motivated by the love of God, by the gift of the Spirit who is God, an understanding of what it is to be God and of what it is to be 'proceeding Love' in God would be necessary. Again, ... to understand [Christ's human nature's] being united to and by the eternal Word who is God, an understanding of what it is to be God and of what it is, in God, to be 'spoken' is required."[11]

Lonergan's expression "ineffable knowledge," then, is roughly equivalent to what McCabe called "God's self-understanding." Beyond all prophecy, beyond even the knowledge of Moses, Jesus expressed "what no eye has seen, nor ear heard, nor the human heart conceived." Beatific knowledge as unimaginable, and therefore not susceptible of being known quidditatively by *any* human mind, may perhaps be most helpfully compared to mystical knowledge, which is also described as immediate insofar as it transcends images and concepts.

According to traditional teaching, then, the pilgrim people "in Christ Jesus" seek to attain the vision of God, but Jesus the pilgrim is the pure instance of grace in human history; he is the only human being who possesses the beatific vision by which we "will know God as we are known by God, face to face" (1 Cor 13:12).

The fact that from the moment he began his human life Jesus did not know in human terms the meaning of his beatific knowledge because that unfathomable knowledge is utterly immaterial accords with the profound impulse motivating the Eastern Christian tradition's insistence on the apophatic starting point for knowing God as incomprehensible mystery. Because of this apophatic dimension, Jesus had to "start from scratch" in learning how to communicate the meaning of the absolute and unconditional love of God for every human being to humankind. Lonergan's statement, "Christ in his humanity did not will means to reach an end, but possessed the end, the vision of God," means therefore that the Word Incarnate made history in Jesus' dedication to communicating to humankind in effable hu-

---

11. Charles C. Hefling Jr., "Revelation and/as Insight," in *The Importance of Insight, Essays in Honour of Michael Vertin*, ed. John J. Liptay Jr. and David S. Liptay, 97–115 (Toronto: University of Toronto Press, 2007), 105.

man terms the mystery of his primordially human, yet ineffable, share in "God's self-understanding." Only if one were oblivious to the fact that, precisely because the vision of God is supernatural and utterly unlike ordinary human knowing by being absolutely unconditioned by space and time, could one coherently suppose that the eschatological gift of the beatific vision violates either the principle that "Christ is like us in all things, apart from sin" or the principle of God's incomprehensibility as beyond the human capacity to understand exhaustively.

The Role of the Holy Spirit in God's Communicating and Our Receiving Salvation

St Paul states the basic Christian teaching of how, in the personal encounter with Jesus, we receive a share in God's self-understanding as absolute love (1 Cor 2:7–13); because the Father through the Son sends the Spirit, St Paul declares in Romans 5:5, "God's love has been poured out into our hearts by the Holy Spirit that has been given to us." The following passage from 1 Corinthians spells out the implications of this for revelation:

But we speak God's wisdom, secret and hidden, which God decreed before the ages for our glory.... But, as it is written, What no eye has seen, nor ear heard, nor the human heart conceived, what God has prepared for those who love him" (Is 64:4)—these things God has revealed to us through the Spirit; for the Spirit searches everything, even the depths of God. For what human being knows what is truly within? So also no one comprehends what is truly God's except the Spirit of God. Now we have received not the spirit of the world, but the Spirit that is from God, so that we may understand the gifts bestowed on us from God. And we speak of those things in words not taught by human wisdom but taught by the Spirit, interpreting spiritual things to those who are spiritual.

Christians believe that the Spirit who "searches everything, even the depths of God" is the Spirit through whom God revealed to us his mysteries as the "spirit of revelation" (Eph 1:17) granted to all believers. A more developed Trinitarian theology teaches that the mission of the Holy Spirit is not merely to lead us to the Incarnate Word by way of instructing and guiding people; as St Paul also says, the Spirit sent into human hearts by the Father through the Son *transforms* us by the graces of conversion, justification, and sanctification. The Holy Spirit transforms us by forgiving our sins (Jn 29:23), indwelling us (Jn 17:26), liberating us (2 Cor 3:17–18), and making us adoptive children of the Father (Rom 8:14–17, Gal 4:6–7), brothers and sisters of Christ, and temples of the Spirit (1 Cor 6:19). Everything the Holy Spirit does supports our claim that the Spirit also brings about what McCabe says regarding that "divinely given disposition of the mind by which we begin to share in God's understanding of himself."

McCabe also wrote: "In faith, we think of the history of humanity and our own life story as centered on the love of God for us as revealed in the Son of God, Jesus Christ, the Word of God made flesh." And so St Paul writes in 2 Corinthians 4:6, "For it is the God who said, 'Let light shine out of darkness,' who shone in our hearts to give the light of the knowledge of the glory of God in the face of Jesus." Yves Congar tells how the Holy Spirit enables Christians to receive a share in God's self-understanding:

The Lord or the Holy Spirit disposes the heart, and opens the ears (Act 16:14; 1 Thess 1:6; Col 4:3). In other words, to the objective revelation there corresponds the subject called to faith. From this viewpoint, which is that of God's operation giving the power of understanding and thus making his Word actual for each person, the revelation is continuous and coextensive with the history of the Word. Jesus, who has the power to reveal to whom he wills (Mt 11:27 par.), incessantly makes the Father known (Jn 17:20).

Congar goes on to recall Augustine's theme of the "interior master,"[12] to speak of the interior anointing by the Holy Spirit (1 Jn 2.27), and then refers to St. Augustine on the theme of the hardening or of blindness of the heart, which we will discuss later.[13]

The Holy Spirit bestows upon receivers of salvation the *lumen fidei,* or light of faith. In summarizing what our quotations from First and Second Corinthians say about the complementarity of the missions of Word and

---

12. *De Magistro* c. 11–14; *Conf.* IX, 9 (32): "docente te magistro intimo in schola pectoris."

13. *Conf.* X, 23.34. See also Yves-Marie Congar, *La Foi et la Théologie*, Le Mystère Chrétien, Théologie Dogmatique 1 (Paris: Desclée, 1962), 16–17. On pages 8 and 9, Congar's reflections on the meaning of the initiative taken by God (of the sort to which the Bible bears witness) to constitute relationships with his creation leads to the following conclusions: that it is *one* work, but it includes diverse projects and different stages; it presents itself both as *one* design and, therefore, as a process in the course of whose realization, the end is accomplished by a unique term.... That term is one of perfect interiority [or union/communion], without either fusion or confusion. The stages involve an ever more intimate communication, with the understanding that God always is entirely present in whatever he does, and that the differences regard only the effects.

Spirit, Lonergan wrote: "Without the mission of the Word, the gift of the Spirit is a being-in-love without a proper object; it remains simply an orientation to mystery that awaits its interpretation. Without the invisible mission of the Spirit, the Word enters into his own, but his own receive him not."[14]

The Analogy of Light: From Faculty Psychology to Intentionality Analysis

Lonergan's Transition to the Perspective of the Primacy of Love

We have seen that God's self-communication is focused upon the life, suffering, death, and resurrection of Christ Jesus as making effable in human terms the ineffable knowledge that is obviously not a matter of theoretical speculation. For years, Lonergan had adhered to the dictum *Nihil amatum nisi praecognitum* (nothing is loved unless it is first known). But as the epigraph for the *Grammar of Assent*—a book Lonergan has said influenced him greatly—St. John Henry Newman had used the maxim of St Ambrose, *Non in dialectica complacuit Deo salvum facere populum suum*.[15] As Lonergan regularly began to quote Newman's motto, *Cor ad cor loquitur* (which he translated, "love speaks to love"),[16] it became clear that the symbol of the heart—as explicated, for example, in Karl Rahner's meditation on it in relation to the Sacred Heart devotion,[17] Hans Urs von Balthasar's *Heart of the World*,[18] and Dietrich von Hildebrand's *The Heart*[19]—signaled a turning point in Lonergan's theological method and his Trinitarian theology.

---

14. This version of the quote, from "Mission and Spirit," *Collected Works of Bernard Lonergan*, vol. 6, *Third Collection*, ed. Robert M. Doran and John D. Dadosky (University of Toronto Press: Toronto, 2017), 36, contains the correction replacing "visible" with "invisible." All other quotations here are paginated from the Paulist Press edition, "Mission and Spirit," in *A Third Collection: Papers by Bernard J. F. Lonergan*, ed. Frederick E. Crowe (Mahwah, N.J.: Paulist Press, 1984), 32.

15. "God has not been pleased to bring about the salvation of his people in dialectic."

16. Bernard Lonergan, *Method in Theology* (New York: Herder, 1972), 113.

17. Karl Rahner, "'Behold This Heart!': Preliminaries to a Theology of Devotion to the Sacred Heart," and "Some Theses for a Theology of Devotion to the Sacred Heart," in *Theological Investigations*, vol. 3, *The Theology of the Spiritual Life*, trans. Karl-H. and Boniface Kruger (New York: Crossroad, 1982), 321–52.

18. Hans Urs von Balthasar, *Heart of the World* (San Francisco: Ignatius Press, 1979).

19. Dietrich von Hildebrand, *The Heart: An Analysis of Human and Divine Affectivity* (South Bend, Ind.: St. Augustine's Press, 2007).

The first crucial shift involved moving to the foreground what had tended to remain rather in the background of his writings, namely, that conscious intentionality is turned toward the world and other persons:

It turns out, however, that the priority of cognitional theory is only relative, and the priority of cognitional operations qualified. The cognitional yields to the moral, and the moral yields to the interpersonal. To make a sound moral judgment one has to know the relevant facts, the possibilities, the probabilities; but with those conditions fulfilled, the moral judgment proceeds on its own criteria and towards its own ends. Again, moral judgments and commitments underpin personal relations; but with the underpinning presupposed or even merely hoped for, interpersonal commitment takes on its own initiative and runs its own course.[20]

The second major change came with his breakthrough to the notion of value:[21]

In *Insight* the good was the intelligent and the reasonable. In *Method* the good is a distinct notion. It is intended in questions for deliberation: Is this worthwhile? Is it truly or only apparently good? It is aspired to in the intentional response of feeling to values. It is known in judgments of value made by a virtuous or authentic person with a good conscience. It is brought about by deciding and living up to one's decisions. Just as intelligence sublates sense, just as reasonableness sublates intelligence, so deliberation sublates and thereby unifies knowing.[22]

The third key shift occurred when Lonergan worked out the link between feelings as intentional responses to values[23] and being in love, whether re-

---

20. Bernard Lonergan, "Variations in Fundamental Theology," in *Collected Works of Bernard Lonergan*, vol. 17, *Philosophical and Theological Papers 1965–1980*, ed. Robert C. Croken and Robert M. Doran (Toronto: University of Toronto Press), 247.

21. Lonergan, "The Notion of Value" and "Judgments of Value," *Method in Theology*, 34–41.

22. Bernard Lonergan, "*Insight* Revisited," in *Collected Works of Bernard Lonergan*, vol. 13, *A Second Collection*, ed. Robert M. Doran and John D. Dadosky (Toronto: University of Toronto Press, 2016), 277. See also "Variations in Fundamental Theology," *Philosophical and Theological Papers 1965–1980*: "[A] distinction may be drawn between sublating and sublated operations, where the sublating operations go beyond the sublated, and a quite new principle, give the sublated a higher organization, enormously extend their range and bestow upon them a new and higher relevance. So inquiry and understanding, stand to the data of sense; so reflection and checking stand to the formulations and hypotheses of understanding; so deliberating on what is truly good, really worthwhile, stands to experience, understanding, and factual judgment; so, finally, interpersonal commitments stand to cognitional and moral operations."

23. Lonergan, "Feelings," *Method in Theology*, 27–34.

ferring to love of intimacy as in friendship and marriage, or of community, neighborhood, or nation, or love of God. As a result, in *Method in Theology*, he recognized that "the question of God is considered more important than the precise manner in which the question is formulated, and our basic awareness of God comes to us not through our arguments or choices but primarily through God's gift of his love."[24] Religious experience, then, is a dynamic state of being in love with God that is conscious (i.e., an experience) but not necessarily known (which would require understanding and judging in addition to the inner experience of God's love). Religious experience is conscious, and Lonergan explains, that it occurs

on the fourth level of intentional consciousness. It is not the consciousness that accompanies acts of seeing, hearing, smelling, tasting, touching. It is not the consciousness that accompanies inquiry, insight, formulating, speaking. It is not the consciousness that accompanies acts of reflecting, marshaling and weighing the evidence, making judgments of fact or possibility. It is the type of consciousness that deliberates, makes judgments of value, decides, acts responsibly and freely. But it is this consciousness brought to a fulfillment, as having undergone a conversion, as possessing a basis that may be broadened and deepened and enriched but not superseded, as ready to deliberate and judge and decide and act with the easy freedom of those who do all good because they are in love. So the gift of God's love occupies the ground and root of the fourth and highest level of man's intentional consciousness. It takes over the peak of the soul, the *apex animae*.[25]

As Lonergan wrote in another place:

Decisions point not only outwardly to our practical concerns but also inwardly to the existential subject aware of good and evil and concerned whether his own decisions are making him a good or evil man. But beyond all these, beyond the subject as experiencing, as intelligent, as reasonable in his judgments, as free and responsible in his decisions, there is the subject in love. On that ultimate level we can learn to say with Augustine, *amor meus pondus meum*, my being in love is the gravitational field in which I am carried along.[26]

These breakthroughs in relation to the fourth level of consciousness as related to the good and values, and leading to the acknowledgment of the prima-

---

24. Lonergan, "*Insight* Revisited," *Collected Works*, vol. 13, 277.
25. Lonergan, *Method in Theology*, 106–7.
26. Lonergan, "Variations in Fundamental Theology," *Collected Works*, vol. 17, 248.

cy of love, yielded Lonergan's reformulation of the psychological analogy for the Trinity:

The psychological analogy, then, has its starting point in that higher synthesis of intellectual, rational, and moral consciousness that is the dynamic state of being in love. Such love manifests itself in its judgments of value. And the judgments are carried out in decisions that are acts of loving. Such is the analogy found in the creature.

Now in God the origin is the Father, in the New Testament named *ho Theos*, who identified himself with *agape* (1 John 4:8, 16). Such love expresses itself in its Word, its Logos, its *verbum spirans amorem*, which is a judgment of value. The judgment of value is sincere, and so it grounds the Proceeding Love that is identified with the Holy Spirit.[27]

Significantly, "the two processions that may be conceived in God ... are not unconscious processes, but intellectually, rationally, morally conscious, as are judgments of value based on evidence perceived by a lover, and the acts of loving grounded on judgments of value."[28] Here are the implications of Lonergan's reformulation of the psychological analogy in which God as Love has the priority:

The two processions ground four real relations of which only three are really distinct from one another; and these three are not just relations as relations, and so modes of being, but also subsistent, and so not just paternity and filiation but also Father and Son. Finally, Father and Son are eternal; their consciousness is not in time but timeless, their subjectivity is not becoming but ever itself; and each in his own distinct manner is the subject of the infinite act that God is, the Father as originating Love, the Son as judgment of value expressing that love, and the Spirit as originated Love.[29]

Religious experience, then, is a matter of conscious awareness, but not at first one of knowledge;[30] it takes place in what Lonergan came to call the world of

27. Lonergan, "Christology Today: Methodological Reflections," *A Third Collection*, 93.

28. Lonergan, "Christology Today: Methodological Reflections," *A Third Collection*, 93.

29. Lonergan, "Christology Today: Methodological Reflections," *A Third Collection*, 93–94.

30. See Lonergan, "The Dehellenization of Dogma," *Collected Works*, vol. 13, 29. See also *Collected Works of Bernard Lonergan*, vol. 12, *The Triune God: Systematics*, trans. Michael G. Shields, ed. Robert M. Doran and H. Daniel Monsour (Toronto: University of Toronto Press, 2007), 215–17. "It is one thing to be conscious, but it is quite another to know, through knowledge in the proper sense, that one is conscious. To be conscious belongs to everyone, for consciousness is

immediacy: "Before it enters the world mediated by meaning, religion is the prior word God speaks to us by flooding our hearts with his love. That prior word pertains, not to the world mediated by meaning, but to the world of immediacy, to the unmediated experience of the mystery of love and awe."[31]

However, according to the Christian understanding of salvation, religious experience also happens in the world mediated by meaning.[32] "The self-communication of the divinity in love"[33] is not only communicative and constitutive; it is also cognitive, as is evident in the words of the simple children's song Karl Barth is said to have recited when asked by a theologian at the University of Chicago to summarize his theology: "Jesus loves me, this I know, for the Bible tells me so." The priority of love is foremost, and God wants everybody to know it. As Hans Urs von Balthasar has expressed it:

God is love; but it is as man that He has chosen to demonstrate this fact; and this is why it is uniquely to Christ that the two precepts of love can be fused into one single precept.... This is equivalent to saying that God, in revealing his face to man, has also revealed to man his own proper human likeness. There was no need for God to make use of man in order to reveal himself; but if he determined to do

---

simply presence of mind to itself. This self-presence is effected by the very fact that our sensitive and intellectual nature is actuated by both apprehending and desiring. It does not matter what object is apprehended or desired, since we as conscious subjects consciously apprehend and desire different things. Nor do we become conscious by adverting to ourselves, since consciousness is on the side of the adverting subject and not on the side of the object adverted to. But when this adverting to ourselves is done, we begin the second step, namely, knowing that we are conscious. For one who is conscious places oneself on the side of the object inasmuch as one understands and conceives consciousness and truly affirms that one is conscious. But unless we define what consciousness is, and unless we truly affirm that we are conscious in the sense of the definition, we do not attain knowledge, properly speaking, of our own consciousness."

31. Lonergan, *Method in Theology*, 112.

32. The "world of immediacy" indicates human conscious intentionality's direct awareness (though not necessarily focal or foregrounded) of the data of the senses or the data of consciousness; the "world mediated by meaning" indicates human conscious intentionality's direct awareness of images, symbols, or words, and its mediate (or indirect) awareness (although, again, not necessarily in a thematized manner) of what the images, symbols, or words signify. To illustrate the difference, contrast the early Husserl's endeavor to isolate acts of "pure perception" with Heidegger's turn toward language (or linguistic phenomenology), so that while pure perception may rarely occur, normally human conscious intentionality is present to the world as symbolic, or "languaged," worded, and spoken — which includes intersubjectivity, intersubjective meaning, artistic, literary, incarnate meaning, gestures, and such — hence the significance of the "as-structure" for hermeneutic phenomenology.

33. Lonergan, "Mission and Spirit," *A Third Collection*, 31.

so, and did so by an in-humanization, then all the dimensions of human nature, known and unknown, are to be assumed and utilized to serve as means of expression for the absolute Person. And so the Christian religion, while remaining sociologically only "one" religion among others, should necessarily coincide with total humanism, and it is only by this title that it can be recognized as fully catholic.[34]

This outward, "in-humanized" Word, as Lonergan said,

has a constitutive role. When a man and a woman love each other but do not avow their love, they are not yet in love. Their very silence means that their love has not reached the point of self-surrender and self-donation. It is love that each freely and fully reveals to the other that brings about the radically new situation of being in love and that begins the unfolding of its life-long implications.[35]

The Distinction between Faith and Belief

When most people say "faith" in a religious context, they probably mean "belief"—holding propositions as true whose veracity depends upon the authority of the one revealing, instead of upon one's own conscious understanding and judging; the truths so believed are dogmas or doctrines, terms which in the post-Enlightenment world have taken on the pejorative connotations of prejudice and superstition. Christians often naturally reacted to this by reframing the *initium fidei* in terms of rational argumentation—operating on the propositions that enter into the *praeambula fidei* (preambles of the faith).[36] In terms of both evangelical import and a more concrete and phenomenological account of the *Glaubenszugang*, or the appropriation of the faith, it becomes clear that receiving God's gift of his love cannot be a

---

34. Hans Urs von Balthasar, "God Has Spoken in Human Language," in *The Liturgy and the Word of God* (Collegeville, Minn.: Liturgical Press, 1959), 33–52.

35. Lonergan, *Method in Theology*, 113, whence I quote footnote 15: "A. Vergote, 'La liberté religieuse comme pouvoir de symbolization,' in *L'Hermeneutique de la liberté religieuse*, ed. E. Castelli (Paris: Aubier, 1968), 383 ff. The presence of another person takes one out of a purely epistemological context. The words he speaks introduce a new dimension to meaning. See also Gibson Winter, *Elements for a Social Ethic* (New York: Macmillan, 1968), 99 ff., applying G. H. Mead on the social origins of meaning."

36. Thomas Aquinas, *Summa Theologica* I, q. 2, a. 2, 3m: The existence and unity of God "are not articles of faith but preambles" ["non sunt articuli fidei sed praeambula ad articulos"]; Guy de Broglie, "La vraie Notion thomiste des 'praeambula fidei,'" *Gregorianum*, no. 3 (1953): 345–389, on the changed conceptualization of this notion in the seventeenth century; "The Preambles of Faith," in *A Theology Reader*, ed. Robert W. Gleason (New York: Macmillan, 1966), 105–14.

matter of people's having been reasoned into loving. "The apologist's task is neither to produce in others nor to justify for them the gift of God's love."[37]

Instead of logical propositions, phenomenology focuses on the prepropositional, preverbal, prejudgmental, preconceptual, thus opening the way to the admission of how beside the point "critically grounding" love is. As soon as he recognized this, Lonergan stopped concentrating on the *analysis fidei* because "in religious matters love precedes knowledge and, as that love is God's gift, the very beginning of faith is due to God's grace." Then "[o]ur capacity for moral self-transcendence has found a fulfillment that brings deep joy and profound peace. Our love reveals to us values we had not appreciated, values of prayer and worship, or repentance and belief."[38]

All these developments allowed Lonergan to distinguish "faith" from "belief," and to define faith as "the knowledge born of religious love." He explained what he meant by knowledge born of love" in this way:

Of it Pascal spoke when he remarked that the heart has reasons which reason does not know. Here by reason I would understand the compound of the activities on the first three levels of cognitional activity, namely, of experiencing, of understanding, and of judging. By the heart's reasons I would understand feelings that are intentional responses to values; ... Finally, by the heart I understand the subject on the fourth, existential level of intentional consciousness and in the dynamic state of being in love. The meaning, then, of Pascal's remark would be that, besides the factual knowledge reached by experiencing, understanding, and verifying, there is another kind of knowledge reached through the discernment of value and the judgments of value of a person in love.[39]

Lonergan therefore calls faith "the eye of being in love with God," which is prior to belief, because, as a love-inspired transvaluation of values, faith is the phenomenologically verifiable condition of the possibility for belief in the truths revealed by God.

37. Lonergan, *Method in Theology*, 123.
38. Lonergan, *Method in Theology*, 122–23.
39. Lonergan, *Method in Theology*, 115.

Sin, Evil, and Redemption: "Love Alone Is Credible"[40]

Sin and Evil

Biblical revelation tells us not only of human fallibility but also of the primordial fall that has become an ongoing legacy—the panoply of human sin and evil that requires the restoration (*anakephalaiosis*) of reality in accord with the purpose of God. If they had not been revealed by God, human beings could not know the mysteries hidden in God; they have, in fact, been revealed in the self-communication of God in love, which, in Lonergan's words, "resides in the sending of the Son, in the gift of the Spirit, in the hope of being united with the Father." We have to explain how this share in God's self-understanding reaches us in spite of the historic distortions caused by sin rooted in the egoism of individuals, group egoisms, and "the overconfident short-sightedness of common sense that corrupts human culture with conflicting ideologies" and that "inflicts on individuals the social, economic, and psychological pressures that for human frailty amount to determinism. It multiplies and heaps up the abuses and absurdities that breed resentment, hatred, anger, violence."[41] In the words of the late poet Philip Larkin, "Man hands misery on to man."

What Lonergan called the "objective surd of sin" or the "social surd and what Eric Voegelin termed "pneumopathology,"[42] spreads contagiously throughout human populations by way of the emotional pressures socially and culturally mediated internally, which breed alienation from oneself and from others, and results in the experience of one's existence as "betrayal," insofar as one's lack of authenticity and moral renunciation involve not just falsehood but a massive lie.

---

40. The marvelous title of one of Hans Urs von Balthasar's favorite of his own books, *Glaubhaft ist Nur Liebe*, Sammlung Christ heute (Einsiedeln: Johannes Verlag, 1963), the translation into English of which is Love Alone Is Credible, or Only Love Is Credible.

41. Lonergan, *Method in Theology*, 117.

42. The political philosopher Eric Voegelin (who had narrowly escaped from the Nazis in Vienna after the *Anschluss*) used the term borrowed from Schelling to distinguish the disease of the spirit as estrangement from the spirit from what may usually be understood by the term "psychopathology" in the context of a lecture delivered on the occasion of having been invited to give a *Vorlesung* at the University of Munich (since published as *Hitler and the Germans*). The lecture, "The German University and German Society," is an analysis of the conditions enabling Hitler's regime, published in *Collected Works of Eric Voegelin*, vol. 12, *Published Essays, 1966–1985*, ed. Ellis Sandoz (Baton Rouge: Louisiana State University Press, 1990), 6.

In Book X, chapter 41 (66) of *Confessions*, St. Augustine prays concerning Truth and the Lie:

You are the truth who preside over all things. In my greed, I did not want to lose you, but together with you I wanted to possess a lie, just as no one wants to speak falsehood such that he himself does not know the truth. Thus did I lose you, because you disdain to be possessed together with a lie.

Earlier in that Book, chapter 23 (34), which is a meditative exegesis on the conditions of the possibility of the twists and turns of his life from birth until the immediate aftermath of his conversion that had been narrated in the first nine books, St. Augustine wrote a passage on love of and hatred of the truth. Here the Bishop of Hippo illustrates how what Lonergan named the sublation of the head (i.e., consciousness as experiencing, understanding, and making judgments of fact) by the heart (consciousness as deliberating, making judgments of value, deciding, and acting) amounts to a transition from concern with factual truth as expressed in propositions to concern with the truth of existence. In responding to the question "why is it that 'truth engenders hatred" in spite of "lov(ing) the happy life, which is simply joy grounded on truth?" Augustine links the "head's" truth vis-à-vis falsehood or error to the "heart's" truthfulness and lying or mendacity when he points out that we can "hate the truth for the sake of the object which [we] love instead of the truth." The terrible result is that we "love truth for the light it sheds," but we "hate it when it shows [us] up" — reprehends, reproves us — "as being wrong."[43]

We are what we are because of what we have been and done. We are responsible for having given in to disordered love of self by deciding to act against what we know would be true to our natural desire to live in harmony with what we are nevertheless aware of as good. Our wish to be the center of the universe instead of being faithful to the one who *is* the center of the universe leads to the destruction of ourselves and of others; we regularly do not want to take responsibility for being and doing these things, so we easily fall into the habit of rationalizing these decisions and deeds. The pure and unrestricted desire to know the truth and be in harmony with the highest good gets displaced by the desire to *be known*. Our illusions about ourselves,

---

43. See St. Augustine, *Confessions*, trans. Henry Chadwick (Oxford: Oxford University Press, 1991), 119–200.

by which we entertain selfish fantasies about the rightness of our desires for comfort and pleasure (the *libido concupiscendi*) and our ambitions for power (the much more serious *libido dominandi*) can turn our moral renunciations into the living lie of sin.

As Lonergan wrote, "Sin is the source of evil in this world insofar as this world is a human creation and a human product. It involves an objective surd and that surd is stopped, it is absorbed, only insofar as there is suffering. Suffering is, as it were, the absorption of the surd of sin." The truth of this is clear: throughout history, people have not needed Machiavelli to tell them that anyone who tries to live in accord with what ought to be rather than with the deformations that actually exist "will work their own ruin." When people "appeal to any conceivable scheme of justice, how could you set that right without causing an equal amount or even more of further suffering?" To be sure, that is the typical way for people to rationalize taking revenge for the atrocities they have suffered.

And yet, as Lonergan said,

Christians know from the incarnation, from the life that the Son of God chose to lead on earth, that he chose suffering and death, and his suffering and death were results of sin. They were the results of sin, the sin of Judas, the sin of the leaders of the people, the sin of the Roman governor who did a shabby job of justice. According to the New Testament, they're the sins of the world: it wouldn't have been part of the divine plan to allow sin so to rise against the God-Man were it not for the sins of all the world.[44]

Moreover, as Lonergan wrote in *The Triune God: Systematics*,

We are conscious in two ways: in one way, through our sensibility, we undergo rather passively what we sense and imagine, our desires and fears, our delights and sorrows, our joys and sadness; in another way, through our intellectuality, we are more active when we consciously inquire in order to understand, understand in order to utter a word, weigh evidence in order to judge, deliberate in order to choose, and exercise our will in order to act.[45]

---

44. Bernard Lonergan, *Collected Works of Bernard Lonergan*, vol. 5, *Understanding and Being*, ed. Elizabeth A. Morelli and Mark D. Morelli (Toronto: Toronto University Press, 2000), 328.

45. Lonergan, *Collected Works*, vol. 12, 139.

The first way of consciousness is directly related to what Lonergan in "Mission and Spirit" called "the passionateness of being," which "has a dimension of its own: it underpins and accompanies and reaches beyond the subject as experientially, intelligently, rationally, morally conscious." Filling in the picture, Lonergan adds:

Its underpinning is the quasi-operator that presides over the transition from the neural to the psychic. It ushers into consciousness not only the demands of the unconscious vitality but also the exigencies of vertical finality. It obtrudes deficiency needs. In the self-actualizing subject it shapes the images that release the insight; it recalls evidence that is being overlooked; it may embarrass wakefulness, as it disturbs sleep, with the spectre, the shock, the shame of misdeeds. As it channels into consciousness the feedback of our aberrations and our unfulfilled strivings, so for the Jungians it manifests its archetypes through symbols to preside over the genesis of the ego and to guide the individuation process from ego to the self.

As it underpins, so it accompanies the subject's conscious and intentional operations. There it is the mass and momentum of our lives, the color and tone and power of feeling, that fleshes out and gives substance to what otherwise would be no more than a Shakespearian "pale cast of thought."

As it underpins and accompanies, so too it overarches conscious intentionality. There it is the topmost quasi-operator that by intersubjectivity prepares, by solidarity entices, by falling in love establishes us as members of community. Within each individual vertical finality heads for self-transcendence. In an aggregate of self-transcending individuals there is the significant coincidental manifold in which can emerge a new creation. Possibility yields to fact and fact bears witness to its originality and power in the fidelity that makes families, in the loyalty that makes peoples, in the faith that makes religions.[46]

This second way of being conscious, which links "the passionateness of being" with intersubjectivity and solidarity as also animated by vertical finality, brings out the priority of the social over the individual. However, St. Paul declared that these dimensions of being human individually and collectively exist under what he called "the reign of sin," or, in Lonergan's reformulation, the probability of sin:

But here we meet the ambiguity of man's vertical finality. It is natural to man to love with the domestic love that unites parents with each other and with their

---

46. Lonergan, "Mission and Spirit," *A Third Collection*, 29–30.

children, with the civil love that can face death for the sake of one's fellowmen, with the all-embracing love that loves God above all. But in fact man lives under the reign of sin, and his redemption lies not in what is possible to nature but in what is effected by the grace of Christ.[47]

The probability of sin is heightened enormously when

to the simpleminded sins of greed there is added the higher organization of sophistry. One must attend to the facts. One must deal with them as in fact they are and, as they are irrational, obviously the mere dictates of reason are never going to work. So rationalization enters the inner citadel. There is opened a gap between the essential freedom all men have and the effective freedom that in fact they exercise. Impotent in his situation and impotent in his soul, man needs, and may seek redemption, deliverance, salvation.[48]

More light has also been cast on this historic probability of sin by the insight René Girard expressed in the neologism "interdividuality"[49] (something Lonergan also examined from a different perspective in terms of the dramatic, individual, group, and commonsense biases). For Girard, the fact of interdividuality goes hand in hand with his account of human desires as mimetic, either for good or for evil. Evil mimesis, as either acquisitive or appropriative, incites mimetic rivalry, victimization, and ultimately, scapegoating. Lonergan remarked that in the life of Jesus, "There are the rather violent denunciations of the Pharisees": "You are from your father the devil, and you choose to do your father's desires. He was a murderer from the beginning and does not stand in the truth, because there is no truth in him. When he lies, he speaks according to his own nature for he is a liar and the father of lies" (Jn 8:44). Since we become caught up in sin, this denunciation *is* true of all of us, to one degree or another.

The Law of the Cross

Lonergan's discussion of the dynamism that is crucial to Jesus' enactment of the law of the cross is what Augustine in the *Enchiridion* spoke of

47. Lonergan, "Mission and Spirit," *A Third Collection*, 30.

48. Lonergan, "Mission and Spirit," *A Third Collection*, 31.

49. René Girard, "Book III: Interdividual Psychology," in *Things Hidden since the Foundation of the World,* trans. Stephen Bann and Michael Metteer (Stanford, Calif.: Stanford University Press, 1987), 283–431.

as the miracle of overcoming evil with good.[50] Lonergan calls this a "law" because it expresses the intelligible historical pattern of redemption and reconciliation articulated in the scriptural narrative of fall and redemption:

There are two solidarities: a first in Adam through sin to death; a second in Christ through death to resurrection. Adam sinned, and through his sin death entered into the world. The death was threefold: there was the spiritual death of the loss of sanctifying grace in the soul; there was the metaphorical death, the curse of Adam, so vivid to us today in the host of the moral and physical evils of the world; finally, there was the material death of the grave where dust returns to dust. Now Christ, the Son of God, knew not sin; still he died, but only to rise again; and as he died for the remission of sin, so he rose again to give us grace (Romans 4:25).[51]

The late Raymund Schwager wrote at length about the drama of Jesus' public life from its beginning as the preacher from Nazareth who in announcing the proximate eruption of the reign of God, called God his Father, and regarded his enemies (sinners) with unconditional readiness to forgive them. He proclaimed a faith that, because it can move mountains, can overcome the walls of separation between human beings and reconcile all enmities.

The situation of radical decision in which Jesus put his opponents did not lead to their conversion. Instead, his challenge unleashed a completely different reaction. The forces of lies and violence that he had laid bare struck back upon him. He was condemned by lies and violently brought to trial, and so turned into a bearer of sins or a scapegoat. In response to the violence threatened and suffered, he did not retaliate with violence. Despite his rebarbative preaching, in his own actions he remained utterly bound by the message of love of enemy and freedom from violence. As the victim of violence, he prayed to his Father for his enemies. Suffering and dying, he raised the claim that his God, even in the face of the supreme injustice and murderous violence, always remains the God of freedom from violence and love of

50. St. Augustine, "What Is Called Evil in the Universe Is but the Absence of God," in *Enchiridion on Faith, Hope, and Love*, trans. J. B. Shaw (Washington, D.C.: Regnery Publishing, Gateway Editions, 1996), 11: "And in the universe, even that which is called evil, when it is regulated and put in its own place, only enhances our admiration of the good; for we enjoy and value the good more when we compare it with evil. For the Almighty God, who, as even the heathen acknowledge, has supreme power over all things, being Himself supremely good, would never permit the existence of anything evil among His works if He were not so omnipotent and good that He can bring good our of evil."

51. See Bernard Lonergan, "The Assumption and Theology," *Collection*, 71.

enemies: "When he was abused, he did not return abuse; when he suffered, he did not threaten; but he entrusted himself to him who judges justly" (1 Pt 2:23).

The one who judges justly uttered his judgment by the fact that he raised the one crucified from the dead. This judgment for the one crucified, however, was not directed *against* his enemies. God instead stood by the very one who interceded for his opponents. In this way, the "heavenly Judge" himself had — without any reservations — defined himself as a God of freedom from violence and of love of enemies. For this reason, he sent the Risen One with his message of peace back to his disciples. Since they — because they had gained greater insight — had become especially guilt-ridden due to their infidelity, the words of Easter peace — "Peace be with you" (Jn 20:21) — proved themselves to be, above all, words of forgiveness.[52]

From another perspective, Lonergan wrote on the same Paschal mystery:

The resurrection of Christ is presented in the New Testament as the work of God the Father. It is the Father who raised the Son from the dead. On the one hand, you have the work of man, as sinning; on the other hand, you have the work of God, raising his Son from the dead.... And that work of the Father is an illustration of those words of St Paul in the eighth chapter to the Romans: to those who love God all things work for good. ["We know that in everything God works for good with those who love him, who are called according to his purpose." (Rom 8:28)][53]

In Lonergan's *De Verbo Incarnato*, the "Theses 15 to 17" elaborate the two central ideas for understanding redemption, satisfaction, and the "just and mysterious law of the cross."[54] The first idea is Thomas Aquinas's explanation of charity on the analogy of friendship (*philia*) based on Aristotle's treatise,[55] and especially, the aspect of my friend as *dimidium animae meae* ('half

---

52. Raymund Schwager, Jesus in the Drama of Salvation: *Toward a Biblical Doctrine of Redemption*, trans. James G. Williams (New York: Crossroads, 1999).

53. Lonergan, *Collected Works*, vol. 5, 376.

54. These theses in Bernard Lonergan's *De Verbo Incarnato* (Rome: Universitas Pontificia Gregoriana, 1964), 445–593, have yet to be published in English. They will soon be published along with a hitherto unpublished and quite substantive "Supplement on the Redemption," written after the publication the above-mentioned Latin treatise by the Gregorian University Press of the *ad usum auditorium* text in vol. 9 of the *Collected Works of Bernard Lonergan* by the University of Toronto Press.

55. See especially Aristotle, *Nicomachean Ethics*, Book 9, 1166a1–29.

my soul"). According to Lonergan, "Love involves a quasi-identification." Here there comes to the fore that type of being conscious through our sensibility, as we undergo rather passively what we sense and imagine, our desires and fears, our delights and sorrows, our joys and sadness connected above with the "passionateness of being" that underpins, accompanies, and overarches human consciousness as inquiring, reflecting, and deliberating. Lonergan glosses this in a more evangelical manner:

When two people are in love their thoughts are about us—what are we going to do, what do we need? It is all spontaneously so. There is a quasi-identification involved. And in the fact that God became man as our savior, there is that same manifestation of love, and it is that aspect of love, of God's love for mankind in the full sense of loving—a self-giving, to which we respond with a self-giving— that there is in charity something way beyond any ethical structure that can be based on the pure desire to know. It presupposes an advance made by God as a lover, in the full sense of loving, and it means ... our response in which we love one another because we love God—and if we don't love one another we don't know God, in the words of St John's epistle. ["Beloved, let us love one another; for love is of God, and he who loves is born of God and knows God. He who does not love does not know God; for God is love" (I Jn 4:7–8).][56]

The second notion central to understanding this experience of Jesus on the cross is the act of contrition in the sacrament of Reconciliation and Repentance. The central experience, mediated by our sympathy with the sufferings our friend Jesus, is the experience of compunction which flows from a sorrow for one's sinfulness motivated by love. My friend and former colleague, Matthew Lamb, has suggested that the Risen Christ sitting at the right hand of the Father is an "upper quasi-operator" affecting us as elemental meaning[57] at the threshold of conscious awareness. Hans Urs von Balthasar reminds us as well that Jesus as manifested in the Book of Reve-

56. Lonergan, *Collected Works*, vol. 5, 377.

57. Lonergan in *Method in Theology* on "elemental meaning": "the meaning of an experiential pattern is elemental. It is the conscious performing of a transformed subject in his transformed world. The world may be regarded as an illusion, but it also may be regarded as more true and more real" (63); "Symbols have their proper meaning. It is an elemental meaning, not yet objectified, as the meaning of a smile, or the meaning in the purely experiential pattern in a work of art. It is a meaning that fulfills its function in the imagining or perceiving subject as his conscious intentionality develops or goes astray or both, as he takes his stance to nature, with his fellow men, and before God. It is a meaning that has its proper context in the process of internal

lation with the wounds still present on his risen body shows that in the end, our Judge in the Last Judgment is also our Victim. How can one refuse his forgiveness?[58]

From a complementary perspective, René Girard wrote, "The Resurrection is not only a miracle, a prodigious transgression of natural laws. It is the spectacular sign of the entrance into the world of a power superior to violent contagion. By contrast to the latter, it is a power not at all hallucinatory or deceptive. Far from deceiving the disciples, it enables them to recognize what they had not recognized before and to reproach themselves for their pathetic flight in the preceding days. They acknowledge the guilt of their participation in the violent contagion that murdered their master."[59] And in Lonergan's words:

In the death and resurrection of Christ we have the tremendous symbol of Christianity that interprets for us the meaning of life. The Christian knows that if the master has suffered, there is nothing incongruous in his own suffering; and he knows that as the master rose again, so the Father is able to transform, to make all things work unto the good. That understanding of the meaning of human life is mediated to us through the death and resurrection of Jesus Christ, as through a symbol, an image, is something on which our intellectual and moral and spiritual lives can develop, and in their development see more and more of its profundity. And that is God's expression of himself to us.[60]

At the center of revelation, then, is the incarnation as a first expression of God's self-donation to us, and to all humanity. The gift of the Holy Spirit—the love poured out into our hearts by the Holy Spirit that is given to us (Rom 5:5)—as Lonergan tells us,

is the personal self-donation of God to the individual soul, and that is charity on God's side, and at the same time it is the infusion of charity.... That gift ... sets up a further good of order in this world, which is the mystical body of Christ and his church. So just as this self-giving of God is something that lies beyond

communication in which it occurs, and it is to that context with its associated images and feelings, memories and tendencies that the interpreter has to appeal if he would explain the symbol" (67).

58. Hans Urs von Balthasar, *Dare We Hope "That All Men Be Saved?" with a Short Discourse on Hell*, trans. Dr. David Kipp and Rev. Lothar Krauth (San Francisco: Ignatius Press, 1988), 90–91.

59. René Girard, *I See Satan Fall Like Lightning*, trans. James G. Williams (Maryknoll, N.Y.: Orbis Books, 2002), 189.

60. Lonergan, *Collected Works*, vol. 5, 376.

... any possible exigence of human nature or conclusion of man's thinking about the world—loving in the full and intimate sense of the word involves a free initiative—so this mystical body of Christ is a further, higher integration of human living. It is the transition from the *civitas terrena* that can be constituted by a pure desire to know, to the *civitas Dei* that is founded on the love of God and the self-revelation of God.[61]

Conclusion

At the beginning of this essay, I quoted Herbert McCabe's definition of faith in *Exploring the Catholic Faith*: "Faith is a divinely given disposition of the mind by which we begin to share in God's understanding of himself. In faith, we think of the history of humanity and our own life story as centered on the love of God for us as revealed in the Son of God, Jesus Christ, the Word of God made flesh." Now, at the end of the chapter, I quote him again: "By the revelation of grace, [Aquinas] says, we are joined to God as to an unknown, *ei quasi ignoto conjungamur* (*ST* Ia, q. 12, a. 13 *ad* 1). God remains the mystery which could only be known by God himself, a sharing which for us in this world is not knowledge but the darkness of faith."[62] So too, according to Lonergan:

What God is—the answer to the question, *Quid sit Deus?* What is God—is something we do not know. We don't know God by his essence in this life. We have only analogous knowledge of him. But that has been God's revelation of himself to us, and insofar as in humility and simplicity we accept things as they are, we can advance to a knowledge of God and an intimacy with God that will leave us convinced that what, as philosophers, we may call his wisdom and his goodness are in truth wisdom and goodness—surpassing wisdom and surpassing goodness.[63]

61. Lonergan, *Collected Works*, vol. 5, 380–81.

62. Herbert McCabe, "The Involvement of God," in *God Matters* (London: Geoffrey Chapman, 1987), 41–42.

63. Lonergan, *Collected Works*, vol. 5, 376–77.

4

Faith, Reason, and Incarnation in Irenaeus of Lyon

KHALED ANATOLIOS

In his Regensburg lecture on "Faith, Reason, and the University," Pope Benedict XVI surveyed some of the decisive fluctuations in the relation of faith and reason within the Christian tradition. In the course of this broad overview, he presents the early Church's performance of this relation as paradigmatic and normative—indeed as "part of faith itself." But he contrasts this exemplary synthesis with later developments within the Christian tradition in which this synthesis is distorted through either a conception of faith that abstracts entirely from human reason or a conception of reason that precludes any positive continuity with faith. He identifies the former relation with the voluntarism of the medieval theologian Duns Scotus, in which God's transcendence and otherness are affirmed at the expense of any analogical reflection in human reason. On the other hand, he diagnoses in modern theology, going back at least to the liberal Protestantism of Adolf von Harnack, a reduction in the scope of reason to the apprehension of the mathematical structure of matter and to experimental verification. This "reduction of the radius of science and reason" not only excludes the question

I am grateful to the editors of *Nova et Vetera* (English edition) for permission to republish this essay, which originally appeared in *Nova et Vetera* 16 (2018): 543–60.

of God from the scope of rational enquiry but also precludes the possibility of rational enquiry into the most fundamental questions of human origin, destiny, and meaning. Pope Benedict concludes his lecture with a call for a renewal of the synthesis of faith and reason in the modern context, a renewal in which the decisive element would be the enlargement of the scope of reason itself.

It would stand to reason, in terms of the logic of Pope Benedict's Regensburg lecture, that the Christian renewal of the proper synthesis of faith and reason should draw upon the resources of the paradigmatic and normative instantiations of this synthesis in the early Church. In this essay, I would like to implement this strategy by reflecting on one significant example of this synthesis in the theology of the great second-century bishop and theologian, Irenaeus of Lyon. There are strong grounds for identifying Irenaeus as the first Christian systematic theologian, the first Christian thinker who explicitly conceived of Christian faith as a coherent body of truth whose very coherence and consistency should be the object of disciplined reflection. Irenaeus's attentiveness to the systematic wholeness of the Christian proclamation was provoked in reaction to what he considered to be the false doctrine of the heretical "Gnostics." Irenaeus attacked the Gnostics both for their misuse and neglect of human reason and for their mischaracterization of the material contents as well as the formal character of Christian faith. He derided what he called their "knowledge falsely so-called" as a perversion of both faith and reason.

In opposition to this Gnostic system, Irenaeus elaborated a conception of authentic Christian knowledge as a synthesis of faith and reason which is grounded in the simultaneous difference and relation between the Creator and the creation, and which comes to full maturity in Jesus Christ, the Word made flesh. In attempting to retrace the synthesis of faith and reason in Irenaeus's theology, this paper will proceed in three main parts. First, I will attempt to draw out some main elements of Irenaeus's critique of the Gnostics on rational grounds; second, I will demonstrate how Irenaeus's construal of the God-world relation determines his own characterization of the proper capacities and limits of human reason; and third, I will show how Irenaeus's understanding of authentic Christian knowledge presumes that the synthesis of faith and reason is consummated only through the Incarnation of Divine Reason in the person of Jesus Christ and is authentically proclaimed only within the communion of the visible and hierarchical Church.

Irenaeus's Rational Critique of the Gnostics

Irenaeus often criticizes his opponents for not making sense. But at the beginning of his five-book treatise, *Against Heresies,* he also seems to suggest that previous defenders of Christian doctrine against the Gnostics did not succeed precisely because they precipitously dismissed Gnostic teaching without probing its *seeming* intelligibility and plausibility, and without acknowledging its demonstrable attractiveness and appeal even to many Christians.[1] For his part, Irenaeus intends to show how the Gnostics don't make sense by directly engaging and refuting the sense they seem to make. Therefore, he spends the entire first book of his five-book treatise on the narration of Gnostic doctrine. There, he tells us that the particular group of Gnostics with whom he was most directly in conflict, called the Valentinians, conceived of a divine realm called the "fullness," or *"pleroma"* in Greek. There are thirty beings, called "aeons," within the pleroma, arranged in male and female pairings that emanate from the first principle, one of whose names is the "Primal Father." At the center of the Gnostic narrative is the account of the misadventures of the youngest member of the pleroma, who is called "Sophia," or Wisdom. Sophia succumbs to an inordinate desire to know the incomprehensible nature of the Primal Father, and this disordered passion results in the generation of a formless substance called "Achamoth." Achamoth is expelled from the *pleroma* but is eventually healed and restored to the divine sphere.

For the Gnostics, the constitution and arrangement of this world is directly the result of the drama of Achamoth's passion and restoration. Achamoth's fear, grief, and anxiety during her exile from the *pleroma* give rise to material substances. Her repentance resulted in the formation of the Demiurge, who is the creator of the intermediate "soul" element within the world. Her post-restoration ecstasy brought forth spiritual substances. Corresponding to this threefold ontological hierarchy are the three different kinds of human beings: the material, who are inescapably destined for corruption; the "soul-ly (*psychic*)," those whom the Gnostics identify as ordinary Christians and who are capable of ascending to an "intermediate space" between this world and the *pleroma*; and the "spiritual/*pneumatics*," who contain a divine element that is destined to be awakened by knowledge of its true origin

---

1. Irenaeas of Lyon, *Against Heresies* (hereafter, *AH*) I.Pref. 1–2.

and end and which ultimately will be restored to the *pleroma*. Despite variations in detail, a fundamental common ground between various Gnostic accounts it that, as a whole, this world is not the direct product of the true and highest god within the pleroma. Rather, its creator is the "Demiurge," who was produced from Sophia's delinquent passion.

Having outlined, in prodigious detail, the particularities of the various versions of Gnostic lore in his first book, Irenaeus proceeds in the second book to criticize Gnostic teaching on predominantly rational grounds before moving on to a positive exposition of Christian faith in the succeeding books. From among the many criticisms that Irenaeus directs against the cogency and plausibility of Gnostic teaching, we can discern three major critiques that characterize Gnostic teaching as simply lacking the form of rational discourse. Each of these critiques presses the point that Gnostic doctrine is irrational and nonsensical, and each of them is correlated with a comparative statement of the superior cogency and rational plausibility of Catholic Christian faith. A brief exposition of each of these critiques and their corrective correlates in Christian faith will thus afford us with a preliminary view of Irenaeus's presentation of the rationality of Christian faith.

(1) The criticism that we should take to be foundational for Irenaeus's program of presenting Gnostic doctrine as irrational is that there is simply no evidence for their god in this world. Now, in making this criticism, Irenaeus's complaint is *not* that the Gnostic "god" cannot be proved on the basis of reason alone. His complaint is that the content of the Gnostic belief system precludes *a priori* any knowledge of God through creation, simply because this creation is not considered to be the work of the true God. Consequently, there can be no epistemological ascent from the apprehension of created reality to any kind of knowledge of the true God. The criterion of rationality that Irenaeus posits in making this argument is that of "witness" or "testimony" (μαρτυρία/testimonium). The god of the Gnostics simply cannot provide any testimony on his own behalf, since in their account there is an ontological disjunction between the realm of creaturely testimony and the realm of the true god. For Irenaeus, this account of the God-world relation necessarily makes Gnostic doctrine pervasively and irredeemably irrational.

To speak rationally of the true God requires that we ascribe a certain truth to creation as providing evidentiary testimony to the God whose very act of creation inscribes a certain knowledge of himself within the very being of creation. To say that God is the creator of this world, for Irenaeus, means to say that "the universe shows forth the One who formed it, and the handiwork suggests its Maker, and the world manifests the One who arranged it."[2] On the other hand, the Gnostic god "has no witnesses" in the realm of creation. Therefore, he concludes, "it is completely irrational (*irrationale*) to set aside the one who is truly God, to whom all things render testimony, in order to inquire whether there is above him another one who does not actually exist and has never been proclaimed by anyone."[3]

In weighing the import of this criticism, we should consider well that the force of its refutation extends beyond the distinctly Gnostic belief that this material world is not the product of the true God. Whenever the analogy of being between this created world and the true God is denied, whenever divinity is construed as disclosed only in the realm of individual interiority, or depicted in strictly negative terms as simply other than creation, then the essential force of Irenaeus's criticism retains all its power. The discourse that posits such a divinity, insofar as it categorically abstracts from seeking evidentiary testimony for the divine from the realm of creaturely being, is, in Irenaeus's terms, foundationally irrational. For Irenaeus, by positive contrast, authentic Christian faith is "reasonable," in the first place, because it seeks to discern the testimony of creation to the God who created it. For the second-century bishop of Lyon, we cannot speak rationally of God without speaking of God primarily as "creator" and as the one who implants and solicits testimony to himself from his creation.

(2) The second critique through which Irenaeus seeks to manifest the unreasonableness of Gnostic doctrine is contained in his plaintive complaint that the Gnostics simply make things up. He attributes the proliferation of the maddening variety of detail within Gnostic accounts to a fundamental epistemological disposition that makes a virtue out of inventiveness of doctrine: "Since they differ so widely among themselves both as respects doc-

---

2. *AH* 2.9.1: "Ipsa enim conditio ostendit eum qui condidit eam, et ipsa factura suggerit eum qui fecit, et mundus manifestat eum qui se disposuit." *Ireénée de Lyon, Contre les hérésies, Livre II*, Texte Critique et traduction par Adelin Rousseau et Louis Doutreleau, SJ, Sources Chretiénnes (hereafter, SC) 294 (Paris: Édition du Cerf, 2011), 84. Unless otherwise noted, translations are my own.

3. *AH* 2.10.1: "Perquam itaque irrationale est, praetermittentes eum qui vere est Deus et qui ab omnibus habet testimonium, quaerere si est super eum is qui non est et qui a nemine umquam adnuntiatus est."

trine and tradition, and since those of them who are recognized as being most modern make it their effort daily to invent some new opinion, and to bring out what no one ever before thought of, it is a difficult matter to describe all their opinions."[4] Irenaeus reiterates this complaint several times in the course of his narration of Gnostic doctrine, saying in another place, "every one of them generates something new, day by day, according to his ability; for no one is deemed perfect who does not develop among them some mighty fictions."[5] The irrationality of this attitude resides in its lack of external and objective accountability, its sheer arbitrariness. It seems that a person can propose as revealed truth just whatever one can dream up. To demonstrate the inherent irrationality of this license to generate doctrine, Irenaeus takes up the mantle of a Gnostic teacher himself and mockingly suggests the following doctrine:

There is a certain "pre-beginning," royal, surpassing all thought, a power existing before every other substance, and extended into space in every direction. But along with [this pre-original power] there exists another power which I term a Pumpkin and along with this Pumpkin there exists a power which I call Utter-Emptiness. This Pumpkin and Emptiness, since they are one, produced ... a fruit, everywhere visible, eatable, and delicious, which fruit-language calls a Cucumber. Along with this Cucumber exists a power of the same essence, which again I call a Melon. These powers, the Pumpkin, Utter-Emptiness, the Cucumber, and the Melon, brought forth the remaining multitude of the delirious melons of Valentinus. For ... if any one can assign these names at his pleasure, who shall prevent us from adopting these names?[6]

We can, I think, discern a logical consistency between Irenaeus's first and second critiques. His first criticism was that the Gnostic system claimed access to a revealed teaching that dispensed with any evidentiary testimony from the realm of creation. His second criticism is really a transposition of the first criticism from the level of ontology and metaphysics to that of human community. Just as the Gnostics are happy to dispense with the universal testimony of creation to their claimed revelation, so they put little stock

4. *AH* 1.21.5; English translation in *The Apostolic Fathers with Justin Martyr and Irenaeus,* Philip Schaff et al., eds., Ante-Nicene Fathers (hereafter, ANF) 1 (Grand Rapids, Mich.: Eerdmans, 2001), 347; cf. *AH* 1.28.1.

5. *AH* 1.18.1 (ANF 1, 343).

6. *AH* 1.11.4 (ANF 1, 332–33); translation slightly altered.

on the value of a universal testimony to that revelation on the part of the community of faith, the Church. By contrast, the reasonableness of Catholic faith is manifest in the correspondence between positing the universal witness of creation to its Creator and performing a universal witness to that revelation in the communion of the Church. The fundamental contrast can be further reduced to that between positing "hiddenness" as the essential formal characteristic of truth, both in the realms of faith and reason, and identifying the essential character of truth with openness, transparency, and communicability.

Catholic faith manifests the openness and accessibility and communicability that characterize all truth through the universality and unanimity and consistency of its witness to revealed truth. That is why the continuity of Catholic faith, across time and space, is for Irenaeus an indispensable sign of the cogency and reasonableness of that faith. Faith knowledge shares with reason the formal characteristic of generating universal attestation. Thus, for Irenaeus, authentic and perfect knowledge, *gnosis*, can only be found in the universal witness of the Church, which can demonstrate its continuity with the Old and New Testaments and with the apostolic preaching and that enacts this universal witness in the communion of all the churches and their common reference to the bishop of Rome. Communion is thus a constitutive characteristic of rationality and truth.[7] It is universal, or catholic communion, a communion that is generated and safeguarded by love rather than mere inventiveness, which is the hallmark of the true knowledge of the Catholic faith:

True knowledge is [that which consists in] the doctrine of the apostles, and the ancient constitution of the Church throughout all the world, and the distinctive manifestation of the body of Christ according to the successions of the bishops, by which they have handed down that Church which exists in every place, and has reached even to us, being guarded and preserved without any forging of Scriptures, by a very complete system of doctrine, and neither receiving addition nor [suffering] curtailment [in the truths which she believes]; and [it consists in] reading [the word of God] without falsification, and a lawful and diligent exposition in

7. For a modern treatment of this theme, from an Orthodox Christian perspective, see John Zizioulas, "Truth and Communion," in *Being as Communion*, 67–122 (Crestwood, N.Y.: St. Vladimir's Seminary Press, 1985). Zizioulas presents some cursory reflections on Patristic resonances of this theme, including some comments on Irenaeus, but does not attend to Irenaeus's concrete ecclesiology.

harmony with the Scriptures, both without danger and without blasphemy; and [above all, it consists in] the pre-eminent gift of love (2 Cor 8:1; 1 Cor 13) which is more precious than knowledge, more glorious than prophecy, and which excels all the other gifts [of God].[8]

As with Irenaeus's first critique, it is not hard to see the relevance of his critique of Gnostic sensibilities for our own times. Ultimately, the question comes down to whether there is such a thing as an objective truth that can transcend the differences between individual subjectivities, not by negating them but by gathering them into communion. If there is not such an objective truth that enfolds individual subjectivities, then inventiveness, in the mode of concoctions of narratives and explanations that reflect and generate subjective experiences, becomes the primary epistemological virtue and the animating principle of discourse. But if there is such a communion-forming, objective truth, then it would naturally manifest itself through a universal witness that transcends the limitless multiplicity of narratives and explanations that individual subjects inevitably project onto reality. Such a universal witness is objectively caused by the self-disclosure of truth and is subjectively maintained through love, which binds together all those who bind themselves to the truth. Irenaeus presumes that a self-standing objectivity is essential to truth and rationality, and that such objectivity manifests itself subjectively in the mode of communion and unanimity of witness. Therefore, the rationality of authentic Catholic faith is bound up with the universal witness of the Church.

(3) The third critique through which Irenaeus seeks to press his characterization of the Gnostics as only seeming to make sense is his complaint that their accounts of the sordid goings-on in the realm of the divine *pleroma*, or fullness, are clearly projections of human experiences onto the divine sphere. The story of Sophia's inordinate desire to know her father, her giving birth without her male companion, her grief, fear, and perplexity, is indeed compelling. If this story seems to make sense—if it seems to carry a certain plausibility, Irenaeus intimates, it is only because it mirrors human experiences and projects them onto the divine. Surely, Irenaeus is right that much of the popularity of Gnostic lore, then and now, is due to its success in projecting onto a transcendent scale primal human experiences of unrequited desire, alienation, escape, and reconciliation. It's a great story line: Sophia

8. *AH* 4.33.8 (ANF 1, 508).

is a single mother with an absent father who gives birth to a delinquent son but then finds her way back to the divine suburbs of the *pleroma*.

The Gnostic strategy of making sense out of human experiences of suffering and alienation by projecting them directly onto the realm of the divine is arguably also operative in some strands of modern Christian theology that follow the Hegelian program of making human suffering and alienation constitutive of a dramatic unfolding of divine life. Against this impulse as manifested in its original Gnostic form, Irenaeus insists that the perception of God that is innate in human reason gives testimony to the indefectible integrity of divine transcendence: "His invisible reality, being powerful, bestows on all a great mental intuition and perception of His sovereign and all-powerful supereminence."[9] Irenaeus thus distinguishes between the seeming sense, the pseudo-rationality of mythology, which projects human psychodrama onto the divine sphere, and the authentic rationality of metaphysical insight, which always factors in the radical difference between God and creation, even as it ascends from knowledge of creation to acknowledgment of the Creator. Genuinely rational metaphysical insight ascends from created to uncreated reality precisely by seeing divine being as the transcendent ground of creation and not merely a part of creation. Consequently, Irenaeus not only insists that creation discloses God but also protests that creation does not mirror God. Created things, he says, are not the direct and symmetrical images of divine things; otherwise, God would be corporeal and simply part of creation, rather than its transcendent ground. It is because the Gnostics ignore this fundamental principle that they end up projecting the drama of human flux and suffering onto the divine sphere:

These things may properly be said to apply to human beings, since they are compound by nature, and consist of a body and a soul.... They are thus describing the affections, and passions, and mental tendencies of human beings, while being ignorant of God. By their manner of speaking, they ascribe those things which apply to human beings to the Father of all ... while, at the same time, they endow Him with human affections and passions. But if they had known the Scriptures, and been taught by the truth, they would have known, beyond doubt that God is not as human beings are; and that His thoughts are not like human thoughts (Is 55:8). For the Father of all is at a vast distance from those affections and pas-

9. *AH* 2.6.1 (SC 294, 60).

sions which operate among human beings. He is a simple, uncompounded Being, without diverse members, and altogether like, and equal to himself, since He is wholly understanding, and wholly spirit, and wholly thought, and wholly intelligence, and wholly reason, and wholly hearing, and wholly seeing, and wholly light, and the whole source of all that is good.[10]

Let us now briefly summarize the three features of the rationality of Christian faith which Irenaeus posits as counterpoints to the irrationality of Gnostic lore. Christian faith is rational, in the first place, because it seeks and finds the testimony of the real world, as we know and experience it, on behalf of the God who is its creator. To dispense a priori from such testimony, says Irenaeus, is to preclude the possibility of any kind of evidence for one's claims, which is fundamentally irrational. Secondly, Christian faith is rational because it also refers to the testimony of a universal community that manifests a unanimity across space and time. Again, to dispense a priori from such a community of witness is to disavow the essential character of truth as a reality that transcends individual subjectivities and brings them into a communion of knowledge, speech, and action. Thirdly, Christian faith is rational because it apprehends created realities as revelatory of their transcendent ground without making that ground simply a mirror of these created realities. Whereas the conflation of the ground of being with the contingent realities brought forth from that ground bears the character of mythology rather than rationality.

It might seem, however, that there is a certain tension, if not outright contradiction, between Irenaeus's insistence that creation gives witness to God and his caveat that creation does not mirror the creator. But for Irenaeus, this tension simply coincides with the structure of rationality itself, which is determined by the real relation between divine and created being. Let us now look more closely at Irenaeus's understanding of this ontological relation, which he presumes to be determinative for the possibilities and limits of human knowledge, as well as its intrinsic openness to divine revelation.

---

10. *AH* 2.13.3 (ANF 1, 373–74).

The God-World Relation and the Structure of Human Reason

For Irenaeus, the most exalted conception of divine transcendence dictates that God is both intimately present to creation and irreducibly other than creation.[11] Irenaeus's equally emphatic insistence on both aspects of this dialectic was directed not only against the Gnostics but was also antithetical to some fundamental principles of the Greek philosophy of his time. Though the lavish mythological veneer of Gnostic lore can seem far removed from the rigorous dialectical exercises of Greek philosophy, one important tenet of Greek philosophy that was foundational for the Gnostic systems was the belief that the highest divinity is not directly involved with the affairs of this world. Aristotle concluded that it was strictly rational to posit a transcendent ground for contingent being, but this divine being who was the Unmoved Mover and Self-thinking Thought can only preserve its perfection by not attending to any realities inferior to it.[12] In the course of his polemic against the Gnostics, Irenaeus tirelessly belittled this kind of conception of divine transcendence. Such a so-called God, whose transcendence is defined as sheer otherness and lack of involvement with the world, would be "a feeble, worthless, and negligent being."[13]

For his part, Plato had maintained that divine goodness is generous and does not begrudge sharing its perfections with lesser beings.[14] Irenaeus evokes this Platonic principle in order to insist that a conception of divine transcendence, conceived most radically as goodness, must entail God's direct engagement with the world. Such divine goodness remains transcendent not by being distant from the world but by containing the world and enfolding it within divine agency. Irenaeus presents this understanding of divine transcendence as self-evident on strictly rational grounds: "That which contains is greater than that which is contained. But then that which is greater is also stronger, and in a greater degree Lord; and that which is greater, and stronger, and in a greater degree Lord—must be God."[15] That God contains

11. I have dealt with the structural importance of this theme and its formative influence on the theology of Athanasius in my *Athanasius: The Coherence of His Thought* (London: Routledge, 1998), 18–24.

12. Aristotle, *Metaphysics* 1072b, 14ff.

13. *AH* 5.4.1 (ANF 1, 530).

14. Plato, *Timaeus* 29E–30A.

15. *AH* 2.1.2 (ANF 1, 360).

all things means, for Irenaeus, that God made creation somehow "in himself."[16] This does not mean that creation alters divine being in any way, but rather that the ultimate forms and intelligible identities of created things have their ground in God's own life: "this God, the creator, who formed the world, is the only God, and there is no other God besides Him—He Himself receiving from Himself the model and figure of those things which have been made."[17] It is because of this unfathomably intrinsic relation of created things to God that creation reveals God and gives testimony to his intelligence, power, and goodness.[18]

Yet for Irenaeus, this grounding and containment of creation in God can never annul the irreducible difference between contingent created being and the transcendent being of the creator. In fact, the two aspects of the relation between God and creation are not at all in competition but are strictly correlative. The difference between God and creation is entirely constituted by God's positive relation to creation as its ground and the source of its ontological sustenance:

The things established are distinct from Him who has established them, and what have been made from Him who has made them. For He is Himself uncreated, both without beginning and end, and lacking nothing. He is Himself sufficient for Himself; and still further, He grants to all others this very thing, existence; but the things which have been made by Him have received a beginning. But whatever things had a beginning, and are liable to dissolution, and are subject to and stand in need of Him who made them, must necessarily in all respects have a different term [applied to them].[19]

It stands to reason, for Irenaeus, that this ontological difference must have epistemological consequences. Indeed, he maintains that the proportion of difference between created and uncreated being must always persist in any creaturely effort to come to knowledge of God: "in the same proportion as he who was formed but today, and received the beginning of his creation, is inferior to Him who is uncreated, and who is always the same, in that proportion is he, as respects knowledge and the faculty of investigating the causes of all things, inferior to Him who made him. For you, O human

---

16. *AH* 2.3.1: "He himself created it who formed it beforehand in himself" (ANF 1, 362).
17. *AH* 2.16.3 (ANF 1, 380).
18. *AH* 2.9.1.
19. *AH* 3.8.3 (ANF 1, 422).

being, are not an uncreated being."[20] Not only that, but since the ultimate truth about created things resides within the divine life itself, human beings cannot of themselves attain to a full understanding of even created being:

Inasmuch as we are inferior to, and later in existence than the Word of God and His Spirit, we are on that very account destitute of the knowledge of His myster- ies. And there is no cause for wonder if this is the case with us as respects things spiritual and heavenly, and such as require to be made known to us by revelation, since many even of those things which lie at our very feet (I mean such as belong to this world, which we handle, and see, and are in close contact with) transcend our knowledge, so that even these we must leave to God. . . . On all these points we may indeed say a great deal while we search into their causes, but God alone who made them can declare the truth regarding them.[21]

Thus, given the simultaneity of positive relation and difference between God and the world, human reason also exhibits a capacity for discerning the presence and activity of God through creation but falls short of the vision of God which it naturally seeks. Moreover, it must always be on its guard against a false similitude of this vision concocted by presuming that created realities directly mirror divine reality. But the good news of Christian faith is that this vision is finally attained when the Word and Reason of God, the Son of the Father, who fully shares in the being of God, becomes human and thus reveals to humanity both God and creation, as well as the relation between them.

Perfect Knowledge and the Incarnation of the Word

As one would expect, Irenaeus and his Gnostic opponents offered very different interpretations of the Prologue of the Gospel of John.[22] The Gnos- tics, with their penchant for projecting multiplicity onto the divine realm,

---

20. *AH* 2.25.3 (ANF 1, 397; slightly altered).

21. *AH* 2.28.2 (ANF 1, 398–99).

22. For a thorough treatment of Irenaeus's treatment of the Gospel of John, see Bernard Mutschler, *Irenäus als johanneischer Theologe*, Studien und Texte zu Antike und Christentum 21 (Tübingen: Mohr Siebeck, 2004). For an analysis of the Valentinian interpretation of the Pro- logue of John's Gospel, see Tuomas Rasimus, "Ptolemaeus and the Valentinian Exegesis of John's Prologue," in *The Legacy of John: Second-Century Reception of the Fourth Gospel*, ed. Tuomas Rasimus (Leiden and Boston: Brill, 2010), 145–71.

take the different divine titles in the Prologue as designating different beings: God, Beginning, Word, Only-begotten, Life, Light, Grace, Truth, are
all different beings in the Gnostic system. Moreover, Gnostic Christologies
typically distinguished between an earthly Jesus, who is created by the Demiurge, and a divine being, called Christ or the Savior, who descends upon
Jesus from the pleroma, and then returns to the pleroma. According to different Gnostic accounts, this divine being descended on Jesus during his
baptism or during the crucifixion; in some accounts, he is laughing at the
side of the cross while the earthly Jesus is being crucified.

For Irenaeus, however, the key disclosure of the Johannine prologue is
that the divine Word and Reason, who always coexists with the Father, has
consummated the union of creator and creation in his becoming flesh. Irenaeus is well aware of the variations in the various Gnostic systems, but for
him, the key touchstone of orthodoxy, whose denial makes them all equi-
distant from authentic Christian revelation, is to be found in the Prologue
of the Gospel according to John. After outlining the variations in Gnostic
Christologies, he concludes: "But according to the opinion of no one of the
heretics was the Word of God made flesh."[23] The epistemological consequences of the Word becoming flesh are central to Irenaeus's concern. We
have seen that for him, the difference between God and creation means that
human beings can never attain to knowledge of God by their own efforts;
they cannot even fully comprehend created realities. At the same time, for
Irenaeus, humanity has never simply been left to its own devices in its efforts
to know the truth of God and creation. On the one hand, Irenaeus contends
that "God cannot be known without God."[24] On the other hand, throughout human history, God has been making himself known through God,
according to the Trinitarian pattern of divine self-disclosure. Irenaeus finds
the foundations for this Trinitarian structure of divine self-communication
in the Prologue of John.

The Prologue of John identifies Jesus as the divine Logos or Intelligence.
Irenaeus presumes this identification as indicating the fullness of the Word's
divinity, since "God is all intelligence, all Word."[25] John's Prologue says, "No
one has seen God. The only-begotten Son has made him known" (Jn 1:18).

---

23. *AH* 3.11.3 (ANF 1, 427).
24. *AH* 4.6.4 (ANF 1, 468).
25. *AH* 2.13.8: "illum totum sensum et totum Verbum" (SC 294, 124); cf. 2.28.5.

Irenaeus seems to be merely paraphrasing this Johannine verse when he declares: "Since it was impossible, without God, to come to knowledge of God, He teaches human beings through his Word to know God."[26] For Irenaeus, the Son's pedagogy of divine self-disclosure reaches its apex when the Word becomes flesh: "For in no other way could we have learned the things of God, unless our Master, existing as the Word, had become human."[27] Going beyond the Prologue of John, and with special reference to the descent of the Spirit on Jesus at his baptism, Irenaeus explains that through the Incarnation, the Son receives the Spirit humanly on our behalf and, in this way, the Spirit of God becomes "accustomed to" dwell in human beings. Thus, the Trinitarian self-communication is complete when the Spirit "furnishes us with the knowledge of the Truth."[28]

While the Incarnation brings about the fullness of divine disclosure, it also simultaneously validates creation itself. Against the Gnostic claim that this material world is the product of a delinquent semidivine being, Irenaeus's persistent argument is that creation's capacity to be the bearer of spirit, truth, and salvation is fulfilled and demonstrated through the Incarnation. Only if this world bore the direct imprint of its divine creator could it bear the full personal presence of divinity in the Incarnation of the divine Word and Reason, the Logos of the Father. If creation in general gives testimony to the presence and activity of God, we can say that God also, in the Incarnation, gives testimony and proof of creation's capacity to carry and communicate the divine presence:

For how could that creation which was concealed from the Father, and far removed from Him, have sustained His Word ... ? How, again, could that creation which is beyond the Pleroma have contained Him who contains the entire Pleroma? Inasmuch, then, as all these things are impossible and incapable of proof, that preaching of the Church is alone true [which proclaims] that His own creation bore Him, which subsists by the power, the skill, and the wisdom of God; which is sustained, indeed, after an invisible manner by the Father, but, on the contrary, after a visible manner it bore His Word.[29]

26. *AH* 4.5.1 (ANF 1, 466; slightly altered).
27. *AH* 5.1.1 (ANF 1, 526).
28. *AH* 4.33.7 (ANF 1, 508).
29. *AH* 5.18.1 (ANF 1, 546).

Irenaeus's interpretation of the Johannine prologue is thus foundational for his conception of the relation between faith and reason. He interprets the Johannine prologue as identifying Jesus to be the intelligence of God and thus, in keeping with Jesus' own words, as the truth itself (cf. Jn 14:6). This identification enables him to apply the Johannine proclamation of the Incarnation to the psalmist's exclamation that "truth has sprung from the earth" (cf. Ps 85:11).[30] But if truth has sprung from the earth, this means that the divine ground of creation is now intelligible in a new way, since this ground has become manifest within creation itself. Moreover, if truth can spring up from the earth, this also means that the earth is a carrier of truth. Faith in the Incarnation, then, validates human rationality while also expanding it beyond its natural limits.

Conclusion

Irenaeus never reflected thematically on the relation between faith and reason in the way that Pope Benedict did in his Regensburg address. But motivated by Pope Benedict's valorization of the synthesis of faith in reason in the theology of the early Church, I have tried to show how Irenaeus performed this synthesis in a way that is exemplary and indeed normative, as Pope Benedict claimed. I would like to suggest that a foundational category in Irenaeus's performance of this synthesis is that of "testimony." We have seen that Irenaeus derides the Gnostic god as devoid of the "testimony" of reality as we know it. On the other hand, he sees the Catholic doctrine of creation as an embracing of creation's testimony to its creator and the doctrine of the Incarnation as indicating the creator's testimony to his creation.

If I may be allowed to follow the trajectory of the letter of Irenaeus's theology into the horizon of the spirit that animates it, I propose that, at its heart, his theological vision presumes that the element of "testimony" or "witness" is intrinsic and even constitutive of rationality and truth, whether in the mode of faith or reason. Intelligence, understanding, reason—however we want to speak of the mystery of the encounter with truth—all of this for Irenaeus is bound up with testimony and witness-bearing. This fundamental intuition is distinctly Christian because it is ultimately Trinitarian. There is no element of testimony or witness that is constitutive of the con-

---

30. *AH* 4.5.1.

ception of ultimate intelligence as self-thinking thought, which is Aristotle's understanding. But the Christian affirmation of Jesus' ultimate identity as the Logos or Reason of the Father, who eternally exists with the Father and eternally "exegetes" the Father, posits Divine Intelligence as intrinsically and constitutively and eternally a communion of testimony or "bearing witness." The Christian God is not merely Intelligence but a communion in which the Son eternally bears witness to the Intelligence of the Father. As the Reason of the Father, the Son does not make the Father rational or intelligent, but his very person is testimony to the perfection of the Father's intelligence and the Son's generation from the Father is coextensive with that testimony.[31] The Spirit too is called the "Spirit of Truth," in the Gospel of John, not because he makes the Son to be the truth and not because he makes the Father generate the truth of the Son, but because he bears witness to the Father's generation of the Son as his self-testimony and to the Son's responsive testimony to the Father, and bears witness also to the mutual love of Father and Son in their mutual testimony. This Trinitarian interactivity of mutual witness is wonderfully expressed in the "troparion" for the Byzantine liturgy of Theophany that commemorates the baptism of Jesus: "When you were baptized in the Jordan, O Lord, the worship of the Trinity was revealed. For the Father's voice bore witness to you by calling you his Beloved Son, and the Spirit, in a form of a dove, confirmed the truth of these words. O Christ God, who has appeared to us and enlightened the world, Glory to You!" Many religions and thought systems envision the divine as intelligent or as intelligence itself, but only the Trinitarian faith of Christianity posits an interactivity of testimony and mutual witness as *constitutive* of divine intelligence.

This emphasis on intra-Trinitarian testimony is, of course, deeply Johannine. It is in John's Gospel that Jesus declares that the Father testifies on his behalf (Jn 5:37) and that the Holy Spirit will also give witness to him (Jn 15:26). Irenaeus does not systematically explicate a theology of testimony based on the exegesis of these Johannine texts. But it seems to me that he presumes this Johannine grammar and that this presumption grounds and permeates his distinctive performance of the synthesis of faith and rea-

---

31. In saying that the Son does not make the Father rational or intelligent, I am essentially reiterating St. Augustine's clarification that the Father is not only wise though begetting wisdom but is himself Wisdom which begets Wisdom, such that the Father is begetting Wisdom and the Son is begotten Wisdom. Cf. Augustine, *De Trinitate* VI.1.2.

son. Ultimately, the most radical differentiation he makes between Catholic Christians and the Gnostics is that the god posited by the latter lacks universal testimony. Catholic faith, on the other hand, is not only a faith in a God who is "all Intelligence" and thus the ground of all rationality but also a faith in the God whose intelligence and rationality is witnessed to extensively throughout creation and intensively in the Church. The *true* God, for Irenaeus, is the God who can evoke this universal witness. We can further add that this true God can evoke this universal witness precisely because witness is eternally constitutive of divine intelligence and divine rationality. Both faith and reason bear witness to this God, and this witness is only a participation in the witness which God gives to himself, as Father, Son, and Holy Spirit. As the evangelist John tells us, "this testimony is true," and in communion with Irenaeus, we can add: "this testimony *is Truth*."

5

Analogy and the *Analogatum Princeps* at Vatican II

THOMAS G. GUARINO

Soon after Vatican II ended, Yves Congar stated, somewhat surprisingly, that while the Council's explicit references to Aquinas are not numerous, and while the great synod more willingly cited Church fathers, earlier councils, and recent popes, nonetheless, "it could be shown ... that St. Thomas, the *Doctor communis*, furnished the writers of the dogmatic texts of Vatican II with the bases and structure of their thought. We do not doubt that they themselves would make this confession."[1] This is a striking statement by one of the principal conciliar periti, appearing to controvert much received wisdom about Vatican II. In his influential book, for example, John O'Malley notes that the Council "largely abandoned the Scholastic framework that had dominated Catholic theology since the thirteenth century."[2]

O'Malley is correct that scholastic *language* was abandoned by the Council. But what about scholastic *ideas*? Was there still some place for them at Vatican II? If not, then how did Aquinas furnish the authors of the Council's dogmatic texts with the "bases and structure" of their thought, as Congar

---

1. Yves Congar, "La théologie au Concile: Le 'théologiser' du Concile," in *Situation et tâches présentes de la théologie* (Paris: Cerf, 1967), 53.

2. John W. O'Malley, *What Happened at Vatican II* (Cambridge, Mass.: Belknap Press of Harvard University, 2008), 46.

insists was the case? In the section that follows, I will discuss briefly how two of Aquinas's central ideas—participation and analogy—were utilized at Vatican II, and how these themes are crucial for the Council's Christocentrism, a theme at the heart of Fr. Robert Imbelli's work.

Participation and Analogical Reasoning
in *Lumen Gentium*

The use of participatory and analogical reasoning is visible throughout Vatican II. For example, in the famous passage from *Lumen Gentium* on the priesthood of the faithful and the ministerial priesthood, it is clearly analogy that serves as the structuring principle. In a well-known sentence, the Council teaches:

Though they differ from one another in essence and not only in degree, the common priesthood of the faithful and the ministerial or hierarchical priesthood are nonetheless interrelated: each of them in its own special way is a participation in the one priesthood of Christ.[3]

Tracing the various drafts of *De Ecclesia* which lead to this sentence, one sees that the council moved from an analogy of extrinsic denomination (with "priesthood" predicated only metaphorically of the baptized) to an analogy of intrinsic attribution (with both the ministerial and common priesthood formally and substantially *participating in* the one priesthood of Jesus Christ.[4] For the dogmatic constitution, Jesus is the prime analogue, the *analogatum princeps*; only he is a priest *per se et per essentiam*. As Gérard Philips, the moderator of Vatican II's Theological Commission and the draughtsman of *Lumen Gentium* later stated: Only Jesus "has by full right the name of priest" even though this attribute is extended to others.[5] Both the ordained ministers and the baptized faithful are priests *per participationem*, secondary analogates who share in the one priesthood of Christ. There is an essential difference between these two analogates (not simply a differ-

---

3. Vatican Council II, *Lumen Gentium*, November 21, 1964, no. 10.

4. I treat this issue at greater length in *The Disputed Teachings of Vatican II: Continuity and Reversal in Catholic Doctrine* (Grand Rapids, Mich.: Eerdmans, 2018). See also, "Analogy and Vatican II: An Overlooked Dimension of the Council?" *Josephinum Journal of Theology* 22, no. 1–2 (2015): 44–58.

5. Gérard Philips, *L'Église et son Mystère au IIe Concile du Vatican*, vol. 2 (Paris: Desclée, 1968), 268.

ence *secundum magis et minus*) because of the nature of the participation exercised by each in the priesthood of the Redeemer.[6]

This brief discussion illustrates a couple of points: 1) Thomist categories—particularly participation and analogy—are essential for fully understanding *Lumen Gentium*'s teaching on the priestly office of Jesus Christ, of his ordained ministers, and of his baptized faithful. In a 1965 article written shortly after the formal promulgation of *Lumen Gentium*, Philips noted that the dogmatic constitution contains the Catholic Church's "first official doctrinal declaration on the subject of the *universal priesthood* of the faithful."[7] A man with his finely honed theological intelligence knew that this teaching, a *novum* in conciliar history, had to be expressed with precision. The classical and scholastic tools of participation and analogical attribution were critical to this task.[8] 2) These tools were utilized by Vatican II in order to honor Christ as the *analogatum princeps*, the unique high priest in whom every other Christian priesthood participates and from whom every other priesthood takes its name.

Another example of participatory and analogical reasoning at the service of Christocentrism may be found in *Lumen Gentium*'s treatment of the term *mediatrix* in no. 62 of the dogmatic constitution. This traditional title caused one of the most divisive discussions within Vatican II's Theological Commission.[9] When Philips presented his draft schema, *De Beata Virgine,* to the

---

6. By insisting on an essential difference between the baptismal and ordained priesthood, Vatican II rejected the univocal predication of Christ's priesthood to the faithful and their ministers. Univocal predication occurs when a single specific form is possessed more or less intensely by a subject, for example, a person who is more or less virtuous, or water that is more or less hot. This type of gradation does not, and it not intended to, overcome univocity. To overcome univocal attribution, *diverse forms* of Christ's priesthood must be specified in the common and ministerial priesthood, even though both constitute intrinsic participations in the one priesthood of Jesus. For a discussion of the diverse forms proper to each priesthood, see Thomas G. Guarino, "*Essentia et non Gradu Tantum Differant*': A Note on the Priesthood and Analogical Predication," *The Thomist* 77 (October 2013): 559–76.

7. See *Primauté et Collégialité: Le dossier de Gérard Philips sur la Nota Explicativa Praevia (Lumen gentium,* chap. III), ed. Jan Grootaers (Leuven: Leuven University Press, 1986), 190. This book contains the French translation of an article by Philips ("La Constitution 'Lumen Gentium' au Concile Vatican II") that originally appeared in the Dutch journal *De Maand* in February 1965, just three months after *Lumen Gentium* was promulgated.

8. As Philips says when commenting on the difference between the common and ministerial priesthoods: "once again, we refer to an explanation *on the basis of analogy.*" See *L'Église,* vol. 1, 143, emphasis added.

9. See Guarino, *The Disputed Teachings,* 82–87.

full commission, it did not include the disputed term. Its absence prompted Archbishop Pietro Parente of the Holy Office to object, arguing that *mediatrix* was a title with which the Mother of God had been traditionally adorned in Catholic theology. Parente asked Philips to edit the text, reconciling two theological trajectories: Mary as Christ's exemplary disciple and Mary as *mediatrix* of graces. Surprisingly, Philips—a man who always sought consensus on the Commissio de Fide—declined to include the term.[10]

Cardinal Ottaviani, the president of the Theological Commission, appointed a subcommittee to resolve the heated dispute. Among the periti on this committee, Karl Rahner and Yves Congar opposed the title *mediatrix*, arguing that it would cause theological confusion and give offense to the separated Christian brethren. But Parente and the Franciscan Mariologist Charles Balić ardently insisted the term must be included in the redrafted schema. Unable to come to an agreement, the subcommittee remanded the matter to the full Theological Commission, which, on June 6, 1964, voted 12–9 to include the word *mediatrix* in the schema.[11]

Of course, the crucial theological issue is obvious: scripture teaches us in 1 Timothy 2:5 that there is *one* mediator between God and man, Jesus Christ. How could the council speak of Mary as *mediatrix* without contradicting pristine biblical truth and without detracting from Christ's unique mediatorial role?

To solve this question satisfactorily, Philips turned to themes he had successfully employed when dealing with the priesthood. As we have already seen, both ministerial priests and the baptized faithful *participate in* the one priesthood of Jesus. Insofar as they share in Christ's priesthood, all Christians are called "priests" *formaliter et substantialiter*. But this attribute belongs preeminently and essentially (*per se et per essentiam*) to Jesus and only secondarily (*per participationem*) to others. As Aquinas had said: Christ alone is the *verus sacerdos*.[12]

10. André-Marie Charue of Namur, Belgium, a vice-president of the Theological Commission, was astonished at Philips' uncharacteristic refusal to compromise, speculating that he had come to know (through Bishop Carlo Colombo, the friend and theological adviser of Paul VI) that the Pope did not want this title in the dogmatic constitution. See André-Marie Chaure, *Carnets conciliaires de l'évêque de Namur A.-M. Charue*, ed. L. Declerck and Cl. Soetens (Louvain-la-Neuve: Faculté de Théologie, 2000), 194.

11. Charue, *Carnets conciliaires*, 204. Philips records the vote as 13–9 in favor of *mediatrix*. See *Carnets conciliaires de Mgr Gérard Philips, secrétaire adjoint de la commission doctrinale*, ed. K. Schelkens (Leuven: Peeters, 2006), 120.

12. Thomas Aquinas, *Summa Contra Gentiles*, IV, c. 36.

Philips invokes this same reasoning when explaining how Mary can be called *mediatrix*. As *Lumen Gentium* states: "just as the priesthood of Christ is *participated in* in various ways by the ministers and by the faithful" (*sicut sacerdotium Christi variis modis ... participatur*) so in the same way "the unique mediation of the Redeemer does not exclude but rather gives rise to a manifold cooperation which is but a *sharing in* this one source (*participatam ex unico fonte*)." In other words, just as Christ is the exemplar of priesthood, so also is he preeminently and essentially the one mediator between God and humanity. But this unique status does not preclude "secondary analogates" who *share in* Christ's mediatorial work—just as creaturely priests are not excluded from sharing in Christ's priesthood.[13]

Ultimately, Philips is arguing, and Vatican II is teaching, that terms such as "priest" and "mediator"—which belong preeminently to Jesus Christ—are not jeopardized when others are called "priests" and "mediators" as long as it is understood that such terms are applied *secondarily and analogically* to those who participate in Christ's unique offices. Once again, the council, in its teaching on *mediatrix*, upholds Christ as the *analogatum princeps*. Jesus is the one mediator between God and men. But just as priests, both ordained and baptismal, participate in the vocation of the one High Priest, so do others participate in the work of the Redeemer.

Vatican II's Christocentric intentions in this matter are illustrated by a journal entry of Philips some six months after *Lumen Gentium* was formally promulgated in November 1964. Looking back on the dogmatic constitution's chapter on Mary, Philips writes:

In the *Communio Sanctorum* all is referred to the Lord, and the cult of the saints is in this sense "relative." That is to say, we venerate the individual person, but this person is only venerable because he or she is referred to Christ as source and fulfillment. The dignity of Mary also comes from Christ. Naturally, no one denies this origin. But the method employed by many does not always take sufficient account of it.[14]

13. Aquinas had said much the same: Although Christ is the one mediator, there exist secondary mediators who assist in uniting God to men. On ministerial priests sharing in the mediatorial work of Jesus, see Thomas Aquinas, *Summa Theologica*, III, q. 26, a. 1.

14. Philips, *Carnets conciliaires*, 147. For Philips, failing to understand the secondary character of the cult of the saints leads to theologies that isolate Mary, as if she could be treated theologically on her own, apart from the Savior. This is one reason Philips, in redrafting chapter 8 of *Lumen Gentium*, decided to surround the word *mediatrix* with other titles (*adjutrix, auxiliatrix*, etc.), so that *mediatrix* would not become the subject of isolated theological reflection. This also explains

The holiness of the Blessed Mother and the saints can only be properly understood in reference to Christ. Once again, Jesus is the prime analogue—*the ontologically dense center of truth and holiness*—while Mary and the saints are "secondary analogates" who participate in the holiness of the Redeemer.[15]

Participatory and analogical thinking—*in service to Christocentrism*—is present in many other places throughout the council—in *Unitatis Redintegratio, Ad Gentes, Gaudium et Spes,* and elsewhere.[16] And this kind of thinking confirms a theme crucial to Fr. Imbelli's thought—that Vatican II purveyed a theology with a rich and vibrant Christological core. In the following section, I would like to illustrate how Fr. Imbelli develops this insight.

Jesus Christ: *Analogatum princeps* at Vatican II in the Work of Robert Imbelli

One of the major themes of Fr. Imbelli's work is his insistence that the documents of Vatican II are "Christologically saturated." Indeed, he contends that the council's singular achievement is "its coherent and defining Christocentrism."[17] We have observed just such a Christocentrism in our discussion above: For the council, Jesus is the prime analogue of the priesthood, and the one mediator par excellence. But neither of these roles precludes secondary analogates who share in his priestly and mediatorial roles.

Jesus Christ (and the Catholic Church) are clearly at the center of Vatican II's teachings, with others—other Christian churches, other religions, and others seeking truth—participating in and related to Christ and his

---

why Philips says of the liturgical expression, *Mirabilis Deus in sanctis*: "Notice, we do not say that it is the saints who are marvelous, but rather that *God is marvelous in his saints*. And for this reason we thank God for his saints." That is, the saints *participate in* the holiness of God, who is himself the source of all holiness and goodness. Philips, *Carnets conciliaires,* 148, emphasis added.

15. This explains why Philips and Congar were disappointed when Paul VI bestowed the title *Mater Ecclesiae* on Mary at the end of the Council's third session. This title, they believed, tended to place Mary *outside* of the Church, thereby making her an object of reflection apart from her status as Christ's exemplary disciple *within* the Church. See Yves Congar, *My Journal of the Council,* trans. Mary John Ronayne and Mary Cecily Boulding (Collegeville, Minn.: Liturgical Press, 2012), 687, 696.

16. See Guarino, *The Disputed Teachings,* chapter 4; Andrew Meszaros, "The Thomistic Underpinnings of *Ad Gentes*," *Nova et Vetera* 13 (2015): 875–901.

17. See Robert P. Imbelli, "The Identity and Ministry of the Priest in Light of Vatican II: The Promise and Challenge of *Presbyterorum Ordinis*," *Josephinum Journal of Theology* 22 (2015): 26.

body. This is the clear message, as earlier noted, of *Unitatis Redintegratio* and *Ad Gentes*. Fr. Imbelli makes the point that even *Gaudium et Spes*, a document which inspired strong objections on the council's Theological Commission, does not lack a strong Christological core.[18] The pastoral constitution teaches,

The Lord [Jesus] is the goal of human history, the focal point of the longings of history and of civilization, the center of the human race, the joy of every heart and the answer to all its yearnings. He it is Whom the Father raised from the dead, lifted on high and stationed at His right hand, making Him judge of the living and the dead. Enlivened and united in His Spirit, we journey toward the consummation of human history, one which fully accords with the counsel of God's love: "To reestablish all things in Christ, both those in the heavens and those on the earth" (Eph 11:10).[19]

Like other conciliar documents, *Gaudium et Spes* has an organizing principle that differs from that of prior ecumenical councils. Rather than the "defensive attitude toward the world that characterized the church in Europe since the French Revolution and the onset of modernity," Vatican II placed its emphasis on what the Catholic Church *shared* with the contemporary world, accenting those attributions and "perfections" that the two hold in common.[20] But this emphasis on similarity did not mean attenuating the Gospel or tailoring it to modern sensibilities. As Imbelli points out, *Gaudium et*

18. For objections to the earlier drafts of *Gaudium et Spes*, see Brandon Peterson, "Critical Voices: The Reactions of Rahner and Ratzinger to 'Schema XIII' (*Gaudium et Spes*)," *Modern Theology* 31 (January 2015): 1–16. Bishop Charue, a vice-president of the *De Fide*, stated that even toward the end of the Council, there remained opposition to *Gaudium et Spes* "by a group of Germans, notably Cardinal Frings under the influence, so it is said, of Ratzinger." See Charue, *Carnets conciliaires*, 262.

19. Vatican II, *Gaudium et Spes*, December 7, 1965, no. 45. Cited in Imbelli, "The Identity and Ministry of the Priest," 34. Imbelli charges postconciliar theology with often "misremembering" Vatican II's strong Christological center, even accusing such theology of proximity to nineteenth-century liberal Protestantism (27, n. 11).

20. Robert P. Imbelli, *Rekindling the Christic Imagination: Theological Meditations for the New Evangelization* (Collegeville, Minn.: Liturgical Press, 2014), 85. A good example of this analogical approach may be seen in the Council's handling of communism. Some four hundred bishops petitioned the Theological Commission to include a condemnation of communism in *Gaudium et Spes*, a reproof that would echo and intensify Pius XI's 1937 encyclical *Divini redemptoris*. But Paul VI, desiring to emphasize what Catholicism *shared* with others, thought that a condemnation would violate the Council's intentions. Nonetheless, to satisfy this large contingent of bishops,

Spes "is radically Christocentric." Jesus is unhesitatingly taught as the fullness of divine revelation, while the modern world is commended for sharing in the quest for truth, justice and peace.[21] Rather than simply accepting the nostrums of modernity, the pastoral constitution urges the Church to "scrutinize the signs of the times," always "interpreting them in the light of the Gospel."[22] In *Gaudium et Spes*, as elsewhere at Vatican II, Christ is always upheld as the fullness of truth, even while others are evaluated in terms of their proximity to the Lord and his Church.[23]

Fr. Imbelli's vigorous argument for Christ as the *analogatum princeps* of the Council is exemplified by this assertion: "I insist that the four Constitutions of Vatican II are Christologically charged, fresh realizations and celebrations of the church's Lord and the world's Savior."[24] Imbelli is entirely

---

Divini redemptoris was mentioned, although relegated to the footnotes. See Guarino, *The Disputed Teachings*, 121.

21. Imbelli, *Rekindling the Christic Imagination*, 84. Imbelli's judgment is shared by Jared Wicks SJ who speaks of the "remarkable *Christological grounding*" of the pastoral constitution. See Jared Wicks, *Investigating Vatican II* (Washington, D.C.: The Catholic University of America Press, 2018), 213. Wicks provides details on those episcopal speeches that argued for a stronger Christological center for *Gaudium et Spes*, concluding that the pastoral constitution contains one of the "great texts on Jesus Christ [no. 10] from a document which has often been 'misremembered' by not taking these lines into account." Wicks, *Investigating*, 218. Just here, Wicks cites Imbelli's comment on the contemporary "misremembering" of key conciliar documents.

22. *Gaudium et Spes*, no. 4. Lukas Vischer, the Swiss Reformed theologian who was the designated observer from the World Council of Churches, strongly criticized the term "signs of the times," which was found more frequently in earlier drafts of *Gaudium et Spes*. Vischer argued that *signa temporum* was an ambiguous phrase. What was urgently needed was a *critique* of the times by the Gospel. See Richard Schenk, "Officium signa temporum perscrutandi," https://www.stthomas.edu/media/catholicstudies/center/ryan/conferences/2005-vatican/Schenk.pdf. See also Carmen Aparicio, "Contributo di Lukas Vischer alla *Gaudium et Spes*," in *Sapere teologico e unità della fede: Studi in onore del Prof. Jared Wicks* (Roma: Editrice Pontificia Università Gregoriana, 2004), 3–19.

23. Joseph Ratzinger famously called *Gaudium et Spes* a "counter syllabus," referring to the Syllabus of Errors issued in 1864. This term does not imply that Christ is not the center of the pastoral constitution, but that the optic for judging the world had changed — from an earlier attitude of condemnation and recrimination to Vatican II's accent on the *partial commensurability* existing between the Church and modernity. In fact, in a speech to the Roman clergy just two weeks before his retirement as the bishop of Rome, Ratzinger/Benedict XVI twice referred to *Gaudium et Spes* as a "great" document. For *Gaudium et Spes* as "counter syllabus," see Joseph Ratzinger, *Principles of Catholic Theology*, trans. Mary Frances McCarthy (San Francisco: Ignatius, 1987), 381–82. For Ratzinger's speech to the Roman clergy, see http://w2.vatican.va/content/benedictxvi/en/speeches/2013/february/documents/hf_ben-xvi_spe_20130214_clero-roma.html.

24. Imbelli, *Rekindling the Christic Imagination*, xxiv. (Page numbers in this section of the chapter refer to this book.)

right that Jesus Christ is at the center of the conciliar documents—all people, all religions, all institutions, and all truth must ultimately be related to him. Scripturally, one sees here the influence of the letter to the Colossians, which teaches that "God's whole plan for creation is embodied in him [Jesus]."[25] Vatican II's theology, Imbelli relentlessly argues, finds its axial principle in Christ, the Redeemer of the world. This is why, despite all the talk that has taken place about the Council's return to scripture and the earliest tradition, Imbelli asserts that "the deepest *ressourcement* the council engaged in was a re-Sourcement: a return to the unique Source who is Jesus Christ" (79).

From Christ, all radiates outward and is analogically related to him. So Mary, the Mother of God, "has lived most intimately and fully the mystery of the church, the sacrament of the paschal mystery of her Son.... She has attained in privileged and preeminent fashion the holiness to which all the baptized are called" (82–83). And that holiness is nothing less than a sharing in Jesus' own life. This sharing in Christ's life—this "Christification," as Imbelli calls it—is the meaning of the well-known scriptural passage that men and women are intended to "become sharers in the divine nature" (2 Peter, 1:4). Christ is the *analogatum princeps,* the source of that divinization in which all are called to participate.[26]

The Christic Center of Vatican II

A particular accent in the writings of Fr. Imbelli is placed on *Dei Verbum*, Vatican II's dogmatic constitution on divine revelation, which speaks lucidly of Jesus as the fulfillment of God's self-manifestation to humanity. For Imbelli, this document must be considered the *primus inter pares* among the four great conciliar constitutions because God's unveiledness is the essential foundation for the Church and the liturgy.[27] But in an article analyzing the

25. Colossians 1:15–20; Imbelli, *Rekindling the Christic Imagination*, 5. On the importance of Paul's letters to the Ephesians and Colossians at Vatican II, see Wicks, *Investigating Vatican II*, 102.

26. See Robert P. Imbelli, "Second Peter: From Periphery to Center," https://www.thecatholic thing.org/2018/06/10/second-peter-from-periphery-to-center/.

27. Imbelli, *Rekindling the Christic Imagination*, xv. After the rejection of the original schema, *De fontibus*, in November, 1962 — and the subsequent difficulties in drafting a replacement schema — some bishops and theologians suggested that the major themes on revelation could be treated in the dogmatic constitution on the Church. This suggestion was strongly resisted by Paul VI, who at the close of the second session (December 4, 1963) spoke of the need for a conciliar document on revelation. Ratzinger asserts that Paul's decision was well-founded. Not only

2000 Congregation for the Doctrine of the Faith (CDF) declaration, *Dominus Iesus*, on the salvific universality of Jesus Christ, Imbelli ruefully notes that "the robust Christocentrism of *Dei Verbum* seems to evoke embarrassment in certain theological and missionary circles of contemporary Catholicism."[28] Indeed, the Church is today faced with the "covert and overt relativizing of Christological normativity." This is the case, even though the conciliar documents themselves speak assuredly, constantly, and consistently of the uniqueness of Jesus Christ.

I fully agree with Fr. Imbelli's emphasis on the Christological center of Vatican II. I would add that when one examines *Nostra Aetate, Lumen Gentium, Unitatis Redintegratio*, and other conciliar documents, one sees both the "center" of the Council, as well as its decided emphasis on others' participatory relationship with that center. Throughout Vatican II, Jesus is presented as the fullness of divine revelation, the Lord of history. But other religions—to take *Nostra Aetate* as an example—are not simply error-laden realities. On the contrary, there exists *partial commensurability* between Christianity and other faiths. This, of course, is particularly true of Judaism, which is the essential foundation of the Christian religion. But such partial commensurability is extended also to Islam, and even to Buddhism and Hinduism, which, although quite different from Christianity, reflect "a ray of that Truth which enlightens all men" (*NA*, no. 2). Vatican II clearly changed the evaluatory optic through which Catholicism judged other realities: from discontinuity and incongruity to partial commensurability and analogical similarity (in varying degrees of intensity). In that sense, there was undoubtedly a shift in perspective (not in fundamental Catholic teaching) at Vatican II. Jesus Christ and his body, the Church, clearly remain at the center. This is why Fr. Imbelli can rightly say, "Failure to recognize the Council's pervasive Christocentrism does scant justice to the Council's 'integral corpus.' Slighting the Council's defining orientation to Christ risks embarking on a misdirection from the very outset."[29]

---

did a document on revelation prevent ecclesio-monism, it made clear that the Church needs, in the first place, to *listen* to the Word of God. See Joseph Ratzinger, "Dogmatic Constitution on Divine Revelation," in *Commentary on the Documents of Vatican II*, ed. H. Vorgrimler (New York: Herder and Herder, 1969), III, 162.

28. Robert P. Imbelli, "The Reaffirmation of the Christic Center," in *Sic et Non: Encountering Dominus Iesus*, ed. Stephen J. Pope and Charles Hefling (Maryknoll, N.Y.: Orbis, 2002), 97.

29. Robert P. Imbelli, "Do This in Memory of Me," *America*, April 22, 2013, 19.

Through the lens of this thorough Christocentrism, Imbelli has also examined Vatican II's decree on the life and ministry of priests, *Presbyterorum Ordinis*. He argues that this document "can only be appreciated in the context of the Council's sublime vision of the uniqueness and originality of Jesus Christ."[30] In other words, only if we keep in mind the dense Christological center of Vatican II can we understand the Council's vision of priesthood, a vision which is neither functional nor pragmatic, but "genuinely 'ontological.'" Unfortunately, Imbelli notes, Vatican II's Christocentric understanding of priesthood has been "if not explicitly denied, certainly relativized in some sectors of the postconciliar Church."[31]

Fr. Imbelli's Christological retrieval of *Presbyterorum Ordinis* is important for several reasons. Only if we understand that Vatican II presents Christ as the high priest par excellence—the priest *per se et per essentiam*—can we understand ministerial priests as formally, substantially, and intensively *participating in* this priesthood, as secondary analogates deeply related to Jesus, the *analogatum princeps* from whom they draw their identity. As *Presbyterorum Ordinis* teaches, Christ "remains always the source and wellspring (*principium et fons*) of their [priests'] lives" (n. 14).[32]

Imbelli's creative retrieval of the *Decree on the Ministry and Life of Priests* is particularly crucial because this document has long been considered to be among the weaker conciliar texts. Yves Congar, for example, noted that the draft schema was "very mediocre, [having] a clumsy message, drawn up in haste in the final period." Although the promulgated document was somewhat better, Congar still stated, "I must admit this text does not correspond exactly to the expectations of priests. I have had to explain it many times."[33]

---

30. Imbelli, "The Identity and Ministry of the Priest," 35.

31. Imbelli, "The Identity and Ministry of the Priest," 36, 38. Richard R. Gaillerdetz has lamented what he calls the "ontological divide" between the clergy and laity. It should be recalled, however, that Vatican II, in accord with the prior dogmatic tradition, firmly rejected the univocal predication of Christ's priesthood to his ministers and faithful. At the same time, this proper distinction need not and should not lead to a "divide." See *An Unfinished Council* (Collegeville, Minn.: Liturgical Press, 2015), 57, 70.

32. The phrase *principium et fons* is reminiscent of a similar comment made by Aquinas, "Christus autem fons totius sacerdotii" (*Summa Theologica* III, q. 33, a. 4) — Christ is the fountainhead of the whole priesthood.

33. *Jean Puyo interroge le Père Congar* (Paris: Le Centurion, 1975), 149. Cited by Lawrence B. Porter, *The Assault on Priesthood* (Eugene, Ore.: Wipf and Stock, 2012), xxxv. Porter's book recounts several stinging critiques of the theological *gravitas* of *Presbyterorum Ordinis*.

Truth be told, I have never heard any priest remark that he has drawn theological or spiritual sustenance from the Council's reflections on the priesthood. As the Church historian Martin Marty famously opined, Vatican II's "winners" were the bishops and laity, while the Church's service ranks—priests and religious—were the "losers." By this, Marty meant that while the Council offered theological advances in understanding the episcopacy and the laity, "no fresh rationales for being a priest or a religious emerged" from Vatican II.[34] Perhaps Marty's judgment on the Council's work is too severe, but his point converges with Imbelli's assessment of the *reception* of Vatican II's teaching on priesthood, a reception that has been tepid at best. Ultimately, Imbelli's pronounced accent on the decree's Christological foundation might allow *Presbyterorum Ordinis* to be reevaluated and perhaps, when taken together with *Lumen Gentium*, to finally bear good fruit in the Church's life.

Conclusion

In conclusion, I would like to make three brief points. First, Vatican II, while scrupulously avoiding scholastic language, used important Thomist ideas—particularly participation and analogy—in order to express how Christ is the center of history and truth, with all other realities related to him. We have already seen that Congar, soon after the Council ended, insisted on the crucial influence of Aquinas's thought on the dogmatic texts of the Council. While not visible on the linguistic surface of the texts, this influence may be discerned in the Council's extensive use of participatory and analogical reasoning in order to show the *proximity* of other realities to Christ and to the Catholic Church. Indeed, analogy so saturates the conciliar documents that if one wishes to speak of a "spirit of Vatican II"—a spirit that finds firm footing in the texts themselves—then analogical thought has a solid claim to the title. This is so much the case that I have called analogy *the philosophical style beneath Vatican II's rhetorical style*.[35]

But the use of analogical reasoning at Vatican II has been obscured because, as Jared Wicks has pointed out, the conciliar speeches again and again

---

34. Martin Marty, "What Went Wrong?" *The Critic* 34 (Fall 1975): 49–53. Cited in Porter, *The Assault on Priesthood*, xxix.

35. Guarino, *The Disputed Teachings*, 27.

appealed to John XXIII's call for a *pastoral* Council.[36] Consequently, the theologians who wrote the documents and the bishops who approved them did not utilize scholastic terminology. This decision was understandable given not only Vatican II's pastoral nature but also John XXIII's strong hopes for Christian unity. Scholastic language would not likely facilitate dialogue with the separated brethren. But precisely because of this emphasis on the pastoral and ecumenical aspects of the Council, the significant role played by participation and analogy—the Thomist "structure" to which Congar referred—has often been overlooked.

Second, Fr. Imbelli's work offers a salubrious reminder that these philosophical ideas were always placed at the service of Vatican II's Christocentrism. As he avers, the most "pervasive and determinative theme [of the council] is that of the lordship of Christ: *Dominus Iesus.*"[37] This is the case because "Christians believe that the Center [of the world] is Christ 'in whom all things hold together' (Col 1:17)."[38] We should not, therefore, understand the Council's invocation of prominent scholastic themes as having occurred simply because of their venerable standing in the theological tradition. We should see this invocation, rather, as an example of the Church using philosophical tools at the service of, and in obedience to, divine revelation.

Finally, I would like to offer a word of caution about the analogical and participatory thinking that pervaded Vatican II. Held not long after the world was profoundly rent by World War II, the Holocaust, and the atom bomb—and while still in the midst of the Cold War—the Council understandably placed its accent on analogy in order to emphasize the *common dimensions* of the human family—what all men and women together shared. This is no doubt why Cardinal Suenens's well-known speech of December 4, 1962—a speech which had been read beforehand by Pope John XXIII and which accented the Council's need to open a dialogue with the Catholic peo-

---

36. In his opening allocution of October 11, 1962, *Gaudet mater ecclesia*, John XXIII referred to the Council as having a "particularly pastoral nature" (*cuius indoles praesertim pastoralis est*). For the influence of this statement, see Wicks, *Investigating Vatican II*, 27. This direction was intensified by the norms for the revision of the texts issued on December 6, 1962, which repeated the pope's accent on the uniquely pastoral character of the Council. See *Acta synodalia sacrosancti concilii Vaticani secundi*, 5 vols. (Vatican City: Typis polyglottis Vaticanis, 1970–1978) I/1, 96–98. An English-language summary of the norms may be found in *Council Daybook* (Sessions 1 and 2), ed. Floyd Anderson (Washington, D.C.: National Catholic Welfare Council, 1965), 114.

37. Imbelli, "Do This in Memory of Me," 18.

38. Imbelli, *Rekindling the Christic Imagination*, 92.

ple, with the separated brethren and with the world itself—struck a deep chord within St. Peter's Basilica.[39]

In retrospect, however, one may wonder if the participatory/analogical approach—with its determined accent on commensurability, that is, on those attributes and "perfections" that Catholicism shares with others—can mask legitimate and important differences. One thinks, for example, of the fiercely negative reaction to the aforementioned declaration issued by the CDF, *Dominus Iesus*—a document to which Fr. Imbelli refers in his work. Is it possible that the declaration's strong affirmation of the uniqueness of Jesus Christ, of Christian revelation, and of the Catholic Church (affirmations fully in accord with Vatican II's teachings) now seemed impolite and even rude? Did the Council's pervasive analogical approach lull some Catholics into thinking the Church should stress only what is *shared* with others —while pointing out profound differences and perceived errors constituted an affront to Christian fraternity and inter-religious rapprochement?

And not only *Dominus Iesus* received a stormy reception. The same is true of the *Catechism of the Catholic Church*. While some theologians voiced concerns that ultimately improved the Catechism, others seemed to be offended at the very idea of a universal catechism proclaiming the *depositum fidei*—as if the Church's claim to the fullness of truth had been abjured by Vatican II and the Catechism represented a temerarious and patronizing assault on other points of view.[40]

But Fr. Imbelli's work has done a service to the Church in consistently calling to mind that Vatican II was not about "changing" the Catholic Church—much less about abjuring the truth which belongs to her essence—but about calling the Church to renewed and more profound faithfulness to her Lord and Master, Jesus Christ.

---

39. See *Acta synodalia*, I/4, 222–25. John XXIII had seen a draft of Suenens' speech and had made some further suggestions. See Léon-Josef Suenens, "Aux origines du Concile Vatican II," *Nouvelle revue théologique* 107 (1985): 3–21.

40. For a discussion of those criticizing the *very idea* of a universal catechism, see Avery Dulles, *Church and Society* (New York: Fordham University Press, 2008), 157–74.

Part 2

THE CENTER
OF THE ECONOMY OF
SALVATION

6

Was Christ "Beautiful in Laying Down His Life" on the Cross?

GERALD O'COLLINS, SJ

He had no form or majesty that we should look at him, nothing
in his appearance that we should desire him.

—Isaiah 53:2

Commenting on a royal wedding song, Psalm 45 (then numbered 44),
St. Augustine of Hippo produced a comprehensive statement on the beauty
of Christ: "for us believers, the Bridegroom is beautiful wherever he meets
[us]." That means that he is also "beautiful under the scourges," "beautiful
on the cross," "beautiful in not shrinking from death," "beautiful in laying
down his life."[1] But how could this be so? In a festschrift honouring a theologian who, like Augustine, treasured the beauty of Christ, it seems worthwhile taking up the passion and crucifixion, a classic challenge to recognizing Christ as beautiful at every stage of his human history.

A poem from Second Isaiah about the Servant of the Lord, who—whether understood primarily as an individual or in a collective sense—suffers
for the sins of "the many" (Is 52: 13–53:12), has deeply shaped thinking and

---

1. Augustine, *Expositions of the Psalms*, 44.3; translation mine.

preaching about the death of Jesus.[2] Early Christians saw the poem as an elaborate prefiguration of Christ in his atoning suffering and death. In the late first century, St Clement of Rome simply quoted the whole of this text when he came to expound the meaning of Jesus' death (1 Clement, 16). In his second-century *Dialogue with Trypho* (no. 13), St Justin Martyr would also cite Isaiah 53 in full. This fourth poem about the Servant of the Lord continued to retain its central place in the Christian imagining of the violent death of Jesus, and remains a key reading in the liturgy of Good Friday.

The language of this poem seems to rule out what Augustine says about Christ being "beautiful under the scourges" and "beautiful under the cross." Claims about the beauty of Christ in his passion and death seem incompatible with (a) what Isaiah says about the Servant being cruelly disfigured and becoming "one from whom others hide their faces" (Is 53:3), and with (b) what the Gospels have to say about Christ being scourged, crowned with thorns, and crucified. Cicero declared crucifixion to be "that cruel and disgusting penalty."[3] The terrible ugliness of the crucifixion appears to rule out any talk of Christ's being attractively beautiful in "laying down his life."[4]

But we should join Thomas Bennett when he speaks of "the dark splendour of the cross," "the glory and the shame of the cross," and the cross being simultaneously "gracious and offensive."[5] What is physically an ugly horror is spiritually beautiful—in Bennett's terms, splendid, glorious, and gracious. In St. Paul's language, "Christ crucified" may be "a stumbling block to Jews and foolishness to Gentiles, but to those who are called ... Christ the power of God and the [beautiful] wisdom of God" (1 Cor 1:23–24). In various ways, Paul and the Gospels lend support to Augustine when he acknowledges beauty in the death of Jesus and in the vulnerable, suffering love

---

2. See Klaus Baltzer, *Deutero-Isaiah*, trans. Margaret Kohl (Minneapolis, Minn.: Fortress Press, 2001), 392–429; William H. Bellinger and William R. Farmer, eds., *Jesus and the Suffering Servant: Isaiah 53 and Christian Origins* (Harrisburg, Pa.: Trinity Press International, 1998).

3. Cicero, *In Verrem*, 2. 5.165. On crucifixion, see Martin Hengel, *Crucifixion*, trans. John Bowden (London: SCM Press, 1977); Gerald O'Collins, "Crucifixion," *Anchor Bible Dictionary*, vol. 1 (New York: Doubleday, 1992), 1207–10.

4. In *Beauty and Revelation in the Thought of Saint Augustine* (Oxford: Clarendon Press, 1992), Carol Harrison discusses the paradox of acknowledging beauty in the ugly, crucified Christ (235–38).

5. Thomas A. Bennett, *Labor of God: The Agony of the Cross as the Birth of the Church* (Waco, Tex.: Baylor University Press, 2017), 1, 3.

it reveals. Support comes in at least three ways: from the accounts of the Last Supper, the passion narrative of Luke, and that of John.

The Last Supper

Convergent evidence from 1 Corinthians 11 and the Gospels makes it historically certain that Jesus celebrated a farewell meal with the core group of his disciples. Faced with murderous opposition and the obvious threat of arrest and execution, he arranged a final meal with them and showed a poignant courage at what has entered history as "the Last Supper."[6] Starting with the washing of the disciples' feet, the account of what Jesus said and did in John 13–17 radiates courageous beauty. To use Augustine's words, he was "beautiful in not shrinking from death." John and the Synoptic Gospels witness in their reports of the Last Supper to the beauty of Jesus "in laying down his life." Here, let me dwell on the institution of the Eucharist, which permanently speaks to the whole Christian Church of the generous and beautiful love that Jesus displayed in the face of imminent death.

Biblical scholars widely agree that the "bread saying" derives from the historical Jesus. Many argue as well that the "cup saying" is also traceable to him. The "words of institution" show Jesus defining his death as a sacrifice that will not only representatively atone for sins but also initiate a new and enduring covenant between God and human beings. The beauty embodied in this gift of the Eucharist was celebrated powerfully by the *Ave Verum Corpus*, an anonymous hymn coming from the fourteenth century and given an exquisite setting by Mozart, the *Adoro Te devote,* probably composed by Thomas Aquinas, and the hymns he prepared for the feast of Corpus Christi: *Lauda Sion, Pange Lingua gloriosi* (also known for its last two verses, which begin *Tantum ergo*), and *Verbum Supernum Prodiens* (best known for its last two verses, which begin *O Salutaris Hostia*). The beauty of the Eucharist comes from the beauty of Christ "in not shrinking from death."

6. On the Last Supper, see François Bovon, *Luke*, vol. 3, trans. James E. Crouch (Minneapolis, Minn.: Fortress, 2012), 148–89; Brendan Byrne, *Life Abounding: A Reading of John's Gospel* (Collegeville, Minn.: Liturgical Press, 2014), 225–91; Joseph A. Fitzmyer, *The Gospel according to Luke X–XXIV* (New York: Doubleday, 1985), 941–53; Andrew T. Lincoln, *The Gospel according to St John* (London: Continuum, 2005), 362–441; Ulrich Luz, *Matthew 21–28*, trans. James E. Crouch (Minneapolis, Minn.: Fortress, 2005), 358–85; Joel Marcus, *Mark 8–16* (New Haven, Conn.: Yale University Press, 2009), 949–74; John Nolland, *The Gospel of Matthew* (Grand Rapids, Mich.: Eerdmans, 2005), 1063–92.

Yet we must ask: how far have the sources of Paul, Mark, and the other witnesses been shaped by early liturgical usages? In 1 Corinthians 11:23–25, the oldest account of the institution of the Eucharist, we read: "the Lord Jesus on the night when he was betrayed took bread and when he had given thanks, he broke it, and said: 'this is my body [which is given] for you. Do this in remembrance of me.' In the same way [he took] also the cup, after supper, saying: 'this cup is the new covenant in my blood. Do this, as often as you drink it, in remembrance of me.'" In Mark's account of the Last Supper, however, the instructions calling for a future repetition of the Eucharist ("do this in remembrance of me" and "do this, as often as you drink it, in remembrance of me") are missing. The qualification of "my body" as being "for you" is also missing. Yet, unlike the Pauline account, Mark describes the blood as being "shed for many." His version runs as follows: "he [Jesus] took bread, blessed and broke it, and gave it to them, and said: 'Take, this is my body.' And he took the cup, and when he had given thanks, he gave it to them, and they all drank of it. And he said to them, 'this is my blood of the covenant, which is shed for many [= for all]'" (Mk 14:22–24).

There are obvious differences between (a) the Pauline tradition (to which, apart from adding, apropos of "my blood," "which is shed for you," and not including, apropos of the cup, "do this in remembrance of me," Luke 22:19–20 approximates) and (b) the Markan tradition (which is more or less followed by Matthew 26:26–28, apart from the latter adding that the blood is shed "for the forgiveness of sins"). Confronted with these differences, some writers back away from relying too much on the words of institution as sources for deciding how Jesus understood his death and its impact. Yet in some form, the words and actions of institution go back to Jesus.

The breaking of the bread, identified as his body, and the shedding of his blood imaged forth the loving, sacrificial surrender of his life, the total self-giving that was about to take place in his violent death. Clearly, those followers present at the Last Supper shared in the body that was being given up to death and in the blood that would be shed. They were lovingly invited to participate in Jesus' destiny and enjoy a new, permanent communion or covenant with him. Whether Jesus spoke of a "new covenant" (Paul and Luke) or only of "a covenant" (Mark and Matthew) that was instituted through his blood, he inevitably evoked key biblical passages (e.g. Ex 24:3–8; Jer 31:31–33) that illuminated his words and gestures. He was making a covenant, sealed and ratified by the shedding of his blood.

Beyond the group present at the Last Supper, whom did Jesus want to benefit from the new covenant? The "for you" of the Pauline and Lukan tradition pointed immediately to his disciples who shared the common cup at the Last Supper. But he clearly intended the group who participated in his final meal to represent others, even innumerable others. Since Jesus called for a *future* repetition of the bread ritual ("do this in remembrance of me"—Paul and Luke) and of the cup ritual ("do this in remembrance of me"—Paul only), he evidently wanted to confer on an indefinite number of others the saving benefits of his life and impending death. Even if Jesus did not literally deliver the directive "do this in remembrance of me," one can reasonably argue that this addition from the Pauline and Lukan churches rendered explicit his intentions. He wanted to establish for countless others his continuing place and presence in the meal fellowship that he was enacting for a small, core group of disciples.

Mark (followed by Matthew) has Jesus speak of his blood shed "for many," an inclusive, Semitic expression for a great multitude or countless number (that is to say, "for all"). But, granted that "for you" and "for many" point to an indefinitely large group, we are still left with the question: did Jesus intend the benefits of the new covenant to be conferred only on all those who were sharing and would share in the ritual and fellowship he was creating? Would the benefits of his sacrificial death "for many" be passed on only to the covenant community, those who would share in the saving power of Jesus' death through eating his "broken body" and drinking from the common cup?

A short answer to those tempted to imagine Jesus limiting the saving impact of the new covenant comes from a feature of his ministry: the meals he shared with all manner of people, not least with the disreputable. That table fellowship conveyed forgiveness to sinners and celebrated in advance the happiness of the heavenly banquet to come, a banquet to which all were invited. The earlier practice of Jesus throws light on his intentions at the Last Supper. It was intended to be "the last supper" or climax of a whole series of meals that revealed his saving outreach to everyone.[7]

At the Last Supper, Jesus linked his imminent death with the divine kingdom: "amen, I say to you, I shall not drink again of the fruit of the vine

---

7. For an account of how Jesus understood his death, see Scot McKnight, *Jesus and His Death* (Waco, Tex.: Baylor University Press, 2005).

until that day when I drink it new in the kingdom of God" (Mk 14:25; see Mt 26:29; Lk 22:18).[8] It is widely agreed that this verse derives from something Jesus said during his last meal. Death is approaching; he will have no occasion again to have a festive meal. But, after his death, God will vindicate the cause of Jesus by fully establishing the divine kingdom. Jesus will be seated at the final banquet—obviously with others at his side—when he "drinks wine new." He looks forward to the time of eschatological feasting.

In this saying, the death of Jesus remains implicit. The resurrection as such is not mentioned, but it is implied that God will rescue Jesus out of death and let him enjoy the final banquet. The saying as such does not attribute to Jesus any redemptive function in the ultimate triumph of God's kingdom. It is not stated, or at least not stated explicitly, that he will restore the fellowship with his disciples that will be broken by death—let alone that he will mediate to others their access to the final banquet.

The saying from Mark 14:25 (and its parallels in Matthew and Luke), taken by itself, leaves much unsaid. Yet it turns up as *the final kingdom saying* from Jesus, a saying about the kingdom that is connected with his approaching death. The saying should be interpreted in the light of what Jesus has already said. He has preached the future reign of God, which will be *the* saving event for all human beings. By linking his imminent death with the coming kingdom, Jesus implicitly interprets his death inclusively, as somehow salvific for all. Through his preaching, he has promised salvation for human beings at large. Now he associates his death with that future salvation and communion at a final banquet in the coming kingdom of God. The kingdom saying at the Last Supper may be laconic, but Jesus charges it with meaning through what he has already said about the coming kingdom.

It is hardly surprising that Jesus made such a positive link between the coming kingdom and his death. The message about the divine reign was inseparable from the person of Jesus. The essential connection between the message of Jesus and his person meant that the vindication of his person in and beyond death entailed the vindication of God's kingdom, and vice versa.[9]

Commenting on the Last Supper, François Bovon remarks: "Jesus' death can be considered from different angles. From one perspective, it corre-

---

8. See John P. Meier, *A Marginal Jew*, vol. 2 (New York: Doubleday, 1994), 302–9, 366–71.

9. For an extensive discussion and bibliography on Jesus and the kingdom of God, see Meier, *A Marginal Jew*, vol. 2, 289–506.

sponds to the high point of human malice; from another angle, it represents the realization of God's plan of redemption."[10] The ritual Jesus establishes—"do this in remembrance of me"— will continue to realize "in the present" the "divine benefits." The disciples at the Last Supper "are not merely spectators of an end; they are also participants of a beginning," which is offered to everyone.[11] Bovon sums up: "this Lord's Supper or Eucharist is a communion with the double characteristic of *looking back* toward the death of Christ as an act of redemption and [the] establishment of a new covenant, and *ahead*, to the kingdom and its joyful banquet."[12]

Bovon's remarks pay tribute to the beautiful event of the Last Supper and gift of the Eucharist. Jesus' core group of disciples was disintegrating in front of him: one of them had decided to betray him, their leader was about to deny him three times, and none of them (except the beloved disciple) would be with him on Calvary. But Jesus himself stood tall and lovingly courageous in turning a hideous miscarriage of justice into the source of supreme blessings for all human beings. What transpired on the night before he died supports Augustine in saying that Jesus was "beautiful in laying down his life."

Commenting on Matthew's passion story, Ulrich Luz observes that, "with the probable exception of Jesus' crucifixion, nothing from the passion narrative has been portrayed in pictures as much as Jesus' Last Supper or the institution of the Christian Eucharist."[13] He supplies and comments on eight portrayals of the Last Supper—from Eastern icons to Western and African paintings, and from the Middle Ages down to an expressionist work created by Emil Nolde in 1909. He points out how these works focus on the historical institution or on the present celebration, how they express Jesus' imminent death as being sacrificial or stress rather the Last Supper as a fellowship meal, and so forth.[14] We should add a further comment: a majestic beauty characterizes the image of Christ not only in the Eastern icons but also in paintings of the Last Supper that Luz supplies from Duccio and Tintoretto. They vindicate Augustine's claim about Christ being "beautiful in laying down his life." The same holds true of portrayals of the Last Supper

10. Bovon, *Luke*, vol. 3, 158.

11. Bovon, *Luke*, vol. 3, 159.

12. Bovon, *Luke*, vol. 3, 163.

13. Luz, *Matthew 21–28*, 365.

14. Luz, *Matthew 21–28*, 365–72.

created by Ghirlandaio, Leonardo da Vinci, Salvador Dalí, and numerous other artists, who pictured the beauty of Christ at the table on the night before he died.

Luke's Passion Story

In Luke's passion story, a beautiful theme runs from the arrest in Gethsemane to the crucifixion on Calvary: Christ's desire to heal, forgive, and save others. This is hardly surprising. From the start of his Gospel, Luke has highlighted the lovely work of salvation. Two majestic prayers enunciate this theme: the *Benedictus* glorifies God for "salvation from our enemies and from the hand of all who hate us," while the *Magnificat* praises "God, my Savior" (Lk 1:47, 71). When Jesus is born, an angel of the Lord announces to the shepherds: "to you is born this day in the city of David a Savior, who is Christ the Lord' (Lk 2:10–11).

Throughout his ministry, Jesus is intent on healing, forgiving, and saving people. Before describing the healing of a paralytic, unlike Mark and Matthew, Luke remarks: "the power of the Lord was there to heal him" (Lk 5:17). Matthew 3:10 recalls how people tried to touch Jesus, but it is only Luke who adds: "power went out of him and he healed them all" (Lk 6:19). Luke shows us how Jesus continues this healing ministry when he moves into the passion. He remains the beautiful Healer and Savior, as we see from eight examples.

(1) In Gethsemane, Jesus makes one last effort to heal and save Judas Iscariot. He acknowledges the traitor personally and speaks to him by name: "Judas, would you betray the Son of Man with a kiss?" (Lk 22:48). It is only in Luke's Gospel that Jesus, at the very moment of betrayal and arrest, acknowledges Judas by name. It is a final, fruitless attempt to change and heal the heart of the traitor. Throughout the passion narrative, "the Lukan Jesus remains one who reaches out in forgiveness to sinners."[15]

(2) As Jesus is being arrested, one of the disciples (Peter, according to John 18:10) draws a sword, strikes at those who have come to seize Jesus, and cuts off the right ear of a servant of the high priest. Jesus says, "enough of that," touches the ear of the wounded man, and heals him (Lk 22:49–51).

---

15. Raymond E. Brown, *The Death of the Messiah: From Gethsemane to the Grave*, vol. 1 (New York: Doubleday, 1994), 259.

The other three Gospels mention the scuffle in which the servant loses his ear. Only Luke reports this act of healing. Raymond Brown comments: "healing was a major part of Jesus' great task in the midst of his own troubles. This is another example of the special Lukan theology of Jesus acting as savior during the passion itself."[16] It is an early example of the beautiful acts of healing and forgiveness that occur before Jesus dies on Calvary.

(3) It is only in Luke's passion narrative that Jesus turns and looks at Peter after the leader of the twelve has denied him. That look makes Peter remember the Lord's warning: "before the cock crows today, you will deny me three times." Peter slips away and begins to weep bitterly. Through his reproachful but healing glance, Jesus has helped Peter to repent and be forgiven (Lk 22:61–62). "When Jesus turns to him, Peter also turns to the Lord," since he remembers the earlier word of the Lord (Lk 22:34). "Luke is concerned to make clear," Bovon reflects, "that the one who speaks the word to Peter, then looks at him, is not simply 'Jesus' but 'the Lord.'"[17] We could add that he is the Lord who shows his beauty by forgiving and healing.

(4) In Luke's passion story, Jesus heals another relationship, that between Herod Antipas and Pontius Pilate. After Jesus is arrested, Pilate learns that he is a Galilean and sends him to the ruler of Galilee. It is only in Luke's Gospel that Jesus is brought before Herod. There follows an ugly scene in which Jesus is mocked, treated with contempt, and then sent back to Pilate. Rather surprisingly, Luke adds: "that same day Herod and Pilate became friends with each other; before this, they had been enemies" (Lk 23:6–12).

Bovon recalls Luke 9:9, where we are told that Herod wanted to meet Jesus. His wish was fulfilled in the unfolding of the passion.[18] Apropos of Herod and Pilate becoming friends, Bovon cites Ephesians 2:11–22, which "celebrates the reconciliation between Jews and pagans that the redemptive death of Christ brought about." He raises a question about the reconciliation between Herod and Pilate: "do we read here a discreet allusion to this victory over hatred and the reconciliation of the nations? What immediately follows (Pilate's cowardice and Herod's disappearance) leads us to answer no. What follows after that, (the declaration of his [Jesus'] innocence, then the crucifixion, and resurrection), encourages us to answer yes."[19] The un-

---

16. Brown, *Death of the Messiah*, vol. 1, 281.

17. Bovon, *Luke*, vol. 3, 233.

18. Bovon, *Luke*, vol. 3, 263.

19. Bovon, *Luke*, vol. 3, 270–71.

expected reconciliation that Jesus brings about between Herod and Pilate symbolizes, albeit strangely, the reconciliation between God's chosen people and the nations.

(5) When Jesus is being led to the place of execution, Luke speaks of his being followed by a multitude of people, which included women "beating their breasts and wailing for him." Jesus turns to them and reveals his loving concern for their future and that of their children:

Daughters of Jerusalem, do not weep for me, but weep for yourselves and for your children. For the days are surely coming when they will say, "blessed are the barren, and the wombs that never bore, and the breasts that never nursed." Then they will say to the mountains, "fall on us," and to the hills, "cover us." For if they do this when the wood is green, what will happen when it is dry (Lk 23:27–31).

The evangelist invites us to recall how "Jesus entered Jerusalem (Lk 19:37–40) amid the rejoicing of a whole multitude of disciples and their singing the blessings of the king." He is "now being led away from the city followed by 'a large multitude of the people' and the women who lament his death."[20]

Jesus reacts by "turning the grief away from his own death towards the death of the city and its inhabitants." Compassion comes through his warning that "no amount of lamenting of what is being done to him can save Jerusalem and its city from the destruction to come." When that happens, children will not be able to protect themselves, and mothers will have "the anguish of seeing those whom they brought into the world destroyed."[21] Using a proverb about different periods of time represented by green wood and dry wood, Jesus warns: "if the Jewish leaders and people treat me like this in a favourable time (when they are not forced by the Romans), how much worse will they be treated in an unfavourable time (when the Romans suppress them)."[22] With stunning self-forgetfulness, Jesus focuses his grief on "the daughters of Jerusalem" and their city.

(6) When the crucifixion takes place, Luke presents Jesus praying for those who are putting him to death: "Father, forgive them, for they know not what they are doing" (Lk 23:34). Reading or not reading this verse, Bovon observes, "poses one of the major textual problems of the Gospel of

20. Brown, *Death of the Messiah*, vol. 2, 921; on the whole passage, see 918–27.

21. Brown, *Death of the Messiah*, vol. 2, 921, 923.

22. Brown, *Death of the Messiah*, vol. 2, 927.

Luke. Was it part of the original text of Luke, or was it added later?" Bovon argues for retaining this "prayer of Jesus in the text of the Gospel of Luke." He adds significantly: "the presence of this prayer confirms the saintliness that the author applies to Christ during his passion,"[23] The loving and beautiful prayer of forgiveness belongs to a pattern inaugurated at the time of his arrest, when Jesus spoke to Judas Iscariot.

(7) While the other evangelists report that Jesus was not crucified alone, it is only Luke who introduces an exchange between Jesus and one of the two criminals who died with him (Lk 23:39–43).[24] "The good thief" acknowledges the guilt he shares with "the bad thief," and turns to Jesus with the prayer: "Jesus, remember me when you come into your kingdom." In the words of Bovon, Jesus "does not wait for an indefinitely postponed enthronement." The "radius of his power is already extended," and he can solemnly promise that "the good thief" will be with him beyond death: "amen, I say to you, today you will be with me in paradise." There can be "no more reassuring divine promise" than this.[25] Jesus promises "a happy future to those who turn to him and trust him. In this moment Jesus is less alone and finds a certain consolation in this criminal."[26] The Lukan portrayal of Jesus' passion lends reciprocity to some acts of healing and forgiving. In all those acts, the Lord shows himself to be "beautiful in laying down his life" and "beautiful on the cross."

(8) A final example of the healing power of Jesus occurs after his death, when Luke speaks not only of female witnesses to the crucifixion but also of the male disciples ("all who knew" Jesus). Admittedly, these men are described as "keeping their distance" and are not expressly called here either "disciples" or "apostles" (Lk 23:49). Nevertheless, despite their failure at the time of Jesus' arrest, a failure supremely exemplified by Peter's denial, Jesus has brought them to be somehow involved in the redeeming event of the crucifixion. With the resurrection and the descent of the Holy Spirit, they will become "authorized witnesses." Here, Bovon comments, "the adjective 'all'

23. Bovon, *Luke*, vol. 3, 306–7.

24. On this episode, see Bovon, *Luke*, vol. 3, 310–17.

25. Bovon, *Luke*, vol. 3, 312. Luke, "as he has done with Lazarus (Lk 16:22), locates the righteous in a place of happiness between their death and the final resurrection. The 'bosom of Abraham' is one way of speaking about it; 'paradise' is another'" (313).

26. Bovon, *Luke*, vol. 3, 317.

is important. No one is omitted in this summons; all can become confirmed disciples."[27]

We have pursued eight details in Luke's passion narrative that lend support to Augustine when he testifies to the beauty of Christ revealed in his suffering and death. We can now appeal also to two passages in John.

John's Passion Story

(1) In the passion narrative of John's Gospel, the beauty of Jesus is divulged through his majestic behaviour, or what we might call the "divine composure" of Jesus. Let us see this exemplified at his arrest (Jn 18:1–11).[28]

In telling the story of Jesus being betrayed and arrested, the evangelist introduces a contrast between light and darkness and between warmth and cold. Throughout the Gospel, Jesus has been pictured as "the Light of the world" (Jn 1:4–9; 3:19; 8:12; 9:3), the true source of warmth and vitality. When Judas led a detachment of Roman soldiers and Temple police into the garden, they came with "lanterns, torches, and weapons." Unlike the other Gospels, John speaks about the arresting party carrying not only weapons but also "lanterns" and "torches."[29] They arrived with their puny lights and arms to arrest the One who is the Light of the world (Jn 18:1–3). Ironically, these forces of darkness and death needed some "illumination"; otherwise, they could not have seen the Light of the world. A similar irony surfaces a little later when Peter warmed himself at a charcoal fire (Jn 18:18). He felt the cold, wanted warmth and light, but went to the wrong source. He relied on a charcoal fire instead of relying on the beautiful Light of the world.

In the Johannine account, Jesus remains in total command. "Knowing all that would come upon him," he does not wait to be kissed and identified but takes the initiative himself. He steps forward and asks the arresting

---

27. Bovon, *Luke*, vol. 3, 329. Brown prefers to identify "all those known to" Jesus as other disciples and friends of Jesus, that is to say, a wider group than the twelve (*Death of the Messiah*, vol. 2, 1172–73).

28. For the Johannine account of Jesus' arrest, see Brown, *Death of the Messiah*, vol. 1, 248–52, 259–62.

29. Mark writes of the arresting party carrying only "swords and clubs" (14:48); that is also what we find in the parallel accounts of Matthew (26:47, 55) and Luke (22:52). John reduces the three words ("swords and clubs") to one word ("weapons"), and assigns two words to the illumination ("lanterns" and "torches").

party: "whom are you seeking/looking for" (Jn 18:4)? Right through the Gospel, people seek Jesus, because—whether or not they realize it at the time—he gifts them with light and life (e.g., Jn 1:38; 20:15). Others seek Jesus because they want to put him to death (e.g., Jn 5:18; 7:1, 19, 25). Those who are bent on his destruction are successful when they look for Jesus in Gethsemane, find him, and arrest him. But, as Raymond Brown observes, this "hostile *seeking*" (and finding with Judas' help) is "not the final word." The "ultimate" question about seeking ("whom are you seeking?") in the Fourth Gospel "will be addressed to a woman disciple, Mary Magdalene (20:15),[30] who will proclaim to the other disciples, 'I have seen the Lord' (20:18)."

When the soldiers and Temple police announce whom they are looking for, "Jesus of Nazareth," he replies: "I am [he] (*egō eimi*)" (Jn 18:5)—a clear evocation of the divine name revealed to Moses at the burning bush (Ex 3:14). Faced with the divine name and its awesome power, all those who had come to arrest Jesus (including Judas)[31] step back and fall to the ground (Jn 18:5–6). In the Johannine story of what happened in the garden, Jesus does not kneel or lie on the ground, not even in prayer. It is those who have come to arrest him who fall to the ground. The worldly might of the Roman and Temple authorities, exercised through their soldiers and police, proves pathetically feeble when confronted with the majestic power of the incarnate Son of God.

The scene anticipates the exchange between Jesus and Pontius Pilate. When Pilate asks, "do you not know that I have power to release you and power to crucify you?," Jesus replies: "you would have no power over me unless it had been given you from above" (Jn 19:10–11). God permits evil but remains sovereignly powerful over all human might.

Another, attractive detail in the Johannine narrative of the arrest of Jesus can catch our attention. He repeats what he has already said and adds significantly: "I told you that I am he [Jesus of Nazareth]. So if you are looking for me, let these others go" (Jn 18:8). This added detail hints lovingly at the whole meaning of Christ's passion; it took place—to echo the Creed—"for us and for our salvation." The others go free, but Jesus will allow himself to be

---

30. This forms an inclusion with what Jesus asks Andrew and his companion at the start of the Gospel: "what are you looking for?" (Jn 1:38).

31. Judas, into whom Satan has entered (Jn 13:27; 13:2) and who has been called "the son of perdition" (Jn 17:12), represents "the power of evil" and "must also fall powerless before Jesus" (Brown, *Death of the Messiah*, vol. 1, 261–62).

arrested and put to death for all others and for their everlasting benefit. He does not try to slip away or shield himself behind the others. He is prepared to be seized and led away to death. The soldiers and the police, along with those who sent them, have no right to touch Jesus, let alone punish him. As he said and will say, he is innocent (e.g., Jn 8:46; 18:23). But, to echo the "bread of life" discourse, he is the bread given and broken for the life of the world (Jn 6:51). The arrest of Jesus enacted the truth: "I have not lost a single one of those whom you [my Father] have entrusted to me" (Jn 18:9; see 10:28; 17:12). Those entrusted to Jesus, we might add, were not merely the few persons with whom he had just shared a last meal, but all men and women of all times and places.

Brown sees in this episode what he calls "the Johannine principle of sovereignty."[32] Jesus lays down his life of his own accord (Jn 10:17–18). Likewise, unlike Mark 14:50 (Mt 26:5), the disciples "do not flee; rather Jesus arranges for their release." This is "another instance of Jesus' sovereignty that governs the Johannine passion narrative. If the disciples fled, they would be acting on their own. Just as Judas could not leave the Last Supper without Jesus controlling the action (13:27: 'what you are going to do, do quickly'), so what the other disciples do in the passion narrative is under Jesus' control."[33]

This exegesis, while true, does not go far enough. The One who exercises this sovereignty is the good or beautiful Shepherd who lovingly lays down his life for his sheep. He arranges for their release, while allowing himself to be captured and put to death. To echo Augustine, he is majestically "beautiful in the story of his arrest."

In his study of the passion narratives, Brown regularly raises the question of historicity. How far do the various episodes and elements in them derive from what actually happened in the final day and hours of Jesus' life? How much historicity should we recognize, for instance, in the Johannine scene of "Jesus' self-identification during his arrest, as compared with the Synoptic account of the Judas kiss?" Brown argues that, "even if John might be historical in indicating that Roman soldiers took part in the arrest of Jesus," he appears to have "moved from history to parable in reporting that

---

32. Brown, *Death of the Messiah*, vol. 1, 279.

33. Brown, *Death of the Messiah*, vol. 1, 290.

those soldiers plus the Jewish police attendants fell back to the ground when Jesus spoke to them."[34]

To hold that Jesus was "beautiful in laying down his life," however, it is enough to establish that the evangelists present the passion and death of Jesus in ways that should be characterized as beautiful (stage three of the Gospels' formation). We can also argue that some or even many of the details to which this chapter appeals go back substantially (through the tradition or stage two) to what Jesus said, did, or suffered (stage one). We did this when discussing the Last Supper and the beauty of Jesus manifested in that episode.

(2) Another episode in John's Gospel that shows Jesus beautiful "in laying down his life" comes after his death when a soldier pierced his side (or even his heart) and "immediately there came out blood and water" (Jn 19:34).[35] Brown invites us to read this passage in the light of John 7:38, "where living water flows from within Jesus." The evangelist has explained that Jesus was referring to the Spirit, which believers in Jesus were to receive (Jn 7:39). Hence in John 19:34, while Jesus' death "is signified by the blood, the promised Spirit flowing from within him is signified by the water." Those who believe in Jesus will receive the Spirit.[36] Understanding this episode in terms of the lovely, life-giving gift of the Holy Spirit obviously helps to picture Jesus as being "beautiful on the cross." Beauty also enfolds later reflections by Church fathers and medieval writers on the pierced side or heart of Jesus symbolizing salvation, divine love, and the sacraments, all of which Brown calls an "incredibly rich development."[37]

Furthermore, we should not neglect the symbolism about *the birth of the Church from the dead Christ*.[38] This symbolism has been prepared by a promise Jesus made to the disciples in his farewell discourse:

You will weep and lament, but the world will rejoice; you will be sorrowful, but your sorrow will turn into joy. When a woman is in labour, she has sorrow, because *her hour* has come. But when her child is born, she no longer remembers the anguish because of the joy of having brought a human being into the world. So

34. Brown, *Death of the Messiah*, vol. 1, 262; elsewhere, Brown distinguishes "the level of storyline" from "the level of history" (*Death of the Messiah*, vol. 2, 1171).

35. Brown, *Death of the Messiah*, vol. 2, 1178–82.

36. Brown, *Death of the Messiah*, vol. 2, 1181.

37. Brown, *Death of the Messiah*, vol. 2, 1178 (with bibliography in fn. 95).

38. On the birth of the Church from the side of Christ, see Bennett, *Labor of God*.

you have sorrow now, but I will see you again, and your hearts will rejoice, and no one will take your joy from you (Jn 16:20–22).

These verses expressed directly the sadness and then joy that the disciples would experience when Jesus suffered, died, and rose from the dead. But do they *also* say something symbolically about Jesus himself, and what he did and endured when "his hour'" had come?[39] Can we join Bennett and such medieval writers as St. Anselm of Canterbury and Julian of Norwich in imagining Jesus on the cross as a woman in labour giving birth to her sons and daughters?[40] That would mean acknowledging Christ's joy in agony or, in Augustine's terms, his beauty on the cross. Here we need to recall some passages from the Old Testament that prepare the ground for this interpretation of John.

The psalmist refers to God as giving birth to creation (Ps 90:2). Moses speaks of God giving birth to the people (Dt 32:18). When enabling the people to return from the Babylonian exile, God compares himself to a woman in childbirth: "now I will cry out like a woman in labour; I will gasp and pant" (Is 42:14). Earlier, Isaiah had used the figure of birth pangs when lamenting the sufferings of the chosen people: "like a woman with child, when she writhes and cries out in her pangs when she is near her time, so were we because of you, O Lord" (Is 26:16). In the third part of Isaiah, Jerusalem would be pictured as giving birth to her children with miraculous speed; she will be a joyful, beautiful mother to those who no longer mourn (Is 66:7–14; see 60:20; and 61:1–3). Isaiah represents the saving action of God as moving from—or enabling his people to move from—pain and sorrow to intense joy at the birth of a child.

Divine salvation would eventually and decisively come through a horribly painful crucifixion. Jesus suffered birth pangs as he brought the Church to life. The image of a woman in labour, whose sorrow will give way to joy when her baby is "born into the world," was exemplified in Jesus himself. He was the woman whose hour had come and who endured the anguish of

---

39. In John's Gospel, Jesus' "hour" regularly indicates his passage through suffering and death to the resurrection and ascension.

40. On Anselm, Julian, and others, see Bennett, *Labor of God*, 9–12. In his *Gospel according to John XIII–XXI* (New York: Doubleday, 1970), Brown writes about John 16:20–22: "Not only are the present sadness and future joy of the disciples compared to the sadness and joy that a woman normally has in the birth of her child, but also there is a reference to a familiar symbolic pattern wherein Jesus' death and victory are portrayed as the woman's birth pangs" (732).

giving birth. With blood and water, he "birthed" the Church and so gave new life to the world. His own mother and two other women assisted at this agonizing childbirth (Jn 19:25).

In a letter to his troublesome Galatians, Paul reaches for the figure of a mother in childbirth to describe his own apostolic experience: "my little children, with whom I am in travail until Christ is formed in you" (Gal 4:19). A similar image in John (16:202-22) encourages us to apply the same birth perspective to Christ's being pierced on the cross, shedding blood and water, and giving birth to the Church.

In the Book of Genesis, God causes a deep sleep to fall upon "the man" and creates "the woman" from the side of "the man" (Gn 2:212-23). In Christian tradition, right down to Vatican II (1962–1965),[41] the piercing of the side of Christ sleeping in death upon the cross and the issue of blood and water symbolized the birth of the Church, the spouse of Christ (see Eph 5:22–33), who is the new Adam (see Rom 5:14; 1 Cor 15:45).

Unlike Paul, the Fourth Gospel does not explicitly invoke the figure of Adam; yet it comes close to doing so in the account of Jesus, taken to be the gardener, appearing to Mary Magdalene in a garden outside his open and empty tomb (Jn 19:42; 20:12–18). Hence, Gregory the Great described her as another Eve,[42] and Leo the Great called her "a figure of the Church (personam Ecclesiae gerens)."[43] The Genesis imagery of Eve being made from the side of Adam stood behind the theme of the New Adam, asleep in death upon the cross, giving birth to the Church.

In justifying Augustine's bold statement of Christ being "beautiful in laying down his life," we have appealed to the accounts of the Last Supper, Luke's theme of healing and forgiveness, and John's accounts of the arrest of Christ and the piercing of his side upon the cross.

41. Vatican Council II, *Sacrosanctum Concilium* (the 1963 Constitution on the Sacred Liturgy), December 4, 1963, 5; *Lumen Gentium* (the 1964 Dogmatic Constitution on the Church), November 21, 1964, 3.

42. *De apparitione Christi Magdalenae facta*, hom. 25. 6, *Homélies sur l'Évangile*, vol. 2, *Sources Chrétiennes* 522, trans. R. Étaix and G. Blanc (Paris: Cerf, 2008), 120–21: "in paradise a woman offered death to a man; from the sepulchre a woman announces life to the men" (translation is mine from the Latin).

43. Leo the Great, *De ascensione Domini sermo* 2. 4, *Sermons III* (38–64), *Sources Chrétiennes* 74, trans. R. Dolle (Paris: Cerf, 2004), 280–81.

Conclusion

Augustine seems audaciously paradoxical when he speaks of Christ being "beautiful under the scourges" and "beautiful on the cross." What Augustine appreciates, however, is that the crucified Jesus challenges the normal indices of beauty. As Tom Casey remarks, "the beauty of Christ is visible most of all at what is seemingly the ugliest moment of all: Jesus' tortured death on the cross. The beauty that shines in the form of Jesus at that moment is the beauty of infinite love." Casey articulates the call of that crucified beauty: "this beauty seeks to touch people and to transform them, to awaken and draw them. The response it elicits is not sensual and momentary but all-encompassing, one that embraces the individual's entire existence. The beauty is a light that pierces the heart." Those who contemplate this beauty are called "to reshape and mould anew an entire life so that it may conform to this new standard of beauty."[44]

The Gospels show Christ's crucified beauty having its impact. Women gather around the cross and attend the death of Jesus. The Roman centurion who has been in charge of the crucifixion blurts out his confession ("indeed this man was the Son of God")—a confession in which, according to Matthew, the other soldiers join (Mt 27:54). An outsider, Joseph of Arimathea, boldly comes on the scene to give Jesus a reverent and honourable burial (Mk 15:42–47). John's Gospel adds Nicodemus, who brings thirty-four kilos of aloes and myrrh to wrap inside the shroud of Jesus (Jn 19:39–40). Quite visibly, the passion narratives show the prophecy of John's Gospel coming true: in his death, Jesus would "gather into one the children of God who had been scattered" (Jn 11:51–52). In his dying and death on the cross, the Beautiful Shepherd already touches, attracts, and reshapes human lives.

Creators of Christian music have revealed their sensitivity to the tragic beauty of the passion and crucifixion. This sensitivity prompted many versions for the *Stabat Mater* ("By the cross her station keeping"), the settings of the Lamentations of Jeremiah composed by Palestrina, and the Tenebrae Responsories created by his younger friend, Tomás Luis de Victoria. The passion oratorios of Johann Sebastian Bach (*St Matthew Passion*, 1727; *St John Passion*, 1724) give supreme aesthetic expression to the heart-breaking beau-

44. Thomas Casey, *Life and Soul: New Light on a Sublime Mystery* (Springfield, Ill.: Templegate, 2005), 107.

ty of the suffering and death of Christ our Savior.[45] Bach has found worthy successors in the passion music of Sir John Tavener (1944–2013) and Sir James MacMillan (b. 1959).

Painters and sculptors, both past and present, have added their witness to Augustine's claim that Christ is "beautiful on the cross."[46] Ulrich Luz has summarized the artistic interpretation of Christ's passion and death—down to the late twentieth-century work of the murdered Cameroonian, Engelbert Mveng.[47]

Finally, without being able to examine here the exquisite language in which they have paid tribute to the suffering and death of the beautiful Christ, we should not pass over in silence the contribution of poets, ancient and modern. Robert Atwan and Laurance Wieder provide nearly fifty pages of poetry inspired by the events from the Last Supper until the burial of Jesus.[48]

Coda

That Christ has been revealed as uniquely beautiful, and not least in his passion and death, carries huge pastoral implications for the beauty of those who live with disabilities and impairments. It is because we can join Augustine in saying that the wounded Christ on the cross is "beautiful in laying down his life" that we should recognize the beauty of disabled men and women.[49] But this would call for another article or chapter.

45. See Jeremy S. Begbie, "Created Beauty: The Witness of J. S. Bach," in *Resonant Witness: Conversations between Music and Theology*, ed. Jeremy S. Begbie and Steven R. Guthrie, 83–108 (Grand Rapids, Mich.: Eerdmans, 2011).

46. See Richard Harries, *The Passion in Art* (Aldershot, Hants: Ashgate, 2004); see also Richard Vladesau, "The Beauty of the Cross," in *Theological Aesthetics after von Balthasar*, ed. Oleg V. Bychkov and James Fodor, 135–51 (Burlington, Vt.: Ashgate, 2008).

47. Luz, *Matthew 21–28*, 515–59.

48. R. Atwan and L. Wieder, eds., *Chapters into Verse: Poetry in English Inspired by the Bible* (New York: Oxford University Press, 1993), 171–216.

49. See Nancy L. Eiesland, *The Disabled God: Towards a Liberatory Theology of Disability* (Nashville, Tenn.: Abingdon, 1994).

7

Trinitarian Christology in the Gospel of Matthew

MATTHEW LEVERING

I offer this essay in tribute to a theologian of whom nothing truer could be said than that he loves the holy Trinity and loves Jesus Christ—Father Robert Imbelli.

In reflecting upon the Trinity and Christology, theologians generally gravitate toward the Gospel of John and the Letters of Paul. For example, discussing whether Christ was sanctified by the Spirit at the first instant of Christ's conception, Thomas Aquinas in his *Summa Theologica* cites Luke 1:35 but enfolds it into the context of John 1:14, John 10:36, and John 3:34.[1] Likewise, in his treatment of the Son of God's becoming man so as to be the mediator between God and humanity (*Institutes of the Christian Religion*, Book II, chapter 12), John Calvin quotes the Gospel of John ten times and the Pauline letters thirteen times, whereas he quotes very little from the Synoptic Gospels. The first paragraph of Calvin's treatment of Christ's true human nature shows the same pattern: quotations from John to show that "the Spirit was given to him without measure," numerous quotations from the Pauline letters and Hebrews, but none from the Synoptic Gospels.[2] Again,

---

1. For discussion, see Dominic Legge, OP, *The Trinitarian Christology of St. Thomas Aquinas* (Oxford: Oxford University Press, 2017).

2. John Calvin, *Institutes of the Christian Religion*, Book II, trans. Henry Beveridge (Grand Rapids, Mich.: Eerdmans, 1989), 410.

when treating of the Trinity as revealed by Christ, Calvin quotes Matthew 28:19, but in general he relies upon the Pauline letters and John's Gospel.[3]

This reliance upon John and Paul, indeed, makes a lot of sense. According to the Gospel of John 1:14, "the Word became flesh and dwelt among us, full of grace and truth; we have beheld his glory, glory as of the only Son from the Father." In John 1:1–3, the evangelist teaches that the Word or Son is "God" and is "with God," and that God (the Father) creates all things "through" his Word or Son. This Son, who has become flesh in Jesus Christ, "is in the bosom of the Father" (Jn 1:18). The Son is one with the Father, as revealed in Christ's testimony that "I and the Father are one" (Jn 10:30). The Father and Son are "one" because they are equally God. Christ proclaims, "before Abraham was, I am" (Jn 8:58)—a reference to Exodus 3:14 (Septuagint), in which God names himself to Moses as "I am." Christ tells his disciple Philip that "I am in the Father and the Father in me" (Jn 14:11), thereby deepening his revelation of the unity of the Father and Son in the Godhead, while also affirming the distinction between Father and Son.

The relationship of the Father and Son to the Holy Spirit, and of Christ to the Spirit, becomes clear in the latter half of the Gospel of John. Christ promises his disciples, "I will pray the Father, and he will give you another Counselor, to be with you forever, even the Spirit of truth" (Jn 14:17). The Father will send the Holy Spirit in Christ's name (Jn 14:26). Christ himself, with the Father, has the power to send the Spirit. Indicating that the Spirit proceeds from the Father through the Son, Christ promises his disciples that "when the Counselor comes, whom I shall send you from the Father, even the Spirit of truth, who proceeds from the Father, he will bear witness to me" (Jn 15:26). Furthermore, Christ is supremely filled with the Spirit. John the Baptist states that "I saw the Spirit descend as a dove from heaven, and it remained on him" (Jn 1:32). Filled with the Spirit, Christ is the true Temple, as shown by his prophecy about his body: "Destroy this temple, and in three days I will raise it up" (Jn 2:19).

Just as the Father (and Christ) will send the Spirit, so also the Father "sent the Son into the world" (Jn 3:17). As Hans Urs von Balthasar points out, this indicates that not only the Son, but also the Spirit, is a distinct divine Person: "An impersonal power cannot be 'sent.'"[4] Filled with the Spirit,

---

3. Calvin, *Institutes of the Christian Religion*, 115–25.

4. Hans Urs von Balthasar, *Theo-Logic: Theological Logical Theory*, vol. 3, *The Spirit of Truth*, trans. Graham Harrison (San Francisco: Ignatius Press, 2005), 51.

the incarnate Son gives his followers this Spirit. At the Feast of Tabernacles, Christ proclaims—speaking about "the Spirit, which those who believed in him were to receive"—"If any one thirst, let him come to me and drink" (Jn 7:38–39). Christ's followers will be "born of the Spirit" (Jn 3:8).

Essentially the same points about the Father, Christ, and the Spirit can be derived from the letters of Paul. Gordon Fee, Wesley Hill, Kavin Rowe, and others have made this clear.[5] For example, citing 1 Corinthians 12:3, Galatians 4:4–6, and 2 Corinthians 3:17, Hill argues that for Paul, "the Spirit's identity is grasped by recognizing his personal identity to be derived from God and Jesus."[6] Spelling out the implications of this point, Rowe states simply: "Trinitarian reasoning works on the level of what must be the case to make theological sense of the way Paul and Hebrews speak of the Old Testament God's salvific act in Jesus Christ through the Holy Spirit."[7]

Yet, rather than focusing on John's Gospel or the Pauline letters, I seek to show in this essay that the Gospel of Matthew also presents a Trinitarian Christology.[8] In undertaking this task, I focus upon passages that may at

5. See Gordon D. Fee, *God's Empowering Presence: The Holy Spirit in the Letters of Paul* (Peabody, Mass.: Hendrickson, 1994); Gordon D. Fee, *Pauline Christology: An Exegetical-Theological Study* (Peabody, Mass.: Hendrickson, 2007); Wesley Hill, *Paul and the Trinity: Persons, Relations, and the Pauline Letters* (Grand Rapids, Mich.: Eerdmans, 2015); C. Kavin Rowe, "The Trinity in the Letters of St Paul and Hebrews," in *The Oxford Handbook of the Trinity*, ed. Gilles Emery, OP, and Matthew Levering (Oxford: Oxford University Press, 2011), 41–54. See also Simon J. Gathercole, "Paul's Christology," in *The Blackwell Companion to Paul*, ed. Stephen Westerholm (Oxford: Blackwell, 2011), 172–87, although Gathercole does not speak of "Trinitarian" Christology and, in discussing whether Paul understands Jesus to be divine, focuses on Jesus' relation to the Father.

6. Hill, *Paul and the Trinity*, 170. Hill's argument is rooted in historical-critical exegesis, but he focuses on showing "that trinitarian doctrine may be used *retrospectively* to shed light on and enable a deeper penetration of the Pauline texts in their own historical milieu, and that it is not necessarily anachronistic to allow later Christian categories to be the lens through which one reads Paul" (171). On this latter point, see also the internet exchange between N. T. Wright and Hill.

7. Rowe, "The Trinity in the Letters of St. Paul and Hebrews," 53.

8. For further discussion, see Roland Deines, "The Holy Spirit in Matthew's Gospel," in *The Earliest Perceptions of Jesus in Context: Essays in Honour of John Nolland on His 70th Birthday*, ed. Aaron White, David Wenham, and Craig A. Evans (Edinburgh: T. and T. Clark, 2018), 213–35. Deines recognizes, "When it comes to the Holy Spirit in the Bible, few people would turn to Matthew's Gospel for inspiration" (213). He focuses therefore on showing "how the topic of the Holy Spirit is made part of the unfolding narrative" of Matthew's Gospel (214). When he comes to Matthew 12:28 and 12:32 (which are central to my essay), he comments on 12:28 that "Jesus insists on his empowerment by the Spirit" and that the Spirit is here presented as wielded by Jesus, and he

first glance seem less than promising. Thus, I do not address in detail two of the passages in Matthew's Gospel that offer prominent support to Trinitarian Christology: Matthew 1:18–20 and 28:19. In Matthew 1:18–20, we learn that Jesus' conception is "of the Holy Spirit." This means that for the Gospel of Matthew, there is never any Christology separated from the Spirit; from the outset, the Spirit is profoundly (if mysteriously) involved. In Matthew 28:19, at the very end of the Gospel, the risen Christ proclaims, "Go therefore and make disciples of all nations, baptizing them in the name of the Father and of the Son and of the Holy Spirit." Christ, having received "all authority in heaven and on earth," commands his followers to be baptized into the name of God: the Trinitarian name, Father, Son, and Holy Spirit. Citing this verse among others, the biblical scholar Jonathan Pennington has shown that Matthew "clearly emphasizes divine fatherhood."[9] Likewise, the biblical scholar Frank Matera argues that Matthew 28:19 "relates Jesus to the Father and the Spirit in an unparalleled way, leaving no doubt about the exalted status and divine nature of the one whom the Gospel presents as the Messiah, the Son of the living God."[10]

I also give only brief attention to Matthew 11:25–27, which concludes, "All things have been delivered to me by my Father; and no one knows the Son except the Father, and no one knows the Father except the Son and any one to whom the Son chooses to reveal him." As is often noted, this passage draws Matthew's Christology close to the Christology of John's Gospel. Equally, I could have given attention to Matthew 4:1, which says that Jesus is led "by the Spirit into the wilderness to be tempted by the devil." This passage occurs right after the Spirit has descended in the form of a dove upon

---

comments on 12:32 that "what makes the saying of Jesus so distinctive is the authority with which he presumed to know precisely which sins can be forgiven and which cannot, and the elevation of the Holy Spirit over the Son of Man" (226–27).

9. Jonathan T. Pennington, *Heaven and Earth in the Gospel of Matthew* (Grand Rapids, Mich.: Baker Academic, 2009), 233.

10. Frank J. Matera, *New Testament Theology: Exploring Diversity and Unity* (Louisville, Ky.: Westminster John Knox, 2007), 41. Matera draws connections between Matthew 28:19 and the Pauline letters, and between Matthew 11:25–27 and John's Gospel. For their part, W. D. Davies and Dale C. Allison Jr. "see no developed Trinitarianism in the First Gospel" (*A Critical and Exegetical Commentary on the Gospel according to Saint Matthew*, vol. 3, *Commentary on Matthew XIX–XXVIII* [London: T. and T. Clark International, 2004], 686). Nonetheless, they suggest as likely the view that in Matthew 28:19 (somewhat paralleling Matthew 3:16–17) "the one divine name — the revealed name of power (Ex 3:13–15; Prov 18:10; Jub. 36:7) — has been shared by the Father with Jesus and the Spirit" (685).

the baptized Jesus (Mt 3:16), and it provides further evidence that Matthew never conceives of Christology in separation from the Spirit's activity. The theophany of the Spirit and the Father—who proclaims "This is my beloved Son" (Mt 3:17)—at Jesus' baptism offers additional valuable evidence for Matthew's Trinitarian Christology, as does the similar theophany at Jesus' Transfiguration (Mt 17:5).

Leaving aside such clearly fruitful passages, I have chosen to concentrate solely upon three verses: Matthew 3:11, Matthew 12:28, and Matthew 12:32. At issue in 3:11 and 12:28 is Jesus' unique ability to act by the divine Spirit. At issue in 12:32 is whether Christ is less than the divine Spirit. In reflecting on Matthew 3:11 and 12:28, my argument is that the Gospel of Matthew shows that through his unique relation to the divine Spirit, we can perceive that Jesus must be the divine Son (of the divine Father). In this light, I then ask whether Matthew 12:32 subordinates the Son to the Spirit.

Although in what follows I make ample use of historical-critical exegesis, I also draw consistently upon Jerome, John Chrysostom, Thomas Aquinas, and John Calvin. If my thesis is correct that Trinitarian Christology belongs to Matthew's Gospel, then the presence of such Christology will be discernible both by historical-critical investigation and by classic Christian exegesis in which the reality of the Trinity is presumed. By examining verses that would not be the first choice for demonstrating Matthew's Trinitarian Christology, I hope to add further reasons—in addition to those found in the more prominent passages such as Matthew 1:18–20, Matthew 3:16–17, and Matthew 28:19—for affirming that Matthew's Christology is Trinitarian.

Trinitarian Christology: Christ and the Spirit in Matthew 3:11, 12:28, and 12:32

Matthew 3:11

In Matthew 3:11, John the Baptist tells the crowd gathered around him, "I baptize you with water for repentance, but he who is coming after me is mightier than I, whose sandals I am not worthy to carry; he will baptize you with the Holy Spirit and with fire." What implied relationship between Christ and the Holy Spirit do we find here?

In commenting on this passage, Jerome reflects upon the nature of the Spirit without addressing the point that it is Christ who has the power to pour out the Spirit.[11] By contrast, John Chrysostom notes that John the Baptist highlights Christ's "great superiority" to the Baptist.[12] The superiority is found in the fact that Christ's baptism "is full of the unspeakable gift," the Holy Spirit. Chrysostom emphasizes that because Christ has the power to bestow the Spirit through his baptism, Christ is immeasurably greater than the Baptist.

Chrysostom adds that rather than describe Christ's preaching, miracles, Passion, and Resurrection, John the Baptist highlights Christ's final work, namely the pouring out of the Spirit (Pentecost). According to Chrysostom, the Baptist considered this final work "the fittest to proclaim His [Christ's] dignity."[13] Drawing also upon John 1:29–34, Chrysostom argues that the divinity of the incarnate Son is best displayed through Christ's power to pour out the Spirit, since only God could give such a gift. On this view, the Baptist established Christ's divine Sonship—Christ's true ontological "rank"—by proclaiming that Christ would bestow "so great a gift" as "the Spirit."[14] Since Christ has "so great power, as ... to give the Spirit,"[15] Christ must be the divine Son able to bestow the Spirit. After making this Christological point, Chrysostom then draws out in detail its soteriological implications.

John Calvin makes a similar Christological point in his commentary on Matthew 3:11 (with its Synoptic parallels). Commenting on the phrase "he who is coming after me is mightier than me," Calvin interprets this as a teaching about Christ's nature. On this view, John the Baptist makes clear that Christ is "far superior in power and rank," and the Baptist seeks to "magnify the glory of Christ."[16] Indeed, for Calvin, John the Baptist indicates in this verse what separates Christ from *all* other ministers of baptism. Only Christ can bestow the Holy Spirit; because of Christ's divinity, only Christ possesses the Spirit so as to bestow it. It is Christ who bestows the

---

11. St. Jerome, *Commentary on Matthew*, trans. Thomas P. Scheck (Washington, D.C.: The Catholic University of America Press, 2008), 70.

12. St. John Chrysostom, *Homilies on the Gospel of St. Matthew*, trans. George Prevost, rev. M. B. Riddle, Nicene and Post-Nicene Fathers, First Series, ed. Philip Schaff, vol. 10 (Peabody, Mass.: Hendrickson, 1995), XI.5, 71.

13. Chrysostom, *Homilies on the Gospel of St. Matthew*, XI.6, 71.

14. Chrysostom, *Homilies on the Gospel of St. Matthew*, XI.6, 71.

15. Chrysostom, *Homilies on the Gospel of St. Matthews*, XI.7, 73.

16. John Calvin, *A Harmony of the Gospels Matthew, Mark, and Luke*, https://www.studylight.org/commentaries/cal/matthew-3.html, nos. 281–82.

Spirit when human ministers perform baptisms: "To men has been committed nothing more than the administration of an outward and visible sign:
the reality dwells with Christ alone."[17] As Calvin says, we must distinguish
between "what is done in baptism by men, and what is accomplished in it by
the Son of God."[18]

For Calvin, there is no difference between John's baptism and later
Christian baptism. Here Calvin recognizes that his interpretation differs from the view that had "long and extensively prevailed," namely "that
John's baptism differs from ours."[19] Thomas Aquinas, among others, dis-
agrees with Calvin on the nature of John's baptism. Nonetheless, Aquinas
and Calvin agree about the Christological implications of "he who is coming
after me is mightier than I." Aquinas maintains that the Baptist's statement
means that Christ does what only God can do: the Baptist is making clear
that there is *no* "resemblance" between him and Christ, *no* shared measure
in terms of their power.[20] Christologically, Calvin and Aquinas agree that
Matthew 3:11 shows Christ's divinity.

What about modern commentators? In his three-volume commentary
on Matthew, the historical-critical exegete Ulrich Luz suggests that the
evangelist Matthew has in view a difference between Christ's baptizing
"with the Holy Spirit" and Christ's baptizing "with fire." Luz notes that the
baptizing "with fire" likely signifies the "annihilating judgment (7:19; 13:40,
42, 50; 18:9)."[21] The annihilating judgment, often symbolized by fire in the
Gospel of Matthew, describes the fate of those who are permanently excluded from God's Kingdom. For example, Jesus teaches in Matthew 13:49–50,
"So it will be at the close of the age. The angels will come out and separate
the evil from the righteous, and throw them into the furnace of fire; there
men will weep and gnash their teeth."

If this devastating judgment is Christ's baptizing "with fire," what then
is his baptizing "with the Holy Spirit"? Luz reasons that the evangelist Mat-

---

17. Calvin, no. 283.

18. Calvin, no. 283.

19. Calvin, no. 282. Calvin adds, "We must learn to form our judgment from the matter as it
stands, and not from the mistaken opinions of men."

20. St. Thomas Aquinas, *Commentary on the Gospel of St. Matthew*, trans. Paul M. Kimball
(n.p.: Dolorosa Press, 2012), 99. In his *Summa Theologica*, Aquinas notes that although in a certain way creatures can be like God, God is in no way like creatures.

21. Ulrich Luz, *Matthew 1–7: A Commentary*, trans. James E. Crouch, ed. Helmut Koester
(Minneapolis, Minn.: Fortress Press, 2007), 138.

thew would have thought "that Jesus himself was the bearer of the Spirit (12:18, 28) and that the baptism with the triadic baptismal formula was commanded by him (28:19)."[22] According to Luz, in the "Q" sayings shared by Matthew and Luke (the "Sayings Source" from which Luz thinks that Matthew draws in 3:11), the "stronger one" is the Son of Man. Thus, when the Baptist speaks of a coming one who "is mightier than I," this statement signals the coming Son of Man.[23] Jesus is therefore the Son of Man who is "the bearer of the Spirit."

Does this mean that the Son of Man is the divine Son, bearing the divine Spirit? Since my interest is in the Christology implied by Matthew 3:11, I want to know what Christ's ability to send the Spirit says about Christ. If the coming Christ is "the bearer of the Spirit," as Luz says, does this imply Christ's divinity?

Luz is somewhat ambiguous on this point. According to Luz in his discussion of Matthew 1:23 — "'his name shall be called Emmanuel' (which means, God with us)" — "the Jewish Christian Matthew has put his story of Jesus in an extremely high christological perspective. Although he did not identify Jesus with God, he probably implied that for him Jesus is the form in which God will be present with his people and later with all nations."[24] Matthew certainly maintains that Jesus should be worshiped, as can be seen in the three uses of προσκυνέω in Matthew 2 and the further use of this verb in Matthew 28:17. As Luz says in commenting on Matthew 2:11, "The proskynesis of the magi directs the readers' attention to the majesty of Christ, the son of David (1:1), the Son of God (cf. 1:21; 2:15), and the Immanuel Jesus."[25] Luz also holds that the audience of Matthew's Gospel were Jews and Gentiles who did indeed worship Jesus. Arguably, the fact that Jesus is not identified with the Father, but has the power to send the divine Spirit and is (as Luz puts it) "the form in which God will be present" indicates at least a proto-Trinitarian Christology. If Jesus is the "bearer of the Spirit" and should be worshipped, then Matthew 3:11 already indicates a (proto-)Trinitarian Christology.

In commenting on the scene of Jesus' baptism in Matthew 3:17, with the Father's voice proclaiming Jesus to be his "beloved Son" and the Spirit's de-

22. Luz, *Matthew 1–7*, 138.
23. Luz, *Matthew 1–7*, 138.
24. Luz, *Matthew 1–7*, 96.
25. Luz, *Matthew 1–7*, 124.

scent upon Jesus in the form of a dove, Luz develops his position further. He affirms, "For Matthew, Jesus was the Son of God from the very beginning, at his birth, and did not become it only at his baptism."[26] The Father's voice is not telling Jesus something Jesus does not know but rather is proclaiming the truth about Jesus to the crowd and thus, says Luz, "to the Christian community."[27] At the same time, Luz argues that Jesus' "divine sonship" need not be interpreted as "pre-existent" Sonship, or indeed as anything other than perfect *obedience*. Luz argues that Jesus' obedient sonship is a path open to all followers of Jesus. He explains, "The way of the disciples is also defined as the way of concrete, earthly obedience. There is no room in Matthew for looking beyond the earthly to heavenly dimensions as in the Johannine Son theology; there is only the way of obedience."[28] Jesus is the "Son" in his perfect obedience, and if we "worship" and follow Jesus, we too can be "sons of God" by obedience.

Here, it seems to me that the exegetical tradition of Chrysostom and Calvin on Matthew 3:11 can add something to Luz's portrait. They emphasized the radical difference between Christ and mere humans. John the Baptist's teaching that the coming Christ "is mightier than I, whose sandals I am not worthy to carry" suggests a difference that goes beyond obedience, because the Baptist, too, is obedient to God's will. The difference that John the Baptist himself identifies consists in the following: John *can* "baptize ... with water," but John *cannot* "baptize ... with the Holy Spirit and with fire." The Holy Spirit is the "Spirit of God" (Mt 3:16), the Spirit who does work that only God can do (see Mt 1:18). As the "Son," then, Jesus differs not only from the Father but also from all fellow humans—and not simply because of obedience. He differs from all his fellow humans because he has the power to bestow the eschatological Spirit of God, a power that indicates that his relation to the Spirit, as to the Father, is constitutive of his identity in a way that goes beyond human capacities.

For Luz, however, such pressing toward Nicene Trinitarianism is not acceptable as a reading of Matthew. In his view, the Synoptics' baptism scene was "a source of embarrassment for the church" because of "the church's altered christology"—namely the Christology according to which "Jesus was

---

26. Luz, *Matthew 1–7*, 143.
27. Luz, *Matthew 1–7*, 143.
28. Luz, *Matthew 1–7*, 144.

the eternal Logos whose real incarnation had taken place long before the baptism and who therefore no longer needed the gift of the Spirit."[29] I find Luz's position here to be contradictory. After all, he has already granted that the baptism scene does not establish Jesus as "Son," but instead proclaims the reality that has existed from the outset. In addition, the idea that the eternal or pre-existent Word, having become human, would not need "the gift of the Spirit," entails a faulty understanding of the incarnate Son's humanity. After all, the pro-Nicene Fathers recognized that the incarnate Son needed the mission of the Spirit to perfect his created humanity. Basil of Caesarea comments that *all* created things "are perfected by the presence of the Spirit", and he adds that "there is no holiness without the Spirit."[30] There is no reason to exclude the Son's *humanity* from the perfective work of the Spirit, even if the Spirit perfected Christ's humanity from the outset. Indeed, according to Matthew 1:18, the Holy Spirit was the creator of Christ's humanity.

If, in the baptism scene, Matthew intends simply to make clear that Jesus is so perfectly obedient that he should be worshiped as the divine Son while being a mere human like us, then the question also arises as to how Jesus can bestow the divine Spirit, which can only come from God. Furthermore, if Jesus is solely human, then the Baptist would have been greatly exaggerating when he said that he was not worthy even to carry the Christ's sandals. Christ would be simply another human instrument through which God acts, and Christ would not be worthy of the worship given to him repeatedly in the Gospel of Matthew. Again, to act with the power of the divine Spirit goes beyond the competence of a mere human, even instrumentally. It requires *divine* action; yet John the Baptist clearly says that Christ himself will baptize with the Spirit.

Thus, we should pause before supposing that Luz's ethical reduction of Matthean faith—a reduction that fits liberal (Enlightenment) Christianity perfectly—fits the Matthean portrait of Christ and the Spirit better than does the viewpoint of Chrysostom, Aquinas, or Calvin.[31] Christ delivers to

29. Luz, *Matthew 1–7*, 144–45.

30. St. Basil the Great, *On the Holy Spirit*, trans. Stephen Hildebrand (Yonkers, N.Y.: St. Vladimir's Seminary Press, 2011), 16.38, p. 71.

31. Luz states, "We too [like the early Church] must understand an individual text of the Bible in light of the entirety of our living, biblical faith. Not until the sense of an individual biblical text in this way becomes *our* sense so that an interpreter cannot only establish what it is but also affirm, proclaim, and live it—not until then is the understanding achieved that the biblical texts

us what Chrysostom calls "the unspeakable gift," the gift that is "fittest to proclaim His [Christ's] dignity," exhibiting his divine "rank" because to give the Spirit is not something that a mere human can do. In Matthew's Gospel, John the Baptist does not say that God baptizes us with his Spirit through Christ. Instead, the Baptist says that Christ will baptize us with the Spirit, which makes sense given that Christ deserves our worship and that Christ is "God with us."

Matthew 12:28

Let me now examine a somewhat similar passage from the Gospel of Matthew, Matthew 12:28, where Jesus says to the Pharisees, "But if it is by the Spirit of God that I cast out demons, then the kingdom of God has come upon you." In the Gospel of Matthew, Jesus links this proclamation with his status as the Son of man: "And whoever says a word against the Son of man will be forgiven; but whoever speaks against the Holy Spirit will not be forgiven, either in this age or in the age to come" (Mt 12:32). These passages are often read for their soteriological import. But what are the implications of these passages for Christology, particularly for the relation of the Son and the Spirit?

This time, I will begin with modern historical-critical exegesis and then move backward in time. In their historical-critical commentary on Matthew, W. D. Davies and Dale Allison hold that Jesus, as an eschatological prophet who believed in the imminent arrival of the Kingdom of God, likely said what is attributed to him in Matthew 12:28. They state, "The authenticity of 12.28 would seem to be one of the assured results of modern criticism. Jesus believed that the power of God was at work in him to overcome evil forces and that his success in fighting the devil and his minions was part of God's eschatological deliverance."[32] But while they affirm its authenticity, they consider that the depth of Jesus' claim needs more attention.

---

themselves have as their goal.... It may be easier for us to find 'our' meaning in the Matthean christology than it was for the ancient church. Connecting the promise of 'Immanuel' with the reification in Jesus' earthly obedience makes it possible to claim in practical living that God can be trusted. This is true for Jesus but also for his followers. The fundamental Matthean story of the obedient Son of God is a 'story of God for living.' If we rediscover it behind the 'high' christology of the church, we also discover that it speaks of God no less centrally than does the classic christology. Its distinctiveness is that it binds the promise of experiencing God to practical obedience in everyday living" (*Matthew 1–7*, 146).

32. W. D. Davies and Dale C. Allison Jr., *A Critical and Exegetical Commentary on the Gospel*

As they point out, Jesus' claim is not simply that he is exorcising demons and therefore the kingdom is at hand. After all, other wonder-workers performed exorcisms. Jesus' point, rather, is that he, *Jesus*, is casting out demons by the Spirit of God. Davies and Allison emphasize that Jesus is asserting "his very presence as the Christ."[33] Yet, as they say, he asserts his presence without making it explicit for his hearers; he invites his hearers to seek out his identity for themselves. He "implicitly asserts the mystery and magnitude of his own person but gives himself no title."[34] He is the Messiah and the Son of man, but his hearers must discover this on their own, since he will not conform to their Messianic expectations.

Davies and Allison, therefore, highlight Jesus' status as the Christ as the key take-away from Matthew 12:28, "But if it is by the Spirit of God that I cast out demons, then the kingdom of God has come upon you." But they do not reflect here upon Jesus' power to act "by the Spirit of God." Instead, they attend to a debate about the Q source, a debate that arises due to the difference between Matthew and Luke in their telling of this story. Luke 11:14–22 includes the words found in Matthew 12:27–28, but with a slight shift: Luke has "by the finger of God" (Lk 11:20) rather than "by the Spirit of God."

Davies and Allison observe, "As to whether Q had 'finger of God' or 'Spirit of God' there has been much discussion."[35] Scholars have drawn a connection to the phrase "finger of God" in Exodus 8:19, where Pharaoh's magicians realize that the living God—rather than a mere human magician—is at work in the plague of gnats. Some scholars have proposed that Luke adapts Jesus' saying (or the Q saying) in order to fit with Luke's theme of New Exodus. Since New Exodus is also a Matthean theme, some scholars maintain that Matthew would have seized upon the opportunity to use

according to Saint Matthew, vol. 2, Commentary on Matthew VIII–XVIII (London: T. and T. Clark International, 2004), 339.

33. Davies and Allison, A Critical and Exegetical Commentary on the Gospel according to Saint Matthew, vol. 2, 339.

34. Davies and Allison, A Critical and Exegetical Commentary on the Gospel according to Saint Matthew, vol. 2, 339.

35. Davies and Allison, A Critical and Exegetical Commentary on the Gospel according to Saint Matthew, vol. 2, 339–40. See also Rafael Rodríguez, Structuring Early Christian Memory: Jesus in Tradition, Performance, and Text (London: T and T Clark, 2010), 195–203. Rodríguez argues that Luke's "finger" presents Jesus' exorcisms as heralding the New Exodus and New Covenant, while Matthew's "Spirit" "links Jesus' exorcisms with the Isaianic vision of restoration, despite the fact that exorcisms do not themselves figure in the Isaianic vision" (203).

"finger of God" had it been present in the Q source of Jesus' sayings. But in the view of Davies and Allison, it is more plausible to hold that Matthew is the one who made the change. Yet, in the end, they argue that it does not really matter, because "the OT equates 'finger of God' with 'hand of God' and 'Spirit of God.'"[36] In this regard, Davies and Allison cite Psalm 8:3, Psalm 33:6, Ezekiel 3:14, Ezekiel 8:1–3, Ezekiel 37:1, and 2 Kings 3:15.

What is the import of these Old Testament verses? Psalm 8:3 praises the divine power to create: "When I look at thy heavens, the work of thy fingers." Psalm 33:6 attributes the work of cosmic creation to God's "breath" or "spirit," as well as to God's "word." Ezekiel 3:14 suggests that God's "Spirit" and "hand" are the same reality; both describe overwhelming divine power. Ezekiel 8:1–3 makes the same point: "He put forth the form of a hand, and took me by a lock of my head, and the Spirit lifted me up between earth and heaven, and brought me in visions of God to Jerusalem." The "hand" of God is not controllable by the prophet. Rather, the "hand" or "Spirit" seizes the prophet and does something that only God can do. The same point comes across in Ezekiel 37:1, where the prophet says that "[t]he hand of the Lord was upon me, and he brought me out by the Spirit of the Lord, and set me down in the midst of the valley; it was full of bones." Only God's Spirit can give the prophet such a visionary experience. God's Spirit (or "hand") takes hold of the prophet, rather than the prophet making use of God's Spirit. Second Kings 3:15 describes "the power of the Lord" coming upon the prophet Elisha. The prophet, moved by the power of the Lord, prophesies. In the Rabbinic Targum, as Davies and Allison point out, 2 Kings 3:15's "power" is changed to "Spirit."

For my purposes, it is not necessary to insist that the Old Testament envisions the Spirit as a distinct, personal divine agent, although I think that certain passages in the Old Testament do support this view.[37] My interest here is in the relation of Jesus and the Spirit, and it seems to me that the most striking aspect of Matthew 12:28 is that Jesus can directly work by the Spirit, which, as shown by the above-cited passages, is nothing less than the divine power.

By contrast, consider Elijah's contest with the prophets of Baal, in the

36. Davies and Allison, *A Critical and Exegetical Commentary on the Gospel according to Saint Matthew*, vol. 2, 340.

37. For further discussion, see my "The Holy Spirit and the Old Testament," *The Thomist* 79 (2015): 345–81.

course of which Elijah prays, "O Lord, God of Abraham, Isaac, and Israel, let it be known this day that thou art God in Israel, and that I am thy servant, and that I have done all these things at thy word. Answer me, O Lord, answer me, that this people may know that thou, O Lord, art God, and that thou hast turned their hearts back" (1 Kgs 18:36–37). The Lord answers by performing a miracle; but the point for my purposes is that Elijah must pray to God in order for God to act with power. Consider, too, the example of Moses—incomparable in Israel (see Deuteronomy 34:10–12)—who is punished by God for performing a miracle in front of the people of Israel while allowing them to think that the ability to work the miracle came from his (Moses') own power. Moses says, "Hear now, you rebels; shall we bring forth water for you out of this rock?" (Nm 20:10). When he does so without crediting God, God tells him, "Because you did not believe in me, to sanctify me in the eyes of the people of Israel, therefore you shall not bring this assembly into the land which I have given them" (Nm 20:12).

Jesus' case is completely different. When Jesus acts, he does so "by the Spirit of God"—not moved by the power of God (as we noted in Ezekiel), nor crediting God for doing something that he prayed God would do (as in the case of Elijah), but acting with the divine power (the divine Spirit) as though that Spirit belongs to him. In my view, this is what is most striking about Matthew 12:28. Jesus works through the divine Spirit as though it is *his* Spirit. This fits with the claim that Jesus is "God with us" and the repeated insistence in the Gospel of Matthew that Jesus should be worshiped. Recall that Moses, in accord with the Decalogue, warns the people of Israel not to worship "the likeness of male or female" or any human figure (Dt 4:16), because "the Lord your God is a devouring fire, a jealous God" (Dt 4:24). But Jesus is worshiped in the Gospel of Matthew, and it seems to me that Jesus' casting out demons "by the Spirit of God" shows that he is the divine Son from the Father, able to act by the divine Spirit.

Davies and Allison are aware of interpretations of Matthew 12:27–28 that emphasize, not primarily Jesus' identity as the Messiah but rather the fact that "Jesus' exorcisms are different because they alone were the work of the Spirit or finger of God."[38] Such interpretations miss the mark, in my view. Jesus does not say that the Spirit of God casts out demons; he does not say that his exorcisms are the work of the Spirit. Rather, he himself is the

---

38. Davies and Allison, *A Critical and Exegetical Commentary on the Gospel according to Saint Matthew*, vol. 2, 341.

one who works. To this extent, Davies and Allison are correct to focus on the revelation here of Jesus' Messianic identity, because Jesus places himself at the center. He takes credit himself for his miraculous deeds. But I would nonetheless highlight the place of the Spirit, precisely because Jesus employs or uses the divine Spirit. Only the divine Son can lay claim to being able to act, on his own, by the divine Spirit. A mere human could call down the Spirit's action but could not act by the power of the Spirit as by his *own* power. Davies and Allison ask, "How else but by God's power could Jewish exorcists cast out demons?"[39] Certainly so, but, as in Matthew 3:11, Jesus is not presented as a Jewish exorcist depending upon God's power. Rather, he acts by the Spirit as by his own power, and this is what distinguishes him as the Messiah. Given that the Spirit is his own, he has authority on his own (by his Spirit) to cast out demons, an authority that he freely and directly exercises.

In John Chrysostom's commentary on Matthew 12:28, John first attends to Jesus' reference to the "kingdom of God." How is it, asks Chrysostom, that it follows from Jesus' exorcisms that "the kingdom of God has come upon you"? Chrysostom answers that the "kingdom" comes when Christ comes. The very fact that Jesus is casting out demons by the Spirit of God means that the kingdom has come, because it means that the Christ has come. In this regard, Chrysostom's emphasis is similar to that of Davies and Allison: the interpretative center of the passage is Jesus' identity as the Christ. Chrysostom then inquires into why it is that Luke's version of the story has "finger of God" whereas Matthew's version has "Spirit of God." He reasons that casting out demons requires the divine power. No mere human can cast out Satan, and one certainly cannot cast out Satan by invoking Satan's own power. The only power that is sufficient is the divine power signified by God's "finger" or "Spirit." Given that Jesus has such power, he cannot be less than God, even though he is not God the Father. Chrysostom observes that Jesus "means indeed that from these things they [the Pharisees] should infer and say, If this be so, then the Son of God is come."[40] The kingdom has come because the Son of God has come; and we know that the *divine* Son has come because Christ performs works that require divine power, wielding the divine power as his own.

Chrysostom perceives that the Christological point is that Christ's pow-

---

39. Davies and Allison, *A Critical and Exegetical Commentary on the Gospel according to Saint Matthew*, vol. 2, 341.

40. Chrysostom, *Homilies on the Gospel of St. Matthew*, XII.2, 265.

er is divine, but he does not specify this further in terms of the relation of Christ and the Spirit. Arguably, however, the reference to the "Spirit of God" does not simply mean the divine power. After all, in addition to passages such as Matthew 3:16, in which the Spirit descends upon Christ in the form of a dove, Matthew 12:18 applies Isaiah 42:1 to Jesus, so as to make clear that God (the Father) has put his Spirit upon his servant Jesus. The Spirit has a distinctive place in Christ's eschatological work, and the risen Christ names the Holy Spirit alongside the Father and the Son in the baptismal formula of Matthew 28:19. Christologically, one who can perform a "work of the greatest power"—in Chrysostom's words—by casting out demons must be the "Son of God," able to act by the "Spirit of God."[41] Matthew 12:28 thus constitutes a further ground for holding that the Christology of Matthew's Gospel is proto-Trinitarian.

This interpretation is made explicit in Jerome's commentary on Matthew 12:28. As do Chrysostom and Davies and Allison, Jerome begins by noting the contrast between "Spirit of God" in Matthew and "finger of God" in Luke. Lest the "finger of God" seem to be doing nothing other than a relatively minor miracle (the gnats of Exodus 8:19), Jerome points out that Moses describes the two tablets of stone, containing the Ten Commandments, as having been "written with the finger of God" (Dt 9:10). Only God can act by his "finger"; likewise, only God (the Son) could act by "the Spirit of God" (Mt 12:28). Jerome compares the Son to "the hand and arm of God," and the Holy Spirit to a "finger" on this hand or arm.[42] Although he does not say it in this passage, Jerome may have in view John 12:37–38 with its quotation of Isaiah 53:1 (the suffering servant): "Though he [Jesus] had done so many signs before them, yet they did not believe in him; it was that the word spoken by the prophet Isaiah might be fulfilled: 'Lord, who has believed our report, and to whom has the arm of the Lord been revealed?'" In the context of John 12, the "arm of the Lord" here is Christ. It makes sense, then, to think of Jesus, the Son of God ("arm") acting by his divine Spirit ("finger"). The missions of the Son and Spirit are united when Jesus, the "beloved Son" (Mt 3:17), acts "by the Spirit of God" to inaugurate "the kingdom of God" (Mt 12:28). Along these lines, Jerome explicitly describes the Trinitarian Christology that he finds in Matthew 12:28: "If, then, the Son is the hand and arm

---

41. Chrysostom, *Homilies on the Gospel of St. Matthew*, XII.2, 265.
42. Jerome, *Commentary on Matthew*, II.12.28, 143–44.

of God, and the Spirit is his finger, then there is one substance of the Father and of the Son and of the Holy Spirit."[43]

Building upon these earlier commentaries, Aquinas likewise places Trinitarian Christology at the center of his interpretation of Matthew 12:28. Aquinas first draws the connection between the Spirit and God's "finger," and between the Son and God's "hand" (more closely connected to the finger than is the arm). Aquinas paraphrases Christ as saying: "it does not follow from this that there is some invocation of the Holy Ghost, but, on the contrary, this happens solely by My [Christ's] own power."[44] In other words, Christ makes clear in Matthew 12:28 that he can cast out demons without needing to invoke the Spirit's aid. He can do it by his own power, and his own power is nothing less than the Spirit of God. This is a Trinitarian Christology.

Aquinas asks the further question of why, if the divine power ad extra is one, casting out demons is attributed uniquely to the Holy Spirit. Why is it not attributed to the one divine power of the holy Trinity? In response, Aquinas explains that the personal property that makes the Spirit distinctive in the Trinity is that the Spirit proceeds as the mutual Love of the Father and Son. Therefore, since it is divine love that drives out demonic power, the Spirit is uniquely manifested by the work of driving out demons.

Recall, too, that for the Gospel of Matthew, the unity of the Father and Son is profound: "All things have been delivered to me by my Father; and no one knows the Son except the Father, and no one knows the Father except the Son and any one to whom the Son chooses to reveal him" (Mt 11:27). The intimacy here is something that would not be possible for a merely human Son. It compares with, but goes far beyond, the "face to face" (Ex 33:11) relationship of God to Moses.[45] Having been told by God that God knows him "by name" and that he (Moses) has "found favor" in God's sight, Moses asks to see God's "glory" (Ex 33:12, 16, 18). In response, God shows Moses the divine "goodness" and the divine "name," but not the divine "face" (Ex 33:19–20). Going much further, Jesus asserts that "no one knows the Father except the Son" and that the Son has received "all things" from the Father. The Father is "the Lord, who made all things, who stretched out the heavens

43. Chrysostom, *Homilies on the Gospel of St. Matthew*, XII.2, 265.

44. Aquinas, *Commentary on the Gospel according to St. Matthew*, 437.

45. For the parallel, see Davies and Allison, *A Critical and Exegetical Commentary on the Gospel according to Saint Matthew*, vol. 2, 283–87.

alone" (Is 44:24). When Jesus says that he alone knows the Father and that he has received "all things" from the Father, this shows, as Frank Matera says, that Jesus enjoys an utterly "unique relationship to the Father" as the Son of God.[46]

Matthew 12:32

Among the many other passages that could be explored in investigating the Gospel of Matthew as a source of Trinitarian Christology, I wish to conclude with Matthew 12:32, "And whoever says a word against the Son of man will be forgiven; but whoever speaks against the Holy Spirit will not be forgiven, either in this age or in the age to come." Does this verse subordinate the Son vis-à-vis the Holy Spirit, indicating that the Spirit may be divine, but the Son is a creature (however exalted or exemplary)?

In his commentary on this verse, Jerome takes the opportunity to insist upon the Spirit's divinity. After all, if a person who "speaks against the Holy Spirit will not be forgiven," then the Spirit cannot be less than God. Although Jerome does not mention it here, recall the commandment of God in the Decalogue: "You shall not take the name of the Lord your God in vain; for the Lord will not hold him guiltless who takes his name in vain" (Ex 20:7). Since speaking against the Holy Spirit will not be forgiven, the principle of the Decalogue regarding blasphemy is applicable to the Holy Spirit. As Jerome notes, in the fourth-century controversy about whether or not the Spirit is divine, "bishops and priests" have "committed blasphemy against the Holy Spirit" by denying the Spirit's divinity.[47] Yet, as Jerome says, the Church forgives these bishops and priests, and even allows them to retain their office. Why does this not contradict Matthew 12:32?

In response, Jerome notes that perhaps Jesus means that speaking against Jesus can be forgiven—because Jesus in the flesh appears to be a mere human—whereas speaking against *what Jesus does in the Spirit* cannot be forgiven, because Jesus' works are clearly shown to be divine. On this view, what *cannot* be forgiven is to say that Jesus' divine works are produced by Beelzebub, because this rejects the clear evidence that he is the Christ who works by the divine Spirit. But what *can* be forgiven are such errors as supposing that because Jesus freely eats and drinks with sinners, he is "a glutton and a drunkard" (Mt 11:19).

---

46. Matera, *New Testament Theology*, 41.
47. Jerome, *Commentary on Matthew*, II.12.32, 145.

Jerome does not address the seeming implication of the verse, namely that the Spirit is superior to Christ. By contrast, John Calvin tackles this implication head-on. In his commentary on Matthew 12:32 (and parallels), he asks, "Why is it said that he who *blasphemes against the Spirit* is a more heinous sinner than he who *blasphemes against Christ*? Is it because the majesty of the Spirit is greater, that a crime committed against him must be punished with greater severity?"[48] To answer this question, Calvin appeals to Colossians 2:9, which teaches that in Christ "the whole fulness of deity dwells bodily." On this basis, he excludes the possibility that Jesus, in Matthew 12:32, might be implying that the Spirit is greater than the Son. He then interprets the verse along the same lines that we found in Jerome: to blaspheme against the Spirit means to reject the clear manifestation of the divine power.

Calvin goes on to point out that it is not really possible to speak against the Spirit unless one has known him through his works. He observes that "no man curses the Spirit who is not enlightened by him, and conscious of ungodly rebellion."[49] Put succinctly, to speak against the Spirit is knowingly to reject the work of divine grace. In accord with his teaching on predestination, Calvin adds that knowingly belittling the Spirit's manifestation of the divine glory is not only a terrible sin but also a sign of everlasting reprobation, which explains why this is an unpardonable sin.

Aquinas's commentary on Matthew 12:32 investigates the Christological problem further. He identifies three ways in which commentators have understood the verse. First, some say that Christ here warns that the people who reject his works—performed by the power of the Spirit—are rejecting the Spirit and are therefore excluding themselves from salvation. Second, some (specifically Hilary of Poitiers) argue rather eccentrically that Christ is here referring to himself, "holy" in his human nature and "Spirit" in his divine nature. Aquinas notes that for some who follow this second path, but who seek to avoid its eccentricity, the meaning of the verse is that "whosoever shall say something out of weakness against the Son and against His human nature, has an excuse; but whosoever speaks against His divine nature, has no reason to be pardoned."[50]

The third path is the one that, among the three, Aquinas favors. When Christ says that "whoever says a word against the Son of man will be forgiv-

---

48. Calvin, §127.

49. Calvin, §128.

50. Aquinas, *Commentary on the Gospel according to St. Matthew*, 440.

en," the phrase "Son of man" here refers to Christ in his human nature. But those who speak "against the Holy Spirit" cannot be forgiven because they see and know that Christ is performing miracles by the Holy Spirit, and they therefore blaspheme Christ in his divine nature: only God can work by the power of God.

Aquinas notes that for Augustine, the central issue raised by Matthew 12:32 is not Christology but rather the scope of divine mercy. How is it that someone can commit a sin so heinous that it cannot be forgiven by God? As noted above, this question also has a significant place for Calvin. What happens if the person repents of the sin and clings to the mercy of Christ? As Aquinas observes, Augustine answers this question by arguing that unforgivable speaking against the Holy Spirit is, quite simply, "the word of impenitence."[51] God can forgive anyone who has sorrow for sin, but not if the person still cleaves to the sin and refuses to seek or accept pardon. Peter Lombard expands upon Augustine by arguing that, along with impenitence, other unforgivable sins include despair, presumption, "obstinacy, resisting the known truth, and envy of our brother's spiritual good."[52] Aquinas identifies these sins as "sins against the Holy Ghost," sins that are unforgivable because the rejection of God's grace is intrinsic to the sin.[53]

Do historical-critical exegetes hold that Matthew 12:32 elevates the Spirit over the Son? The "Son of man" is Jesus, and he casts out demons "by the Spirit of God" (Mt 12:28, 32). What do exegetes today say about the seeming problem that Jesus, in Matthew 12:32, may appear to give a higher standing to the Spirit than to himself?

The Reformed theologian and biblical scholar Peter Leithart suggests that to ask such a question is to miss Jesus' point. Instead, we should recognize that during Jesus' earthly ministry, the Spirit has not yet been poured out. After Jesus' death and Resurrection, by contrast, the Spirit will be fully poured out. In his eschatological discourse in Matthew 10, Jesus points forward to this time, which will be a time of persecution but also a time when the Spirit will speak through those who are testifying to Christ. Leithart maintains that in Matthew 12:32, Jesus is distinguishing between the time of his coming (his public ministry) and the time of the Spirit's coming. In

51. Aquinas, *Commentary on the Gospel according to St. Matthew*, 442.

52. Aquinas, *Commentary on the Gospel according to St. Matthew*, 443.

53. Aquinas, *Commentary on the Gospel according to St. Matthew*, 444.

this vein, Leithart states, "He is the Son of Man, and He comes in humility. Those who reject Him will have a chance to repent. The Jews will put Jesus the Son of Man on the cross and kill Him, but once the Spirit comes at Pentecost, the Jews are told again and again what they've done, and many repent and are forgiven."[54] Regarding those who do not repent at Pentecost, Leithart considers that they have in fact hardened themselves against the works of the Spirit and therefore will not be forgiven.

By contrast, the Catholic exegete Donald Senior simply argues that Matthew 12:32 means that "to attribute Jesus' power to Satan rather than to the Spirit of God is a 'blasphemy' or insult against God so perverted in the eyes of the Gospel and so closed to the truth that it leaves no room for repentance or forgiveness either 'in this age or in the age to come.'"[55] But if this is so, then why would insulting Jesus not be equivalent to insulting the Spirit by which Jesus works? If insulting the Spirit is unforgivable, and if Jesus works by the Spirit, then why would insulting Jesus not also be unforgivable? Another Catholic historical-critical exegete, Rudolf Schnackenburg, recognizes the problem. His answer is to highlight the human lowliness implied by the phrase "Son of man" in the Gospel of Matthew. He recalls Matthew 8:20, "the Son of man has nowhere to lay his head," and Matthew 11:19, "the Son of man came eating and drinking, and they say, 'Behold, a glutton and a drunkard, a friend of tax collectors and sinners!'" Both of these verses show the humanness, the vulnerability, of Jesus, as well as the ease of misidentifying him. In his humble humanity as the "Son of man," says Schnackenburg, Jesus' "power in the Spirit is not altogether clear."[56] Even so, there are those who recognize that he is doing divine works by the Spirit; for those who recognize this, and who nonetheless "ascribe the workings of the Holy Spirit to Satan," their sin is a sin of malice, and because their malice rejects Christ's work of divine mercy, their sin stands outside the divine mercy.[57] On this view, rather than positing that the Son is lesser than the Spirit, Matthew 12:32 points to the difficulty of recognizing the divine Son in his humble humanity, a difficulty that becomes an impossibility if we refuse to countenance the works that he does by divine power.

54. Peter J. Leithart, *The Gospel of Matthew through New Eyes*, vol. 1, *Jesus as Israel* (Monroe, La.: Athanasius Press, 2017), 256.

55. Donald Senior, *Matthew* (Nashville, Tenn.: Abingdon Press, 1998), 142.

56. Rudolf Schnackenburg, *The Gospel of Matthew*, trans. Robert R. Barr (Grand Rapids, Mich.: Eerdmans, 2002), 117.

57. Schnackenburg, *The Gospel of Matthew*, 117.

Conclusion

In the above, I have raised various exegetical issues that pertain to Matthew 3:11, Matthew 12:28, and Matthew 12:32. My purpose has not been to answer all the theological questions that arise in these texts (most notably, the thorny problem of the unforgiveable sin). Rather, I have attempted to show that the tradition of Christian exegesis helps us to perceive more fully the Gospel of Matthew's Trinitarian Christology. Regarding Trinitarian Christology, Robert Imbelli has observed that "[u]nless God has revealed himself fully through Jesus Christ in the Holy Spirit, then the church is without foundation."[58] As Imbelli reminds us, "It is Jesus Christ who, by his passion, death, and resurrection, has redeemed the world."[59] This can only be the case if Christ acts as the divine Son in the fullness of the divine Spirit, so that the Son and the Spirit together draw the fallen (but now redeemed) world to the Father.

The biblical scholar Simon Gathercole has defended the view that the Synoptic Gospels affirm the preexistence of Christ as the divine Son.[60] Yet, Gathercole admits that "the idea of pre-existence is neither as prominent nor as extensively defined in the Synoptics as it is elsewhere [i.e., in Paul, Hebrews, and the Johannine literature]," and he also notes that "none of the Synoptic Gospels stresses the coeternity of Father and Son as does the Johannine tradition."[61] At the same time, he insists that the divine preexistence and divine status of the Son is present in the Gospel of Matthew, notably in Matthew 28:19, Matthew 23:37, Matthew 11:27, and elsewhere. He maintains that Matthew frequently speaks of the Spirit's divine agency (as distinct from the Father and the Son), for example in Matthew 1:20, Matthew 3:16, and Matthew 4:1. As he says, Matthew 28:19 "identifies the Spirit as personal: the Spirit partakes of a *name*" and indeed "shares the *divine* name" with the Father and Son.[62]

---

58. Robert P. Imbelli, *Rekindling the Christic Imagination: Theological Meditations for the New Evangelization* (Collegeville, Minn.: Liturgical Press, 2014), xv.

59. Imbelli, *Rekindling the Christic Imagination*, 83.

60. Simon J. Gathercole, *The Pre-Existent Son: Recovering the Christologies of Matthew, Mark and Luke* (Grand Rapids, Mich.: Eerdmans, 2006).

61. Simon Gathercole, "The Trinity in the Synoptic Gospels and Acts," in *The Oxford Handbook of the Trinity*, ed. Gilles Emery, OP, and Matthew Levering (Oxford: Oxford University Press, 2011), 61.

62. Gathercole, "The Trinity in the Synoptic Gospels and Acts," 67.

In this essay, I have employed Matthew 3:11, 12:28, and 12:32 to enrich the case that Gathercole and others make for Matthean (proto-)Trinitarian Christology. As we have seen, Jesus is the one who uniquely acts by the Holy Spirit. The Holy Spirit is Jesus' own Spirit; he freely acts by the Holy Spirit. As the humble "Son of man," he is also the Father's "beloved Son" who alone knows the Father. By the Spirit, he does divine works; and when we recognize this, we see his divine unity with his Father. By the Spirit, the Son inaugurates the eschatological kingdom, which, as Matthew emphasizes, is *from heaven* and is unlike any earthly kingdom, including the one that the Jewish people were expecting the Messiah to bring.[63] Jonathan Pennington states that "for Matthew, the kingdom of heaven did critique and promise to overthrow the Roman Empire—but via God's irruption into the world from heaven."[64]

This irruption, in Christ and his Spirit, is at the heart of the Church's Trinitarian Christology.[65] As Pennington concludes, drawing not only on Matthew 28:16–20 but also on Matthew 16:13–20, for Matthew "Jesus is the divine Christ,"[66] sent by the divine Father and empowered with the divine Spirit. This Christological truth is what I have sought to make manifest in this essay, in light of biblical exegesis past and present.

---

63. See Pennington, *Heaven and Earth in the Gospel of Matthew*.

64. Pennington, *Heaven and Earth in the Gospel of Matthew*, 339.

65. Thus, Pennington states, "Jesus' identity (Christology) as well as that of his people (ecclesiology; New Covenant) and their ultimate goal and hope (eschatology) can all be understood as part of the heaven and earth disjuncture; in each case, these realities are depicted as being on the 'heaven' side of the heaven versus earth equation" (343).

66. Pennington, *Heaven and Earth in the Gospel of Matthew*, 346.

8

The Trinitarian Shape of the Mystical Body of Christ
in the Theology of Isaac of Stella

NATHANIEL PETERS

The Cistercian abbot Isaac of Stella (c. 1100–c. 1170) is an obscure figure of medieval theological history, best known today for appearing occasionally in the Office of Readings and searches through the Patrologia Latina. Born in England, he studied in the French schools and became abbot of Stella, a small community near Poitiers, in 1147. He spent the rest of his life there except for a brief period on the Île de Ré. For scholars of medieval monastic thought, Isaac is best known as one of the most speculative Cistercian theologians. His doctrine of God, anthropology, and Eucharistic thought are profound meditations on the person of Christ at the center of the mysteries of the Christian faith, especially Christ as the head of his mystical body, the Church. Isaac also shows how the relations of the persons of the Trinity shape their economic activity in that mystical body, especially in the mystery that constitutes its unity, the Eucharist. For Isaac, the rational faculties of the soul serve as the point of union with God through a sharing in the knowledge and affective life of the Trinity. That union with God takes place through the soul's union with the Son by being made a member of his mystical body, the Church. The Eucharist is the means by which that body's members are united to each other. It is its food and fills the faithful with the love of the Holy Spirit, in whom they are united to Christ their head.

Sharing in Divine Knowledge and Affectivity

Neoplatonic metaphysics influenced Isaac's conception of the relationship between the body, the soul, and God. Within human beings, he writes, the mind is the summit of the soul, the image of God that can connect to the Spirit. Likewise, Christ is the summit of humanity that permits its union with God. The personal union of Creator and rational creatures is realized in him.[1] Christ therefore has two aspects: an immanent, hidden one that expresses the Father and an economic one that reveals the Word, and by the Word, the Father.[2] The Son's incarnation serves as the conjunction of God and human beings, but his death and resurrection serve as the culmination of his salvific action. Our fallen state has resulted in a double death of soul and body and a double separation of body from soul, and the two from God. In Christ, too, there are two bonds: body and soul, humanity and divinity. The latter bond could not be broken, and the former did not deserve to be. But Christ loosens the bond between his soul and body in his death, so that with his resurrection he can retie ours. His death and resurrection are "an effective type of ours, and not simply a figure or symbol."[3] Christ's incarnation, death, and resurrection serve as complementary parts of human redemption, which takes place by reconnecting the bonds severed by sin so that human beings made whole can be reunited with God.

Redemption takes place when Christ has become the object of the human mind's knowledge and love in a way analogous to that of the Word in the mind of the Father. In his sermons for Sexagesima, Isaac develops his understanding of the Word as the rational thought of the Father, an import-

1. Robert Javelet, *Image et ressemblance au douzième siècle: de Saint Anselme à Alain de Lille*, vol. I (Paris: Éditions Letouzey & Ané, 1967), 235.

2. See also *Sermo* 8. All citations from Isaac's sermons are taken from his *Sermons*, ed. Anselm Hoste and Gaetano Raciti, trans. Gaston Salet, vols. I–III, SC 130, 207, and 339 (Paris: Les Éditions du Cerf, 1967, 1974, and 1987). English translations are taken from *Sermons on the Christian Year*, trans. Hugh McCaffery, Cistercian Fathers Series (CF) 11 (Kalamazoo, Mich.: Cistercian Publications, 1979), and Isaac of Stella, *The Selected Works of Isaac of Stella: A Cistercian Voice from the Twelfth Century*, ed. Dániel Deme (Burlington, Vt.: Ashgate, 2007), unless otherwise noted.

3. Leonard Gaggero, "Isaac of Stella and the Theology of Redemption," *Collectanea Cisterciensia* 22 (1965): 33. See also *Sermo* 40.

ant aspect of his Trinitarian thought. When Isaac considers the mind of God from which creation proceeded, he concludes that the mind of God cannot be other than God himself: "These two truths go together then: He is and he has Mind. He is being and has what, belonging to and proceeding from his being, is himself."[4] The Son is the Word and Wisdom of God, who proceeds from the Father, differing in personal property but not in essence.[5] As such, he is the object of the divine mind's self-knowledge and the source of all created things, the efficient principle of their existence.[6]

This rational aspect of God's nature is the point of connection by which God allows created beings to share in the divine life. Therefore, the purpose of rational faculties is to seek union with God through knowledge and love of him:

When the indivisible Trinity willed eternally and undividedly the existence of beings able to receive God, to have part in his delight, gladness, peace, joy, then the Trinity created from nothing the rational mind made in God's image.... Rational spirit has no other purpose than to enjoy and share God's delight in God and in all else. Rationality is his that he may be able to seek God himself in himself and in everything.[7]

Again, Isaac writes:

Rational minds are the first and only beings made in God's image, thanks to the gift God wills to make of his Joy. They are for that reason the only creatures capable of sharing his knowledge and love. Their intellects and wills, faculties that enable them to understand and to love, fit them to share God's communicable nature. These faculties are, as it were, receptacles and tools belonging to their nature that the first gift of grace puts in being and the further gift of grace fills against both emptiness and the wrong kind of content.... Created minds are the receptacles into which God's Wisdom and Power pours himself, filling them with

---

4. "Duo quidem occurrunt, ipsum esse et aliquid habere; ipsum esse et ipsius aliquid, quod tamen de se sit et hoc quod ipse" (*Sermo* 23.4; CF 11, 190).

5. *Sermo* 23.6–7.

6. *Sermo* 23.14; 22.23.

7. "Fecit itaque, quando voluit, quae velle numquam coepit, indivisa Trinitas indivise naturam sui capacem, suae delectationis et iucunditatis et pacis et gaudii participio habilem, mentem rationalem videlicet ad imaginem suam de nihilo.... Ideo igitur factus est spiritus rationalis ut congaudeat et condelectetur Deo de Deo et de omnibus in ipso solo. Rationalis quidem factus, ut ipsum Deum in se et in omnibus investiget" (*Sermo* 25.3–5; CF 11, 206).

knowledge and love of him. Each of them is a field in which the Wisdom and Power of God sows himself, the Seed, from which comes the light of knowledge and the fervor of love.[8]

These passages reveal key aspects of Isaac's anthropology and Trinitarian theology. First, Isaac's anthropology is marked by a deep sense of receptivity. The soul's rational faculties are made to receive Christ, the Word and Wisdom of God, in a manner analogous to that of the mind of God, which has the Word as its object. Union with God takes place through the Son sowing himself in rational minds, an image taken from the parable of the sower in Matthew 13 and Luke 8. The Son sows himself from the bosom of the Father "freely, that is, by the gift of the Holy Spirit" to the angels in heaven, to Adam and Eve, to the Israelites in the desert, and to the whole world in the person of Jesus.[9]

Second, joy and delight serve as two important characteristics of God's nature, both of which are also associated especially with the Holy Spirit. When Isaac first treats the Spirit in the Sexagesima sermons, he describes him as "God's internal joy and delight in his light and with his light." As such, the Spirit belongs both to the Father, who rejoices, and to the Son, because of and in whom he rejoices: "God's joy in his Son makes both of them [the Father and the Son] the principle of their unique joy."[10] Since the Father and the Son are one being, Isaac continues, it follows that this joy shares their being and is the love that exists between them, as well as their sweetness, peace, and delight.[11] As Javelet notes, one could make of Isaac's conception of the Trinity a Trinity of joy, because the unity of the three persons is precisely the joy of

8. "Naturali dono communicabilis gaudii sui facta a Deo mens rationalis, sicut prima et sola eius suscipit imaginem, ita potest cognitionem et amorem. Facta est enim capax capabilis Divinitatis per rationem et voluntatem, id est intelligendi et amandi facultatem, tamquam per vasa quaedam aut instrumenta naturalis conditionis, quae sicut primum gratiae donum creat ut sint, sic secundum replet ne vacua sint aut male plena.... Ipse ergo, sicut vas cui se sapientia et virtus Dei, ut cognitione ac caritate ipsius perfundat, infundit, ita est et ager ubi se sapientia eadem ac virtus seminat, quatenus de tali semine cognitionis lux ac dilectionis fervor exsurgat" (*Sermo* 26.1, 3; CF II, 211–212).

9. "id est dono Spiritus sancti" (*Sermo* 26.II, 18; CF II, 214).

10. "Si enim intus de hac sua luce et cum sua luce gaudet ac delectatur, gaudium illud ac delectationem de utroque procedere manifestum est: de illo scilicet qui gaudet et de illo de quo et cum quo gaudet. Utrumque enim principium constat esse gaudii quod huius de illo est" (*Sermo* 24.9; CF II, 199).

11. *Sermo* 24.10–11.

that fullness that breaks out in the Trinitarian embrace. Still, spiritual joy is especially associated with the Spirit, who is charity.[12]

This joy is the communion into which those who receive the Spirit are invited. In the economy of salvation, the Holy Spirit is poured out into the hearts of human beings through the Son as a gift of that same love and light.[13] Indeed, Isaac sees him as "closer to the creature in some sense as the one who, proceeding from both, is Gift and Power."[14] Likewise, in his *De anima*, Isaac writes that every enjoyment of God that we have comes from the gift of the Spirit, "for he is the natural gift existing in God, by means of which God can be given to and enjoyed by every nature, as it was said above."[15] The Spirit bears the image of the Father and the Son and is thereby able to conform those who receive him to that image. He fills their hearts with that same charity that exists between the Father and Son, giving them the likeness of the Trinity and thereby uniting them to God and giving them a share in divine joy.[16] Isaac understands the soul's union with God to be a participation in divine affectivity through the infusion of the Spirit into the rational faculties made to receive him.

Like other ancient and medieval exegetes, Isaac sees this union in terms of the kiss from the opening verse of the Song of Songs. It is a union with the Father, through the Son (by filial adoption into the whole Christ), in the Spirit, who is light and gift.[17] He especially associates the Son with forgiveness and liberation from slavery, and the Spirit with favor and friendship. Hence, the Spirit is the kiss of friendship given to the soul by the Son, the mouth of the Father.[18] The Son and Spirit work together, but each has his own particular mission:

12. Javelet, *Image et ressemblance au douzième siècle*, I:418.

13. *Sermo* 24.21–22.

14. "creature tamen quodammodo quasi proprior videtur esse spiritus sanctus quipped qui de utroque munus est utriusque" (Caterina Tarlazzi, "L'Epistola de Anima di Isacco di Stella: studio della tradizione ed edizione del testo," *Medioevo* 36 (2011): 547–49; *The Selected Works of Isaac of Stella*, 156).

15. "nobis autem omnis diuinitatis usus ex munere. Est enim in deo munus naturale quo ipse donabilis et fruibilis est omni, ut superius dictum est, nature" (Tarlazzi, "L'Epistola de Anima di Isacco di Stella," 547–49; Isaac of Stella, *The Selected Works of Isaac of Stella*, 156).

16. Javelet, *Image et ressemblance au douzième siècle*, I:93–95; 440.

17. Gaetano Raciti, "Isaac de l'Étoile," in *Dictionnaire de Spiritualité*, vol. 7 (Paris: Beauchesne, 1971), 2031.

18. *Sermo* 45.13.

In this perspective Christ is to an extent a mediator of forgiveness, the Spirit is a mediator of friendship. Christ mediates verity, the Spirit mediates charity. Through Christ comes forgiveness, through the Spirit comes fortitude. Pardon through Christ, perseverance through the Spirit. Through Christ comes loosing, through the Spirit comes binding together. Nonetheless Christ and the Spirit do it all inseparably. For the Father and the Son and the Holy Spirit actuate in one and the same way, being one without composition and three without division.... The Son, as atonement and advocate, mediates between the one found guilty and the Judge who judges justly; while the Spirit, as assuage and advocate, mediates between the weakness of the one at peace and the greatness of the one appeased.[19]

In each of these pairs, Christ provides the prior attribute required for what the Spirit provides, though Isaac makes clear that they do this "inseparably," with respect to attribution and without temporal sequence *ad extra*. Still, as the Son proceeds prior to the Spirit, who proceeds from him, so his economic activity is prior to the Spirit's.

The Mystical Body of Christ

Isaac's teaching on the mystical body of Christ, into which individual members are drawn and in which they are sustained by the Holy Spirit, shapes his understanding of how union with God takes place. His ninth sermon describes his understanding of the union of particular souls with God and the relationship between that union and the mystical body of Christ. The sermon is for the first Sunday after the Octave of Epiphany, whose gospel reading is the wedding feast at Cana. Isaac distinguishes between three kinds of wedding feast: an outer feast of the flesh joining human beings, an inner feast joining flesh and spirit in human beings, and a higher feast above human beings joining spirit and spirit. The first feast, matrimony, unites two persons in one flesh. The second, conception, unites rational soul

---

19. "Christus itaque mediator quodammodo est ad iustitiam, Spiritus ad amicitiam. Christus ad veritatem, Spiritus ad caritatem. Christus ad remissionem, Spiritus ad conservationem. Christus ad indulgentiam, Spiritus ad perseverantiam. Christus ad absolutionem, Spiritus ad colligationem. Omnia tamen Christus, et omnia Spiritus indivise operantur. Omnia enim Pater et Filius et Spiritus sanctus simul et similiter operantur, qui sine confusione sunt unum et sine divisione tres.... Inter iniquitatem rei et aequitatem iudicis, Filius reconciliator et advocatus intercedit; inter infirmitatem reconciliati et maiestatem placati, Spiritus delinitor et paraclitus intervenit" (*Sermo* 45.14–15; Isaac of Stella, *The Selected Works of Isaac of Stella*, 122).

and flesh and results in a person. In the third, deification, the spirit clinging to God becomes one with God and becomes what God is. This unity is what Christ meant when he prayed that they may be one as we are one. It precedes, surpasses, and outlives every other; it is both source and purpose of all that is and the everlasting glory of existence itself.[20]

So far, Isaac's schema is a standard description of mystical union. However, he then adds another kind of marriage between the second and third feasts, that between the Word and man: "That this built-in bent towards God should in due time and through God's grace find fulfillment, there took place a mysterious marriage, intermediate between the second and third kinds and far distant from the first, a marriage whereby the Word and our nature, Christ and the Church were joined."[21] This third marriage takes place for the sake of the fourth. That is, Christ's incarnation, passion, and resurrection take place to wed Christ to the Church so that the members of the Church can be joined to God, allowing them to enter the Trinity without it becoming a quaternity.[22]

In a way that many other mystical theologians do not, Isaac expressly underscores that mystical marriage takes place first between the Church and Christ, then between souls in the Church and God. He also shows how these unions or feasts depend on each other sequentially, with later feasts serving as the fruit or fulfillment of previous ones. In rightly ordered sexual relations, matrimony unites a man and a woman in one flesh, which serves as the foundation for the conception of a new human life. That union of soul and flesh is perfected in and through the union of the Word and human nature in the marriage of Jesus Christ and the Church. The incarnate, mystical body enables the union of its members with God, bringing it to completion at the end of time.

In Sermon 11, Isaac explains how the Church's forgiveness of sins in the sacrament of penance is the logical result of her union with Christ.[23] Be-

---

20. *Sermo* 9.9–10.

21. "Sed ut pervenire possit aliquando per gratiam quo semper tendit per naturam, factae sunt quaedam mysteriales nuptiae inter secundas et tertias, a primis longe remotae, Verbi et carnis, Christi et Ecclesiae" (*Sermo* 9.10; CF 11, 76).

22. *Sermo* 9.17.

23. "Sponsus itaque cum Patre unum, cum Sponsa unus; quod in Sponsa reperit alienum, abstulit, affigens cruci, ubi peccata sua pertulit super lignum, et abstulit per lignum; quod naturale et proprium assumpsit et induit, quod ipsius sui proprium et divinum contulit. Abstulit enim

cause Christ and the Church hold everything in common, Isaac continues, Christ gives the Church the power to forgive sins. The Church's authority comes from her intimate union with Christ, who willed forgiveness to be granted through her.[24] To put it another way, if the right to forgive sins does not belong to the Church, it does not belong to the whole Christ.[25] The union between Christ and the Church grants the Church the power to celebrate the other sacraments as well:

It follows that apart from Christ the Church cannot grant forgiveness and that Christ has no will to forgive apart from the Church.... Doubtless, Christ need accept no restraints to the power of his baptizing, consecrating the Eucharist, or-daining ministers, forgiving sins, and the like, but the humble and faithful bride-groom prefers to confer such blessings with the cooperation of his Bride. "What God," then, "has joined together, let no man put asunder" (Mt 19:6). "I say this is a great mystery and refers to Christ and the Church" (Eph 5:32). The sacrifi-cial turtle-dove's neck might not be completely severed from its body (Lev 5:8); no man may separate Christ, the Head, from his Body.... To remove the Head from the Body were to ruin the whole Christ irreparably. Christ apart from the Church is no more the whole Christ than the Church is complete if separated from Christ. Head and Body go to make the whole and entire Christ.[26]

The mystical union of Christ and the Church is the foundation of her sacra-mental activity, the reason that when the Church's ministers act, it is Christ acting through their words and deeds. In all instances, it is Christ who

---

diabolicum, assumpsit humanum, contulit divinum, ut omnia Sponsae sint Sponsi" (*Sermo* 11.10; CF 11, 94).

24. "Pour avoir le Christ tout entier et tel qu'il est, il faut le prendre dans l'Église: pour avoir le pardon du Christ totalement et réellement, il faut donc le recevoir dans le pardon de l'Église" (Émile Mersch, *Le corps mystique du Christ*, 2 vols. [Paris: Desclée de Brouwer, 1944], II:153–54).

25. *Sermo* 11.11.

26. "Nihil ergo potest Ecclesia sine Christo dimittere, nihil vult Christus sine Ecclesia dimittere. Nihil potest Ecclesia, nisi paenitenti, id est quem prius Christus tetigit, dimittere; nihil vult Christus Ecclesiam contemnenti dimissum servare. Omnia per se potest omnipotens Christus, id est baptizare, Eucharistiam consecrare, ordinare, peccata dimittere, et similia; sed nihil vult sine Sponsa humili et fidelis Sponsus. Quod igitur Deus coniunxit, homo non separet. Ego dico, sac-ramentum hoc magnum in Christo et in Ecclesia. Noli caput turturis prorsus abrumpere, noli ca-put corpori detruncare. Non enim decollari voluit Christus, sed cruce extendi, distendi, suspendi, ut ima, summa, media copularet. Noli ergo corpori caput subtrahere, ut nusquam sit totus Chris-tus; neque enim totus Christus sine Ecclesia usquam, sicut tota Ecclesia sine Christo nusquam. Totus est enim et integer Christus, caput et corpus" (*Sermo* 11.14–15; CF 11, 96).

performs the sacraments to bring souls into union with his mystical body, through which he operates.[27] Likewise, the action of the Church is nothing other than the action of Christ operating through it, bringing her members to be joined to God sacramentally, just as the Son is naturally joined to him and Christ's humanity is personally joined to him.[28]

In Sermons 9 and 11, we see how the important themes of Isaac's theology come together in his theology of the mystical body. In the person of Christ, the Word through whom the universe was created is joined to human nature, the highest point of creation. The whole Christ unites "the entirety of relations in himself" and is himself the nexus of relations between God, the universe, and human beings.[29] The members of the mystical body of Christ ascend in and through him, toward fuller adoption into the sonship he has received by nature. As Deme puts it: "The Son of God ascends through himself to himself, yet man can ascend only at the discretion of Christ, and even that only up to a point after which no one is able to follow."[30] How exactly the mystical body becomes one with God through Christ remains, on the deepest level, a mystery. However, the sacraments serve as the visible means of that unifying grace.

The giver of that grace is, of course, the Holy Spirit. As much as Isaac's theology of the mystical body is evidently Christocentric, it is also deeply pneumatological and brings his Trinitarian theology into contact with the other elements of his theology. As Deme notes, "The central concept of the 'Whole Christ' from this perspective is just as much a pneumatological term as it is Christological. It is the Spirit that instructs and leads the Church to Christ, and it is here that the Body finds its unity with the Head."[31] In a variation on the metaphor of the vine and branches in John 15, Isaac also describes the Spirit as the life of a tree:

27. As Beumer notes, the authority of the Church is nothing other than the authority of Christ, who wants to complete everything through the Church (Johannes Beumer, "Mariologie und Ekklesiologie bei Isaak von Stella," *Münchener Theologische Zeitschrift* V [1954]: 53–54).

28. *Sermo* 42.12.

29. Dániel Deme, "Introduction to the Theology of Isaac Stella," in *The Selected Works of Isaac of Stella*, 193.

30. Deme, "Introduction," 203.

31. Deme, "Introduction," 219. See also Antonio Piolanti, "La nostra soledarità soprannaturale nel pensiero di Isacco della Stella," *Palestro del Claro* VII (1956): 304; Henri de Lubac, *Corpus Mysticum: The Eucharist and the Church in the Middle Ages: A Historical Survey*, trans. Gemma Simmonds et al. (Notre Dame, Ind.: University of Notre Dame Press, 2007), 88.

Nonetheless just as verdure and vigor come, as life itself comes only from the life of the Root to the whole Tree, so the whole Body of the Church lives, feels and moves in complete dependence on the one Holy Spirit of Christ and of our God. The life of the root of a tree does not belong to any but to its own tree and to the whole of it; the Spirit of Christ, in our present context, extends his influence only and completely to the Body that belongs to him, so that the whole of it lives and moves because of and in him.[32]

The Holy Spirit is therefore not an afterthought in Isaac's understanding of the mystical body. Rather, he is the life of that body that flows from Christ, its head, the power by which Christ brings the Church to the final consummation of eschatological union.

The Eucharistic Theology of Isaac's Sermons

The culmination of Isaac's theology of the Trinity and the mystical body lies in the act by which that body is constituted: the Eucharist. Just as Isaac's Sexagesima sermons are important for his Trinitarian theology and doctrine of God, so his sermons for Easter, the Ascension, and Pentecost[33] are important for his Eucharistic theology. In Sermon 44, Isaac writes of the altar of Christ nourishing the faithful with Christ's body and blood. Like baptism, this must be received with charity, otherwise neither profits. However, Isaac goes on to describe the banquet that Wisdom has prepared (Pr 9:2–4), where the bread is truth and the wine is charity. He later ascribes Charity to the Holy Spirit, Truth to the Son, and Power to the Father. By Truth and Charity, we come to Power—that is, by the Son and Spirit, to the Father.[34] This is more than just one allegory stacked on top of the others. Rather, it demonstrates the broader Cistercian interest in the role of the Son and the Spirit in the Eucharist and the way in which that is determined by their roles in the economy of salvation as a whole.[35]

A concluding passage from the *De anima* further elaborates on these

32. "Verumtamen, sicut de sola vita radicis in totum arboris corpus viror et vigor vita que procedit, sic de solo Christi et Dei nostri sancto Spiritu totum Ecclesiae corpus vivit, sentit, movetur" (*Sermo* 34.7; Isaac of Stella, *The Selected Works of Isaac of Stella*, 91).

33. *Sermo* 41–44.

34. *Sermo* 44.12–14.

35. See also Nathaniel Peters, "The Trinitarian Dimensions of Cistercian Eucharistic Theology" (PhD diss., Boston College, 2017), and, more generally, Lawrence Feingold, *The Eucharist:*

roles. There, Isaac outlines the way in which gifts proceed from God to human beings and from human beings back to God:

just as divine gifts descend to us from the Father through the Son and the Spirit, or in the Spirit ... so through the Spirit to the Son, and through the Son to the Father human gifts ascend. For upon the departure of the Son the Paraclete Spirit is sent that he might unite the body to the head, that is, to Christ, and Christ to God.... Therefore the Spirit rules, consoles, instructs, and leads the Church to Christ. And Christ at the same time offers it, without spot or blemish as a kingdom to his God and Father. May the glorious Trinity deign to fulfill this in us. Amen.[36]

Even though the Eucharist is not explicitly mentioned here, it is the greatest human gift offered to the Father by the Church and is clearly implied. The Son becomes present through the power of the Spirit and offers himself back to the Father through that Spirit's working through those whom the Spirit has formed into the Son's mystical body. Members of the mystical body are incorporated into the Son's own self-offering to the Father in one simultaneous action, according to the relations of the Trinitarian persons.

In a sermon for the Second Sunday of Easter, Isaac clarifies that the Son's self-offering is not only to the Father but to the other persons of the Trinity as well. While discussing Christ's prayers on the night of the Last Supper, he describes him as: "My teacher and Lord Jesus Christ, true God, true priest, true sacrifice, who offered himself as victim and oblation to himself and to the Father and to the Holy Spirit."[37] This passing remark pertains directly to the Passion. But given Isaac's theology of the mystical body, we can

---

Mystery of Presence, Sacrifice, and Communion (Steubenville, Ohio: Emmaus Academic, 2018), 337–39, 510–16.

36. "Itaque, licet indifferens sit natura coequalis trinitatis, tamen sicut ad nos a patre per filium et spiritum vel in spiritu diuina descendunt, iuxta quod dicitur 'baptizantes eos in nominee patris et filii et spiritus sancti,' ita per spiritum ad filium et per filium ad patrem humana ascendant. Ideo namque abeunte filio mittitur paraclitus spiritus, qui corpus capiti uniat idest Christo, et ipse deo, sicut scriptum est: 'Caput mulieris uir, uiri Christus, Christi deus.' Spiritus igitur regit et consolatur et erudite et perducet ecclesiam ad Christum, quam ipse simul sine macula et ruga offeret regnum deo et patri. Quod in nobis adimplere dignetur gloriosa trinitas. Amen" (Tarlazzi, "L'Epistola de Anima di Isacco di Stella," 562–72; Isaac of Stella, *The Selected Works of Isaac of Stella*, 156–57).

37. "Doctor et Dominus meus Iesus Christus, verus Deus, verus sacerdos, verum sacrificium, qui se sibi et Patri et Spiritui sancto pro nobis hostiam et oblationem effecit" (*Sermo* 36.20; the translation is my own).

also see that it applies to the Eucharist. When the body of Christ performs sacramental actions, it is Christ himself who acts through the members of his body, who are empowered by the gift of the Holy Spirit. The greatest of these, Isaac writes, is the confection of the Eucharist.[38] Hence, Christ serves as priest and sacrifice in the Eucharist as well as the Passion. But this text also brings to the fore another paradoxical doctrine: Christ's sacrifice on the cross and in the Eucharist is offered to all the persons of the Trinity.[39] Christ is priest, sacrifice, and recipient of his own self-offering. The persons of the Trinity receive this offering according to their work in the economy of salvation: through the Spirit, Christ's members are assembled into one body, which is then joined to its head, and presented to the Father.

Isaac's sermon on the Ascension joins these ideas from different sermons and the *De anima* together. He begins with an exposition of the doctrine of the mystical body and the unity of the body with its head. All the members form one body, which is united to Christ the Head of the body. Together, the two make up the whole Christ. Isaac then turns to Paul's comparison of the union between husband and wife, Christ and the Church, and Christ and God.[40]

The head then to which a wife is united through her husband is Christ; the head to which a husband is united through Christ is God. It follows that God is the head to which wife, husband and Christ are united. All therefore joined with God are one God; the Son being so naturally, the Son of Man being so personally, while the Body is so sacramentally (cf. Eph 5:32).[41]

38. "Ad hanc etenim potestatem pertinere dignoscuntur quae a sacerdotibus vel praesulibus aut praelatis fiunt benedictiones, consecrationes, ordinationes, exorcizationes et manuum impositiones, praelationes, praedicationes, baptizationes, absolutiones, excommunicationes quoque, et maxime maxima potestas eucharistiae confectionis" (*Sermo* 43.12; Isaac of Stella, *The Selected Works of Isaac of Stella*, 112).

39. In twelfth-century Byzantium, a vigorous debate arose over whether the Eucharist was offered to the Trinity as a whole, not simply to the Father. The councils of Constantinople in 1156 and 1157 concluded that it was. For more information, see John Meyendorff, *Christ in Eastern Christian Thought* (Washington, D.C.: Corpus Books, 1969), 152–55.

40. "Since the head to which a wife is united is her husband, just as the head to which every individual is united is Christ; so too the head to which Christ is united is God" (1 Cor 11:3).

41. "Caput igitur, mediante viro, mulieris Christus; caput viri, mediante Christo, Deus. Caput ergo mulieris et viri et Christi, Deus. Itaque et omnia cum Deo unus Deus, sed Filius Dei cum Deo naturaliter, et cum ipso Filius hominis personaliter, cum quo suum corpus sacramentaliter" (*Sermo* 42.12; Isaac of Stella, *The Selected Works of Isaac of Stella*, 108).

What Christ is by nature, those incorporated into him are by fellowship (*consortio*); what he has fully, they have by participation. In this sense, they can claim to be God's son and even God, just as Isaac's own foot and tongue can claim to be Isaac.[42] And the fellowship by which they are constituted as one body—such that they could claim to participate in the attributes of Christ—is a sacramental one.

Isaac then considers the threefold way in which Christ is born. According to his divine nature, Christ is born from the beginning from the Father without a mother. According to his humanity, he is born in time from a mother without a father. Christ's third birth in the human soul comes about according to sacrament or mystery (*secundum vero sacramentum*) from God the Father through the Holy Spirit, and from the virgin mother Church. Isaac goes on to say that it is by this same Spirit, by whom Christ was born of the Virgin, that we are reborn in the waters of baptism and made into children of God and the body of Christ. His focus with respect to the sacraments remains on baptism and its spiritual birth and forgiveness of sins. Yet, having described Christ taking on the sins that baptism removes and bearing them on the cross, Isaac writes, "Offerer and Offering and God, by offering himself to himself he has reconciled himself through himself to himself and to the Father and to the Holy Spirit."[43] That sacrifice took place on the cross, but is re-presented in the Eucharist, where the Spirit joins the ecclesial body of Christ to its head in offering to the Trinity. The Eucharist, therefore, is the way by which the initial birth of baptism is brought to its fruition. It is the oblation to which baptism is ordered and the means by which the mystical body participates in its head's offering of himself to himself, the Spirit, and the Father.

The Eucharistic Theology of *De officio missae*

Isaac further develops his Eucharistic theology in his letter *De officio missae*. The letter opens with a statement of the purpose and occasion of the work. John, the bishop of Poitiers, had asked Isaac to explain "what our purpose is in the sacred canon when we are celebrating the holy mysteries," and

42. *Sermo* 42.14.

43. "Sacerdos et sacrificium et Deus, qui se sibi offerens, se per se sibi sicut Patri et Spiritui sancto reconciliavit" (*Sermo* 42.18; Isaac of Stella, *The Selected Works of Isaac of Stella*, 110).

Isaac is at last answering his request.[44] He begins by noting that practically everything can be divided into a three-fold action, and, while he does not offer justification for this division, Trinitarian imagery is an obvious reason. In the canon of the Mass, then, Isaac distinguishes "three principal actions which, one might say, take place on three altars, served by a priest performing three functions, and offering a three-fold sacrifice."[45] This is foreshadowed with Moses and the tabernacle in the desert. The tabernacle has an altar of bronze in the forecourt, where animals are sacrificed; an altar of incense within the tent where incense is burned; and the holy of holies, in which is the throne of mercy. The veil that hung between the two altars was torn during the passion of Christ, so that the throne of mercy lay open to the gaze of all. Christ's body is that throne of mercy, naked and nailed to the cross.

These sacrifices are how God's tabernacle is made not with men, but in men, Isaac continues. They are reflected in the canon of the Mass, where the three sacrifices of the slave, the free man, and the man united to God are offered. In the first part of the canon, the priest offers bread and wine to God. This offering of the physical sustenance of life symbolizes the offering of our physical life to God: "We put the knife of abstinence and fasting against our throat when we offer to God our total sustenance. Afterwards, only out of necessity, and sparingly and reverently, do we eat from our sustenance, as though from the altar of God."[46] The priest next comes to the words of institution, which give new spiritual life. Jesus himself is a new priest who offers a heavenly sacrifice of his own flesh and blood. He offers "the pure victim, holy victim, immaculate victim, the holy bread of eternal life, the chalice of everlasting salvation," which makes us pure, holy, immaculate, which is spiritual and not temporal or corporeal, and which is able to satisfy and save eternally.[47]

44. "quomodo in sacrum canonem, dum sacrosancta celebramus, intendimus" (*De officio missae*, PL 194, 1889B; Isaac of Stella, *The Selected Works of Isaac of Stella*, 158).

45. "Tres enim distinguuntur in sacro canone principales actiones, quibus quasi tria deserviunt altaria, quibus quasi trinus assistit sacrifex, cum quodammodo tribus sacrificiis" (*De off*, 1890C; Isaac of Stella, *The Selected Works of Isaac of Stella*, 159).

46. "Formam vero attende, quam subtiliter et eleganter expressit, dicens: Fige cultrum in gutture tuo. Cultrum quippe abstinentiae et inediae quasi in gutture figimus, dum qui totum victum nostrum Deo obtulimus, de eo postmodum parce et timide quasi de altari Dei ad necessitatem sumimus" (*De off*, 1893C; Isaac of Stella, *The Selected Works of Isaac of Stella*, 161–62).

47. As Schaefer notes, Isaac compares the transformation of the bread and wine into the body and blood of Christ to the Resurrection, which is more common in Byzantine liturgiology than in

Since flesh and blood profit nothing (John 6:63), the priest seeks something higher: "Nothing will content him until he is united through the body to God in heaven and is joined to divinity through humanity."[48] However, the priest cannot accomplish this union on his own. In the *supplices te rogamur*, therefore, he asks that his sacrifice may be united to the body of Christ in heaven, where Christ the eternal high priest offers sacrifice to the Father. To signify this, he bows before the altar, kisses it, and rises up. Isaac writes:

For just as we partake of the bread and wine of the first altar by the fact that he looks down upon it, so he now asks that, by the power of the sacrament, he may communicate in the truth of that flesh and blood from this second altar, which is beyond the veil in heaven.... So the priest asks to be united with the supreme head through the Spirit. For the head of Christ is God."[49]

For Isaac and his contemporaries, this language was not mere metaphor. Jungmann notes that other theologians of this period—under the influence of the Gallic liturgy—also conceived of the transfer of the gifts to the heavenly altar as a real activity in which the sacrifice of the Mass attains its completion. The *Supplices* thereby becomes a sort of epiclesis, "and actually there is a plea that the power of God might touch our sacrificial gift, but in reverse order, not by the descent of the Spirit, but by the ascent of the gift."[50] The *Supplices* and Eucharistic reception mark the completion of the Spirit's offering of souls by which they are incorporated into the mystical body.

Through that participation in the sacrifice of Christ, those who receive the Eucharist and live lives of sacrifice are brought into communion with God. More accurately, that participation in Christ's self-offering to the Fa-

---

Western liturgiology (Mary Schaefer, "Twelfth Century Latin Commentaries on the Mass: Christological and Ecclesiological Dimensions" [PhD diss., University of Notre Dame, 1983], 300).

48. "Amplius autem, quia caro et sanguis non prodest quidquam, secundum verbum, quia spiritus et vita sunt, altius adhuc aliquid expetit, cui donec per corpus in coelo Deo uniatur, et per humanitatem divinitati conjungatur, nihil sufficit, quippe qui scalam sibi erexit, ascendere utique satagit" (*De off*, 1894C; Isaac of Stella, *The Selected Works of Isaac of Stella*, 163).

49. "quatenus sicut per ipsum quod hoc inspicit, panis et vini de primo altari sumimus, et in veritate carnis et sanguinis de secundo ultra velum in coelo benedictione olim semini Abrahae promissa, et gratia Mariae allata, virtuti sacramenti ipsius communicet, id est summo capiti per spiritum uniatur. Caput enim Christi Deus" (*De off*, 1895A; Isaac of Stella, *The Selected Works of Isaac of Stella*, 163).

50. Joseph Jungmann, *The Mass of the Roman Rite: Its Origin and Development (Missarum Sollemnia)*, vol. 1, trans. Francis Brunner (New York: Benziger, 1951), 438.

ther *is* this communion. Schaefer adds that unlike other medieval authors, Isaac does not focus on the way in which the Mass represents the historical events of Christ's passion. Rather, like Odo of Cambrai, Isaac sees the Canon of the Mass as containing Christ's self-offering, and thereby the self-offering of the Church, his mystical body: "The threefold action of the Mass, which inserts us into the mystery of Christ, allows us to ascend with him to the Father. Isaac's analysis of the Mass is in keeping with the ascetical-mystical ascent of the soul to union with God which was the driving force behind the monastic reform movement of the twelfth century."[51] The transfer of the sacrifice from the earthly to the heavenly altar in the *Supplices*, together with reception of the Eucharist, serve as the culmination of this union. The joining of the earthly sacrifice of the Church to the heavenly sacrifice of Christ is an essential part of our communion with God: "It is because of the union of the Church's sacrifice with Christ the High Priest in heaven that we are able to be divinized.... Christ is the means whereby we attain union with God. By taking the visible bread and wine from the 'altar outside,' at the level of the visible rite, we receive from the second, the altar within the temple, the truth of the flesh and blood of Christ. This joins us to Christ in heaven; divinized, we are united to God."[52]

This is what Louis Bouyer intuited when he called Isaac's understanding of the triple sacrifice of the Mass the "full and concrete development" of his doctrine of our assumption into the mystical body and the way in which the Church's election is realized in time.[53] For Isaac, the Eucharist is the means of joining one's own self-sacrifice to that of the Church's, which becomes Christ's. This is the sense in which Isaac espouses the common doctrine that the fruit of the Eucharist is the unity of the Church: "For by means of the divine mysteries we are freed from the slavery of the devil through the Son, so that we may be united with the Son to the Father of the family.... All the action of the heavenly sacraments is designated to serve this end: that we may be united to one God and through Christ and find our joy forever in him. For though we are many, in this sacrifice we are one bread, one body; and we have only one Head; and he has God for his head."[54]

51. Schaefer, "Twelfth Century Latin Commentaries," 301–2.

52. Schaefer, "Twelfth Century Latin Commentaries," 305–6.

53. Louis Bouyer, *The Cistercian Heritage*, trans. Elizabeth A. Livingstone (Westminster, Md.: The Newman Press, 1958), 183–85.

54. "Ad hoc enim per divina sacramenta a servitute diaboli per Filium liberamur, ut ipsi Patri-

Isaac's emphasis on the mystical body of Christ also helps explain his unusual depiction of the Spirit offering the Eucharistic sacrifice. One usually thinks of Christ the high priest offering the sacrifice of his body in the Eucharist. But Isaac focuses on the fact that the Spirit is the person of the Trinity at work in the lives of the faithful, conforming them to the likeness of Christ, the head of the body. The Spirit empowers them to make a sacrifice of their lives and joins that sacrifice to Christ's eternal sacrifice to the Father. After the Ascension, Christ's offering takes place in heaven, where he sits at the right hand of the Father. Hence the importance of the *Supplices*, when the Spirit completes the unification of the earthly sacrifice with the heavenly one, the presentation of the faithful to the Father as members of the body of the Son. Thus, Isaac's theology of the mystical body underscores how all three persons of the Trinity are working through the Church in the Eucharist, drawing her members into their joy.

Conclusion

By studying Isaac's Eucharistic theology together with his doctrine of God and anthropology, we can better understand his view of the Son and the Spirit in the mystical body of Christ and the economy of salvation as a whole. Human beings are made with the capacity to love and know so that they can enter into union with God through those faculties. The rational faculties are receptacles by which they receive God, the anthropological foundation for union with him. Since sin severed the bond between God and humanity, the Son came to restore it in his own person and by his reconciling passion, death, and resurrection. Those who are joined to the Son's body the Church are thereby joined to its head, and through him to God the Father. They have Christ sown in their minds and hearts and are capable of knowing and loving him in a manner analogous to self-knowledge and

---

familias cum Filio uniamur. Sic nempe pro servis Filius loquitur Patri: Volo, Pater, ut sicut ego et tu unum sumus, ita et isti sint unum nobiscum (Jn 17). Omnis ergo actio sacramentorum coelestium huic fini deservire dignoscitur, ut sine fine uni Deo per Christum uniti, in Christo delectemur. Ideo unus panis, unum corpus multi sumus; sed non multa capita habemus, sed unum, et cujus caput Deus" (*De off*, 1892B–C). Gaggero argues that this passage's opening sentence provides the core of Isaac's thought on redemption (25). But Gaggero does not treat the sacrament as an essential means of redemption, as this chapter does. For more on the unity of the Church as the fruit of the Eucharist, see de Lubac, *Corpus Mysticum*, 83.

self-love of the persons of the Trinity. This union takes place in the Holy Spirit, who joins particular believers to the body of Christ and makes his life and benefits their own. With the Spirit in them, the members of the body are filled with the joy and delight characteristic of the Trinitarian communion. Their participation in Trinitarian knowledge and love leads to a participation in Trinitarian affectivity.

The Eucharist plays an important role in this process. Incorporation into the body of Christ begins with baptism but is sustained by the Eucharist. The Eucharist is the way by which Christ joins his members to the mystical body by filling them with the love of the Holy Spirit. That growth in love takes place by the work of the Son and the Spirit, who operate in the Eucharist according to their intra-Trinitarian relations and their missions in the world. The Son performs the work of redemption by the cross and resurrection and is himself the point of union between God and humanity. He bestows the Spirit to join others to him so that they will know and love God as God does, filled with the love and joy that is the Spirit. In the Spirit, they are joined to the Son and, through him, to the Father. In these ways, Isaac shows how the persons of the Trinity draw human beings into relationship with them in a manner reflective of their own relations—that is, how the mystical body of Christ has a Trinitarian shape.

Part 3

THE CENTER OF THE CHRISTIAN LIFE

9

Deus adorans, Homo adorans

Joseph Ratzinger's Liturgical Christology and Anthropology

CHRISTOPHER RUDDY

I would like to begin with an almost banal statement: liturgy is central to the life and thought of Joseph Ratzinger. He has written three books and dozens of articles on liturgy, and the first volume of his collected works to appear was on liturgy. As Pope, he expended significant ecclesial capital in issuing *Summorum pontificum* and reshaping papal liturgies.[1] And, in the introduction to the liturgical volume of his collected works, he writes, "The liturgy of the Church has been for me since my childhood the central reality of my life,"[2] while his memoir *Milestones* likewise reveals the lasting imprint

1. One might also note his 2009 Apostolic Constitution *Anglicanorum coetibus*, which opened the way for, among other things, the riches of the English-Anglican liturgical tradition to be reintegrated into the fullness of Catholic communion.

2. Joseph Ratzinger, *Joseph Ratzinger: Collected Works*, vol. 11, *Theology of the Liturgy: The Sacramental Foundation of Christian Existence*, ed. Michael J. Miller, trans. John Saward, Kenneth Baker, Henry Taylor et al. (San Francisco: Ignatius, 2014), xvi. See also his similar statement in his memoirs: "The inexhaustible reality of the Catholic liturgy has accompanied me through all phases of life." See *Milestones: Memoirs 1927–1977*, trans. Erasmo Leiva-Merikakis (San Francisco: Ignatius, 1998), 20.

of childhood liturgies, missals, devotions, and pilgrimages on his heart and mind. That much is evident.

It may be less evident, though, that Ratzinger also sees the present crisis—or crises—in the present-day church as ultimately rooted in liturgical crises. In *Milestones*, for instance, he writes, "the crisis in the Church that we are experiencing today is to a large extent due to the disintegration of the liturgy.... This is why we need a new Liturgical Movement, which will call to life the real heritage of the Second Vatican Council."[3] Still more boldly and starkly, he wrote the following in the 2015 preface to the Russian edition of his volume on liturgy:

The Church's existence lives from the proper celebration of the liturgy and ... the Church is in danger when the primacy of God no longer appears in the liturgy nor consequently in life. *The deepest cause of the crisis that has upset the Church lies in the obscuring of the priority of God in the liturgy.* All this led me to devote myself to the theme of the liturgy more fully than previously because I knew that the true renewal of the liturgy is a fundamental condition for the renewal of the Church (italics added).[4]

Such claims may sound hyperbolic, irresponsible, and even dangerous, however, in the light of the renewed outbreak of sexual abuse scandals in the Church. One might ask, "Does Ratzinger really think that liturgical abuse is the biggest problem? How can he possibly think that?" His argument *is* dangerous if one thinks of liturgy and liturgical abuses primarily as a matter of rubrics, vestments, music, translations, etc.—or if one thinks of liturgy as something secondary or even marginal to believers' "real" work in the so-called "real world."

Ratzinger, however, locates liturgy at the deepest level possible: God himself. For Ratzinger, the human person is fundamentally a liturgical person, a *homo liturgicus*, a *homo adorans*. More deeply than that, however, he also sees Jesus Christ as *the* worshipper, *the* pray-er, *the* contemplative and beholder. He is *Deus adorans, homo adorans*, the Son who offers perfect worship to his Father and who makes possible our perfect worship of his Father. Nothing could possibly be more fundamental, more essential, or more needed

---

3. Ratzinger, *Milestones*, 148.

4. The Italian preface to the Russian edition of his *Theology of the Liturgy* (2015) can be found here: http://www.fondazioneratzinger.va/content/dam/fondazioneratzinger/contributi/Prefazione%20Papa%20emerito%20edizione%20russa%20Opera%20omnia.pdf, accessed May 15, 2019.

today. Ratzinger puts it this way: "For the liturgy is not about us, but about God. Forgetting about God is the most imminent danger of our age. As against this, the liturgy should be setting up a sign of God's presence."[5]

To this end, my chapter will explore Ratzinger's liturgical Christology and anthropology. First, I present some key themes of his liturgical thought (e.g., sacrifice, vicarious representation, glorification-adoration). Next, I look at his Christology, centered on Jesus as the Son who is in constant prayerful communication with his Father and who offers perfect worship to that same Father. Third, I show how this liturgical Christology extends into a liturgical anthropology in which the *homo adorans* blossoms forth in pro-existence. Finally, I conclude with some brief reflections on some possible contributions that Ratzinger's thought might offer us today, in the midst of awful scandal and evil within the Church.

I

Why is liturgy so central? Ratzinger's own experience at Vatican II offers a reason. The Council's decision to begin its work with the drafting of *Sacrosanctum Concilium*, the Constitution on the Sacred Liturgy, was clearly a pragmatic one: the nascent liturgical movement had received significant papal approbation by Pius X and Pius XII, the preparatory draft was in good shape, and there was broad agreement among the Council fathers. The Council would thus be able to get off to a relatively uncontroversial start. But for Ratzinger, the pragmatic was complemented by the providential:

---

5. Ratzinger, "The Organic Development of the Liturgy," *Collected Works*, vol. 11, 593. See also Benedict XVI, "Letter to Bishops on Lifting of Excommunications of Lefebvrite Bishops," *Origins* 38 (March 26, 2009): 647: "In our days, when in vast areas of the world the faith is in danger of dying out like a flame which no longer has fuel, the overriding priority is to make God present in this world and to show men and women the way to God. Not just any god, but the God who spoke on Sinai; to that God whose face we recognize in a love which presses 'to the end' (cf. Jn 13:1) — in Jesus Christ, crucified and risen. The real problem at this moment of our history is that God is disappearing from the human horizon, and, with the dimming of the light which comes from God, humanity is losing its bearings, with increasingly evident destructive effects.... Leading men and women to God, to the God who speaks in the Bible: This is the supreme and fundamental priority of the Church and of the Successor of Peter at the present time."

It was a very good idea to begin with the liturgy because in this way the primacy of God could appear, the primacy of adoration. *Operi Dei nihil praeponatur*: this phrase from the Rule of St. Benedict (cf. 43:3) thus emerges as the supreme rule of the council. Some have made the criticism that the council spoke of many things but not of God. It did speak of God! And this was the first thing that it did, that substantial speaking of God and opening up all the people, the whole of God's holy people, to the adoration of God, in the common celebration of the liturgy of the body and blood of Christ.

In this sense, over and above the practical factors that advised against beginning straight away with controversial topics, it was, let us say, truly an act of providence that at the beginning of the council was the liturgy, God, adoration.[6]

Still more concisely, as he puts it the introduction to his collected works on liturgy, "Beginning with the liturgy tells us: 'God first.'"[7] Liturgy, then, points—or should point—ineluctably to the primacy of God.

Ratzinger's opening meditation on the Exodus in *The Spirit of the Liturgy* underscores the primacy of worship. The "only goal" of the Exodus, he writes, is worship. The Promised Land is ordered to true worship: "mere possession of the land, mere national autonomy, would reduce Israel to the level of all the other nations."[8] The land becomes a true good only in being ordered to worship, to being the place where God reigns.

Israel, however, must learn over and over again to worship truly and to reject idolatry. The purpose of its wandering in the wilderness was to teach it how to worship God rightly. It must learn to look at God:

[In the wilderness] Israel learns how to worship God in the way he himself desires. Cult, liturgy, in the proper sense, is part of this worship, but so too is life according to the will of God; such a life is an indispensable part of true worship. "The glory of God is the living man, but the life of man is the vision of God," says St. Irenaeus (cf. Adv. Haer. 4, 20, 7), getting to the heart of what happens when man

6. Benedict XVI, "Speech on the Interpretation of the Second Vatican Council," *Origins* 42 (February 28, 2013): 604.

7. Ratzinger, *Collected Works*, vol. 11, xv. A fuller quote is apposite here: "By starting with theme of liturgy, God's primacy, the absolute precedence of the theme of God, was unmistakably highlighted. Beginning with the liturgy tells us: 'God first.' When the focus on God is not decisive, everything else loses its orientation. The saying from the Rule of St. Benedict 'Nothing is to be preferred to the liturgy' (43, 3) applies specifically to monasticism, but as a way of ordering priorities it is true also for the life of the Church and of every individual, for each in his own way."

8. Ratzinger, *The Spirit of the Liturgy*, trans. John Saward (San Francisco: Ignatius, 2000), 17.

meets God on the mountain in the wilderness. Ultimately, it is the very life of man, man himself as living righteously, that is the true worship of God, but life becomes real life only when it receives its form from looking toward God. Cult exists in order to communicate this vision and to give life in such a way that glory is given to God.[9]

Presaging his *Jesus of Nazareth*, Ratzinger states that only when our relationship with God is right, can our other relationships be right.[10] In this sense, worship is the indispensable element for right human existence in the world. Conversely, when Israel fails to worship rightly—to be truly orthodox—it falls into idolatry and apostasy. This idolatry manifests itself in two ways. First, Israel uses God for its own ends; it cannot bear the otherness of God and so seeks to make him visible and controllable; God must appear on command, so to speak. Second, Israel's worship becomes self-generated and self-seeking; the community becomes closed in upon itself. Ratzinger notes that even legitimate worship can become idolatrous. In the story of Aaron and the golden calf, such idolatry is subtle: the Israelites remain outwardly attached to God, and their worship is orderly and rubrically correct. But such worship is "apostasy in sacral disguise. All that is left in the end is frustration, a feeling of emptiness. There is no experience of that liberation when man encounters the living God."[11]

Having spoken of Ratzinger's understanding of the primacy and purpose of liturgy, we can now approach its content, so to speak. Three aspects are especially pertinent here: sacrifice, vicarious representation, and glorification-adoration.

First, although sacrifice "is at the heart of worship" in all religions,[12] Ratzinger locates the essence of sacrifice not so much in destruction but rather in a "way of being"[13] that consists of self-giving love.[14] Ever the

9. Ratzinger, *The Spirit of the Liturgy*, 17–18.

10. See *The Spirit of the Liturgy*, 21. See also Ratzinger, *Jesus of Nazareth: The Infancy Narratives* (III), trans. Philip J. Whitmore, (New York: Image, 2012), 44: "Man is a relational being. And if his first, fundamental relationship is disturbed — his relationship with God — then nothing else can be truly in order. This is where the priority lies in Jesus' message and ministry: before all else, he wants to point man toward the essence of his malady and to show him — if you are not healed *there*, then however many good things you may find, you are not truly healed."

11. Ratzinger, *The Spirit of the Liturgy*, 23.

12. Ratzinger, *The Spirit of the Liturgy*, 27.

13. Ratzinger, *The Spirit of the Liturgy*, 28.

14. See Ratzinger, *Introduction to Christianity*, trans. J. R. Foster and Michael J. Miller (San

Augustinian, he notes that the true sacrifice is the "*civitas Dei*, that is, love-transformed mankind, the divinization of creation and the surrender of all things to God."[15] Furthermore, Jesus reverses the flow of sacrifice; sacrifice is not so much what humanity gives to God, but what God gives to us: "It is not man who goes to God with a compensatory gift, but God who comes to man, in order to give to him.... [Jesus] took from man's hands the sacrificial offerings and put in their place his sacrificed personality, his own 'I.'"[16] Accordingly, our response to the divine sacrificial initiative must be receptivity, thanksgiving, *eucharistia*:

We worship him by dropping the fiction of a realm in which we could face him as independent business partners, whereas in truth we can exist at all only in him and from him. Christian sacrifice does not consist in a giving of what God would not have without us but in our becoming totally receptive and letting ourselves be completely taken over by him. Letting God act on us—that is Christian sacrifice.[17]

Second, Christian sacrifice is bound up with representation. Where previous sacrifices were mere "replacements" (*Ersatz*) in which the "real thing is missing,"[18] in Christ genuine representation happens: he is the true Lamb who stands at the "center of the heavenly liturgy ... and makes replacement liturgies superfluous."[19] Such representation is, for Ratzinger, the "fundamental law" of salvation history: the "one" or the "few" act on behalf of the "many"—Israel for the Gentiles, Jesus for all humanity.[20] But, this (unique)

Francisco: Ignatius, 2004), 291: "It is not pain as such that counts but the breadth of the love that spans existence so completely that it unites the distant and the near, bringing God-forsaken man into relation with God. It alone gives the pain an aim and a meaning. Were it otherwise, then the executioners around the Cross would have been the real priests; they, who had caused the pain, would have offered the sacrifice. But this was not the point; the point was that inner center that bears and fulfills the pain, and therefore the executioners were not the priests; the priest was Jesus, who reunited the two separated ends of the world in his love (Eph 2:13f)."

15. Ratzinger, *The Spirit of the Liturgy*, 28.

16. Ratzinger, *Introduction to Christianity*, 282, 287; see also *Jesus of Nazareth: Holy Week: From the Entrance into Jerusalem to the Resurrection* (II), trans. Philip J. Whitmore (San Francisco: Ignatius, 2011), 231–32.

17. Ratzinger, *Introduction to Christianity*, 283. See Joel Hodge, "Recovering the Liturgical Background to Christian Atonement: The Approach of James Alison and Joseph Ratzinger," *Irish Theological Quarterly* 81 (2016): 284–305.

18. Ratzinger, *The Spirit of the Liturgy*, 36.

19. Ratzinger, *The Spirit of the Liturgy*, 38.

20. Ratzinger, *The Meaning of Christian Brotherhood* (San Francisco: Ignatius, 1993), 79; see

representation does not exclude, but rather gives rise to, participation in Christ's liturgical, salvific action:

Solus Christus numquam solus, one would say here: Christ alone saves, certainly, but this Christ who alone saves, is never alone, and it is characteristic of his saving action that he does not make others into mere passive recipients of a self-contained gift, but introduces them into his own activity: the human person is saved in cooperating in the salvation of others. We can thus say saved for others and in this sense also by others.[21]

Third, liturgy is ordered to glorification and adoration. "Orthodoxy" is literally the right worship and glorification of God:

In the word "orthodoxy," the second half, "-doxa," does not mean "idea" but, rather, "glory": it is not a matter of the right "idea" about God; rather, it is a matter of the right way of glorifying him, of responding to him. For that is the fundamental question of the man who begins to understand himself correctly: How must I encounter God? Thus learning the right way of worshipping — orthodoxy — is the gift par excellence given to us by the faith.[22]

Furthermore, true worship, true glorification issues forth in adoration. In his homily at the closing Mass of World Youth Day in Cologne in 2005, just a few months after his election as pope, Benedict noted that adoration has different resonances in Greek and Latin. The Greek *proskynesis* refers to "submission, to the recognition of God as the true measure of our lives."[23] The Latin *adoratio* means "mouth-to-mouth contact, a kiss, an embrace, and hence, ultimately love." In this context, "submission becomes union, because he to whom we submit is love."[24] External submission to a norm is transformed into interior communion. Such communion is the very fruit of true worship.

---

also "Vicarious Representation," trans. Jared Wicks, *Letter and Spirit* 7 (2011): 209–20. For the centrality of this theme in Ratzinger's thought, see Christopher Ruddy, "'For the Many': The Vicarious-Representative Heart of Joseph Ratzinger's Theology," *Theological Studies* 75 (September 2014): 564–84.

21. Ratzinger, "Kein Heil außerhalb der Kirche?" in *Das neue Volk Gottes: Entwürfe zur Ekklesiologie* (Düsseldorf: Patmos, 1969): 358.

22. Ratzinger, *Collected Works*, vol. 11, xv–xvi.

23. Benedict XVI, "Eucharist: Setting Transformations in Motion," *Origins* 35 (September 1, 2005): 202.

24. Benedict XVI, "Eucharist: Setting Transformations in Motion," 203.

II

Given his emphasis on worship and idolatry, it does not seem accidental that Ratzinger begins the first volume of *Jesus of Nazareth* with another reflection on the Exodus. Deuteronomy tells of God's promise of a new prophet, of a new Moses who will lead "an even more radical kind of exodus."[25] The true prophet follows the way of faith, of trust in God's promise. The soothsayers and magicians without and even within Israel, though, follow the way of idolatry, of attempting to "seiz[e] control of the future."[26]

What distinguishes Moses above all, according to Ratzinger, is not so much his deeds, miracles, or sufferings, but that he "spoke with God as with a friend."[27] His prophetic office consisted above all in showing Israel the face of God and of the path by which they must follow him. The prophet calls Israel to reject idolatry and to worship the one true God. Unlike Moses, though, Jesus sees the face of the Father. And he does so "not just as a friend, but as a Son; he lives in the most intimate unity with the Father."[28] This is, for Ratzinger, the decisive, essential reality of Jesus: He is the Son who lives in unceasing dialogue and communion with his Father.[29] He worships and adores his Father.[30]

At the heart of Jesus' filial identity is his prayer to his Father: "Jesus' prayer is seen also by John to be the interior locus of the term 'the Son.' Of course, Jesus' prayer is different from the prayer of a creature: It is the dialogue of love within God himself—the dialogue that God *is*.... The term 'Son,' along with its correlate 'Father (Abba),' gives us a true glimpse into

25. Ratzinger, *Jesus of Nazareth: From the Baptism in the Jordan to the Transfiguration* (I), trans. Adrian J. Walker (New York: Doubleday, 2007), 3.

26. Ratzinger, *Jesus of Nazareth* (I), 2.

27. Ratzinger, *Jesus of Nazareth* (I), 4.

28. Ratzinger, *Jesus of Nazareth* (I), 6. Later in this book, Ratzinger presents this unity as one of being, knowledge, and will (340–43).

29. Among numerous instances, see, for instance, *Jesus of Nazareth* (I), 345, 354; Ratzinger, *Behold the Pierced One: An Approach to a Spiritual Christology*, trans. Graham Harrison (San Francisco: Ignatius, 1986), 36.

30. Ratzinger's thought is paralleled by Herbert McCabe: "You might say that as he lived and gradually explored into himself, asking not just the questions 'Who do men say that I am?' but 'Who do *I* say that I am?', he found nothing but the Father's love.... However he would have put it to himself (and of this we know nothing), he saw himself as simply an expression of the love which is the Father and in which the Father delights" (*God Matters* [London: Geoffrey Chapman, 1987], 95).

the inner being of Jesus—indeed, into the inner being of God himself. Jesus' prayer is the true origin of the term 'the Son.'"[31]

Behold the Pierced One, a collection of Ratzinger's Christological addresses and homilies, begins with a gem of a chapter, "Taking Bearings in Christology." The article is built around seven theses, the first of which is, "According to the testimony of Holy Scripture, the center of the life and person of Jesus is his constant communication with the Father."[32] The second thesis is, "Jesus died praying. At the Last Supper he anticipated his death by giving of himself, thus transforming his death, from within, into an act of love, into a glorification of God."[33] His death was an act of prayer and of worship. He offered himself completely as the perfect sacrifice. And, in this total prayerful communication with his Father, he overcame death, which is, in Ratzinger's words, "the destruction of every communication," and thus transformed death into an "act of self-communication.... death ... itself becomes a word, becomes the place where meaning communicates itself."[34] Even death becomes, in Jesus, an act of prayer and worship.[35]

Finally, Jesus' sonship and worship manifest themselves in his proexistence. This theme is present throughout Ratzinger's writings,[36] but it receives its climactic presentation in the *Jesus of Nazareth* trilogy. Nowhere does he state it more directly and concisely than in Part II:

Recent theology has rightly underlined the use of the word "for" in all four accounts [of the words of institution], a word that may be considered the key not only to the Last Supper accounts, but to the figure of Jesus overall. His entire being is expressed by the word "pro-existence"—he is there, not for himself, but for others. This is not merely a dimension of his existence, but its innermost essence and entirety. His very being is a "being-for." If we are able to grasp this, then we have truly come close to the mystery of Jesus, and we have understood what discipleship is.[37]

---

31. Ratzinger, *Jesus of Nazareth* (I), 344; also, Ratzinger, *The Feast of Faith: Approaches to a Theology of the Liturgy*, trans. Graham Harrison (San Francisco: Ignatius, 1986), 26–27. For a parallel, see McCabe, *God Matters*, 220: "[Jesus] is not first of all an individual person who then prays to the Father, his prayer to the Father is what constitutes him as who he is. He is not just one who prays, not even one who prays best, he is sheer prayer."

32. Ratzinger, *Behold the Pierced One*, 15.

33. Ratzinger, *Behold the Pierced One*, 22.

34. Ratzinger, *Behold the Pierced One*, 25.

35. See, for instance, *Introduction to Christianity*, 286–87.

36. For instance, the "principle of 'for'" in Ratzinger, *Introduction to Christianity*, 251–54.

37. Ratzinger, *Jesus of Nazareth* (II), 134.

In sum, the Son who is his prayer to the Father is the one whose entire being is directed away from himself toward his Father and toward all humanity.

III

Ratzinger's liturgical anthropology flows out of his liturgical Christology. Jesus Christ is the "definitive human being.... In him alone appears the complete answer to the question about what the human being is."[38] True humanity, according to Ratzinger, is rooted in a grateful affirmation of creaturely dependence upon God, in an awareness that creation itself is ordered to worship. Sin is a denial of such dependence, a rejection of relationality. It manifests itself in a particularly insidious way through the "slavery of activity,"[39] which rejects Sabbath rest and reflects an idolatrous desire for control and manipulation of creation, humanity, and God himself.

Jesus, as the Second or New Adam, salvifically reverses the route of the first Adam, becoming dependent, enslaved, humble, and even passive to a certain extent.[40] He follows the path of love, not power. He reveals the path of true, Christian humility: "a humility of being, not a merely moralistic one: being as receiving, accepting oneself as created and dependent on 'love.'"[41] Much as Ratzinger ceaselessly criticizes those who try to "make" liturgy, to create worship (which is, in reality, idolatry), rather than receiving it as a divine gift, so too does he see the human person's redemption in his or her humble receiving of the gift of creation, his or her "yes" to creation. This assent is what he characterizes as holiness: the Son's eternal yes to the Father, Mary's yes to the angel Gabriel, the human person's assent to his or her creation, redemption and, ultimately, glorification. In short, all of creation exists for the sake of worship, and the human person is never more human than when he or she recognizes one's dependence upon God and lovingly sings his praise.

---

38. Joseph Ratzinger, *"In the Beginning ...": A Catholic Understanding of the Story of Creation and the Fall*, trans. Boniface Ramsey and Helen A. Saward (Grand Rapids, Mich.: Eerdmans, 1995), 48.

39. Ratzinger, *"In the Beginning ..."*, 32.

40. Ratzinger, *"In the Beginning ..."*, 75–77. For arresting commentary on Jesus' Passion as a movement from "unfettered freedom to total constraint" (27), see W. H. Vanstone, *The Stature of Waiting* (New York: Morehouse, 1982).

41. Ratzinger, *"In the Beginning ..."*, 99.

It is partly due to this conception of creation, sin, and freedom that, in his commentary on *Gaudium et Spes*, written only a few years after Vatican II's close, Ratzinger was occasionally quite critical of the Pastoral Constitution. He deemed it to be, in various sections, somewhat semi-Pelagian or even Pelagian,[42] insufficiently Christocentric,[43] and lacking thick or even sufficient presentation of sin and of human freedom.[44]

However, his comments on Section 22 — the famous "only in the mystery of the incarnate Word does the mystery of man take on light," so beloved of John Paul II — move in a much more positive direction. In his view, "A new type of completely Christocentric theology appears.... The generally theologically reserved text of the Pastoral Constitution here attains very lofty heights and points the way to theological reflection in our present situation."[45] He continues with a remarkable reflection on adoration:

[*Gaudium et Spes* No. 22] ends with the thought of our incorporation into Christ by which we become sons in the Son.... A text which to some appears at first far too humanist in tendency, thus culminates in the idea of adoration. Christ truly shows himself, even from the theological point of view, as the way and the mediator who in the end brings men before the face of the Father. Thereby finally the Pauline form of Christocentrism finds expression, characterized by the little word "per"; it knows Christ to be the centre and has its goal in the Father. Precisely this culmination in adoration, in theology in the strictest sense of the term, justifies the anthropological endeavour of our chapter, which does not lead to an unacceptable form of anthropocentrism but, by taking man seriously, recognizes him as the being who is constituted to be not merely in himself, but above and beyond himself, and who is in full possession of himself only when he has gone forth from himself: Abba, Father.[46]

One sees in this passage the convergence of Ratzinger's liturgical, Christological, and anthropological thought. The Son adores the Father, and men and women — only through and in the Son — become sons and daughters capable of beholding, adoring, and worshiping the Father. We are never more

---

42. Ratzinger, "The Dignity of the Human Person," in *Commentary on the Documents of Vatican II*, vol. V, ed. Herbert Vorgrimler (New York: Herder and Herder, 1969), 138.

43. Ratzinger, "The Dignity of the Human Person," 120–21.

44. Ratzinger, "The Dignity of the Human Person," 136–38.

45. Ratzinger, "The Dignity of the Human Person," 159.

46. Ratzinger, "The Dignity of the Human Person," 163.

human — or more divine — than when we worship and adore our Father. For Ratzinger, this is the human person's and the Church's "highest task": "the glorification of the living God, from whom comes mankind's salvation."[47] Adoration — which Ratzinger describes in *Introduction to Christianity* as "that disinterested love which glorifies God himself" — is "man's highest possibility; it alone forms his true and final liberation."[48] Adoration spills forth in pro-existence. Love of God generates love of neighbor. And, thus when we are truly orthodox — that is, when we rightly glorify God — then we become like the Son, whose entire being is pro-existence: wholly from God and wholly for our brothers and sisters.

Corresponding to such pro-existence is Ratzinger's warning against the danger of moralism. Moralism, as he presents it, is not a rejection of norms of moral behavior but rather a distorted emphasis or primacy given to what we do for God rather than what he does for us; it raises the specter of Pelagianism. Ratzinger sees in the Gospel of John's account of Jesus' foot-washing both the temptation to, and the overcoming of, such moralism. One may read that account simply as Jesus commanding us to follow his example of humble service, which we accomplish simply through our own energies. Instead, Jesus goes before us and already does what we have to do. He has opened the way to God and become himself the bridge to God, a way that we could never traverse by our own efforts alone.[49] The "new commandment," then, is "not simply a new and higher demand: it is linked to the newness of Jesus Christ — to growing immersion in him.... The gift — the *sacramentum* — becomes an *exemplum*, an example while always remaining a gift. To be a Christian is primarily a gift, which then unfolds in the dynamic of living and acting in and around the gift."[50] Gift always precedes task in the Christian economy. As Ratzinger put it shortly before his election to the papacy, "to be workers of true justice, we must be workers who are *being made just* by contact with him who is justice itself: Jesus of Nazareth. The place of this encounter is the Church, nowhere more powerfully than in her sacraments and liturgy."[51]

---

47. Ratzinger, *The Feast of Faith*, 153.
48. Ratzinger, *Introduction to Christianity*, 288.
49. See Ratzinger, *The Spirit of the Liturgy*, 59.
50. Ratzinger, *Jesus of Nazareth* (II), 65; see also *The Spirit of the Liturgy*, 59.
51. Joseph Ratzinger, Homily for the Fortieth Anniversary of *Gaudium et Spes*, March 18,

IV

I would like to conclude by looking briefly at some ways that Ratzinger's liturgical thought might help us address contemporary crises and scandals in the Church today. Many will be familiar with his famous Christmas Day address of 1969, wherein he spoke about the Church of the future likely being a small flock, divested of its infrastructure and temporal influence.[52] I want to look, instead, at two other programmatic addresses: his 2008 address in Paris to the French "world of culture" and the final address from his 2011 trip to Germany, delivered in Freiburg to German Catholic leaders.

In its reflection on the Christian and specifically monastic roots of Western culture, the Paris speech shows the primacy of the *quaerere Deum*: the search for God.[53] Pope Benedict notes that the early monastics did not start out by trying to create or even preserve culture. They first sought God— "to go from the inessential to the essential, to the only truly important and reliable thing there is"—and from that search flowed the development of a Christian culture. The French philosopher Rémi Brague, commenting on Benedict's address, says that "culture is a by-product of praise."[54] As Ratzinger muses elsewhere, while shouting all too often prevails on earth, right worship

teaches [us] silence and singing again by opening [us] to the depths of the sea and teaching [us] to fly, the angels' mode of being. . . . One recognizes right liturgy by the fact that it liberates us from ordinary, everyday activity and returns to us once more the depths and the heights, silence and song. . . . It sings with the angels. It is silent with the expectant depths of the universe. And that is how it redeems the earth.[55]

2005, http://www.vatican.va/roman_curia/congregations/cfaith/documents/rc_con_cfaith_doc_20050318_ratzinger-gaudium-spes_en.html.

52. Ratzinger, "What Will the Future Church Look Like?" in *Faith and the Future* (San Francisco: Ignatius, 2009), 101–18; see also Christopher Ruddy, "'Smaller but Purer'?: Joseph Ratzinger on the 'Little Flock' and Vicarious Representation," *Nova et Vetera* 13, English edition (2015): 713–41.

53. Benedict XVI, "France Visit: Address on Culture," *Origins* 38 (September 25, 2008): 248–53.

54. Rémi Brague, "From What Is Left Over," *First Things* 275, August/September 2017, 44.

55. Ratzinger, "The Image of the World and of Human Beings in the Liturgy and Its Expression in Church Music," in *A New Song for the Lord: Faith in Christ and Liturgy Today*, trans. Martha M. Matesich (New York: Crossroad, 1996), 160.

There are many concrete steps that can and must be taken now in the face of the various scandals presently facing Catholicism—a renewed commitment to justice and transparency concerning clerical sexual abuse; the release of all relevant documentation, both in the United States and in the Vatican, concerning the rise and fall of Theodore McCarrick; efforts at clerical, episcopal, and curial reform; and so on—but lasting reform will occur only when such efforts are joined to a renewed emphasis on the liturgical recognition of the primacy of God. Without right worship, we lose sight of God. And when we lose sight of God, the consequences are all too evident.

Second, Benedict's "farewell" address in Freiburg in August 2011 is perhaps his most concise and penetrating statement of the Church's life and mission in the West.[56] The Church, he notes, arises out of and is sustained by the *sacrum commercium*, the "unequal exchange" between God and humanity: Christ takes our sins, and gives us his grace and life; he empowers us and makes us sharers in his saving work. The unequal exchange is nowhere effected more powerfully—or regularly—than in the Church's worship, supremely so in the Eucharist. Such a Church, he notes, is "always on the move," always in mission, always "immersed" in Christ's outreach to humanity.

However—and with Ratzinger there is usually a however!—the Church is perennially tempted to turn inwards, to become self-referential and self-satisfied, to take refuge in institutional and structural self-maintenance. In such ecclesial worldliness, the primary, true *skandalon* of the Cross is obscured, and the "secondary scandals" of unworthy preachers conceal the "true demands of the Christian Gospel." In this situation, when "secularizing trends" result in the loss of church property and privileges, the Church is called to shed its worldliness and embrace the poor "destiny" of the tribe of Levi, which had no ancestral land or possessions of its own, but "[took] as its portion only God himself, his word and his signs." It is not coincidental, I think, that the ancient Levites were central to Israel's temple worship. Like the Israelites wandering in the wilderness and the desert, the Levites' true Promised Land was their true worship of God, their orthodoxy.

To return to the beginning of this chapter, Ratzinger's claim that liturgical problems and crises are at the heart and even root of the Church's present

---

56. Benedict XVI, "Germany Visit: Meeting with Catholics Active in Church and Society," *Origins* 41 (October 13, 2011): 305–7. All quotations in this and the following paragraphs are taken from this address.

crisis may seem overblown and dangerous. But, can there be much — if any — doubt that a Church whose gaze is turned to the Lord and which is humbled, stripped of its possessions and even good reputation, can be the most powerful form of witness to the crucified love of Christ? A Church whose believers are utterly turned in worship to, and dependent upon, the Father? A Church devoted to its "vocation to the ministry of divine worship and service of neighbor"?[57] That is, a Church turned to its Lord in worshipful adoration will be a Church turned to its neighbors in pro-existent service. And, in the beauty of its holiness, such a worshipping Church will offer convincing witness to the saving truth of Christianity:

The only really effective apologia for Christianity comes down to two arguments, namely, the saints the Church has produced and the art which has grown in her womb. . . . If the Church is to continue to transform and humanize the world, how can she dispense with beauty in her liturgies, that beauty which is so closely linked with love and with the radiance of the Resurrection? No. Christians must not be too easily satisfied. They must make their Church into a place where beauty — and hence truth — is at home. Without this the world will become the first circle of hell.

A theologian who does not love art, poetry, music and nature can be dangerous. Blindness and deafness toward the beautiful are not incidental: they necessarily are reflected in his theology.[58]

This emphasis on beauty — liturgical, artistic, Christic, human — was evident at a Mass of Thanksgiving on the occasion of Father Robert Imbelli's fiftieth anniversary of priestly ordination, celebrated in 2015 at Sacred Heart Parish in Newton Centre, Massachusetts, where he lived and served for almost thirty years while teaching at Boston College. His homily took as its theme a line from Psalm 84 (83): "How lovely is your dwelling place, O Lord of Hosts." After reflecting on the beauty of Sacred Heart's art and architecture, he turned to the beauty of the parish's people:

For, however lovely this building, these windows, the Lord's true dwelling place is in the hearts, minds, and bodies of his priestly people: they form a holy temple, the very body of Christ. We form a holy temple, the very body of Christ.

57. Benedict XVI, "Germany Visit: Meeting with Catholics Active in Church and Society," 306.
58. Joseph Cardinal Ratzinger with Vittorio Messori, *The Ratzinger Report: An Exclusive Interview on the State of the Church*, trans. Salvator Attanasio and Graham Harrison (San Francisco: Ignatius, 1985), 129–30.

It is our faith, our generosity, our hoping against hope — all in Christ — that is the true beauty that shines so splendidly.... We, priests and people, are irrevocably united in the one body of Christ. For the ordained priest is a baptized Christian anointed and consecrated to serve the priestly life of his brothers and sisters in the Lord. Our priestly service, gathered around the altar, is to unite, through the ordained priest, our personal offering of praise and thanksgiving, to the one perfect sacrifice of Jesus, the true Priest of the new covenant between God and his people.... This Eucharistic meal we share is made possible by the sacrifice Jesus offered two thousand years ago on Calvary, but present now both in heaven before the Father and on earth on every altar where Christ's sacrifice is remembered/re-presented.

For over two decades, Robert Imbelli has been my friend and trusted confidant. He, more than anyone else, has taught me that Christianity is about Christ. As the Catholic Common Ground Initiative (of which he was a founding member) put it in its mission statement, "Called to Be Catholic: Church in a Time of Peril": "Jesus Christ, present in Scripture and sacrament, is central to all that we do; he must always be the measure and not what is measured."

That commitment to the person of Christ (and not simply to his example or his cause), to Christ the Center and the Tree of Life, has been the *leitmotiv* (a word that the lifelong opera lover would surely appreciate!) of his life, ministry, and scholarship. I imagine a certain elderly Bavarian hierarch-theologian nodding his head in agreement with Father Imbelli's words elsewhere in his golden anniversary homily:

Of course, sin tarnishes the beauty — today, as it did when this church was built. Each of the inscriptions on the windows is not only a testament of love, but also of regret; not only of loss, but of failure: of things done or left undone.

They and we are Christ's body bearing witness to God's love and mercy in Christ, not only in our wholeness, but also in our brokenness: ordained priests and priestly people together.... The names today may be different. The faces are certainly more diverse and colorful. But the faith, hope, and love are the same. For "Jesus Christ is the same: yesterday, today, and forever."

The Incarnate Word in Catholic Moral Theology

The Christocentric Visions of Pope John Paul II and Robert Imbelli

RYAN CONNORS

On August 6, 2000, the Congregation for the Doctrine of the Faith issued the "Declaration *Dominus Iesus*: On the Unicity and Salvific Universality of Jesus Christ and the Church."[1] The publication of this text did not win universal acclaim. In fact, a trusted source reported that critics alleged the Pope had been kept ignorant of the text's content. This report seemed odd in light of the fact that the Pope had approved the official text before its publication. The controversy required the Pope to express his personal support for the truths expressed in the declaration. Indeed, Pope St. John Paul II used a Sunday Angelus address to make his position clear.[2] He even lamented that "so many erroneous interpretations" of the document had obscured its reception.[3]

In the United States, *Dominus Iesus* did not find many supporters. One

1. Congregation for the Doctrine of the Faith, "Declaration *Dominus Iesus*: On the Unicity and Salvific Universality of Jesus Christ and the Church," August 6, 2000.

2. See Tarcisio Cardinal Bertone, *The Last Secret of Fatima*, trans. Adrian J. Walker (New York: Doubleday, 2008), 102.

3. Pope John Paul II, Angelus address, October 1, 2000.

notable exception was Father Robert Imbelli. This Boston College professor of theology chose to defend the magisterial text. He broke with many of his university colleagues who had argued that the objectives of *Dominus Iesus* were foreign to Catholic theology and, indeed, to the vision of Vatican II.[4] Imbelli for his part found the magisterial text consonant with the great tradition. He insisted that "Christological normativity, the uniqueness and salvific universality of Jesus Christ, was not invented by the Congregation for the Doctrine of the Faith. It is simply the doctrine of the faith."[5] With these words, Imbelli set himself against the established orthodoxies of the religious studies departments of most Catholic universities.

Dominus Iesus bears the publication date of August 6, the feast of the Lord's Transfiguration. Pope John Paul II also chose the feast of the Transfiguration for another important teaching document of his pontificate. August 6, 1993, saw the publication of *Veritatis splendor*, an encyclical letter on fundamental questions of moral theology. The coincidence of publication dates indicates a correlation between the two documents. Both documents highlight the central place that the person of Christ holds in the proper exercise of Catholic theology, whether in dogma or morals.

Dominus Iesus confronts the widespread relativization of Christ that one encounters among the practitioners of much contemporary Catholic theology. This error poses serious dangers for a proper exposition of soteriology as well as other themes in dogmatic theology. For example, Christology and sacramental theology suffer when theologians relativize Christ and his Church. *Dominus Iesus* refutes the claim that the Catholic Church offers one path among others for salvation. Few commentators, however, have observed the extent to which the relativization and subsequent displacement of Christ in contemporary thought has affected moral theology. Such harm, however, merits close attention. For his part, Father Imbelli has labored to keep Christ at the center of all Catholic theology.

Pope John Paul II established in *Veritatis splendor* a firm ground for a proper approach to Catholic moral theology. This ground corresponds with how the Church understands Christ and his mission. The Second Vatican Council's Decree on Priestly Training anticipated the work of *Veritatis*. The

---

4. See, for example, several of the essays in *Sic et Non: Encountering Dominius Iesus*, ed. Stephen J. Pope and Charles Hefling (Maryknoll, N.Y.: Orbis Books, 2002).

5. Robert Imbelli, "The Reaffirmation of the Christic Center," in *Sic et Non: Encountering Dominius Iesus*, ed. Stephen J. Pope and Charles Hefling (Maryknoll, N.Y.: Orbis Books, 2002), 99.

Decree *Optatam totius* called specifically for a renewal of moral theology. The text insisted that "special care must be given to the perfecting of moral theology."[6] It furthermore held that the theological disciplines should "be renewed through a more living contact with the mystery of Christ and the history of salvation."[7] One can assume that the Church recognized the need for "a more living contact with the mystery of Christ" in order to counter the deficiencies of the moral theology in vigor in the immediate preconciliar period.

By and large, Catholic theologians relied on the system of moral casuistry from the sixteenth-century Council of Trent until the mid-twentieth century.[8] The encyclical *Veritatis splendor* marked an end of modern casuistry and restored virtue-based reasoning to Catholic moral thought. While certain commentators have praised the encyclical for its refutation of moral theories incompatible with Catholic theology, *Veritatis*'s connection to the Pope's broader Christocentric vision has drawn less attention.[9] In order to honor a dear mentor, Father Robert Imbelli, this essay examines what Imbelli describes as the "Christic center" and its role in the proper exercise of Catholic moral theology. What follows examines three aspects of the Christocentric vision of the moral life emphasized in *Veritatis splendor*. Taken together, these elements of Catholic moral thought find a common theme that *Dominus Iesus* sets down. The bold text merits close attention: "Christ even now associates the believers to himself in a living manner in the Spirit and gives him the hope of resurrection."[10]

Christ Embodies the Excellent

The moral theology of St. Thomas Aquinas receives its most complete treatment in the *Secunda Pars* of his *Summa Theologica*. This part of the *Sum-*

---

6. Vatican Council II, *Optatam totius* [Decree on Priestly Training], October 28, 1965, no. 16.

7. *Optatam totius*, no. 16.

8. For an elaboration of the deficiencies of the casuist system, see Servais Pinckaers, OP, *The Sources of Christian Ethics*, trans. Sr. Mary Thomas Noble, OP (Washington, D.C.: The Catholic University of America Press, 1995), especially 254–79; Romanus Cessario, OP, *Introduction to Moral Theology* (Washington, D.C.: The Catholic University of America Press, 2001), 229–42.

9. One author who has stressed Pope John Paul II's Christocentric vision of moral thought is Cardinal Avery Dulles. See Cardinal Avery Dulles, SJ, *The Splendor of Faith: The Theological Vision of Pope John Paul II* (New York: The Crossroad Publishing Company, 2003), especially 186–204.

10. *Dominus Iesus*, no. 12.

ma includes commentary on man's happiness, human acts, the passions, the treatises on law and grace, and an extended reflection on the theological and moral virtues. In the immediate postconciliar period, some theologians wrongly criticized Aquinas's moral theology as presented in the *Summa* for failing to pay sufficient attention to the Incarnate Word. Informed exegetes of Aquinas, however, have pointed out the Christological axis of St. Thomas's moral theology.[11] In fact, Thomists especially recognize the full truth about the moral life and its necessary connection to the person of Jesus Christ. *Veritatis splendor* picks up on this theme. The encyclical unfolds within the context of an exposition of the pericope of the rich young man.[12] For Pope John Paul II, Christ's encounter with his well-to-do inquisitor offers the best context for understanding what lies beneath moral matters. The Pope dissuades Christians from approaching the moral life as an effort to observe rules and obligations and persuades us to embrace an on-going personal transformation with a view toward achieving complete human flourishing.

Historians of moral theology identify two false extremes in the discipline that conscientious confessors and sound theologians attempt to avoid. On the one hand, adherents of tutiorism counsel erroneously that one should always pursue the most rigorous option in the moral life. The tutiorist fears the occasion of sin at every turn. At the other extreme, laxist moral theologians adopt a minimalist approach to moral obligations. When a theologian turns his attention to Christ, he sets himself on a path that avoids both the rigorist and laxist errors. One hardly needs to argue that rigorism enjoys few supporters today. Those who do succumb to this error, however, fail to recognize the authentic freedom Christ introduces into the world. Why? Rigorists identify moral probity with constraint, whereas the New Testament announces liberation: "For freedom Christ set us free" (Gal 5:1). Those transformed by grace should be free from anxiety or needless worry that every movement may implicate them in sinful activity. As the "Woe" texts of Luke indicate, Christ promises liberation from the crippling strictures of moral legalism (see Lk 11: 37–54).

Laxism stands out today as the more prevalent error among moral theorists. We need to hear again Pope John Paul II's cry, "Be not afraid, open

11. See, for example, the essays of Jean-Pierre Torrell, OP, in his *Christ and Spirituality in St. Thomas Aquinas*, trans. Bernhard Blankenhorn, OP (Washington, D.C.: The Catholic University of America Press, 2011).

12. Pope John Paul II, *Veritatis splendor*, August 6, 1993, no. 6–27.

wide the doors to Christ." The Pope directs believers to embrace Christ and thereby to prefer the morally excellent. Moral excellence never succumbs to ethical minimalism. Post-Tridentine moral casuistry generated both tutiorist and laxist extremes. Indeed, laxism enjoys a long history. One look at the pages of Denzinger that treat the post-Tridentine period reveals that casuistry requires constant ecclesiastical supervision to escape the laxism to which rule-based moral theories are prone. The condemnations of Pope Innocent XI in 1679 offer many examples that illustrate papal intervention to correct laxist moral theories.[13] Contemporary theologians fail to escape this laxist error when they prefer a moral analysis that stresses the mitigating factors that may lessen moral culpability rather than an evaluation of the quality of the object of the human act.[14]

Optatam totius sounds a different note when this text of the Second Vatican Council requires that moral theology "should shed light on the loftiness of the calling of the faithful in Christ."[15] Likewise, Pope John Paul II later urges the faithful "not to stop at the minimum demands of the Law."[16] When theologians and believers heed the lofty call of Christ to moral excellence, they escape minimalist understandings of what is required for Christian living. The antidote to laxism arises from a believer's sustained reflection on the call to Christian perfection. Those who embrace Christ strive to become "perfect as [the] Heavenly Father is perfect" (Mt 5:48).

Consider further that rule-based moral theories in use during the casuist period paid scant attention to the virtue of fortitude. Servais Pinckaers identifies the reason.[17] The strict obligations of courage prove difficult to classify. An obligation-based moral theory is unable to explicate fortitude without abandoning fundamental principles of moral casuistry. The moral manual of the Capuchin Heribert Jone offers only one reference to fortitude in his entire volume.[18] Christocentric instruction in moral theology, on the

13. For a full treatment of one of these condemnations, see Andrew McLean Cummings, *The Servant and the Ladder: Cooperation with Evil in the Twenty-First Century* (Leominster: Gracewing, 2014).

14. For an exposition of the essential continuity between the method of moral casuistry and that of proportionalism, see Christopher Kaczor, *Proportionalism and the Natural Law Tradition* (Washington, D.C.: The Catholic University of America Press, 2002).

15. *Optatam totius*, no. 16.

16. *Veritatis splendor*, no. 18.

17. Pinckaers, *The Sources of Christian Ethics*, 24–27.

18. See Heribert Jone, OFM Cap, *Moral Theology,* trans. Urban Adelman, OFM Cap (Westminster, Md.: The Newman Bookshop, 1951), § 112.

other hand, draws students to imitate the courage of Christ. Contemporary challenges, especially those regarding the protection of human life and the sanctity of marriage, require of Christians a robust fortitude. The vaunted precision of rule-based moral theories proves illusory. The one who turns to Christ, however, reflects upon his virtues and sees in him the model for Christian living. To continue with the two examples, prolife advocates and supporters of traditional marriage can discover by their fruitful meditation on the Gospel right courses of action to follow. This discovery, to repeat a favorite theme of Servais Pinckaers, occurs under the inspiration of the Holy Spirit, which Christ promises to his disciples (see Lk 12:12: "The Holy Spirit will teach at that moment what you should say").

For his part, Pope John Paul II urges believers to attend to the person of Christ in moral matters. "Following Christ is thus the essential and primordial foundation of Christian morality," he declares.[19] Indeed, "people today need to turn to Christ once again in order to receive from him the answer to their questions about what is good and what is evil."[20] Unlike the rich young man, Christians today must act on the truth they discover in conversation with Christ and take comfort in the knowledge that, as Pope John Paul II often taught, Christ sheds light on man and his integral vocation.[21] The remark from the Pope reflects *Gaudium et Spes*, no. 22: "The truth is that only in the mystery of the incarnate Word does the mystery of man take on light."[22] One comes to know the full and supernatural truth about the human person only in reference to Christ. No wonder the Second Vatican Council boldly proclaimed that Christ alone "reveals man to himself."[23] Though the Christian moral life finds its foundation in the precepts of the natural law, its fulfillment appears only in the Risen Christ. Human reason provides authentic knowledge of the natural moral law; however, Christ's light provides the believer with a suprarational illumination. The loftiness of the Christian calling takes up these natural moral precepts, even

---

19. *Veritatis splendor*, no. 19. Other spiritual authors have described the posture of looking to Christ for guidance in moral matters as the *sequela Christi* or even the *imitatio Christi*. For an outstanding treatment of this matter, see "Imitating God as His Beloved Children: Conformity to God and to Christ in the Works of St. Thomas Aquinas," in Torrell, *Christ and Spirituality in St. Thomas Aquinas*, 110–25.

20. *Veritatis splendor*, no. 8.

21. *Veritatis splendor*, no. 8.

22. Vatican Council II, *Gaudium et Spes*, December 7, 1965, no. 22.

23. *Gaudium et Spes*, no. 22.

as this same calling elevates the believer's mode of fulfilling them (see Mt 5:22). The Christian vocation exposes the full flowering of the theological life, where the theological virtues reach down to shape human activity.[24] Contrary to what many may think, Christianity is not a mere humanism. A revealed assessment of the moral life locates its ultimate aim in the following of Christ and one's imitation of him.

The doctrine of the imitation of Christ enjoys a long history in Catholic thought. *Christ and Moral Theology* by the Toulouse Dominican Louis B. Gillon (1901–1987) merits praise as the groundbreaking treatment of the question in the twentieth century.[25] In his capacity as professor in Rome at what would later become the Pontifical University of St. Thomas Aquinas, Gillon served as the dissertation director for Servais Pinckaers.[26] Following the work of Gillon, Servais Pinckaers, in his singular achievement, *The Sources of Christian Ethics*, explained virtue-based Christocentric moral theology to the postconciliar Church.[27] Pinckaers's achievement shows that Gillon's progeny attained success in pointing out that, in order to present a full vision of Catholic moral thought, moral theologians should attend to the face of the Risen Christ. Truth to tell, Gillon's book picks up the late-medieval theme of the imitation of Christ. Subsequently, some spiritual authors interpreted this Christological exemplarism in an extrinsic fashion, a kind of mimetic moralism divorced from the inner transformation necessary for authentic Christian discipleship. Unfortunately, some mistakenly believe that the imitation of Christ stops short at an extrinsic model. In extreme instances, such a spiritual paradigm could resemble the Pelagian claim that Christ's only benefit remains his setting of moral example.

Both Gillon and Pinckaers, of course, rejected such a reductionism. They insisted that in order to live like Christ one must draw near to him, live in him, and abide in his friendship. Pope John Paul II makes this truth his own. In *Veritatis,* he teaches: "Following Christ is not an outward imita-

---

24. See *Catechism of the Catholic Church* (hereafter, *CCC*), no. 1813 and 2686.

25. Louis B. Gillon, OP, *Christ and Moral Theology*, trans. Cornelius Williams, OP (Staten Island, N.Y.: Alba House, 1967).

26. For reflections on the importance of Servais Pinckaers for the renewal of moral theology, see both Romanus Cessario, OP, "On the Place of Servais Pinckaers (+7 April 2008) in the Renewal of Catholic Theology," *The Thomist* 73 (2009): 1–27; Michael Sherwin, OP, "Eulogie pour le P. Servais Pinckaers, O.P.," *Nova et Vetera*, English edition, 84 (2009): 133–36.

27. See Pinckaers, *The Sources of Christian Ethics.*

tion, since it touches man at the very depths of his being. Being a follower of Christ means becoming conformed to him who became a servant even to giving himself on the Cross."[28] Precepts play a role but are not the last word in the moral life. Christian virtue arises from an interior renewal that is the fruit of a transformation by grace. The human person's graced transformation always bears fruit in concrete human actions. As the apostle James reminds us, "Faith of itself, if it does not have works, is dead" (Jas 2:17).

Contrary to the view of some authors, an inner transformation through grace remains incompatible with grave moral failings. According to the received understanding of St. Thomas Aquinas, the transformation that Christ works in the souls of the justified sinks down to the sense powers of the human soul. This transformation allows the believer to follow Christ without interference even from unruly emotional upset. When the rich young man asks of Christ, "What still do I lack," (Mt 19:20), he seems to grapple with divided emotion. *Veritatis splendor* offers counsel to those who find themselves in similar moral circumstances. The text speaks about a "path of perfection" that entails personal integrity: "Conscious of the young man's yearning for something greater, which would transcend a legalistic interpretation of the commandments, the Good Teacher invites him to enter upon the path of perfection."[29] Christ would hardly point out a path to perfection that left men troubled by appetitive turmoil.

Virtue and the Moral Life

The latter half of the twentieth century witnessed a renewed interest in the category of virtue in ethics and moral theology. Important figures who discussed virtue, albeit in different philosophical contexts, include Josef Pieper, Peter Geach, and Alasdair MacIntryre. Thinkers who took up the theme of moral virtue returned to the work of Thomas Aquinas, whose insights they considered useful for modern ethics. Of course, Thomist scholars, such as another Toulouse Dominican, Michel Labourdette, and the aforementioned Servais Pinckaers, also mined Aquinas's writings on the virtues for their own theological purposes.[30] Some of this theological

28. *Veritatis splendor*, no. 21.

29. *Veritatis splendor*, no. 16.

30. The recently published course notes of Michel Labourdette, OP, demonstrate the virtue-based moral theology he taught during his decades in Toulouse (1940–1990). See Michel

reflection found its way into the 1993 encyclical *Veritatis splendor*.[31] The virtue-based moral thinking of *Veritatis* emphasizes the ultimate end of human activity, the habits or dispositions necessary for human flourishing and the interaction of the natural and supernatural orders that gives Christian moral theology its specificity.[32] By the turn of the twenty-first century, these themes had taken firm hold on the best of moral instruction, especially in Catholic seminaries.

Because Aquinas treats the virtues in the *Secunda Pars* of his *Summa Theologica*, and therefore before he treats Christ in the *Tertia Pars*, certain critics have argued that Thomas's description of the virtues lack an intrinsic connection to the mystery of Jesus Christ. Aquinas's ordering of his materials, however, imports no such separation. On the contrary, Aquinas insists that the virtues of Christian living find their completion in Christ. The virtues as habits of being allow Aquinas to account for the New Testament promise that grace transforms human nature. Moral theories that exclude the virtues find it difficult to account for the transformation of the human person in grace. One may observe that those ethical theorists who eschew virtue find themselves preoccupied with the evaluation of isolated acts. A moral theology that places the person of Christ at its center easily accounts for the power of grace to transform the whole person. Recall that virtues include those of the sense appetites. Against those who charge Aquinas with neglecting the place of Christ in the moral life, Joseph Warwrykow retorts that in order to grasp St. Thomas's complete teaching on moral matters one

Labourdette, OP, *Cours de théologie morale: Tome 1, Morale fondamentale* (Paris: Parole et Silence, 2010) and *Cours de théologie morale: Tome 2, Morale special* (Paris: Parole et Silence, 2012). The classic entry of Thomas Deman, OP, "Probabilisme," in the *Dictionnaire de theologie catholique*, 417–619 (Paris: Letouzey et Ane, 1936), also stands as a prophetic testament to the Thomist tradition in moral theology. For at least a partial defense of the Dominican approach to moral questions during the casuist period, see Benedict Ashley, OP, *The Dominicans* (Wilmington, Del.: Michael Glazier Inc., 1991), 174–75.

31. See, for example, *Veritatis splendor*, no. 52.

32. For a strong case for the integrity of nature found in the Thomist tradition, see Lawrence Feingold, *The Natural Desire to See God in St. Thomas Aquinas and His Interpreters* (Ave Maria, Fla.: Sapientia Press, 2010), and Steven A. Long, *Natura Paura: A Rediscovery of Nature in the Doctrine of Grace* (New York: Fordham University Press 2010). For an alternative perspective, see Henri de Lubac, *Surnaturel: etudes historiques* (Paris: F. Aubier, 1946), as well as John Milbank, *The Suspended Middle: Henri de Lubac and the Debate concerning the Supernatural* (Grand Rapids, Mich.: Eerdmans, 2005), and Denis Bradley, *Aquinas on the Twofold Human Good* (Washington, D.C.: The Catholic University of America Press, 1997).

must not limit his search to the *Secunda Pars* of the *Summa Theologica*. Since Aquinas explains that Christ is the way through which man moves toward God, the full exposition of his moral teaching also requires the work of the *Tertia Pars*.[33] In the same fashion, Father Pinckaers explains that just as the Blessed Sacrament can be found in only one place in a Cathedral, yet the Lord's presence "radiates throughout the edifice," so too, while St. Thomas treats Christ in a specific section of his *Summa* is his presence felt throughout.[34]

One advantage to moral theorists' attention to the virtues appears in the stress this approach places on the passions of the soul. Alternative ethical theories that focus exclusively on concrete acts find it difficult to explain the ordering of the sensitive appetites.[35] Conversion to Christ enacts a full transformation, including at the appetitive level. Therapists may help persons to avoid certain malevolent actions. New life in Christ, on the other hand, promises a true inner renewal of the self. One should not confuse the graced reality of personal transformation with the fact that a person may control disordered passions in a voluntaristic fashion. Will power alone does not ensure promptness, ease, and, above all, joyfulness in doing good. In a word, Christian sanctification runs deep.

Moral teaching that places Christ as its center identifies the Sermon on the Mount as the starting point for doing Christian moral theology. Recognition of this relationship dates back at least from the patristic period, when authors begin to regard the fifth chapter of Matthew's Gospel as a paradigm of the moral life. Practitioners of modern casuistry, on the other hand, failed to assimilate this key biblical text into their moral questions and answers.[36] When moral theologians focus their attention on one of Christ's principal

33. See Joseph Wawrykow, "Jesus in the Moral Theology of Thomas Aquinas," *Journal of Medieval and Early Modern Studies* 42 (2012): 17. Wawrykow writes, "[T]o get the full moral theology of the *Summa*, one must keep reading, into the Tertia Pars."

34. See Pinckaers, *The Sources of Christian Ethics*, 170.

35. For an account of Aquinas's teaching on human emotion, see Nicholas E. Lombardo, *The Logic of Desire* (Washington, D.C.: The Catholic University of America Press, 2011), and Robert Miner, *Thomas Aquinas on the Passions: A Study of Summa Theologiae, 1a2ae 22–48* (Cambridge: Cambridge University Press, 2009). For the role of the passions in the development of virtue, see Servais Pinckaers, OP, *Passions and Virtue*, trans. Benedict M. Guevin, OSB (Washington, D.C.: The Catholic University of America Press, 2015).

36. For a full treatment of the place of the Sermon on the Mount in Christian moral teaching, see Pinckaers, *The Sources of Christian Ethics*, 134–67.

moral instructions, their teachings acquire an evangelical amplitude that question-and-answer-based theories lack. The Sermon offers a high vision of Christian living: "Be perfect just as your Heavenly Father is perfect" (Mt 5:48). No one who reads the Lord's Sermon on the Mount comes away with a minimalist view of Christian life. The Sermon on the Mount begins with the Lord's announcement of the Beatitudes. These Beatitudes form the sermon's essential core. As Father Pinckaers points out, however, the Beatitudes were displaced by authors of the casuist period. Fundamentally, the Beatitudes describe Christ as the one truly poor in spirit, authentically meek, and fully pure of heart. As the *Catechism* puts it, the Beatitudes paint a picture of Christ.[37] Again, Christian living means to live in Christ. Futility marks the attempt to achieve this perfection in any other way. A believer's struggle to imitate Christ as if he were only an exterior model never works. Throughout the New Testament, we read about one's being conformed to Christ, configured to Christ, and conjoined to Christ. These expressions aim to demonstrate the closeness that Christ promises to those who seek him.

No one should reduce living in Christ to mere ethical behavior. Philosophers treat ethics, while full transformation in Christ expresses itself through the exercise of the theological and infused moral virtues.[38] The *Catechism of the Catholic Church* observes: "The theological virtues are the foundation of Christian moral activity; they animate it and give it its special character. They inform and give life to all the moral virtues."[39] Alternatively, moral systems that avoid speaking about conformity to Christ fail to ascribe to the theological virtues their full moral import. When this happens, the distinctive acts of faith, hope, and charity lose their immediacy to the moral life. In this circumstance, Catholic moral theology becomes difficult to distinguish from a generic form of religious ethics.

Christ's Gift of Grace

Students new to a Catholic seminary are often surprised to learn that theologians trained in moral theology tend to be assigned as instructors for the course on grace. For virtue-based moral theologians, the reason for this

37. *CCC*, no. 1717.
38. See *Veritatis splendor*, no. 64.
39. *CCC*, no. 1813.

assignment is simple. Divine grace provides a topic for theologians who discuss human actions. This association explains why St. Thomas Aquinas locates his treatise on grace within the *Secunda Pars* of his *Summa Theologica*, which, as noted above, contains his treatment of the virtues.[40] Among the benefits of Aquinas's disposition of his materials, one recognizes the strongly anti-Pelagian tenor that imbues his thought. The practice of restricting discussions of grace to courses in dogmatic theology makes it difficult to describe adequately the specifically Christian dynamics of morality. When the Church teaches that Baptism confers the whole panoply of Christian perfections, she warns against trying to describe the Christian life apart from the indispensable helps of divine grace. Within the history of moral theology, one can discover tendencies to identify Christian living with unaided personal effort or rely exclusively on legal categories to define its contours. In the latter case, moral theology oftentimes became preoccupied with moral dilemmas.[41]

Catholic moral theology flourishes when, as *Veritatis splendor* urges, it attends to the place of Christ in the moral life. In *Veritatis*, Pope John Paul II explains that "Christ dwells by faith in the heart of the believer, and thus the disciple is conformed to the Lord."[42] The Pope offers the reason for this happy thought when he affirms that "[t]his is the effect of grace, of the active presence of the Holy Spirit in us."[43] The Christian who dwells on his being conjoined to Christ quickly moves to consider the gifts Christ bestows. The pages of the New Testament repeatedly announce promise that Christ makes to his people when he pledges them his divine help. This assistance comes in the form of the seven virtues of the Christian life. Since the theological virtues have God as their object, only God's grace can account for their proper activities. The gift of divine grace also includes the infused moral virtues that enable a person to live out a rounded human existence on a supernatural plane. This supernatural plane appears, for instance, in

---

40. See Thomas Aquinas, *Summa Theologica*, Ia-IIae q. 109–14.

41. See, for example, the remark of Thomas Slater, SJ, *A Manual of Moral Theology for English Speaking Countries*, vol. 1 (New York: Benzinger Brothers, 1925), v: "Manuals of moral theology ... are not intended for edification, nor do they hold up a high ideal of Christian perfection for the imitation of the faithful. They deal with what is of obligation under pain of sin; they are books of moral pathology."

42. *Veritatis splendor*, no. 21.

43. *Veritatis splendor*, no. 21.

acts of penitential fasting and the clerical observance of chaste celibacy. The Gospels point to this reality when they speak of those who "renounce marriage for the sake of the Kingdom of God" (Mt 19:12). In every case, infused virtues elevate and transform ordinary human actions into meritorious conduct worthy of heavenly reward.

Christian living requires the divine assistance. Its gift character makes this plain. Divine assistance, however, should not be thought of as an external aid to right-living. Grace does more than provide an aid for right conduct. Instead, God's grace penetrates every aspect of the redeemed believer. Actions flow from being; meritorious actions from redeemed being. How ill-informed are those critics who interpret the Christian moral life as gilded fulfillment of natural law precepts. Rather, transformative grace accounts for the "new man" (see Col 3:10) and the thoroughly new actions that he performs. The person who lives "in Christ" acts in Christ and brings him into the world.

Within the context of the proper understanding of the transformative power of divine grace, one can consider the performance of human acts as those that come under the influence of the gifts of the Holy Spirit. According to the classical teaching of theologians, the gifts aid the exercise of the theological and moral virtues.[44] The gifts of the Holy Spirit come to the believer as divine impulses to act according to a suprarational mode of conduct. The gifts represent a new divinely bestowed source of human activity that enables a person to accomplish meritorious acts. No theological text can account for the multiplicity of situations in which modern man finds himself. These divine helps move a person to implement virtuous action within a variety of sometimes difficult circumstances. The Catholic moral tradition recognizes a kind of knowledge that comes about as a result of the actor's connaturality, which in this context means that the moral agent under the impulse of the Holy Spirit operates from a felt closeness with God's law. It should be observed, again, that authors working in the casuist period remained skeptical about knowledge by connaturality. They opined that such connaturality could result in the agent's unwarranted self-dispensation from observing the moral law. Pope John Paul II clearly does not share this misgiving. On the contrary, in *Veritatis splendor,* he explains: "[I]n order

44. See Robert Edward Brennan, *The Seven Horns of the Lamb: A Study of the Gifts Based on Saint Thomas Aquinas* (Milwaukee, Wis.: Bruce, 1966).

to 'prove what is the will of God, what is good and acceptable and perfect' (Rom 12:2), knowledge of God's law in general is certainly necessary, but it is not sufficient: what is essential is a sort of 'connaturality' between man and the true good."[45] Furthermore, the Pope explicitly teaches about the relationship that the gifts of the Holy Spirit enjoy with the virtues of the Christian life. "Such a connaturality," he asserts, "is rooted in and develops through the virtuous attitudes of the individual himself: prudence and the other cardinal virtues, and even before these the theological virtues of faith, hope and charity."[46] One may observe at this juncture that these texts from *Veritatis splendor* point out a feature of Catholic moral thought ignored by those theorists who rely exclusively on practical reasoning in order to determine a proper course of moral action.

The lasting value of *Veritatis splendor* resides not so much in its refutation of inadequate moral theories as in its positive presentation of how Christians should approach moral matters. The Pope does not restrict himself to the denunciation of erroneous views. Instead, he sets forth in *Veritatis* a program by which Christians can develop a well-formed conscience that is able to "make judgments and lead to decisions in accordance with the truth."[47] By means of his positive proposal, the Pope comforts Christians who face challenging moral dilemmas. He reassures such believers that Christ himself remains a steadfast guide for the moral life.[48] Indeed the very structure of *Veritatis splendor* urges its readers to enter into dialogue with the Lord (chapter 1) and to seek strength from his cross (chapter 3). Affective union with Christ remains the sure bulwark for the person who seeks to escape temptation's power. The need to rely on Christ holds true both for the individual Christian and the Church herself. Pope John Paul II could not express better his confidence in the moral guidance that Christ gives to his Church and her members than this significant text from the encyclical: "Each day the Church looks to Christ with unfailing love, fully aware that

45. *Veritatis splendor*, no. 64.
46. *Veritatis splendor*, no. 64.
47. *Veritatis splendor*, no. 85.
48. *Veritatis splendor*, no. 85. Not only does the Pope urge Christians to discover moral direction from their union with Christ, he also acknowledges that the Church herself depends on Christ for her mission of preaching the truth. See *Veritatis splendor*, no. 85: "[T]he Church finds its support — the 'secret' of its educative power — not so much in doctrinal statements and pastoral appeals to vigilance, as in constantly looking to the Lord Jesus."

the true and final answer to the problem of morality lies in him alone."[49] Christocentrism has become an inescapable feature of Catholic moral life.

Tribute to a Master

Father Robert Imbelli's lifetime of ecclesial service witnesses to the centrality that Christ holds in the life of the Church. He highlights what he calls the "Christic imagination" as the effective means to shape one's moral compass. Father Imbelli recognizes that practitioners of sound Catholic theology cannot proceed apart from their adherence to the person of Christ. He insists that the power of Christ can shape a believer's moral awareness. A transformed heart bids the Lord Christ to enter in. The kind of imagination that Father Imbelli envisages enjoys the advantage of both moving beyond the legal categories of moral casuistry and, at the same time, inoculating against culturally deformed truisms. The one blessed with the Christic imagination recognizes what is morally defective in those proposals that gain cultural, and even political, ascendency. Christic imagination would be unintelligible apart from the invisible mission of the Holy Spirit in which the believer discovers authentic freedom (Rom 8:21). The Christian believer who discovers authentic freedom grows from strength to strength. In such a person, we discover the transformation characteristic of Christ's saints.

In both his university teaching and published works, Father Robert Imbelli has illustrated the various dimensions of moral transformation in Christ. Christic imagination provides a shorthand for this program for Christian life.[50] Imbelli further asserts that the one possessed of a Christic imagination goes forth with Christ occupying the center of his or her existence. "Once the Christic center is firm," Imbelli assures his readers, "we can venture forth to the peripheries without fear of losing the way."[51] Faithful to his priestly identity, Father Imbelli has applied his Christic imagination norm to the area of interreligious sensitivity. He holds that only those Christians firmly committed to the person of Jesus find themselves apt to dialogue with those who do not share the Christian faith. It remains a testimony to Father Imbelli's pastoral prudence and fortitude that his teaching

---

49. *Veritatis splendor*, no. 85.

50. Robert Imbelli, *Rekindling the Christic Imagination: Theological Meditations for the New Evangelization* (Collegeville, Minn.: Liturgical Press, 2014), especially 91–95.

51. Imbelli, *Rekindling the Christic Imagination*, 95.

and writing have always placed the person of Christ at the center of theological instruction and social engagement. To his true credit, Father Imbelli has not failed to remind the theological community that salvation in Christ remains possible only through the Paschal mystery. He unwaveringly upholds that salvation comes from a participation in the paschal mystery of Christ. Again, he declares, "to speak of salvation in Christ is to speak especially of the paschal pattern of salvation."[52] Father Imbelli's voice has not gone unheeded. Indeed, the essays in this volume bear witness to the influence he has exercised on theologians old and young. His students at Boston College—now scattered throughout the globe in service to the Church—attest to his influence on them. For my part, I would add that one appreciates Father Imbelli's personal warmth and pastoral charity. I note also his unique ability to remain in touch with many of his students. This thoughtful communication reminds us to remain firmly grounded in the Christic center— that is, in Christ himself the *Splendor of truth*.

---

52. Imbelli, "The Reaffirmation of the Christic Center," 105–6.

11

"To weep with those who weep and to rejoice with those who rejoice"

Signature Divine Affectivity Humanly Expressed in Hugh of St. Victor

BOYD TAYLOR COOLMAN

Paul's Mystical Participation in the Affectivity of Jesus

In his letter to the Philippians, Paul makes a remarkable (yet seemingly seldom remarked) claim as he expresses his intense feelings for the community there: *For God is my witness, how I long for* (ἐπιποθῶ) *all of you with the* σπλάγχνοις *of Christ Jesus* (Phil 1:8 NRSV). *Splangchna* is not easily rendered from Greek, as the variety of terms chosen by translators over the centuries reveals: Latin: *visceribus*; KJV/Douay-Rheims: "the bowels"; NKJV: "affection"; AS: "tender mercies"; 3rd Mil: "compassion"; New Living: "tender compassion"; Good News: "the heart of Christ Jesus himself." In the LXX, the earliest Greek translation of the Old Testament, the term itself translates a Hebrew word, *rahamim*, which can refer to the heart, or to the stomach, or more broadly to a feeling in one's "guts" or even the womb. The older translations are thus not wrong to suggest the more physical translation of viscera or bowels.[1]

But what feeling is it, precisely? In one sense, it is an affective identification with or participation in the pain or suffering of another, hence the common English translation, "compassion" or "tender mercy." But there also seems to be a further dimension that expands the sense of "fellow feeling" to encompass an emotional connection to and investment in not just another's pain but in their entire existence, their whole person, as it were, hence the translation "affection," which could be a synonym for compassion, literally "to be affected by, to undergo with," but which here has the broader connotation of deep care and concern for another "in weal and woe."[2] This becomes evident when paired in Paul's phrasing with the verb ἐπιποθῶ, or in Latin, *cupiam*. His feeling is not merely a passive response to suffering; rather, it is a desire or yearning for someone, distinct from but akin to sexual desire—hence "longing." This is Paul's feeling for the Philippians: he craves or yearns with the gut-wrenching pain of intense solicitude for their flourishing; his heart aches with longing for their wellbeing.

Perhaps even more remarkable here is that Paul, who never knew Jesus in his earthly ministry, never watched Jesus interact with those whom he fed, healed, and taught, and whose letters seem mostly devoid of interest in the events of Jesus' life apart from the paschal mystery, clearly finds it self-evident, needing no explanation, to connect this feelings with that of Jesus: Paul feels *the splangchna of Jesus*. Thirty years after his earthly ministry, the impression of this particular disposition (emotion, feeling, affection) in Jesus was seemingly still actively remembered and perhaps cultivated, still of interest in the accounts of his life and ministry. The synoptic gospels

1. Elizabeth R. Achtemeier, "Mercy, Merciful; Compassion, Pity," *The Interpreter's Dictionary of the Bible*, ed. G. A. Buttrick (New York: Abingdon, 1962–76), 3:352–54: "The Hebrews regarded [the bowels] as the center of the tenderer affections, especially of kindness, benevolence, and pity. The bowels were for them equivalent to our heart as the seat of compassion. When Jesus was confronted with human need, the New Testament therefore says he was moved in his bowels—i.e., he had pity and compassion."

2. See William Barclay, *New Testament Words* (Louisville, Ky.: Westminster John Knox, 1974), 276: "So then in classical Greek the *splagchna* mean the inner parts of man, which are the seat of the deepest emotions. It is from that idea that the verb *splagchnizesthai* was formed in later Greek. It means *to be moved with compassion*, and, from its very derivation, it can be seen that it describes no ordinary pity or compassion, but an emotion that moves a man to the very depths of his being. It is the strongest word in Greek for the feeling of compassion."

convey this impression too, frequently noting the *splangchna*, typically translated "compassion," of Jesus.[3] Perhaps not insignificantly, Jesus himself attributes this feeling to the exemplary figures in two of his most beloved parables in Luke 15:20: the Good Samaritan responds with compassion (*esplagchnisthe*) to the suffering he sees and the father of the Prodigal Son is "moved with compassion" (*esplagchnisthe*) as he sees his son returning home. Safe to say that the New Testament evinces a pronounced concern with the compassion of Jesus.[4]

This New Testament interest in Jesus' *splangchna* may be an ingredient in its conviction about his very identity. It may well be that the experience of this disposition in Jesus was integral to the core conviction that in him, God was "with us," present and acting decisively, as "the Messiah in whom divine mercy is present."[5] Zechariah's prophecy of the coming of the Messiah in Luke's Gospel 1:78–79 NRSV concludes by noting:

By the tender mercy (διὰ σπλάγχνα ἐλέους; *per viscera misericordiae*) of our God,[6] the dawn from on high has broken upon us,[7] to give light to those who sit in darkness and in the shadow of death, to guide our feet into the way of peace.

In some sense, Jesus is the incarnation of divine *splangchna*, however that should be interpreted.

---

3. Cf. Matthew 9:35–38, 14:13–14, 15:32, 20:29–34; Mark 1:35–44, 6:34, 8:2; Luke 7:11–17, 10:33, 15:20. Mark's Gospel records two miraculous feedings of thousands and in both instances, especially the latter, Jesus feeds the crowds, not to demonstrate divine power or to perform impressive, attention-getting tricks, but because of his felt compassion on the hungry crowds. In the first instance, they are like sheep without a shepherd and moved by compassion Jesus teaches them; in the second, they have been listening without eating for three days and moved by compassion he feeds them.

4. See James Gustafson, *Can Ethics Be Christian?* (Chicago: University of Chicago 1975), 101: "an affective sensibility which made [Jesus] identify with the needy, the immoral person, the victim of prejudice."

5. Helmut Köster argues that the term's (*splagchnon, splagchnizomai*) application to Jesus is meant to characterize him as "the Messiah in whom divine mercy is present" See *Theological Dictionary of the New Testament, Volume VII*, ed. Gerhard Kittel, trans. Geoffrey W. Bromiley (Grand Rapids, Mich.: Eerdmans, 1971), 554.

6. King James Version: "bowels of the mercy"; Holman Christian Standard version: "because of our God's merciful compassion"; Good News version: "Our God is merciful and tender"; Douay-Rheims version: "Through the bowels of the mercy of our God."

7. Adopting the alternative reading found in some ancient manuscripts. Other versions read: "will break upon us."

Also striking about Paul's self-description is his claim to possess, or perhaps even to be possessed by, this feeling of Christ's own compassion. It does not seem to be a casual observation about his own emotional state or about its apparent inspiration. That he feels this way is so important that he summons God as his witness, almost as if such a feeling were the necessary condition for and qualification of his apostolic authority. Could it be that this is not only the messianic affectivity, the proof of divine presence, the signature affection of Jesus and of the Father who sent him but also the telltale disposition of his true followers? However that may be, Paul's claim seems stronger than a mere comparison of his feeling to Christ's or even that he somehow is imitating the Lord. Rather, he seems to say: I participate in that present, living reality that we all recognize as the *splangchna* of Jesus.

Lastly, *splangchna* can have a connection to a mother's womb, and by extension to the deep solicitude a mother has for her children, sometimes rendered "womb-pain." This too is foreign neither to Paul nor to Jesus. At various points, Paul uses maternal imagery to talk about his apostolic labors, sometimes actually referring to himself as a mother: *I am in labor pains until Christ is formed in you*, he tells the Galatians in 4:19, and toward the Thessalonians: he acts *like a nurse caring for her own children,* as related in 1 Thessalonians 2:7.[8] Here, too, a precedent lies in the life of Jesus, who once compared himself to a mother hen desiring to gather her chicks under her wings (Mt 23:37; Lk 13:34).[9]

Noteworthy is that this affective disposition is not merely descriptive in Paul's writings; it is also prescriptive: Believers must strive to cultivate this moral and spiritual trait. A later Pauline writing (Col 3:12) exhorts its readers to "put on compassionate mercy" (*splánchna oiktirmoú*; *viscera misericordiae*) and, most importantly for present purposes, Paul tells the Roman believers "to weep with those who weep and to rejoice with those who rejoice" (Rom 12:15), expanding this maternal solicitude to include a crucial positive aspect to this maternal disposition: to rejoice with the joy of another.

8. See Beverly Roberts Gaventa, *Our Mother Saint Paul* (Louisville, Ky.: Westminster John Knox, 2007).

9. In *Jesus of Nazareth: From the Baptism in the Jordan to the Transfiguration* (New York: Doubleday, 2007), Pope Benedict XVI observes, regarding the Good Samaritan of the Gospel parable: "His heart is wrenched open. The Gospel uses the word that in Hebrew had originally referred to the mother's womb and maternal care. Seeing this man in such a state is a blow that strikes him 'viscerally,' touching his soul. 'He had compassion' — that is how we translate the text today, diminishing its original vitality" (197).

To what extent the subsequent history of Christian discipleship took this affectivity as exemplary, imitable, even requisite cannot be assayed here, but it may surprise both casual and learned readers alike to learn that at a particular moment in the high Middle Ages, namely, during the so-called "twelfth-century renaissance," interest in this affectivity (linked to Jesus and Paul) rose to apparently unprecedented intensity. This chapter hopes to highlight that moment by demonstrating that various twelfth-century thinkers, but especially Hugh of St. Victor (d. 1141), who prized a bivalent capacity for fellow-feeling, conceived of not only as a capacity to cosuffer another's pain but also as a complementary capacity to copleasure another's joy. The first of these they often called *compassio*—to suffer in some way the pain of another; the second, they often termed *congratulatio*—to celebrate, rejoice with, take pleasure in the wellbeing of another. These were not merely esteemed human feelings; for many, they constituted the signature affectivity of humanness itself.

The importance of this observation lies in part in the fact that while theoretical reflection on compassion figures centrally in much contemporary ethical theory (e.g., Davies, Wyschogrod, Nusbaum), congratulations (corejoicing, copleasure) are virtually neglected (note the absence of a meaningful modern English term), though it would seem to have as much ethical value as the former.

Maternal Affectivity in the Twelfth Century: "Breasts of Compassion and Congratulation"

Twelfth-century interest in this bivalent affectivity should be located within the broader contemporary phenomenon of interest (devotional and doctrinal) in the humanity of Jesus, especially his suffering humanity,[10]

10. Cf. Boyd Taylor Coolman, "Hugh of St. Victor on Jesus Wept: Making Christological Sense of Jesus' Tears and Conceiving Ideal *Humanitas* in the Twelfth Century," *Theological Studies* 69, no. 3 (2008): 528–56: "toward the end of the eleventh century, interest in the humanity of Jesus surged markedly throughout Europe. Poets, preachers, artists, and monks, in places such as London, Paris, and Rome, gave expression to this apparently deep and widespread shift in religious feeling." The literature on this theme is immense. In the middle of the previous century, R. W. Southern observed: "This power of St. Anselm and St. Bernard to give varied and coherent expression to the perceptions and aspirations which they shared with their contemporaries is most clearly seen in their treatment of the central theme of Christian thought: the life of Christ and the meaning of the Crucifixion. The theme of tenderness and compassion for the sufferings

concomitant with a shift toward loving kindness, tenderness, and solicitude, which some have styled a feminization of piety that valorized motherhood and the various dispositions associated with mothering. "In the later middle ages, Christian men were increasingly measured against more 'feminine' standards of godliness placing new value on love, compassion, forgiveness, mildness, sweetness, and nurturing."[11] Beginning in the late eleventh century, a "thin stream of compassion and tenderness" became a "flood which, in the later centuries of the Middle Ages, obliterated the traces of an older severity and reticence."[12]

As Caroline Walker Bynum noted many years ago, this shift in sensibility is well-exemplified by the writings of Anselm of Canterbury at the dawn of the period under consideration.[13] Attentive reader of scripture that he was, Anselm espied the above-noted maternal dispositions in Paul and Jesus, in his meditational prayer to them:

> O St Paul, where is he that was called the nurse of the faithful, caressing his sons? Who is that affectionate mother who declares everywhere that she is in labor for her sons? O mother of well known tenderness, may your son feel your viscera of maternal piety.... And you, Jesus, are you not also a mother? Are you not the mother who, like a hen, gathers her chickens under her wings? ... For, longing to bear sons into life, you [Jesus] tasted of death, and by dying you begot them.[14]

---

and helplessness of the Saviour of the world was one which had a new birth in the monasteries of the eleventh century, and every century since then has paid tribute to the monastic inspiration of this century by some new development of this theme" (R. W. Southern, *The Making of the Middle Ages* [New Haven, Conn.: Yale University, 1953], 231). See also Rachel Fulton, *From Judgment to Passion: Devotion to Christ and the Virgin Mary, 800–1200* (New York: Columbia University, 2002). For later developments in this regard, see Ellen M. Ross, *The Grief of God: Images of the Suffering Jesus in Late Medieval England* (New York: Oxford University, 1997), and Paul Gondreau, *The Passions of Christ's Soul in the Theology of St. Thomas Aquinas*, Beiträge zur Geschichte der Philosophie und Theologie des Mittelalters, NF, 61 (Münster: Aschendorff, 2002).

11. Robert Baldwin, "Shifts in Late Medieval Culture," unpublished essay.

12. Southern, *Making of the Middle Ages*, 233: "it was the Cistercians who were the chief agents in turning into the flood which, in the later centuries of the Middle Ages, obliterated the traces of an older severity and reticence. In this expression of an ever-heightening emotion all countries in western Europe had a share, and at different periods led the way. In the twelfth century leadership belonged to France, and probably, one should add, England."

13. Bynum, *Jesus as Mother: Studies in the Spirituality of the High Middle Ages* (Berkeley: University of California, 1982).

14. Anselm of Canterbury, *Prayers and Meditations of St Anselm*, trans. Benedicta Ward (London: Penguin Books, 1973), 152–56.

For Anselm, it is especially yearning desire that signals the presence of this maternal trait, a trait that is found preeminently in Jesus and then made available to Paul:

Then both of you are mothers.... You [Jesus] by your own act, you [Paul] by his power.

Therefore you are fathers by your effect and mothers by your affection. Fathers by your authority, mothers by your kindness. Fathers by your teaching, mothers by your mercy.

Then you, Lord, are a mother and you, Paul, are a mother too.[15]

Anselm's interest in this maternal theme, when noticed at all, is typically paired with a similar theme in the writings of Julian of Norwich, who famously spoke of Jesus as Mother. But he stands at the headwaters of a stream of spirituality flowing directly into the immediately subsequent generations.

One striking aspect of this development in affectivity is the widespread tendency to see the maternal breast of a mother (not a lover!) as an image or symbol of these twin dispositions of compassion and congratulation. Writing in the late eleventh century, for example, the often impatient reformer, Cardinal Peter Damian, found it obvious to link the better-than-wine breasts of the bride in the Song of Songs with the Pauline injunction in Romans 12:15 to weep and to rejoice. For Peter, Paul's words "depict the whole of religion" and "with these breasts, mother Church suckles those making progress and nourishes the perfect."[16] Pauline rejoicing occurs when the mind, "affixing of the whole affect of its desire in the high point of divine contemplation ... rejoices in the Lord," and "the soul exults in its God,"[17] as Isaiah 61 relates. This "is the breast of congratulation (*mamilla congratulationis*), from which the milk of exhortation pours fourth, by which the perfect

---

15. Anselm of Canterbury, *Prayers and Meditations*, 152–56.

16. Peter Damian, "Sermon 29 – On Saint Mary Magdalene" (PL 145.660d–661a): "*Vere meliora sunt ubera sponsae vino isto* (Cant. I). Quaenam autem sunt illa? Procedat in medium Paulus apostolus, et ubera felici lacte manantia nobis assignet. '*Gaudere*, inquit, [661A] *cum gaudentibus, et flere cum flentibus*' (Rom XII). O quam brevi sermunculo totius religionis depinxit insigne, tam eleganti clausula proposuit pietatem, aequitatem statuit, submovit invidiam. His uberibus mater Ecclesia lactat proficientes, perfectos nutrit."

17. Peter Damian, "Sermon 29 – On Saint Mary Magdalene" (PL 145.661b): "et in divinae contemplationis acumen totum desiderii sui figens affectum, gaudens, gaudet in Domino, et exsultat anima sua in Deo suo (Isa. LXI)."

are nourished."[18] Pauline weeping, conversely, is a "religious sadness that grieves over sin, either one's own or another's."[19] One disposed thus knows

how to instruct sinners in a spirit of leniency, to suspend vindictiveness, and [to give succor] in their viscera to a sinner with full affection. From this breast of compassion [*mamilla compassionis*] flows forth the milk of consolation, and with this milk the Apostle fed those who were not mature enough for solid food.[20]

In the first half of the twelfth century, Bernard of Clairvaux used the same imagery and terms but to make a different point, orienting both aspects of this affectivity to the circumstances of others: "She [the abbot who is a true mother] knows how to rejoice with those who rejoice and to be sad with those who sorrow [Rom 12:15], pressing the milk of encouragement without intermission from the breast of joyful sympathy, the milk of consolation from the breast of compassion."[21] For Bernard, as Bynum noted, "breasts are a symbol of the pouring out toward others of affectivity or of instruction and almost invariably suggests to him a discussion of the duties of prelates or abbots."[22] In the middle of the same century, another Cistercian abbot, Gilbert of Hoyland (d. 1172), admonished other abbots: "Let the feeling of compassion and congratulation be born within you, but let it flow … as through breasts to nourish your hearers."[23] For, "breasts of grace, breasts of consolation, are better than the wine of austerity and harshness, because they are more effective, better able to change sad and exasperated feelings,

18. Peter Damian, "Sermon 29 – On Saint Mary Magdalene" (PL 145.661c): "Haec est mamilla congratulationis, de qua lac exhortationis effunditur, quo nutriuntur perfecti (Isa. LXVI), ut cum avulsi fuerint a lacte isto, epulentur ab introitu gloriae Dei."

19. Peter Damian, "Sermon 29 – On Saint Mary Magdalene" (PL 145.661c): "Religiosa enim tristitia, aut alienum peccatum luget, aut proprium."

20. Peter Damian, "Sermon 29 – On Saint Mary Magdalene" (PL 145.661d): "Beati quorum luctus in hac intentione versatur, quia consolatoriam possunt exspectare dulcedinem. Quam leni et dulcissimo spiritu imbibitus est spiritus illius, qui novit in spiritu lenitatis peccantes instruere, suspendere vindictam, et affectuosis officiis in viscerare sibi peccatorem, donec vitae reddatur. De hac compassionis mamilla lac consolationis effunditur, et hoc lacte pascit Apostolus illos qui solido cibo vesci non possunt (I Cor. III)."

21. Bernard of Clairvaux, "Sermon 10," par. 3 (*Sancti Bernardi Opera* 1:49–50; trans. Walsh, *Song* 1:62–63).

22. Bynum, *Jesus as Mother*, 115.

23. Gilbert of Hoyland, *Sermons on the Song of Songs I–IV*, vol. 2, *Sermons super Cantica Canticorum*, trans. Lawrence C. Braceland, 3 vols., Cistercian Fathers 20 (Kalamazoo, Mich.: Cistercian Publications, 1979), 31.4.

and to strengthen weak and tender feelings. They persuade more readily and encourage more gently."[24] About the same time, Aelred of Rievaulx (d. 1167) exhorted recluses: "Thus clasp the whole world to your breast of love, there at once contemplate and rejoice in those who are good, gaze upon and weep for those who are evil."[25]

As noted, this construction of ideal (masculine) *humanitas*, by appropriating traditional maternal imagery, reflects a certain feminization of ideal *humanitas* in the twelfth century, as "admiration for qualities that were regarded as distinctively feminine, such as piety, mercy, and tenderness" emerged and "the warm, tender, loving qualities associated with ... mothers generally, were admired in men no less than women,"[26] in contrast with harshness (*crudelitas*), anger, wrath, cruelty, and envy.

While Cistercian authors figure prominently in the affective developments noted above and have thus garnered the lion's share of scholarly attention, Hugh of St. Victor also singled out these twin maternal affections for special consideration: "There are two breasts of clemency: compassion from which flows the milk of consolation, by which the weak are nourished; congratulation, whence flows the milk of encouragement, by which the strong are sustained."[27]

Compassion: "To weep with those who weep"

Hugh's most sustained discussion of the nature and importance of compassion occurs in his treatment of it in the human nature of Jesus Christ.[28] There, Hugh attributes to Jesus' human nature a human willing, which he

24. Gilbert of Hoyland, *Sermons on the Song of Songs I–IV*, vol. 2, 31.5.

25. Cited in Bynum, *Jesus as Mother*, 95.

26. Giles Constable, *The Reformation of the Twelfth Century* (Cambridge: Cambridge University Press, 1998), 66. Constable notes: "the works of Cabassut, McLaughlin, and Bynum have shown the importance of the devotion to Christ our mother, but much research remains to be done on the broader use of maternal and feminine imagery ... which were current already in the early twelfth century" (67).

27. Hugh of St. Victor, *Miscellanea*, 116 (PL 177.744a–b): "Duo clementium esse ubera. Duo sunt clementium ubera: compassio de qua fluit lac consolationis, quo nutriuntur infirmi; congratulatio, [744B] unde fluit lac adhortationis, quo sustentantur validi."

28. Hugh of St. Victor, *On the Four Wills in Christ* [*De quatuor voluntatibus in Christo libellus*] PL 176.841b–846c (hereafter, *Quat. Volunt.*). All translations are mine. Only six columns in the Patrologia Latina, this short work appears to be the first medieval treatise devoted to the theme of Christ's compassion. Lactantius' (240–320) fourth-century *Divinae Institutiones* (6.10–16) contains what appears to be the closest prior (and perhaps singular) instance of similar attention to

calls the "will of tender pity" (*voluntas pietatis*). With that will, Jesus "sighed deeply over another's evil through compassion."[29] Hugh finds two Gospel warrants for positing this will in Christ. The first is Luke's account in 19:41 of Christ weeping over Jerusalem: *When he approached Jerusalem, seeing the city he wept.*[30] Hugh asks: "Why did Jesus weep if he was not mourning?" What was Jesus mourning? The perdition of the city's inhabitants: "If he was mournful concerning the perdition of [the city's inhabitants], he did not will their perdition."[31] Hugh interprets Jesus' tears as an expression of felt sorrow over the eternal fate of Jerusalem's unbelieving inhabitants, which he does not wish, according to his compassionate will (*secundum pietatis*).

The second text is the account of Jesus' emotional turmoil at the death of Lazarus in John 11. Hugh notes with care the language with which John describes Jesus' emotional response to his friend's death. Hugh's text reads: *Jesus groaned in spirit and troubled* (turbavit) *himself.* "Attend to this," Hugh admonishes: "How did he trouble himself? What was that troubling by which Jesus troubled himself?" This *turbatio*—literally, "a disturbance"—was, he argues, *pietas*, which he then glosses as "commiseration" (*miseratio*). He then asks: "Is he who is moved by *pietas* rightly troubled with a good troubling?" Hugh's answer is yes: Jesus troubled himself as he "willingly (*sponte*) received commiseration."[32] Hugh concludes: "So also Jesus, in his assumed humanity, while he willed to bear it passibly, endured both passion in body and compassion in mind, through the property of his humanity."[33]

---

this theme. Aquinas cites Hugh's *De quatuor voluntatibus* in both the *Scriptum* on the *Sentences* [*In III Sent*, d. 17, a. 1 sol. 3, obj 6; d. 17, a. 3, sol. 4 ad 2] and in the *Summa Theologica* [3, q. 18, a. 3 c].

29. Hugh of St. Victor, *Quat. Volunt.* (PL 176.841b–c): "voluntas pietatis per compassionem in malo alieno suspirabat."

30. Hugh of St. Victor, *Quat. Volunt.* (PL 176.842b): "Cum appropinquaret Jerusalem videns civitatem flevit super eam (Lk 19)."

31. Hugh of St. Victor, *Quat. Volunt.* (PL 176.842b): "Quare flebat si non dolebat? Ergo noluit quod doluit. Quid doluit? perditionem. Si doluit de perditione illorum, noluit perditionem illorum."

32. Any anxiety over such a disturbance in Christ is removed for Hugh by the fact that Jesus actively, willingly gave himself over to this emotion rather than being passively afflicted by it. Hugh compares the situation to Jesus' betrayal by Judas [*Quat. Volunt.* (PL 176.846a)]: "Sicut tradidit semetipsum, quando Judas tradidit eum: sic turbavit semetipsum quando miseratio turbavit eum" [Just as he gave himself over, when Judas gave him up: so he troubled himself when commiseration troubled him].

33. Hugh of St. Victor, *Quat. Volunt.* (PL 176.845b–c): "Scriptum est: Jesus autem infremuit spiritu et turbavit semetipsum (Jn 11). Hic intendite: Turbavit semetipsum (Jn 11). Quomodo

Hugh is impressed as much with Jesus' compassion as with his passion, as is evident in the rhetorical cadence of this passage:

For this reason, the God-man, who came to remove both suffering and co-suffering, endured both. He took on suffering in the flesh; he took on co-suffering in mind. In both, he willed to languish for us, so that he might heal us who were languishing. He was weakened by suffering in his penalty; he was weakened by co-suffering for another's misery. He bore his passion that he might die for those were going to die; he bore compassion that he might weep for those who were going to perish. For the sake of misery, he handed over his flesh to suffering; for the sake of heart-misery, he stirred up his own soul to co-suffering. In his own flesh he was pained for us by his passion; in his own mind he co-sorrowed for us by compassion.[34]

Hugh is patently moved himself by Jesus' tears and willing acceptance of commiseration and compassion for fallen humanity. His consistent pairing of passion and compassion suggests that for our Victorine, the intensity of the latter matches that of the former: to whatever extent Jesus suffered physically, he also cosuffered psychically, that is, through compassion.

With Christ serving as exemplar, Hugh turns to this theme in human beings generally. What can be said? First, Hugh refers to this as an *affectus compassionis*, a feeling of compassion. "In a heart-wretched way," he says, "tender pity willed not the perdition of the miserable, according to the feeling of compassion."[35] Again, "there is a certain feeling of compassion" that

---

turbavit? Quae fuit ista turbatio qua semetipsum turbavit Jesus? Pietas ipsa, miseratio ipsa fuit turbatio. Bona turbatio, bene turbabatur qui pietate movebatur? Turbavit seipsum. Miseratio turbavit eum, et ipse semetipsum turbavit, qui miserationem sponte suscepit. Sicut tradidit semetipsum, quando Judas tradidit eum: sic turbavit semetipsum quando miseratio turbavit eum.... Sic itaque Jesus in humanitate assumpta quandiu eam passibilem portare voluit secundum proprietatem humanitatis et passionem in carne et compassionem in mente portavit."

34. Hugh of St. Victor, *Quat. Volunt.* (PL 176.844d–845a): "Propterea Deus homo, qui utrumque tollere venit utrumque toleravit. Suscepit passionem in carne; suscepit compassionem in mente. In utroque aegrotare voluit propter nos, ut in utroque nos aegrotantes sanaret. Infirmatus est passione in poena sua; infirmatus est compassione in miseria aliena. Eousque passionem sustinuit, ut pro morituris moreretur, eousque compassionem suscepit, ut pro perituris lacrymaretur. Propter miseriam carnem suam tradidit ad passionem, propter misericordiam animam suam turbavit ad compassionem. In carne sua doluit pro nobis patiendo, in mente sua condoluit nobis compatiendo."

35. Hugh of St. Victor, *Quat. Volunt.* (PL 176.842d): "Similiter et pietas quod secundum affectum compassionis in poena vel perditione miserorum misericorditer noluit."

prompts us to "commiserate with" others.[36] What is the nature of this *affectus compassionis*? Noting the various terms Hugh employs sheds light. In addition to *compassio*, which we have noted, Hugh often employs the verb *condolore*, meaning to cosorrow or comourn, to describe it: "For just as illness of the flesh is suffering, so sorrow of the mind is compassion."[37] Used more or less synonymously is the verb *miserare*, to commiserate. Etymologically related to *miserare* is the noun *misericordia*, used throughout the Latin Vulgate to render the Greek *splánchna*, referring to the innards or bowels, from which deep human emotions might emanate.[38] Hugh says that the proper object of the will of tender pity is *misericordiam*, perhaps best rendered as "wretchedness of heart."[39] Or again: the will of tender pity "loved *misericordia*, which was its own."[40] Each of these terms has classical, biblical, and patristic resonances, which cannot be pursued.[41] Suffice to say that Hugh's use of them creates a rich semantic field surrounding Christ's compassionate affectivity.

Second, Hugh imbues compassion with a basic moral significance, both for those who proffer and for those who receive it. "In this life," he says, "to be compassionate is of virtue."[42] Later, he distinguishes between vicious, natural, and virtuous compassion.

36. Hugh of St. Victor, *Quat. Volunt.* (PL 176.844c): "Est tamen quidam compassionis affectus ... secundum quem ... naturae non exstinguendae miseremur."

37. Hugh of St. Victor, *Quat. Volunt.* (PL 176.844d): "Sicut enim aegritudo carnis est pati, ita aegritudo mentis est compati."

38. See Introduction, above.

39. Hugh of St. Victor, *Quat. Volunt.* (PL 176.842c): "voluntas humanitatis misericordiam" [the human will (toward) tenderheartedness].

40. Hugh of St. Victor, *Quat. Volunt.* (PL 176.843a): "sed quod suum erat amavit misericordiam."

41. George H. Williams, "Mercy in the Grounding of a Non-Elitist Ecological Ethic," 29, observes: "Classical Latin had a close equivalent of the Septuagintal and New Testament *splánchna* in misericordia. Already in Cicero this meant literally wretchedness in the heart or the breast (pericardium) of someone who knows sorrow and is acquainted with grief. When Jerome rendered the Old and the New Testament in Latin as the authoritative Vulgate, misericordia was his main term for rachamim, *splánchna*, mercy. 'Have mercy upon me' of Psalm 51:1 and elsewhere became the supplicatory imperative, Miserere. In the parable of the prodigal son, for example, where the Greek had the verbal form of *splánchna*, Jerome has the father 'moved by misericordia' (Lk 15:20). Even the Stoic emotionless clementia of superior mercy acquired in Christian usage and later in the Romance languages the component of compassion, taking it over from misericordia. The Latin language and its vernaculars have refined the terminology for what emotionally takes place among people and also what is thought to have been revealed about God himself."

42. Hugh of St. Victor, *Quat. Volunt.* (PL 176.843b): "Hic compati virtutis est."

The mode of compassion is threefold. For compassion is either from vice, from nature, or from virtue. Compassion from vice is when the affect is touched by a reprehensible sorrow there, where it was earlier held fast by an illicit love. Compassion from nature is when from the affect of piety implanted within itself, the soul co-sorrows the distress of another, as often as it sees nature oppressed or afflicted against the measure of pity or humanity. Compassion from virtue is when, for God's sake, we co-suffer the sorrow/pain of another, that is, when we see the just oppressed or the innocent afflicted. Compassion from vice is culpable; compassion from nature is not reprehensible; compassion from virtue is praise-worthy. The first is reprehended; the third is praised. But the second does not have guilt, since it is from nature; neither does it have reward, since it is not from virtue.[43]

For Hugh, the necessity of compassionating the suffering of others is itself, like suffering itself, part of the penalty inflicted on fallen human beings: "to suffer and to co-suffer are both punishments." Yet there is this difference between them: "Suffering is given to human beings for iniquity, while co-suffering is commanded for goodness."[44] And here the moral dimension emerges, as Hugh explains:

For it is just and right before God that the one who suffers should also co-suffer, in order that sin may be removed through suffering and that goodness may be increased through co-suffering. For this surely pertains to the goodness of mortal life, that one conform oneself to the conditions of others and be made a participant in another's suffering through co-suffering, in order that, as that which is suffered is a necessity, so that which is co-suffered might be a work of goodness.[45]

43. Hugh of St. Victor, *Quat. Volunt.* (PL 176.844a–b): "Triplex enim compassionis modus est. Est quippe compassio, alia ex vitio alia ex natura, alia ex virtute. Compassio ex vitio est quando affectus illic reprehensibili dolore tangitur, ubi illicito prius amore tenebatur. Compassio ex natura est quando ex insito sibi pietatis affectu animus alienis aerumnis condolet, quoties contra pietatis vel humanitatis mensuram naturam opprimi sive affligi videt. Compassio ex virtute est quando propter Deum alienis doloribus compatimur cum scilicet vel justitiam premi vel innocentiam affligi videmus. Compassio ex vitio, culpabilis est; compassio ex natura, irreprehensibilis; compassio ex virtute laudabilis, prima reprehenditur, tertia laudatur. Secunda autem nec culpam habet, quia ex natura est; nec praemium, quia ex virtute non est."

44. Hugh of St. Victor, *Quat. Volunt.* (PL 176.843b): "Pati et compati utrumque poena est. Pati datum est homini pro iniquitate; compati autem praeceptum est pro bonitate."

45. Hugh of St. Victor, *Quat. Volunt.* (PL 176.843b): "Justum est enim et aequum coram Deo, ut qui patitur compatiatur, ut per passionem deleatur iniquitas, per compassionem exerceatur bonitas. Hoc siquidem ad bonitatem pertinet vitae mortalis, ut se in aliis conditioni suae accommodet, et alienae passionis per compassionem particeps efficiatur, ut sicut id quod patitur necessitatis

Hugh does not elaborate regarding the nature of this goodness, but the implication seems to be that even though co-suffering is technically a punishment that afflicts fallen human beings,[46] it is nonetheless a moral good to be cultivated.[47]

Third, for Hugh, compassion is strictly a this-worldly virtue, because cosuffering can exist only in the presence of suffering, and only while the soul itself is passible, that is, in this present life, can it undergo compassion. In the next life, neither suffering of the body nor cosuffering of the mind will be possible.[48] So Hugh notes the proper time and context of compassion. "If you seek the time: we ought to co-suffer as long as we are able to suffer."[49] The proper context for compassion is where there is still hope: "the misery of compassion ought to be shown forth there, where the pity of suffering is not yet to be despaired of."[50]

---

est, ita id quod compatitur opus sit bonitatis." Again, *Quat. Volunt.* (PL 176.843c): "Hic compateris voluntate, moveris pietate, condoles bonitate" [In this life, you will co-suffer through the will, you will move through tender pity, you will co-sorrow through goodness].

46. Similarly, Thomas Aquinas, *Summa Theologica*, 3 q. 15, a. 6 ad 3: "All sorrow is an evil of punishment; but it is not always an evil of fault, except only when it proceeds from an inordinate affection."

47. Hugh's distinction between natural and virtuous compassion seems to anticipate a similar distinction emphasized in the early modern period. See Jennifer A. Herdt, "The Endless Construction of Charity: On Milbank's Critique of Political Economy," *Journal of Religious Ethics* 32, no. 2 (2004), 301–24. Herdt notes that, while some early modern thinkers (e.g., late seventeenth-century Latitudinarian divines) championed the superiority of natural, involuntary compassion, "insofar as a trend does appear over time, it was away from sympathy as an involuntary instinct and toward imaginative understanding as an intentional practice that builds on natural sympathetic impulses" (305).

48. Hugh of St. Victor, *Quat. Volunt.* (PL 176.843a–c): "pietas amore compassionis passibiliter movetur, praesenti tantum vitae debitum est ... tunc utique sicut carnem nec passio neque timor passionis ullius affliget; sic mens nullam ex compassione alieni doloris poenam suscipiet.... Sic itaque compati esse non potest, nisi illic tantum ubi pati esse potest, quoniam et ipsum compati, pati est" [that tender pity is moved passibly by co-suffering love, is owed only in the present life ... for in the next life, just as neither suffering nor the fear of any suffering will afflict the flesh, so the mind will endure no punishment from co-suffering for another's sorrow.... And so co-suffering thus is not possible, except there alone where suffering is possible, since co-suffering is itself suffering].

49. Hugh of St. Victor, *Quat. Volunt.* (PL 176.844b–c): "Si igitur tempus compassionis quaeris, quandiu pati possumus compati debemus."

50. Hugh of St. Victor, *Quat. Volunt.* (PL 176.844c): "Si locum quaeris, illic compassionis miseria exhibenda est, ubi adhuc passionis misericordia desperanda non est." Hugh adduces a biblical example to confirm his point: "David, aegrotante filio, lacrymas fudit; mortuo faciem

In the proper time and context, compassion is also to be cultivated and exhibited rightly. For Hugh, this means that in its compassion, the soul must not "transcend the measure of justice,"[51] in so far as this is known. Where someone suffers for violating a clear precept of divine law, Hugh demurs regarding compassion: "But where the intention of divine justice is revealed as immutably fixed, against that . . . the place of tender pity is not owed."[52] The Victorine suggests, however, that in this present life, certainty regarding divine justice often eludes human understanding, and in such situations, justice should always give way to compassion:

But in this life, where we can neither know nor foreknow perfectly the meaning of divine justice, we also can without injustice will certain things which are not just according to divine justice; but let this alone pertain to us that, where we are ignorant of what pleases God more, we should choose above all that which concords with tender pity.[53]

For Hugh, it is always better to err on the side of mercy and compassion.

All of this leads Hugh to his strongest endorsement of compassion. At the very outset of his Christological analysis, as he introduces Christ's will of tender pity (*voluntas pietatis*), he observes that this is also called simply the *voluntas humanitatis*, the "will of humanity," or more simply the "human will." Earlier, he had spoken of tender pity as "pertaining to true humanity." Here, he elaborates:

---

lavit (2 Kgs 12), ut ostenderet quod tandiu compassionis miseria portanda est quandiu passionis misericordia desperanda non est. Est tamen quidam compassionis affectus qui naturam etiam perditam miseratione prosequitur, secundum quem in nostri generis similitudine sicut culpae non corrigendae irascimur ita naturae non exstinguendae miseremur" [As long as his son was sick, David poured forth tears; after he died, David washed his face (2 Kgs 12), in order to show that the misery of co-suffering was to be borne, so long as the pity of suffering was not to be despaired of. Yet there is a certain feeling of co-suffering, which follows fallen nature in misery, according to which in the likeness of our kind, just as we are angered at guilt not yet set aright, so we commiserate nature not yet extinguished].

51. Hugh of St. Victor, *Quat. Volunt.* (PL 176: 844b): "animus in compassione justitiae mensuram non transcendit."

52. Hugh of St. Victor, *Quat. Volunt.* (PL 176: 844a): "Ubi autem divinae justitiae sententia immutabiliter praefixa ostenditur, contra eam deinceps pietati locus non debetur."

53. Hugh of St. Victor, *Quat. Volunt.* (PL 176: 843d–844a): "In hac autem vita ubi ejusdem divinae justitiae sententiam perfecte nec scire nec praescire possumus, quaedam etiam quae secundum ipsam justa non sunt sine injustitia velle possumus; quia hoc solum ad nos pertinet ut ubi nescimus quid potius Deo placet, hoc potissimum eligamus quod pietati concordat."

For that tender pity is called humanity, and they are called human who pity tenderly, and [who] readily compassionate the miseries of others. For it is proper to humanity to compassionate and to be moved with tender pity by the misery of others. An animal can suffer, but to compassionate is the property of humanity. For this reason the will of tender pity is called the human will, because it is of a human being to be moved with tender pity.[54]

Evident here is how central compassion is to Hugh's conception of ideal human nature, preeminently in that which Christ assumed,[55] but also in that which humans bear generally. To have such a will is to compassionate the misery of others, and to be so moved is basically and properly human.

Congratulation: "To rejoice with those who rejoice"

Of the two maternal affections under consideration here, compassion garners the larger share of attention among twelfth-century authors, including Hugh. But he does not neglect the other one, whose ethical significance, as noted above, would seem to be just as robust, namely, congratulations—"to rejoice with those who rejoice."

That Hugh and the Victorine tradition emanating from him identify this as a distinct and spiritually/morally significant feeling or affection is apparent in a catalogue of such affections that Hugh describes in a short treatise on prayer. For him, interestingly enough, the power or efficaciousness of prayer stems from the intensity of the affections that prompt and accompany it: "Since therefore all the power of prayer is in the affections of piety (*affectibus pietatis*), let us enumerate those ... that are praiseworthy and acceptable to God."[56] Among the nine that he lists, Hugh includes "the feel-

---

54. Hugh of St. Victor, *Quat. Volunt.* (PL 176.842b): "Nam ipsa pietas humanitas vocatur, et dicuntur humani qui pii sunt, et facile alienis miseriis compatiuntur. Proprium est enim humanitatis compati et moveri pietate in miseria aliena. Bestia pati potest, compati autem humanitatis est proprium. Idcirco voluntas pietatis, voluntas humanitatis vocatur, quia hominis est pietate moveri."

55. Hugh of St. Victor, *Quat. Volunt.* (PL 176.842b): "Et haec similiter secundum naturam humanitatis in Christo invenitur."

56. Hugh of St. Victor, *Virtute Orandi* 14 (152–56:391–436). *L'œuvre de Hugues de Saint-Victor, I: De institutione novitiorum; De virtute orandi; De laude caritatis; De arrha anime*, ed. and trans. H. B. Feiss, P. Sicard, D. Poirel, and H. Rochais, Sous la Règle de Saint Augustin (Turnhout: Brepols, 1997): "Quia igitur in affectibus pietatis est omnis virtus orandi, enumeremus aliquot ex ipsis, et exemplis demonstremus, ut quia omnes enumerare non possumus (infiniti enim sunt affectus) quid tamen in omnibus laudabile sit, et Deo acceptum, ex quibusdam conjiciamus."

ing of congratulation," which emerges when "the mind is filled with a kind of cheerfulness upon seeing something acceptable or well-pleasing,"[57] or arises "from the commemoration of certain prosperous events and felicitous deeds."[58]

One example of such sources of congratulation is the divine nature itself and its activity in the economy of creation and salvation. Strikingly, given the theme of this essay, another Hugonian text orients this human feeling of rejoicing in good things toward the awareness of divine compassion toward sinful human beings: the devout mind

marvels at the divine pity which caused the divine majesty to have compassion on us; it marvels at the divine majesty that did not allow such pity to be affected by our compassion and disturbed by our care. [For if there were such goodness but not such majesty, our evils would overwhelm God; but if there were such majesty but not such goodness, his goodness would not have condescended to us.] Let us rejoice in the goodness of such majesty for its own sake, lest it be affected for us; let us rejoice in the immensity of such goodness for our sake, that it compassionated us.[59]

More directly germane to the moral or ethical dimension of this feeling, though, is Hugh's directing it toward the good that one encounters in another. While *compassio* is directed at the evil or suffering (*malum*) that befalls another, *congratulatio* focuses on the good (*bonum*) of another, whether the goodness of another's moral virtue or the benefits or blessings—good things—that another possesses: "For truly if you love the virtuous, whatever

---

57. Hugh of St. Victor, *Virtute Orandi* 14 (152–56:391–436): "Est affectus congratulationis, cum acceptabile aliquid et beneplacitum videns, quadam hilaritate perfunditur."

58. Hugh of St. Victor, *Virtute Orandi* 14 (152–56:391–436): "De istis affectibus primi tres ad istud praecipue genus Scripturarum pertinent, in quo fit laudatio. Quia scilicet ex commemoratione bonitatis, surgit affectus dilectionis, ex commemoratione potentiae et fortitudinis surgit affectus admirationis, ex commmemoratione autem alicujus prosperi eventus et facti felicis surgit affectus congratulationis."

59. Hugh of St. Victor, *Misc.*, 1.120 (PL 177.545d–546a): "Mens pia jugi contemplatione Creatoris sui reficitur, et quanto magis ejus bonitatem cogitat, tanto amplius ejus amore inflammatur. Miratur pietatem quae tantam majestatem ad nostram compassionem inflectit; miratur majestatem, quae tantam pietatem nostri compassione et providentia affici et perturbari non sinit. Si enim tanta bonitas esset, et tanta majestas non esset, mala nostra ad Deum redundarent. Si autem tanta majestas esset et tanta bonitas non esset, bona ejus ad nos non descenderent. Congratulamur [546A] ergo bonitati de tanta majestate propter ipsum, ne pro nobis afficiatur; congratulamur immensitati de tanta bonitate propter nos, ut nobis compatiatur."

blessing comes to them makes the charity which is in you rejoice (*gratulatur*) as though the benefit were yours and not another's."[60] Most fundamentally, *congratulatio* loves the good regardless of where it is found, and loves it *as if* it were its own. That is, in true *congratulatio*, the ego boundaries that typically create and maintain the distinction between "mine" and "yours" cease to exist. One simply delights and rejoices in the good, *simpliciter*. It is not that one loses one's self, that is, that the self ceases to exist; rather, the self expands, is literally magnanimous—"large souled"—not in the sense that one is generous to others (as the term magnanimous is often defined, though of course that is not excluded) but more literally in that one has become *affectively* one with others.

But Hugh goes further. This "affective identification" with others is also exponentially expansive of the affectivity that produces it. Speaking of an individual's experience of the love of God, Hugh observes that such bliss increases and multiplies the more that it is shared:

Indeed it would be blessed to enjoy this love alone, but it is much more blessed to delight in it with the co-rejoicing [lit. *congratulatio*] of many good individuals, for, when in those also who are co-participants the feeling of love is expanded, the joys of charity and sweetness are amplified.[61]

Hugh here describes an affective unity among individuals that is not only noncompetitive, not a "zero-sum game" in the possession of finite goods, but the opposite. In this mutual and reciprocal affective participation, the experience is not "divvied up," parceled out, or diluted, but is intensified and magnified in each one. The underlying principle is this:

Spiritual love, in effect, is more perfectly known to each when it is shared by all. It is not lessened by this participation of many, for its delights are realized completely and uniquely by each of them.[62]

In short, congratulation effects a spiritual "multiplier effect" and draws a return increased according to a spiritual principle of "compound interest."

The full force of Hugh's insight here is clarified and deepened in light of his discussions of the vices of pride and envy, which in effect are the vi-

60. Hugh of St. Victor, *De arrha anime* 1:246.314ff.
61. Hugh of St. Victor, *De arrha anime* 1:246.314ff.
62. Hugh of St. Victor, *De arrha anime* 1:246.314ff.

cious opposites of congratulation. Hugh defines pride as "the love of one's own excellence, when the mind loves only the good which it possesses, that is, without Him from whom it receives the good."[63] In the simplest terms, pride loves the good, which it has received from God, *as if* it had not received it from God, *as if* it were *its own*. Such a one loves "the gift apart from the giver," and thus "perversely claims for himself the part of the good which is given to him from [God]."[64] The problem of pride is not that it loves its own excellence, but rather, the way it does so — *as if* it were its own. Adopting an Augustinian intuition, Hugh sees pride as born in a refusal to acknowledge creaturely dependency and the resulting willful divorce of gift from Giver, of creaturely possession from gratuitous reception. Thus, pride manifests itself as a perverse affection funded by a false intellection: that is, a misconstrual of the gift-nature of creaturely existence leads to a perverse love for one's own excellence, as if it were one's own. Rejecting the inexorable link between created gift and divine Giver, pride issues in the love of the latter apart from the former.

The effect of pride's perverse affection is the loss of the capacity to relate with proper affectivity to that which it has received from God and also to God himself:

He is not able to possess *usefully* that which he has, as long as he does not love it in Him from Whom he has [received] it. For just as every good is truly from God, so no good can be possessed *usefully* apart from God. But rather that very thing which man has is lost through this: that what he has is not loved in God, and with God, and from God.[65]

The essential character of this loss of creaturely good is that it ceases to be a cause of the soul's delight in God. This loss of useful possession of creaturely excellence refers to the lost capacity for delighting in God on the basis of

63. Hugh of St. Victor, *De quinque septenis*, 58–62 (ed. *Six opuscules spirituels*, Introduction, critical text, French translation, and notes by Roger Baron, Sources Chrétiennes, 155 [Paris: Editions du Cerf, 1969]): "Superbia namque est amor propriae excellentiae, quando mens bonum quod habet singulariter diligit, id est sine eo a quo bonum accipit."

64. Hugh of St. Victor, *De quin.*, 66–69: "Hoc profecto tu agis, cum doces donum extra datorem diligere, ut qui partem boni, quod ab illo datum est, perverse sibi vindicat."

65. Hugh of St. Victor, *De quin.*, 70–75: "nec id quod utiliter habere possit, dum illud in eo a quo habet non diligit. Sicut enim omne bonum veraciter a Deo est, ita nullum bonum extra Deum utiliter haberi potest. Immo vero per hoc id ipsum, quod habetur, amittitur; quod in eo, et cum eo, a quo habetur, non amatur."

what one has received from God and what one truly possesses only in and with God. For the proud, creaturely excellence ceases to be God-referential and becomes self-referential, and such a one thereby becomes a kind of viciously circular, self-enclosed contradiction. The immediate fruit of pride, therefore, is the loss of God: "pride carries man away from God."[66]

For Hugh, pride naturally gives birth to envy. For, as soon as one's own excellence is loved *as one's own*, and not as from God, then all the goods of others become rival excellences.[67] Hugh's insight here is that when human goods are loved as from God, then such delight is possible regardless of who possesses such goods. Loved in this way, another's excellence is no less a source of my delight in God as my own excellence. By contrast, the one who "does not wish to love the good common to all, now rightly pines with bruises for another's good."[68] And this "bruising longing" is envy. Another's success "burns" the envious one, says Hugh, because he does not possess through love "Him in Whom is every good." The envious one considers "another's good to be alien from himself," when he does not through love "possesses his own good and another's good together" in God.[69] Thus, the lost affectivity of pride with respect to God gives birth to a lost affectivity with respect to the neighbor, "since [the soul] is not delighted at the good of another through charity." Rather than loving the neighbor as corecipient of gratuitous goods, envy burns and pines for the goods of the neighbor as a rival competitor. And, just as the perverse affection of pride separated the self from God, so envy's perverse affection severs him from his neighbor too.[70]

---

66. Hugh of St. Victor, *De quin.*, 58: "Diximus, quod superbia aufert homini Deum."

67. Hugh of St. Victor, *De quin.*, 80–83: "Et idcirco superbiam semper invidia sequitur; quia qui illic amorem non figit, ubi omne bonum est quantum de suo perverse extollitur, tanto gravius de bono alieno torquetur" [And for this reason, envy always follows pride; for he who does not attach his love there, where every good is, the more gravely he is turned away from the good of another, to that extent is he perversely lifted up concerning himself].

68. Hugh of St. Victor, *De quin.*, 84–86: "Invidia, quae quia commune omnium bonum diligere noluit, recte nunc boni alieni livore tabescit."

69. Hugh of St. Victor, *De quin.*, 86–90: "Quam profecto alienae felicitatis successus non ureret, si illum, in quo omne bonum est, per amorem possideret. Nec enim alienum a se iudicaret bonum alterius, si suum ibi diligeret, ubi et suum et alterius bonum simul possideret."

70. Hugh of St. Victor, *De quin.*, 90–93: "Nunc ergo quantum se per elationem contra Creatorem extollit, tantum per livorem sub proximo cadit; et quantum ibi fallaciter erigitur, tantum hic veraciter praecipitatur" [Now, therefore, to the extent that he lifts himself up against the Creator through his elation, to that extent he descends below/falls under his neighbor; and to the extent that he is falsely lifted up there, to that extent there is he truly brought low].

By contrast, the virtue of *congratulatio* "rejoices with those who rejoice," thus reflecting and affecting the affective identity that unites one with others.

The force of Hugh's claim here can perhaps be more fully appreciated when contrasted with the casual use of the English term "congratulations!" in contemporary American usage. When someone extends "congratulations!" to another on the occasion of a good achieved or received, the meaning is typically something like "well done!" or "that's great for you!" But we don't typically assume that the congratulator is rejoicing with the congratulated *as if* that good were her own, *as if* she also were now in possession of it, as if the experienced pleasure of the newly possessed good were greater and more intense for both persons in light of their affective unity. Indeed, the casual expression "congratulations" often conceals either jealousy or even envy in the one extending them.

Conclusion

A collection of texts emanating from Hugh of St. Victor and his school contains a fitting passage with which to conclude this brief foray into medieval theology:

To rejoice with those who rejoice, to weep with those who weep (Rom 12:15). These words express in brief the affection of mothers, since mothers can neither weep nor rejoice with children apart from those whom they have begotten. For a mother has two breasts, from which she offers her children two kinds of milk. The first breast is congratulation, the second is compassion. The first milk is exhortation, the second is consolation. From the breast of congratulation, a good pastor produces the milk of exhortation to those making progress; from the breast of compassion he offers the milk of consolation to the disheartened, buffeted by the force of temptation.[71]

---

71. Hugh of St. Victor, *Misc.*, 3 (PL 177.812c–d): "De ubere maternae affectionis. Gaudete cum gaudentibus, flete cum flentibus (Rom. XII). Materni breviter exprimuntur affectus, quia nec dolere nec gaudere parvuli absque ea quae genuit [812D] possunt. Habet enim duo ubera, ex quibus duplex filiis lac porrigit. Primum uber est congratulatio, secundum compassio. Primum lac exhortatio, secundum consolatio. Ex ubere itaque congratulationis pastor bonus producit lac exhortationis proficientibus; ex ubere compassionis porrigit lac consolationis pusillanimis ex vi tentationis concussis."

The focus here is on those in positions of supervision and leadership in religious communities and thus has a particular pastoral focus, but the passage reflects well the moral and spiritual significance the Victorines attached to these twin dispositions in general and also how they conceived of them in relation both to Paul's injunction and to the maternal imagery used to express them. Ultimately, for Hugh, compassion and congratulation are the preeminent and signature symptoms of Christian *caritas*. Animated by charity, compassion and congratulation identify affectively (literally in and through the *affectus*) in some profound way with another, such that another's evil and good are experienced as one's own.[72] As another Victorine text puts it: "It is proper characteristic of the elect to bewail another's evil as their own. For just as by co-rejoicing with good persons, they come to participate in their merits, so also by co-sorrowing with sinners through compassion, they generate profit for themselves from the perdition of the sinners."[73] Still another observed that the spiritually mature "rejoice spiritually for those who advance from the right, just as if their grace were their own; they feel compassion for those who fall from the left into some fault, temptation, or trouble of mind or body, just as if they themselves were suffering ... from the right by congratulation, from the left by compassion."[74] This double sentiment is already present, of course, in Paul's words to the Corinthians, in 1 Cor-

72. Though Hugh may well be drawing on a patristic tradition here. See Jordan Joseph Wales, "Contemplative Compassion: Gregory the Great's Development of Augustine's Views on Love of Neighbor and Likeness to God," *Augustinian Studies* 49, no. 2 (2018): 199–219. In his *Pastoral Rule*, Gregory writes of the ideal pastor: *Regola Pastorate*, ed. Floribert Rommel, *Opere Di Gregorio Magno* 7 (Rome: Citta nuova, 2008), 28; *The Book of Pastoral Rule*, trans. George E. Demacopoulos, Popular Patristics Series 34 (Crestwood, N.Y.: St. Vladimir's Seminary Press, 2007), 43: "He should be quick to forgive through compassion ... [but also] deplore the evil perpetrated by others as though it were his own. In his own heart, he must suffer the afflictions of others and likewise rejoice at the fortune of his neighbor as though the good thing were happening to him" [Qui ad aliena cupienda non ducitur, sed propria largitur. Qui per pietatis uiscera citius ad ignoscendum flectitur, sed numquam plus quam deceat ignoscens, ab arce rectitudinis inclinatur. Qui nulla illicita perpetrat, sed perpetrata ab aliis ut propria deplorat. Qui ex affectu cordis alienae infirmitati compatitur, sicque in bonis proximi sicut in suis prouectibus laetatur].

73. Hugh of St. Victor, *Adnotatiunculae elucidatoriae in threnos Jeremiae* (PL 175.286c–d) Proprium est electorum aliena mala tanquam sua plangere. Sicut enim bonis congaudendo in eorum meritis participes fiunt, ita quoque malis per compassionem condolendo, de [286D] illorum perditione sibi lucrum faciunt.

74. Achard of St. Victor (d. 1170), Sermon: "For the Dedication of a Church," *Achard of St. Victor: Works*, trans. Hugh Feiss (Kalamazoo, Mich.: Cistercian Publications, 2001), 242.

inthians 12:26, which seem both descriptive and prescriptive: *If one member suffers, all suffer together with it; if one member is honored, all rejoice together with it.* Perhaps more fundamentally, *congratulatio* and *compassio* together reflect a divine attribute that fuses or integrates the two modes into which love is often analyzed, often in opposition to one another, namely, *eros-amor* and *agape-caritas*. In Christ (and those conformed to his paradigmatic affectivity), there is a fundamental yearning (desire, longing, craving) for another, not to possess him erotically but to promote his flourishing. It is *amorous caritas*: the fusion of the nuptial and the maternal. It is what Paul saw (and emulated) in Christ when he said in Philippians 1:8: "I long for you all with the compassion of Christ Jesus."

As seen earlier, in an arresting and evocative image, namely, the *ubera compassionis et congratulationis*, some twelfth-century writers construed these two affective dispositions as maternal breasts, "located" no less strikingly on male figures such as Jesus and Paul. Invoking the biblical injunction "to weep with those who weep and to rejoice with those who rejoice," as Romans 12:15 commands, these writers constructed an ideal *humanitas* in which a bivalent capacity for fellow-feeling was paramount. This emerging ideal of *humanitas* privileged such affective capacities as tenderness, gentleness, patience, condescension, a readiness to console and to nourish, in contrast to austerity, harshness, anger, wrath, and cruelty. As Hugh said it: "they are called human who pity tenderly, and [who] readily compassionate the miseries of others."

While it may seem arbitrary to focus on Hugh of St. Victor and some of his contemporaries in this regard, his (and their) insights on this topic seem to be pioneering and innovating in Christian history, at least in the West.[75] This is perhaps best appreciated by noting the evolution of the meaning of

75. Far beyond the scope of this chapter is an investigation of parallel transformations of culture in contact with the Gospel. For example, in "The Triple Heritage of the Christian Theological Literacy in Africa," Aloysius M. Lugira writes: "Such leaders, both church and civil, felt the need of an African homegrown Christianity which, while drawing on the patrimony of the apostolic, patristic, exegetical and theological tradition, should be suited to the wisdom, the human values, the character, the genius and the culture of Africa. Such contemporary Christianity was ideally expected to accommodate the ideals expressive of the African heritage as summarized in the concept of **Ubuntu**, encapsulated by Archbishop Desmond Tutu as "a concept difficult to render.... You know when it is there and it is obvious when it is absent. It has to do with what it means to be truly human, it refers to gentleness, to compassion, to hospitality, to openness to others, to vulnerability, to be available for others and to know that you are bound up with them

the classical term *pietas*, the classical term for ideal Roman *humanitas*, from the classical period to the Renaissance. To put it very simply, the *pietas* that for Vergil was primarily "the dutiful or loving conduct of the devout toward the divine and toward the public good" had become by the time of Dante the "compassion that is the dominant sense of the derivative *pietà* in medieval Italian,"[76] and in the other Romance languages *piedad* (Spanish), *pitié* (French), and finally the English "pity." Between the classical period and the later Middle Ages and the Renaissance stand Hugh of St. Victor and his twelfth-century contemporaries. At the same time, their seemingly utterly original insight regarding the positive expression of fellow-feeling, namely, *congratulatio*, appears entirely unprecedented and perhaps also not successfully passed along to succeeding generations, at least as an explicitly cultivated moral virtue or spiritual disposition. As one modern commentator has noted: "sympathy with suffering (*Mitleid*) and sympathy with joy (*Mitfreude*) are two kinds of sympathy. The latter, for which we have no name, has been very much neglected in ethical discussions, although it would appear to have as much ethical value as pity."[77] Here, a verbal commonplace conceals beneath its banal ubiquity the values and insights of an earlier age; a word no longer noticed harbors an insight that should not be ignored. Such it is with "congratulations."

If, in sum, "the history of compassion is yet to be written,"[78] a crucial chapter in that narrative will need to include conceptions of ideal *humanitas* that proliferated in twelfth-century Europe and found expression in writers such as Hugh of St. Victor. It will also need to encompass both *compassio* and *congratulatio*, both "weeping with those who weep and rejoicing with those who rejoice," as written in Romans 12:15.

---

in the bundle of life, for a person is only a person through other persons" (*The Rainbow People of God: The Making of a Peaceful Revolution* [New York: Doubleday, 1994], 125).

76. James D. Garrison, *Pietas from Vergil to Dryden* (University Park, Pa.: Pennsylvania State University Press, 1992), 2.

77. V. J. McGill, "Scheler's Theory of Sympathy and Love," *Philosophy and Phenomenological Research* 2, no. 3 (March 1942): 276.

78. Karl F. Morrison, *I Am You: The Hermeneutics of Empathy in Western Literature* (Princeton, N.J.: Princeton University Press, 1988), xix.

Part 4

THE CENTER OF
EVANGELIZATION

12

Augustine the Preacher

Practicing the Rhetoric of Love

BRIAN E. DALEY, SJ

St. Augustine was, above all, a preacher. We tend to think of him, perhaps, as more of a controversialist: questioning the narrow, sectarian Donatist conception of the Church and its sacramental life, or challenging the
conception of divine grace and its relation to human free effort promoted
in his time by the monk Pelagius and his disciples. Or we may conceive of
his intellectual work primarily in terms of his great spiritual or apologetic
or speculative enterprises: the *Confessions*, the *City of God*, and *The Trinity*.
These are the monumental literary and theological achievements, of course,
that established Augustine's reputation as one of the most influential Christian thinkers of the West, and as one of the greatest Latin prose writers of all
time. Yet what he did, week in and week out, for the last thirty-nine years

I am especially delighted to contribute this essay to a volume honoring Fr. Robert Imbelli:
my dear friend and wise counselor since our days of studying Latin literature together at Fordham
University and searching together, in the Fordham College Sodality, for ways of bringing the
Word of Christ to today's world. A shorter, earlier version of this essay was presented as the John
S. and Virginia Marten Lecture in Homiletics at St. Meinrad Seminary and School of Theology
on October 3, 2017.

of his life—first as a presbyter in the busy North African port city of Hippo Regius, and then, from 395 until his death in 430, as its bishop—was to preach about the scriptures to congregations of ordinary Christians as they gathered for the liturgy: to struggle to let the Word of God, which had just been read to them, take hold powerfully in their hearts and continue the unending divine work of inner transformation.

To be an effective preacher, Augustine would argue, it was extremely helpful also to be a trained rhetorician, as he was. For many centuries, after all, classical Greek and Roman society was fascinated to the point of obsession by words. In the absence of digital media and video games, people seem to have spent a great deal of their business and leisure time listening and talking; to speak correctly, beautifully, persuasively was the key to professional and political success, the ultimate mark of a cultured person. So the normal shape of general education for boys—and sometimes for girls as well—began with learning how to read and write in the local primary school, then moving on (around the age of twelve) to the study of classical literature with a *grammaticus* and learning to recognize and appreciate good style, and finally reaching its formal climax (beginning around age fifteen) in the study of rhetoric: learning how to construct a cogent argument, how to remember one's line of reasoning—without notes—and even how to project one's voice, all as part of the larger task of learning how to convince a public gathering, or a court of law, by appealing to the heart as well as the mind. To be a good speaker was the main key to success in a competitive, power-hungry world that was still an oral society; rhetoric was the long-cultivated art and science of effective public speaking.

But rhetoric, as Augustine also knew, and as we are still well aware of, is a skill that can all too easily be misused. Quintilian, the celebrated Roman teacher and orator of the first century AD, declares in his classic textbook, *Instructions in Oratory (Institutio Oratoria)*:

The orator whom we are forming should be the person Marcus Cato describes as "a good man, skilled in speaking." So what he places first is, in the nature of things, more urgent and more important than anything else: namely, to be a good man.[1]

---

1. Quintilian, *Institutio Oratoria*, 12, I.1, ed. Michael Winterbottom and Tobias Reinhardt (Oxford: Clarendon Press, 1970), 692 (my translation).

Quintilian goes on to reflect on the ways criminally motivated people can misuse the art of effective speaking; he then insists, in contrast:

We are not training just some resource for the law-courts, some voice for hire, nor – to avoid harsher language – just a useful advocate whom people tend to call a legal hack, but someone outstanding for his natural talent, who has deeply grasped all the most refined arts in his own mind, yet who is committed to human affairs: someone whose like no earlier age has known, unique and perfect in every way, supremely noble in sentiment, supremely noble in speech.[2]

This often did not happen, as one might guess. Augustine, commenting on his own literary training as a teenager three centuries later, laments the emphasis placed by the Roman society of his time on cultured and elegant speech, even when its content may be morally questionable; he adds: "Your praises, Lord, your praises expressed through your Scriptures would have upheld the tender vine of my heart, and they would not have been snatched away by empty trifles,"[3] but, like many others, he seems to have initially been put off by the often rough language and confusing narratives of the Latin Bible. As someone formed by his own culture to be fascinated by good style, even at the expense of real content,[4] Augustine eventually became skilled enough himself to "sell eloquence" to others[5] and to hope that his own proficiency in speaking – coupled with the right connections – would eventually lead to a major public office.[6] Whatever the classical description of rhetorical skill might have been, Augustine had learned from his own experience as a young professional teacher of the arts that it needed to be consciously focused on conveying the truth to become a force for good.

In any case, when he returned to Africa in 388 as a newly baptized Christian thirty-something, hoping to dedicate himself to a quiet life of ascetic contemplation and writing in his native town of Thagaste with fellow "ser-

2. Quintilian, 12, I.25, 697. Quintilian may be thinking here of Cicero or some other earlier hero of Roman public life.

3. Augustine, *Confessions* I, trans. Henry Chadwick (Oxford: Oxford University Press, 1991), 20.

4. See, for example, Augustine, *Confessions* IV, iii. 5 (he enjoyed conversing with the physician Vindicianus, even though his Latin style was not sophisticated); IV, xiv. 21 (dedication of treatise to the celebrated rhetorician Hierius, whom he had never met, but whose style he admired); V, xiv. 24 (first attraction to Ambrose as preacher was because of his style, not his message).

5. Augustine, *Confessions* IV, ii. 2.

6. Augustine, *Confessions* VI, xi. 19.

vants of God," it was probably inevitable that Augustine's training in eloquence and his wide reputation would not remain hidden for long. For a few years, he tells us in a later sermon on the clerical way of life, he avoided towns where the bishop's office was vacant, knowing that even his casual presence might start people thinking of him as a likely successor. On a visit to Hippo in 391 to talk to a friend about the possibility of setting up a quasimonastic Christian community there, however, this strategy failed. The elderly bishop, Valerius—a native Greek speaker from southern Italy, who was not a particularly competent public speaker—had apparently mentioned in a homily that he was looking to find a *priest* who could help him instruct the people by sharing his duties of preaching, a practice that was apparently still rare in Africa at the time. Despite his efforts to stay anonymous, Augustine recounts, he apparently was pointed out to Valerius as the man he was looking for: "I was caught!" he says; "I was made a priest, and by way of this grade I eventually came to the episcopate."[7] It was the end of his years of quiet prayer and reflection. After a short "sabbatical" granted to him by Valerius to put his affairs in Thagaste in order and study in greater depth the scriptures he would have to expound, Augustine began a round of preaching that did not cease until his death in 430: first as presbyter-assistant to Valerius, then—after 395—as the bishop of Hippo himself, the tireless leader and teacher of his own community, the collaborator of Aurelius, the primate of Carthage, and soon the most celebrated voice of the Catholic Church in Africa.

As a bishop in the late Roman Empire, he was a significant public figure in a number of ways: acting as a local magistrate who was expected to arbitrate disputes over property or inheritances too small to catch the interest of provincial judges; being a participant in the wider disputes on Christian doctrine that were increasingly capturing the attention of governors and emperors; and being a promoter of peace and unity within the whole Christian body—especially in North Africa, then riven by the schism with the Donatist Church. Above all, however, in an age where few ordinary priests had sufficient education to be asked to interpret scripture in public, being a bishop meant, by a kind of default, being the community's preacher.

Augustine exclaimed, at the beginning of a sermon likely delivered at

7. Augustine, Sermon 355.2, *The Works of St. Augustine* III, vol. 10, *Sermons*, trans. Edmund Hill, OP (Hyde Park, N.Y.: New City Press, 1995), 166.

the shrine of St. Cyprian in Carthage in the early summer of 424, "I am a servant of the word: not mine but God's, of course—our Lord's, whom nobody serves without honor, nobody ignores without punishment."[8] To speak God's Word accurately and powerfully, to allow it to challenge and shape the faith and practice of his Eucharistic community, was the bishop's central responsibility. In fact, we still possess around a thousand of Augustine's sermons, most of them delivered without notes before a wide variety of congregations, and written down by a team of clerical stenographers: sermons which dealt with a wide variety of Scriptural texts—including comprehensive series on the Gospel and the First Letter of John and on the entire Book of Psalms. Undoubtedly, all of these represent only a fraction of his actual output of homilies over thirty-five years as bishop.[9]

With his training and experience as a prominent professor of rhetoric, Augustine soon became Africa's leading theoretician and reformer of Christian preaching as well. Shortly after he had succeeded Valerius as bishop in Hippo, Augustine and his old friend and colleague Alypius—now bishop himself in Thagaste, Augustine's hometown—wrote a joint letter to Aurelius of Carthage, congratulating him in lofty phrases on his "holy idea" of systematically preparing priests to share in the preaching of the Gospel.[10]

May you rejoice in the Lord in such men (Augustine and Alypius write enthusiastically). May he deign to hear you praying for them, as you do not refuse to hear him speaking through them. . . . May the way of these sacred ants glow with activity; may the work of these sacred bees give forth fragrance; may they bear fruit in patience, persevering to the end unto salvation.[11]

Toward the end of the letter, Augustine and his friend suggested to the bishop of Carthage "that you order such of their sermons as you direct to be written and corrected and sent to us."[12] It seems likely from this that Augustine and Alypius, both accomplished rhetoricians themselves, offered to be part of Aurelius's program, by reading and evaluating sample sermons of

---

8. Augustine, Sermon 114.1, 188.

9. Dom Cyrille Lambot, the great Belgian scholar of Augustine's preaching, estimates his extant sermons may only amount to 10 percent of his total preaching oeuvre.

10. See Augustine, Epistle 41, *The Works of St. Augustine* II, vol. 1 (Hyde Park, N.Y.: New City Press, 2001), 153.

11. Augustine, Epistle 41.

12. Augustine, Epistle 41.

these presbyters in training. A systematic initiative for forming preachers was apparently under way.

Significantly, it was in these first few years of his ministry as bishop that Augustine apparently began his own major treatise on the art of Christian biblical interpretation for potential preachers, perhaps as his contribution to the realization of Aurelius's "holy idea": his four books *On Christian Learning* (*De Doctrina Christiana*), which were to become one of his most influential works for the development of a Christian culture in the West.[13] In the prologue to the treatise, Augustine points out that "rules" have been developed for "opening up the hidden secrets of the divine literature" of Scripture, and for proclaiming those secrets to others, and which students—presumably students training to be preachers—would do well to learn. Some people may simply not understand what he plans to write, Augustine continues, and some may think they understand it but be unable to use it profitably. So be it! His real concern is to convince a third group of possible readers, who may feel that studying classical literary techniques, as strategies for interpreting and proclaiming the Bible—strategies for preparing homilies—is a waste of time, and that one simply needs to entrust oneself to the inspiration of the Holy Spirit. Augustine gently reminds his readers that all of us had to learn to read and speak our language correctly as children, that

13. On the continuing influence of *De Doctrina Christiana*, see especially the classic study of Henri-Irénée Marrou, *Saint Augustin et la fin de la culture antique*, 4th edition (Paris: E. de Boccard, 1958). In *Retractationes* 2.28–29, Augustine lists the *De Doctrina Christiana* after his two books *To Simplicianus* and his *Against the Error of Mani*, which he says were the first two works he wrote after becoming a bishop. Those works are usually dated to 396–397. They and *De Agone Christiano* (also written in 396) appear with the first two books of *De Doctrina* in what is clearly the oldest manuscript containing Augustine's works: Leningrad Q.v.1,3, which can be dated by its writing to north Africa in the late fourth or early fifth century. The fact that only the first two books of *De Doctrina* appear there confirms Augustine's own report, in *Retr* 2.31.1, that he had originally stopped the work of composition at III, 25.36 — presumably in 397 — and only finished it, completing Book III and adding Book IV, near the end of his life, in 426 or 427.

In Epistle 41, Augustine also briefly reminds Bishop Aurelius that he has asked for his opinion on the "seven keys" or rules for interpreting biblical metaphors worked out a few decades before by the Donatist exegete Tychonius. This may explain why Augustine broke off composition of *De Doctrina* at this particular point in the 390s, since his eventual adaptation of Tychonius's "keys" for Catholic preachers, in *De Doctrina*, follows almost directly after the hiatus at III, 25.36. So in the absence of a timely reply from Aurelius, giving him official encouragement to use this interpretive proposal by a schismatic author, he may simply have postponed further work on the treatise, only to return to it — and to Tychonius's ideas — much later. See Edmund Hill, "*De Doctrina Christiana*: A Suggestion," *Studia Patristica* 6 (Berlin: Texte und Untersuchungen, 1962), 443–46.

Moses took his father-in-law's advice, and that Paul and the other Apostles received instruction from their colleagues. To read the scriptures with understanding, to dig out the hidden meaning of an obscure passage and to communicate that meaning clearly and powerfully to others, are in large degree learnable skills, he suggests, which can draw on a long and honorable tradition of classical literary and rhetorical training. One simply needs to "know the rules"—even the rules of secular interpretation of classical texts. "Let us not be too proud," Augustine remarks characteristically, "to learn what has to be learned with the help of other people, and let those of us by whom others are taught pass on what we have received without pride and without jealousy."[14] Studying, especially as an adult, can be a laudable exercise in Christian humility!

The work that follows, in its final form, is an elaborate adaptation of the classical tradition of literary and rhetorical study to form articulate interpreters of the Christian scriptures: Books II and III of the treatise are devoted to what was traditionally called "grammar"—the art of deciphering, pronouncing, and understanding the writing on a page, despite whatever linguistic and literary obstacles may lurk in the text—and Book IV focused on "rhetoric," the art of communicating the text's meaning to others persuasively and beautifully. As Augustine puts it, we need first to "discover what needs to be understood" and then "find a way to put our discoveries across."[15] Before turning to the technicalities of interpretation and oral composition, however—to those skills so finely honed in ancient society, in which Augustine himself had become a world-renowned expert and teacher—he turns at some length to address the hermeneutical framework in which Christian scriptural interpretation and persuasion has to take place: the content of Christian faith and hope, the Christian imperative to love. Only from a sense of the whole Christian message, as received in the community of believing disciples, can one discover the message of a particular scriptural passage in either testament and communicate it in depth without distortion or diminishment.

The first book of *De Doctrina* is a condensed but substantial survey of what Augustine understands as the whole body of Christian teaching—of

---

14. See St. Augustine, *Teaching Christianity* [*De Doctrina Christiana*], Prologue 5, trans. Edmund Hill (Hyde Park, N.Y.: New City, 1996), 102.

15. Augustine, *Teaching Christianity* I, 1.1, 106.

doctrina in our modern sense, the *content* of what we are taught—before he turns to the strategies one can learn in the ancient classroom for finding the meaning of individual scriptural passages, and to the techniques of proclaiming that meaning appropriately. Augustine begins his survey with a famous distinction—later welcomed by Ludwig Wittgenstein, among others—between "things" (*res*) and "signs" (*signa*): a sign being a kind of thing, but precisely one whose role is to *point* to another thing.[16] *Words*, of course—the things Augustine studied and used so expertly—are classic examples of signs: their purpose and whole rationale as things, as sounds we make and marks we scratch out on paper (or hammer out today on a keyboard), is to *point* to other things, to *signify*. Secondly, Augustine points out, some of the *things* we encounter are realities we desire simply for their own sakes, to possess or *enjoy* them for themselves, while others are realities we *make use of* in order to possess those things we hope to enjoy. It is the distinction between means and ends: "things that are to be *enjoyed* make us happy," as Augustine put it; "things which are to be *used* help us on our way to happiness." Like the previous distinction, this one seems at first obvious, but it lays the foundation for all that follows in Book I, which discusses in a remarkably concise way what Augustine understands to be the agenda that God has proposed to humanity for genuine and lasting enjoyment, and what he takes to be the divinely revealed way to that end—the tools to be used, in a cautious and intentional way, as we travel toward it.

Augustine begins the main expository section of Book I with a bold statement: seen from the perspective of faith, *God* is the only reality, the only *thing* (if we can speak that way), we are made simply to *enjoy*:

The things that are to be enjoyed (he writes) are the Father and the Son and the Holy Spirit—in fact the Trinity, one supreme thing, and one which is shared in common by all who enjoy it.[17]

Yet everyone who thinks seriously about God will realize that God is *above* our ability to think or describe in normal categories of speech: "all agree that God is whatever they put above all other things."[18] So those who desire to enjoy God as the ultimate reality desire in some way to participate in God's life by sharing in unchangeable wisdom. Augustine concludes:

16. Augustine, *Teaching Christianity* I, 2.2, 106.
17. Augustine, *Teaching Christianity* I, 5.5, 108.
18. Augustine, *Teaching Christianity* I, 7.7, 109.

That is why, since we are meant to enjoy that truth which is unchangeably alive, and since it is in its light that God the Trinity, author and maker of the universe, provides for all the things he had made, our minds have to be purified, to enable them to perceive that light and to cling to it once perceived. We should think of this purification process as being a kind of walk, a kind of voyage towards our home country.[19]

Life, while we are still on the way toward sharing God's wisdom is, for Augustine, a matter of seeing the world as an interwoven complex of signs, all pointing the way to him. Faith, and the communication of faith to others, depends on knowing how to read and interpret those signs.

Augustine goes on to point out that although the wisdom of God is always present in the world, shaping the signs of our history, most humans have been incapable of perceiving her. Echoing the prologue to John's Gospel, he writes of this divine wisdom: "So she came where she already was, because she was in the world.... How did she come, if not by the Word becoming flesh and dwelling amongst us?"[20] Like the words in our mind that take on a concrete, spoken form in order to be communicated to others, God's Word has now been spoken in time, has himself become the sign of signs, so that we might be healed and united to him. So faith, based on the conviction that Christ—God's Word made flesh—is risen from the dead, is transformed into hope for our own future transformation and resurrection. And the community formed by faith and hope in Christ is the *Church*, his Body, which has been entrusted with the "keys" of forgiveness and which, as a whole, is "on the way" to share fully in the healing of sin and eternal life.[21]

In the context of this sketch of ultimate reality, of the "things" truly worth desiring and enjoying, Augustine then turns to reflect on *love*, as the driving force of human choice and action. Clearly God, as the ultimate ground of reality, is to be loved and desired uniquely, but how are we to love ourselves and each other, how are we to love the other things that surround us in the world? Augustine suggests here that our love for creatures can never be ultimate; they must always be contextualized in the recognition that their goodness is a gift of God, who is the source of all good.

19. Augustine, *Teaching Christianity* I, 10.10, 110.
20. Augustine, *Teaching Christianity* I, 12.12, 111.
21. Augustine, *Teaching Christianity* I, 16.15–21.19.

So if you ought not to love yourself for your own sake, but for the sake of the one to whom your love is most rightly directed as its end, other people must not take offense if you also love them for God's sake and not their own. This, after all, is the rule of love that God has set for us: "You shall love," he says, "your neighbor as yourself"; God, however, "with your whole heart and your whole soul and your whole mind." (Mt 1:31, 30)[22]

So the two "great commandments" articulated in Deuteronomy, and in the words of Jesus, really leave no aspect of our moral obligation, as travelers in the world, untouched. The command is not to reject anything that is genuinely loveable but simply to love in the right *order,*

so that you do not love what is not to be loved, or fail to love what is to be loved, or have a greater love for what should be loved less, or an equal love for things that should be loved less or more, or a lesser or greater love for things that should be loved equally.[23]

To love God above all things, with all our energy and our conscious commitment; to love our neighbor as ourselves, and nonhuman creatures less than our human neighbor, in ways appropriate to their place in creation, is to respond to the value of creation itself, of the "things" whose being and lovability is grounded in the absolute being and lovability of God, the ultimate "thing." "And the supreme reward," Augustine insists, "is that we should enjoy him"—possess God as our good—"and that all of us who enjoy him should also enjoy one another in him."[24]

All of these reflections on God and the world, on the proper objects of our faith and our hope and our love, which he has developed at some length, are put on this earth, Augustine reminds us at the end of Book I of *De Doctrina Christiana*, because they constitute the real content of the scripture that the preacher is called upon to interpret and proclaim.

So if it seems to you that you have understood the divine Scriptures, or any part of them, in such a way that by this understanding you do not build up this twin love of God and neighbor, then you have not yet understood them. If on the other hand you have made judgments about them that are helpful for building up this love, but for all that have not said what the author you have been reading actually

22. Augustine, *Teaching Christianity* I, 22.21, 115.
23. Augustine, *Teaching Christianity* I, 27.28, 118.
24. Augustine, *Teaching Christianity* I, 32.35, 122.

meant in that place, then your mistake is not pernicious, and you certainly cannot be accused of lying.[25]

Preachers who make such interpretive mistakes need to be corrected, Augustine goes on to insist: "but if they are mistaken in a judgment which is intended to build up charity," they are mistaken like people who leave the main road to take "a rough path," but are still generally headed in the right direction.[26] The main road of good exegesis is clearly the better way, but the most important thing is to reach one's destination: the love of God, and of creatures in God.

What is the point of beginning a closely packed, frankly academic treatise on scriptural interpretation and preaching with this broad reflection on the content of revelation and the purpose of human life? For Augustine, it seems, only such a reflection can give an adequate context for what Christian interpreters and preachers, with all their carefully acquired skills, set out to do. The things that surround us, the signs that point beyond themselves to other things of value, and ultimately to the thing we all yearn for, which is union with God, are together the setting for the journey of human life. Only if the preacher has an awareness of that landscape, only if he knows where he is and where he is heading, will his linguistic efforts amount to more than the "noisy gong and clanging cymbal," as Paul warns of in 1 Corinthians 13:1. If the scriptures are God's word to us, then our words of interpretation have to begin from a sense of who God is.

In Book II, Augustine turns to more technical issues: to human techniques for making sense of scripture's signs, when their meaning seems immediately to elude us. Like a good classical literary critic or *grammaticus*, Augustine reflects on the nature of the Bible as a collection of texts, on the challenges of its language, the puzzle and delight of its metaphors, the reasons for the Bible's frequent obscurity. Augustine begins with the basic rule—articulated also by Origen in the preface to his work *On First Principles*, almost two hundred years earlier—that what God really expects all humanity to know and hope for and do he has caused to be put clearly in scripture. If some other passages and sayings seem wrapped in obscurity, this is simply God's providential way of preventing scripture's interpreters

---

25. Augustine, *Teaching Christianity* I, 36.40, 124.
26. Augustine, *Teaching Christianity* I, 36.41, 124.

from getting bored.[27] The central rule is: "Instances from the plainer passages are used to cast light on the more obscure utterances, and the testimony of some undoubted judgments is used to remove uncertainties from
those that are more doubtful."[28] Revelation is presumed to be consistent,
in other words; so we must use clearer parts of the Bible to interpret the less
clear ones.

In the rest of Books II and III, Augustine draws on his experience as a
sophisticated reader of classical literature and a man of broad liberal education to sketch out the kinds of learnable knowledge that will help a person read the scriptures well: knowledge of other languages, of the habits of
scribes and the art of correcting manuscripts; a nodding acquaintance, at
least, with history and natural science, mathematics and music; an understanding of the rules of reasoning and the principles of sound argument—
much of which we grasp intuitively before we learn their formal structures.
Augustine's overall advice, emphasized in the last few chapters of Book II,
is that secular learning is clearly of great value for our life in the world, and
even for our ability to understand the Bible, but must never be allowed to
become an end in itself or a cause for self-satisfaction. If a person "does not
turn all this to the praise and love of the one God from whom he knows it
all proceeds, such a person can seem to be very *learned*, but in no way at all
can he be *wise*."[29]

In Book III, Augustine moves on to discuss what he calls the "ambiguous signs" in scripture: words and phrases whose meaning in their biblical
context is unclear, even though their normal signification is familiar. Here
the main task is to discuss the various types of figurative language one finds
in the Bible: metaphors and other types of verbal tropes that most of us tend
to use intuitively in everyday speech. The problem for interpreters is taking
what may be meant to be a literal assertion in the Bible in a figurative way,
or vice versa. Augustine's general strategy, again, is to reach back to what he
has outlined in Book I, the content of Christian biblical revelation summarized in the Church's "rule of faith," as the key to his proposed hermeneutic.
He writes:

27. Augustine, *Teaching Christianity* II, 6.8; 9.14.
28. Augustine, *Teaching Christianity* II, 9.14, 135.
29. Augustine, *Teaching Christianity* II, 38.56, 158.

Here, quite simply, is the one and only method: anything in the divine writings that cannot be referred either to good, honest morals or to the truth of the faith, you must know, is said figuratively. Good honest morals belong to *loving* one's neighbor, the truth of faith to *knowing* God and one's neighbor.[30]

And while the fundamental task of scripture scholars, in Augustine's view as in our own, must certainly be to try to grasp what the *original author* of a passage intended to say, and if we assume that these authors were guided by the Holy Spirit for our instruction—that scripture as a whole, canonical collection is, as we say, inspired—then the Christian reader must assume that a multiplicity of possible interpretations of some passages is actually *intended*, by God's design:

The author, in fact, possibly even saw this very meaning [i.e., the figural meaning] in the same words which we wish to understand; and certainly the Spirit of God who produced these texts through him foresaw without a shadow of a doubt that it would occur to some listener or reader, because it is upheld by the truth.[31]

In Book IV of *De Doctrina*, Augustine finally moves on to discuss how one might effectively *preach* what one has found to be scripture's providentially intended meaning. Augustine makes it clear from the start that he has no intention of producing a full, formal treatise on the art of persuasion, since abundant examples were already available in the rhetorical works of his time. He simply insists that anyone who hopes to proclaim God's Word to the Christian body should not shrink from the effort to grow in eloquence, adding the caution that most of this relies on an intuitive, aesthetic grasp of language that cannot be taught.[32]

Augustine's method of teaching eloquence to preachers here is not to examine classical examples of beautiful Latin or Greek prose but to analyze passages in the Bible—Old Testament and New—that represent the recognized strategies for intentionally powerful speech. So he quotes passages from Paul that illustrate the oratorical practice of the *klimax*—words and phrases tantalizingly piled up to increase the intensity of a passage's

---

30. Augustine, *Teaching Christianity* III, 10.14, 176.

31. Augustine, *Teaching Christianity* III, 27.38, 185–86. See also Augustine's similar conclusion about the variety of meanings possible to find in Genesis's reference to "heaven and earth" in *Confessions* XII, xvi. 23–xxiv. 33.

32. Augustine, *Teaching Christianity* IV, 2.3–3.4, 201–2.

thought—or "periodic" sentences, which suspend the completion of an idea until the end of a long series of clauses, both of these strategies being finished off with a short, crisp statement to summarize the point being made.[33] Augustine insists, however, that while scripture is occasionally obscure, the preacher's task is not to be: he must strive for clarity, even at the expense of art.[34]

Rhetorical treatises traditionally distinguished three main purposes of artful speech: to *teach* (*docere*) or convey information, which requires clarity above all; to *delight* (*delectare*) and thus to engage the hearer, which calls for elegance and grace of literary form; and to *move* (*flectere*) the hearer to action, which calls for still more emotionally powerful engagement on the part of the speaker.[35] Corresponding to these three aims are the three "styles" of speaking classically distinguished by ancient rhetorical theory: the "calm manner" (*submissa dictio*), suitable for conveying information clearly, in simple terms; the "moderate manner" (*modica dictio*), which adds an element of aesthetic embellishment by balance, rhythm, and tastefully colorful phrases; and the "grand manner" (*dictio grandis*), which Augustine characterizes as "not so much a matter of elegantly stylish language as of the impetuous expression of very deep feelings."[36] Augustine offers substantial examples of each of these styles from Paul's letters, plus a few further examples from the Latin ecclesiastical writers Cyprian and Ambrose.[37] But, he adds (echoing Quintilian), while a skillfully composed sermon may certainly convey the truth and power of scripture to a congregation, even when the preacher's life does not notably conform to this truth, such a contrast between a speaker's words and life is clearly not ideal.

What therefore does it mean to speak not only eloquently but wisely, if not to provide words that are sufficient in the plain style, brilliant in the moderate, vehement and forceful in the grand manner, but still for saying true things that really need to be heard? But if anyone is unable to do both, let him say wisely what he does not say eloquently, rather than say eloquently what he says unwisely. If however he cannot even do this, let him so conduct himself that he not only earns

---

33. Augustine, *Teaching Christianity* IV, 6.97.14, 205–9.

34. Augustine, *Teaching Christianity* IV, 8.2210.25, 212–15.

35. Augustine, *Teaching Christianity* IV, 12.2728, 215–16.

36. Augustine, *Teaching Christianity* IV, 17.34–20.44, 220–27.

37. Augustine, *Teaching Christianity* IV, 21.45–50, 228–33.

a reward for himself, but also gives an example to others; and so his manner of life can itself be a kind of eloquent sermon.[38]

In the end, the most successful form of preaching is behavior that embodies the Gospel.

A few years after beginning this remarkable treatise on the literary and rhetorical skills that build on faith and love to form the good preacher, Augustine composed another, shorter work on the technique of Christian communication that is no less condensed, but also no less remarkable: his treatise *On Catechizing the Uninstructed (De Catechizandis Rudibus)*, apparently written sometime late in 403.[39] As Augustine explains at the beginning of the work, he is writing in response to an agonized letter he has received from a Carthaginian deacon, with the characteristically pious North African name of Deogratias. The deacon, as Augustine observes, is apparently recognized in Carthage as someone skilled in summing up Christian faith for inquiring outsiders, and is often visited by adults who would like to know more about the faith, in a quick summary, before formally deciding to enter the catechumenate. Deogratias has written to Augustine, famous now both as bishop and as rhetorician, because he is, as he says, never quite sure how to balance the elements of biblical narrative and moral doctrine *(praecepta)* in his summary, and because he has given his presentations so often now that he bores and disappoints even himself as he makes it! Augustine responds with a work that both summarizes his own understanding of what one needs to say when communicating the faith to inquirers and makes concrete suggestions on how to continue finding joy *(hilaritas)* in this vital ministry.

Augustine observes at the start that he, too, is often deeply dissatisfied with his own preaching and teaching. One reason, he suspects, is that in all of us, "the tongue is unable to keep up with the intellect."[40] We seem to grasp the meaning of the Gospel in a sudden flash of insight, but our speech lags behind, and "while speech is still spinning out its words, that intellectual insight has already vanished into its secluded domain."[41] Yet, however frustrated we can be with our own efforts at communicating the faith, Au-

---

38. Augustine, *Teaching Christianity* IV, 28.61, 238–39.

39. For a discussion of the dating this work, see the introduction to the recent English translation by Raymond Canning, *Instructing Beginners in Faith* (Hyde Park, N.Y.: New City, 2006), 9–11.

40. Augustine, *Instructing Beginners in the Faith* 2.3 (Canning, 56).

41. Augustine, *Instructing Beginners in the Faith* 2.3 (Canning, 56).

gustine observes, the fact that listeners keep coming to us suggest that they, at least, are finding substance and even joy in what we say. Still, a positive attitude clearly enhances the vitality of our words, and calls for cultivation.[42]

Augustine begins the body of his treatise on catechesis with a sustained reflection on what is involved in communicating the narrative *(narratio)* of our faith: essentially the story told by the canonical Bible. This is what the preacher-catechist has to proclaim: not in detail, of course, at a first meeting, but in a way that brings out the crucial turning points in God's history. Augustine's perspective is clear: if the Bible, in its present form, is one book, then

everything that we read in the holy Scriptures that was written before the coming of the Lord was written for the sole purpose of drawing attention to his coming and of prefiguring the future Church. That Church is the people of God throughout all the nations; it is his body, and also included in its number are all the faithful servants who lived in the world even before the Lord's coming, believing that he would come, even as we believe that he has come.[43]

The point of the whole narrative, Augustine insists, culminating in the death of God the Son, is, quite simply, to prove that God loves us, "his purpose being that we should love one another," and love him above all things.[44] If we discover that we are loved by someone else, particularly when that someone else is of a significantly higher status than we are, we can hardly avoid being stirred up to love in return. And so it is with the biblical story:

Thus, before all else, Christ came so that people might learn how much God loves them, and might learn this so that they would catch fire with love for him who first loved them, and so that they would also love their neighbor *(proximum)* as he commanded and showed by his example — he who made himself their neighbor by loving them when they were not close (literally, "not neighbors," *non proximum*) to him, but were wandering far from him *(longe peregrinantem)* — and if all of the divine Scripture that was written before the Lord's coming was written to announce that coming, and everything that has since been committed to writing and invested with divine authority tells of Christ and calls us to love, then it is plain that on the two commandments of love for God and neighbor hinge not only the law and

42. Augustine, *Instructing Beginners in the Faith* 2.4 (Canning, 56).
43. Augustine, *Instructing Beginners in the Faith* 3.6 (Canning, 65).
44. Augustine, *Instructing Beginners in the Faith* 4.7 (Canning, 67).

the prophets … but also all the other books of divine writings which were later dedicated to our salvation and handed down to us.[45]

The message of the whole of scripture, Augustine here passionately insists, is a message of love: God's love for all of us, summoning forth our love for God and each other. And if the great obstacle to loving (as Augustine always held) is *pride*, which generates the narrow-minded self-preoccupation he calls "envy" (*invidentia*), then it is God's loving humility, revealed in the self-emptying service of the Son, which is our ultimate cure: "a proud humanity is a great misery," he says in summary, "but an even greater mercy is a humble God."[46] So the love at the heart of this biblical story must be, for the preacher and catechist, "the goal of all you say": "Recount every event in your historical exposition in such a way that your listener, by hearing it, may believe, by believing may hope, and by hoping may love."[47]

Augustine goes on to reflect on the best way to go about communicating this radiant summary vision of the Church's biblical faith: one should keep one's remarks rooted in the biblical narrative; one should draw from it some sketch of the Christian hope in resurrection, judgment, and recompense; one should also deal briefly with the basic principles of Christian behavior (*honesta conversatio*): a Christian "is to love himself and us, and all the others whom he holds dear as friends, *in* the one and *because of* the one who has loved him as an enemy, so as to justify him and make him a friend."[48] In offering this rapid summary of the Christian faith and life, Augustine goes on to advise, it is essential for a catechist to size up his listener as accurately as he can, to get some sense of what the listener already knows of Christianity from others, and so avoid repeating the familiar; to approach an educated person—especially someone trained in literature and rhetoric—in a more familiar, culturally refined way than a person with little education.

In the end, Augustine also suggests here, the only antidote to our own boredom and frustration in this central ministry of proclaiming the Gospel to beginners is to take the story seriously ourselves: to focus on the call to do what we are doing as a ministry of fraternal love—as a humble form of service, communicating the service of a humble God.

---

45. Augustine, *Instructing Beginners in the Faith* 4.8 (Canning, 67).
46. Augustine, *Instructing Beginners in the Faith* 4.8 (Canning, 72).
47. Augustine, *Instructing Beginners in the Faith* 4.8 (Canning, 72).
48. Augustine, *Instructing Beginners in the Faith* 7.11 (Canning, 80).

We will even be glad to endure troubles for the sake of our work of mercy, if it is not our own glory that we seek there. For a work is truly good only when the will of the one who performs it is struck with the shaft of love (*cum a caritate jaculatur agentis intentio*) and when, returning as it were to its proper place, the will comes again to rest in love.[49]

Like a parent or an older sibling teaching familiar material to a young child, our sense of having been here before is best overridden by our joy in the act of loving communication itself: "When our listeners are touched by us as we speak, and we are touched by them as they learn, each of us comes to dwell in the other, so that they as it were speak in us what they hear, while we in some way learn in them what we teach."[50] Only love for the message itself, and love for the person to whom we are communicating it, can overcome the tedium of constant repetition in our ministry.

Only love formed by the love of Christ in us can give us, as preachers or teachers, real joy.

≪

What can we, as struggling twenty-first-century preachers and cate-chists, learn from Augustine's reflections on the ministry of communicating God's Word? Obviously, we live in a different time and a different culture. Rhetoric is still central to human communication, but now it is the rhetoric of TV politics, of tweets and texting, rather than that of the Roman law court and the forum. We still seek to put our thoughts in attractive and beautiful forms, to move those who listen to us to conversion and action, but the limitations on our forms of self-expression (sometimes as few as 130 characters!) and the norms by which we judge each other's speech to be credible, are massively different from what they were in the fifth century. The approach to certainty, too, and to verifiability that we have inherited from the Enlightenment, make any form of credible communication—especially a message based on biblical narration, on sacred or even human history—open to new doubts, or at least new questions, before it can be heard as convincing. Knowledge for us consists in the analysis of evidence, in the deconstructing of what seems to be a presupposed whole, rather than in proposing grand syntheses. How, then, can we find in Augustine's reflections on preaching anything more than a historical curiosity?

---

49. Augustine, *Instructing Beginners in the Faith* 11.16 (Canning, 96).
50. Augustine, *Instructing Beginners in the Faith* 12.17 (Canning, 97).

1. We can learn from Augustine, surely, that preaching, in its broadest sense, should be above all *biblical*: drawn from thoughtful reflection on and study of the biblical text. Liturgical preaching and catechetical instruction are not simply a way of sharing our personal insights — such as they are — on contemporary problems, let alone a time to tell heartwarming stories about our past. It is meant to be an extension and application, a self-effacing interpretation, of the biblical text that has been set before us as a witness to the fundamental content of Jewish and Christian faith. As Vatican II's *Constitution on the Liturgy* puts it, using the metaphor of a banquet, in the homily "the treasures of the Bible are to be opened up more lavishly, so that a richer fare may be provided for the faithful at the table of God's word."[51] It is, by its very nature, a kind of condiment to the Bible: expository speech that develops what is contained in the Word of scripture, and that is seen by faith as reaching its climax in the life of the Word made flesh.

2. Preaching, as Augustine's works constantly remind us, thus involves not just skill in self-expression but also the ability to interpret the Bible in an intelligent, unabashedly Christian way. For the post-Enlightenment reader, biblical interpretation is a complex process. Thanks to two centuries of historical criticism of the biblical text, we are more aware than early Christian scholars were of the layers of composition and redaction, the incorporation of earlier sources into a later, changed context, that have shaped our present biblical books; we are aware, too, of the fluid nature of our biblical canon, and of the fact that the major Christian traditions today have somewhat different conceptions of what the canonical Bible is. Our awareness of this complexity, of the "blurry borders" and conjectured origins, of the present biblical text, is not something we can simply lay aside when we turn to the proclamation of the biblical message; yet proclamation of the Gospel also cannot simply be historical-critical exegesis — the explanation of scripture's complexity and fluidity. You can't preach the *Jerome Biblical Commentary*!

3. Preaching, then, is a *theological* as well as an exegetical task. Based on an understanding of the text that draws consciously on all the contemporary literary knowledge and skills available to us — as Augustine urged his own contemporaries to do — preaching and catechesis are ultimately a proclamation of the *mystery of salvation in Christ*. "Jews demand signs and Greeks seek

---

51. *Sacrosanctum Concilium* 51, trans. Sean Collins and Austin Flannery (Northport, N.Y.: Costello, 1996), 136.

wisdom," Paul remarks, "but we preach Christ crucified" (1 Cor 1:22–23). The content of Christian preaching has to be the central content of Christian faith itself, rooted in the whole of our scripture and adapted to the circumstances in which preacher and public find themselves: the news of God's mysterious being and God's presence in history, the message that in Jesus God the Son has entered our human race at a definite point in time and space to offer himself for us, and to reconcile us to his Father. The news, Augustine reminds us, is always *Christ*, the divine love for humanity he reveals and the call given to ancient Israel and to Jesus' disciples to love as God loves us. And the purpose of proclaiming this news of Christ, as movingly as one is able to do, is not just to provide it with a contemporary thoughtful context but to move the hearers to prayer, to contemplation of what God has done for us all, and to deeper personal engagement with the Church's faith.

4. Preaching, as Augustine and most of his early Christian contemporaries assumed, always takes a *figural* as well as an analytical or literal approach to interpreting biblical texts. As an act done in and for the Church, preaching sets out to interpret, in a powerfully motivating way, the texts that the Church has recognized as constituting, together, the norms for our faith and moral obligation. What we call the Hebrew Bible, along with the four Gospels, the letters of Paul, and the other works we regard as sketching out a "New Testament," have been generally recognized since the late second century as being authoritative for the Church's faith and practice in ways that no other texts, however valuable, are thought to be — this is why we bind them together as one volume, which we call "the Bible." And the perspective from which all of them are read and are thought to form a single, canonical whole is that we take them as forming together a zigzag narrative, a patchwork instruction, whose climax and resolution, as Augustine reminded the deacon Deogratias,[52] is Christ himself. St. Irenaeus, more than two centuries before Augustine, had made the same point:

If anyone reads the Scriptures with attention, he or she will find in them language about Christ, and a foreshadowing of our new calling (*vocatio*). For he is "the treasure hidden in the field" (Mt 13:44) — that is, in the world, "for the field is the world" (Mt 13:38) — but also hidden in the Scriptures, since he was pointed out there by means of types and parables.[53]

---

52. Augustine, *Instructing Beginners in Faith* 4.8, 70.

53. *Adversus Haereses* IV, 26.1, ed. Adelin Rousseau, Sources Chrétiennes 100 (Paris: Cerf, 1965), 712 (my translation).

To see in the writings of the whole canonical Bible a broad Christological reference that does not abrogate the original intention of its authors or our original understanding of a passage's social context, but which offers to the whole collection a wider, more ultimate meaning in the context of the community that now receives it in faith as Holy Scripture, is the heart of Christian figural reading—the hermeneutical key both to our present Catholic lectionary and to many centuries of theological reflection.

In the twenty-fourth chapter of Luke's Gospel, the risen Jesus is presented as walking along with two of his disciples as they make their way to the village of Emmaus on the evening of his resurrection. Although at first they do not recognize him, he converses intensely with them about the Hebrew scriptures—about "Moses and the prophets"—to show that in fact they had pointed to his own crucifixion and resurrection. It is only in the context of the "breaking of the bread" that "their eyes were opened" and they recognized him, Luke tells us in 24:13–35, but when that recognition takes place, they realize that even as they listened to him speak about scripture, "their hearts were burning within them." Preaching, as scriptural interpretation within a liturgical context, reaches its fulfilment in the celebration of the Eucharist, at which Christ is always the hidden presider. But even on the way to that fulfilment, it is intended to set our own hearts burning with love for Christ, who is the central content of all of faith's mysteries, and who walks with us still.

13

Spirit of Christ, Spirit of the Kingdom

Christocentrism and a Pneumatology for Mission

ANDREW SALZMANN

To befriend Robert Imbelli is to receive, in the midst of the meditative homilies, the convivial meals, the long conversations punctuated by short quips, many "gentle invitations" to encounter the Lord in shared beauty and in silence: an invitation to a performance of Handel's *Messiah,* the gift of a picture of a classic work of art, the sharing of a photocopied passage, just read. Henri Nouwen describes Andre Rublev's famous icon of the Holy Trinity as one such gentle invitation, an invitation

to participate in the intimate conversation that is taking place among the three divine angels and to join them around the table. The movement from the Father toward the Son and the movement of both Son and Spirit toward the Father become a movement in which the one who prays is lifted up and held secure. During a hard period of my life in which verbal prayer had become nearly impossible ... a long and quiet presence to this icon became the beginning of my healing. As I sat for long hours in front of Rublev's Trinity, I noticed how gradually my gaze became a prayer. This silent prayer slowly made my inner restlessness melt away and lifted me up into the circle of [their] love.[1]

1. Henri J. M. Nouwen, *Behold the Beauty of the Lord: Praying with Icons* (South Bend, Ind.:

In the opening chapter of this volume, Andrew Meszaros lays out the importance of Imbelli's Christocentricism to a theology that is supportive of the New Evangelization. Evangelization proclaims the *kerygma* of Christ's paschal mystery and prompts us to make a doxological, liturgical, personal response, even as it offers us the "space" to do so.[2] Thus, evangelization must offer not an abstract or "notional" picture of God but Jesus Christ as God in the flesh, God made fully visible (Jn 14:9) and impressed upon the imagination through scripture, service, devotions, and, of course, the arts. Cast Christocentrically, doctrines are no hindrance to the proclamation of the Christian message; rather, when "imaginative" enough to suggest the experience of Christ, dogmas become like the words of a Zen *koan*, those admittedly mysterious verbal formulae that, when accepted and pondered, constitute the precondition for a moment's silent realization—or, in the case of dogma and the Christian, for an encounter with "the Person about whom those teachings tell us something."[3]

The Problem of Christomonism?

But to return to Rublev: What about the Trinity? If Christocentricism is a virtue, perhaps it has not only the possibility of defect (the Christological amnesia prophetically decried by Imbelli) but also that of excess? Indeed, the Christocentric revival of Christian theology initiated by Karl Barth and introduced into Catholic thought by Hans Urs von Balthasar has long prompted charges of "Christomonism."[4] Yet, what is Christomonism? For Jacques Dupuis, SJ, "Christomonism" is merely the stigmatization of a Christocentricism that is legitimate in itself but which must be paired with a counter-

---

Ave Maria Press, 1987), 20–21. For Imbelli's appreciation of Nouwen's reflection on Rublev's icon, see his "For my shield this day a mighty power," *Priests and People* (April 1999): 133–37.

2. On the centrality of the paschal mystery in the relationship between Christology and Pneumatology, particularly in dialogue with the "Spirit Christology" of Roger Haight, see Robert P. Imbelli, "The New Adam and Life-Giving Spirit: the Paschal Pattern of Spirit Christology," *Communio* XXV, no 2 (Summer 1998): 233–52.

3. See Meszaros, "Christocentrism in Theology and Evangelization in the Thought of Robert P. Imbelli," chapter 1 in this volume.

4. Imbelli speaks of an "exclusive Christocentricism" prior to Vatican II that "risked consigning the Spirit to the status of 'forgotten person' of the Trinity" in his "Christ, the Giver of the Spirit," *Priests and People* 10, no. 4 (April 1996): 129.

balancing "Pneumatocentricism."[5] For Paul Althaus, it referred to God's limitation of all revelatory action to Christ alone.[6] For G. C. Berkouwer, Christomonism means that "all questions of the ultimate state of creation ... are resolved through the triumphant application of an unbounded grace found in Jesus Christ." In Barth's own response to the accusation of Christomonism, we find a fourth definition of Christomonism: the charge that he reduces the human race to Jesus alone, against which Barth insisted that he believed God and humanity exist as two realities united in Jesus Christ. In a fifth definition, John Cobb used the term to describe Barth's methodology, by which "every doctrine within the traditional systematic *loci* is processed and viewed through the lens of Christology"; this definition of "Christomonism" echoes the description offered by Meszaros of Imbelli's Christocentric theology, which presents "all of the questions considered in theological discourse ... [in] reference to" Jesus Christ. In presenting these last three definitions of Christomonism, David Guretzki also refers to a sixth way in which "Christomonism" is used: to refer to a Christological (and institutional) emphasis that wrongly edges out pneumatological themes, resulting in a "binitarianism" that focuses on Father and Son alone.[7] This last definition of Christomonism is of particular concern, clearly representing the possibility of a Christological "excess" that eclipses Trinitarian and pneumatological themes.

Here we face an irony that Imbelli is not shy to point out repeatedly: Vatican II was praised for its personalist interpretation of Jesus Christ as the

---

5. Jacques Dupuis, "Western Christocentrism and Eastern Pneumatology," *Clergy Monthly* 35 (1971): 191.

6. Paul Knitter, "Christomonism in Karl Barth's Evaluation of Non-Christian Religions," *Neue Zeitschrift für systematische Theologie une Religionsphilosophie* 13 (1971): 99. Knitter goes on to summarize Barth's reasoning: "since God has spoken only in Christ, therefore he speaks nowhere else, therefore there is the abyss between God and man" (106). Cf. Paul Althaus, *Die Christliche Wahrheit,* 7th ed. (Glütersloh: Glütersloh Verlaghaus, 1966), 56–60.

7. David Guretzki. *Karl Barth on the Filioque* (New York: Routledge, 2009), 42–43, esp. n. 131; on binitarianism, cf. 26 n. 108; duplicate word omitted from quote. Cf. Robert W. Jenson, "You Wonder Where the Spirit Went," *Pro Ecclesia* 2/3 (1993): 296–304.

Dupuis describes this last version of Christomonism: An emphasis on Christ and forgetfulness of the Spirit, which ends in "a juridical approach to the life of the Church as against a charismatic approach, a hierarchical conception against a more communal view, Roman centralism versus 'Sobornost', etc.... Full justice is not done to the Spirit as principle of life by which the Church not only is endowed with power but truly comes to existence. His function seems reduced to infusing life into a juridical structure, pre-established and set up by Christ" (192).

fullness of God's revelation; indeed, in the right context, all of its supporters still do. But in the decades after the Council, "the robust Christocentrism of *Dei Verbum* seems to evoke embarrassment in certain theological and missionary circles," which oppose its Christological normativity as recapitulated in the 2000 declaration *Dominus Iesus*.[8] This Christocentricism, Imbelli reminds us, was "not invented by the Congregation for the Doctrine of the Faith," which cited *Dei Verbum* seven times.[9] Yet, for as much as Imbelli can describe his Christocentrism as the heart of the Council, von Balthasar can call Vatican II no less than the "Council of the Spirit":

It has been a *Council of the Holy Spirit*, like no other Council. For the Spirit proceeds from the Father and the Son from the Father who created the world and its ordinanaces, and from the Son who redeemed the world through the Cross and through utter renunciation. But these are not two spheres that simply lie alongside one another, for the Father created all things in view of the Son, and the Son redeemed all things in view of the Father, in order to lay the completed kingdom at his feet (1 Cor 15:23).[10]

Thus, for von Balthasar, Vatican II is the "Council of the Spirit" because "the entire reform within the Church in the spirit of the Council" is "oriented to the great movement of the Church's mission" to bring unity to the human family in truth and love.[11] Despite offering a catalogue of passages in which Vatican II gives a more robustly pneumatological account of the Church, Jacques Dupuis's judgment of the extent to which the Council treated the Holy Spirit adequately is more negative· The Council, while growing "towards a fuller awareness of the function of the Spirit in the creation and life of the Church" from the notable inadequacy of *Sacrosanctum Concilium* to *Gaudium et Spes*'s vivid awareness "of the all-pervasive action of the Spirit in the Church's life and activity," did not give full recognition to the Spirit "as the one without whom the Church would not exist."[12] He writes,

---

8. Robert P. Imbelli, "The Reaffirmation of the Christic Center," in *Sic et Non: Encountering "Dominus Iesus*," ed. Stephen J. Pope and Charles Hefling (Maryknoll, N.Y.: Orbis, 2002), 97. As Imbelli writes elsewhere, "It is not faceless or anonymous Spirit we invoke, but the Spirit of Jesus Christ, poured out through Christ's Paschal Mystery" ("Christ, the Giver of the Spirit," 133).

9. Imbelli, "The Reaffirmation of the Christic Center," 98–99.

10. Hans Urs von Balthasar, "The Council of the Holy Spirit," *Communio* 17, no. 4 (1990): 608.

11. Balthasar, "The Council of the Holy Spirit," 602.

12. Dupuis, "Western Christocentrism," 194–95.

Christocentricism and Pneumatocentricism, far from being opposed, call for each other. For, if through His glorification Christ has become the universal principle of life, the exercise of His sanctifying power consists entirely in giving His Spirit to the Church.... It is the Body of Christ because Christ's Spirit is its soul.... Thus there is no dichotomy but perfect complementarity between the functions of the divine persons.... The Christ-event is at the center of the history of salvation, but it becomes operative in the economy of the Spirit.[13]

Dupuis's "complementarity" of Christ and Spirit speaks of their work in tandem, of "the economy of Christ *and that* of the Spirit," the "work of Christ *and that* of the Spirit."[14] While he regrets that a "situation progressively developed which eventually would lead to an option between the economy of Christ and that of the Spirit, between the role of Christ and that of the Spirit," which he considers a false dichotomy, the ease with which he speaks of the separate spheres of Christological and pnuematological activity seem to set up the very separation he laments.[15] How to integrate their work?

Josiah Royce on the Work of Son and Spirit

Imbelli submitted his dissertation, "Man's Quest for Salvation in the Thought of Josiah Royce," to Yale in 1973—a work that, while unpublished, won university recognition.[16] Josiah Royce (1855–1916) was a philosopher close to Charles Sanders Peirce and William James, and, like James, was interested in defending Christianity by articulating an account of faith which spoke to the modern condition. Unlike Peirce and James, however, Royce moved away from Pragmatism, concerned that, as an epistemological system, it was dangerously individualistic. Under some influence from Augustine, Royce believed that liberal Christianity was incapable of answering the exaggerated individualism of his time, and he sought, in the Pauline doctrines of sin and of Christ's atonement, to provide a response to the liberal Protestant rejection of these doctrines. He grounds this attempt in his analysis of the structure of the human will and in an attempt to articulate

---

13. Dupuis, "Western Christocentrism," 196–98.

14. Dupuis, "Western Christocentrism," 190, 191.

15. Dupuis, "Western Christocentrism," 191.

16. Robert P. Imbelli, "Man's Quest for Salvation in the Thought of Josiah Royce," PhD diss. (Yale University, 1973).

a metaphysics of community. For Imbelli, who had studied in Rome during the Council and returned to the United States in its aftermath, and who dissertated under Hans Frei and George Lindbeck, the search for a post-liberal Christology must have seemed timely, to say the least. However, before arriving at Royce's account of the relation of Christology and Pneumatology, or the Christocentricism that it requires, an anthropological prolegomenon is necessary.

Royce sought to correct notions of the self which made community secondary to individualism. Central to this project is Royce's account of the construction of the self, which occurs through the act of interpretation. In the first place, the act of interpretation involves articulating a purpose that one seeks to realize through action; in the second place, this sense of purpose or meaning comes from joining one's past, present, and intended future into a unifying harmony.[17] To this extent, then, Royce's account of the self is voluntaristic, or focused on the will. It is not, however, either Romantic (the self does not exist already in the depths of one's interiority, an ahistorical and unmediated pure emanation waiting to be found) or Rationalist (the self is not the preexistent building block of which community is then formed); for Royce, both philosophies would render true community secondary to individualistic accounts of an autonomous self.[18] Nor is it Empiricist, in which consciousness or the sense of self would come to exist through the mere accumulation of raw experience: Because a sense of selfhood only arises by the act of interpretation, which meaningfully connects one's past, present, and future (and choice between alternate futures), selfhood arises from conscious acts of judgment; thus, consciousness and will (beyond mere experience) are necessary constituents of the self.[19] Experience only results in selfhood when mediated through consciousness and will, which are therefore prior to experience and preconditions of the construction of the self.[20]

While this voluntaristic account of selfhood, because it places priority on the will in the construction of the self, may seem doomed to end in the very individualistic solipsism and relativism that Royce sought to avoid,

---

17. Imbelli, "Man's Quest for Salvation," 113. For Royce, the question of possible futures is the most important; the future has a priority in the construction of self because it is the primary field in which the will still operates (112).

18. Imbelli, "Man's Quest for Salvation," 109.

19. Imbelli, "Man's Quest for Salvation," 80.

20. Imbelli, "Man's Quest for Salvation," 76–77.

Royce believed that the structure of the will itself reveals the inadequacy or falseness of individualisms that place the existence of self prior to the existence of community. Indeed, it was Royce's discussion of the will's structure that led to his rejection of pragmatism. The pragmatist is revealed as an individualist because the pragmatist asserts that if I observe a truth claim to function in the world, that claim is thereby validated as true; but as a description of the phenomenology of knowing, the pragmatist's account is false. In reality, when I observe a truth claim to function in the world, I turn to others around me and ask, "Did you see that, too?" The will's intuitive awareness that it "ought" to find verification in the experience of others amounts to an additional condition for establishing truth, beyond functionality.[21] This condition is, moreover, social: The will is such that it relies on verification before making those judgments and interpretative acts which constitute not only my beliefs but my very personality.[22] As a result, the construction of the self through interpretation is a fundamentally communal act.[23] What is more, the will, by its very structure, strives not simply to validate its conclusions but to act on and for what is thus validated as true. This teleological structure of the will means that "the worlds which the will's action creates—the worlds of the material, the political, the scientific ... are ordered worlds, subject to the ought which directs all ordering activity according to the logos of the will itself."[24] In its drive for companionship in judgment and desire for order, the will tends not toward relativism or solipsism but toward the establishment of interpretive communities grounded in socially verified truth claims about what ought to be sought and why.[25] Royce considers this question—how the human subject realizes itself authentically through the will's interpretive work—to be the very question of salvation, in which the will actualizes the self by truth and community.[26]

Royce's investigation into the will's structure and its role in the development of personality lays the groundwork for his metaphysics of community.

21. Imbelli, "Man's Quest for Salvation," 84.

22. Imbelli, "Man's Quest for Salvation," 90.

23. Imbelli, "Man's Quest for Salvation," 111.

24. Imbelli, "Man's Quest for Salvation," 93.

25. Cf. Imbelli, "Man's Quest for Salvation," 114.

26. Imbelli, "Man's Quest for Salvation," 96. As Royce himself explains, "'If life as a whole is to have worth,' then the conflicts which divide a man inwardly and alienate man must 'be brought to an end'" (66).

The same work of interpretation that creates the self also creates the shared world in which selves live and construct themselves, again creating the context for meaningful community by linking its present to its past and possible futures at a social level, work that Royce believes is the basis of any community.[27] Indeed, cultures and societies are formed based on "their common projection of a teleological vision of the real," and as a result, philosophy, reflecting on the logos in the structure of its day, always belongs to its own context and time, even as the philosophies of all nations and periods are connected to the common attempt to articulate the shape and purpose of reality (as it is itself a product of the logos of the will).[28] Communities are further helped in this work of interpretation by their histories (which are the stories of the community's will in the past) and their art (which is the symbolic expression of the community's will for what it desires to become); both help to realize concretely what the community willed or wills for itself in the abstract.[29] It should be clear by now that the community's act of interpretation, by which many people cooperate in judgment about what good should be sought through collective action, amounts to a kind of reconciliation or mediation between the individual wills of the members of the community.[30] This work of mediation, reconciliation, or at-one-ment requires a mediator, whose work "is essentially an education in the art of understanding various minds, and in discovering how to bring them together."[31] The success of a community is never the result of structural socioeconomic processes but rather depends entirely on the quality of the mediator who attempts this community-creating interpretative work; the "mutual interpretation" by which a community agrees on the significance of the past and the goal of the future depends upon the "spontaneity and creativity" of the mediator's work, which, in doing the work of the establishment of a new community, "introduces novelty into the social system."[32]

The outlines of a Christology thus begin to take shape. Given this understanding of community, we can imagine a perfect community, one in which the individual person is shown how to find one's self authentically

27. Imbelli, "Man's Quest for Salvation," 107–8.
28. Imbelli, "Man's Quest for Salvation," 51.
29. Imbelli, "Man's Quest for Salvation," 47; cf. 33.
30. Imbelli, "Man's Quest for Salvation," 53.
31. Imbelli, "Man's Quest for Salvation," 54.
32. Imbelli, "Man's Quest for Salvation," 53; cf. 58.

in the collective interpretive act of a community in which each lives for the whole. Royce calls this the Beloved Community, a term he uses for the Kingdom of God, a community marked by holy living, living "not for Self, but for the quelling, the putting down of Self, and for the building up of peaceful, harmonious, but entirely unselfish life."[33] It is this spirit that distinguishes the Beloved Community. If the Kingdom of God required a justice in which each has what is needed for self-realization, it might easily collapse into a solipsistic concern for self or an uninhibited right to pure self-determination. Rather, what is needed is a love that integrates the self into a community, a love Royce identifies as the Holy Spirit. The Holy Spirit makes this possible by "helping us to interpret ourselves according to a common past (*anamenesis*) and future (hope), helping us to speak as 'we' not 'I' or many 'I's,'" moving us to act corporately, to "mutual identification of the members with one another through deeds which are performed and reciprocally appropriated."[34] The Spirit actualizes Christ's mediating work.

Here, Royce's postliberalism emerges in a twofold caution against careless language about the nature of love. In the first place, it is not love itself that is important but a specific kind of love; in the second place, it is extremely difficult to know the true nature of the correct kind of love, and therefore it must be shown or revealed by the example of Christ. This emphasis on the need for the revelation of the correct nature of love or proper order of relationships was Royce's reaction against the emotional tones of Romanticism; considering that "disordered love cannot give birth to the true order of community" and aware that "only redeemed love can build genuine community," Royce asked not whether he loved or hated his neighbor but rather whether his love of others had "the quality of the love that saves" and which Jesus reveals.[35] The love which saves has been transformed by Jesus' example into what Royce calls "loyalty," or the love which is "of a self for an united community."[36] "Loyalty" is not simply love for another individual or set of individuals — even an infinite set of individuals — but for the life of the community. Loyalty in particular is necessary because it is self-transcending; no individualist ethic, however benevolent, will suffice. Loyalty is love transformed into a *communitarian* love, in which the life of the community "be-

33. Imbelli, "Man's Quest for Salvation," 67.
34. Imbelli, "Man's Quest for Salvation," 320–22.
35. Imbelli, "Man's Quest for Salvation," 313, 312.
36. Imbelli, "Man's Quest for Salvation," 313.

comes the determining relation which orders all of one's other pursuits and projects."[37] It must be Christ who interprets the Holy Spirit for us, taking on the role of mediator or atoner (at-one-r).

The nature of the role of the atoning interpreter is unique within the community, however. Precisely because it is the atoner or mediator who models the new relations of personality which construct the new self, and because the construction of selfhood is a communal project, the atoner does not merely relate selves to other selves, individuals to other individuals, but relates community to itself by relating selves to some common third point shared by all: This common point is the Atoner himself.[38] The Atoner connects the many to "the commitment to the 'we' of interpersonal communion, the new creation Royce calls 'Man the community.'"[39] This direct relation to the Atoner allows "the Christic pattern" of loyalty to permeate "the life of the members" and for the Community to build itself up through a "liberating con-spiracy."[40] As a result, the Atoner becomes the Community in miniature; Jesus Christ must be the Kingdom of God in his person, because he is the logos (or form) which orders the relationships of all those in the community, possessing, living, and modelling the Holy Spirit for all.[41] And because the Atoner is the Beloved Community (or because Christ is the kingdom), the Beloved Community must share not only the Atoner's Holy Spirit but also the Atoner's own mission: "the mission of so furthering the work of loyalty that all humanity might be at-oned in the unity of the Spirit. It is the commitment and devotion to the task of 'inventing and applying the arts which shall win men over to unity, and which shall overcome their original hatefulness by the gracious love, not of mere individuals, but of communities.'"[42] The Spirit joins us to Christ's work; their work is not parallel.

As far as I know, Imbelli has not quoted Royce is his other writings, but Royce's influence is present there in ways other than the role of art in constructing the self. This very pattern of the relationship between Christians, Christ, and the Spirit seems to reproduce itself throughout Imbelli's subsequent work. In his response to the Spirit Christology of Rog-

---

37. Imbelli, "Man's Quest for Salvation," 315.
38. Imbelli, "Man's Quest for Salvation," 315–16.
39. Imbelli, "Man's Quest for Salvation," 316–17.
40. Imbelli, "Man's Quest for Salvation," 322.
41. Imbelli, "Man's Quest for Salvation," 311.
42. Imbelli, "Man's Quest for Salvation," 323.

er Haight, SJ, Imbelli returns to the theme of sharing in the life-giving Adam, whose death becomes the model of Christian personhood and allows one to become like Christ, "no longer the autonomous individual, but person-in-relation."[43] Elsewhere, Imbelli reminds us that salvation is "not merely a new situation," in which the death we fear has been definitively vanquished; rather, salvation "is a new self being transformed into the likeness of Christ," an incorporation of persons into Christ which is "the work of the Holy Spirit."[44] The Spirit does not only actualize Christ's work in our lives, however; our relationship with the Spirit is modeled by Christ.

In the next section, I would like to suggest that we find in Imbelli's presentation of Royce the fundamental insight for integrating Christology and Pneumatology in such a way that Christocentricism cannot be Christomonism: a Christology which is sufficiently kenotic to allow for a robust account of the centrality of the role of the Spirit in the earthly life of the Christ.[45] Recall that it was precisely the division between the work or economy of Christ and that of the Spirit which allows Christocentricism and Pneumatocentricism to exist in tandem and enter into direct competition.[46] An account of Christ's dependency on the Spirit in his earthly mission will now help us to integrate them, hopefully banishing the possibility of one displacing the other in the process. By no means a "low Christology," it will allow Christ's empowering anointing with the Spirit to model our own relation both to the Spirit and to the mission of proclaiming the kingdom.

43. Imbelli, "The New Adam and Life-Giving Spirit," 249.

44. Robert Imbelli, *Rekindling the Christic Imagination: Theological Meditations for the New Evangelization* (Collegeville, Minn.: Liturgical Press, 2014).

45. In his "Dwelling Place for God in the Spirit," *Dunwoodie Review* 6, no. 2 (1966):175–206, Fr. Imbelli offers an account of the Spirit which anticipates some of the work which would be done in his dissertation: the Spirit is active throughout history, and Church does the work of interpreting the Spirit's work across history in the light of its privileged disclosure in Christ and his suffering on the Cross, by which the history effected by our alienation from God is finally destroyed and reversed when the body of the Church is conformed to its Head.

46. As Raniero Cantalamessa, OFM Cap, laments, "Pneumatology tends to part company with Christology and locate itself after the latter, rather than within it," in *The Holy Spirit in the Life of Jesus: The Mystery of Christ's Baptism*, trans. Alan Neame (Collegeville, Minn.: Liturgical Press, 1994), 9.

The Anointed's Proclamation of the Kingdom of God:
The Spirit in the Life of the Christ

Although Josiah Royce is usually described as a philosopher of religion, Imbelli argues that Royce was also a philosophical theologian in the proper sense precisely because he confesses that he cannot give a full philosophical account of that new spiritual impulse with which the Mediator empowers the Beloved Community, that is, of the Holy Spirit. I would like to give a more explicitly theological summary of Royce's insight. If integrating the work of Christ and the work of the Spirit will overcome the dualism which forces us to fall either into Christomonism or a Pneumatology unmoored from Christ because it places the work of Christ and Spirit in tandem, and if the key to this integration lies in a deeper appreciation of the Spirit empowering Christ's redeeming mission during his earthly life, then a starting point for considering this more integrated view will be the title "Christ" itself. Christ's redeeming mission is, of course, the proclamation of the Kingdom of God; the opening words of Jesus' public ministry proclaim, not his arrival, but the arrival of the kingdom: "The kingdom of God is at hand. Repent!" (Mk 1:15; cf. Mt 4:17). Luke introduces the kingdom with Jesus' own exegesis on Isaiah 61 in the synagogue at Nazareth:

The spirit of the Lord God is upon me, because the Lord has anointed me; He has sent me to bring good news to the afflicted, to bind up the broken hearted, To proclaim liberty to the captives, release to the prisoners, To announce a year of favor from the LORD and a day of vindication by our God; To comfort all who mourn; to place on those who mourn in Zion diadem instead of ashes, To give them oil of gladness instead of mourning, a glorious mantle instead of a faint spirit. (Is 61:1–2; cf. Lk 3:18–19).[47]

In taking up Isaiah's hopes for a restored Israel and naming them "the Kingdom of God," Jesus has already done something new: He has modified the messianic hopes from a world in which Israel reigned over the nations into a new order in which God actively reigns over all.[48] By the Kingdom of God,

47. While "Kingdom of God" is not a phrase which Isaiah himself uses, the Old Testament, in emphasizing a coming reign of God "not only over nature, but also over history," contains an "implied Kingdom of God ... not equivalent to the kingdom of Israel" (*Anchor Bible Dictionary* [hereafter, *ABD*], IV.5). Imbelli considers this inaugural sermon to be of "primordial importance" to contemporary Christology ("The New Adam and Life-Giving Spirit," 236).

48. Geerhardus Vos, *The Teaching of Jesus Concerning the Kingdom of God* (New York: American

Jesus means that it will at last be "on earth as it is in heaven" (Mt 6:10), indicating not only the moral renewal by which human rebelliousness against God would cease but also the final destruction of all the ways in which the created world falls short of God's will for it and suffers (Mt 13:41). "Death"—the painful limits of the human condition which stand in what seems to be a final judgment against the value of our lives—and the fear of death are destroyed.[49] This is also a common challenge to a Christocentric view of the Gospel: The centrality of the Kingdom of God in Jesus' preaching has led many to point out that Jesus proclaimed "not himself, but the Kingdom."[50] Against any "Christomonistic" neglect of the Holy Spirit, it must be admitted that the Spirit is at every juncture essential to the coming of the Kingdom of God: To understand the person and message of Jesus, we must understand the anointing by which he is the Christ, and by which he accomplishes his mission. Indeed, to understand our relationship with the Lord Jesus, we must understand how we share in that anointing and that mission.

Readers and friends of Fr. Imbelli will know the importance that the Transfiguration, that great Trinitarian theophany, has to his Christology. In a similar spirit, I would like to continue this reflection on the nature of Christ's anointing by turning to another great Trinitarian theophany, the one which marks the beginning of Jesus' ministry: the baptism in the River Jordan.[51] The baptism of Jesus can be confusing, even theologically awkward. The first point of confusion seems shared by John the Baptist himself: What need has Jesus for a baptism of repentance? The questions only continue with the descent of the Spirit upon Jesus. What exactly descended upon Jesus in the form of the dove? Early in Christian history, this passage was sometimes used as a justification for the Gnostic heresy of adoptionism, the claim that the human person of Jesus was adopted at some point (perhaps his birth, perhaps now, at the baptism) by the divine person of the Logos.[52] If

Tract Society, 1903), 15–24. For an appraisal of this work's influence, see Danny Olinger's introduction to its 2017 reprint by Fontes Press, xviii–xxv.

49. Cf. Imbelli, "The New Adam and Life-Giving Spirit," 246–48; Imbelli, *Rekindling the Christic Imagination*, 11–15, 55–56, 59–61.

50. Cf., for example, Karl Rahner, *Foundations of Christian Faith*, trans. William Dych (New York: Crossroad, 2002), 250–51.

51. For Fr. Imbelli's use of the Transfiguration, see, for example: "The Reaffirmation of the Christic Center," 104–6.

52. Cf., for example, Riemer Roukema, *Jesus, Gnosis and Dogma* (New York: T and T Clark, 2010), 53.

we reject the adoptionist claim, then what did Jesus receive in this baptism? Did he not already possess the Holy Spirit? What is more, as fully human and fully divine, what exactly does the Holy Spirit empower the all-powerful Word to do?

These questions certainly exercised the church fathers.[53] Irenaeus of Lyon resolves any adoptionist or Gnostic interpretations of Jesus' anointing with the Spirit at his baptism by speaking of Christ's two anointings. As summarized by Kilian McDonnell, OSB, the Word is anointed with divinity from all eternity; in the theophany at Jordan, the Holy Spirit "descends and anoints the Lord at the Jordan," a second anointing that "comes out of the prophetic tradition which promises that the Spirit of God will descend on the Expected One," so that from this moment, Jesus—who from his conception was already the divine Word united to flesh—is now anointed in his flesh with the power of the Spirit and "is called 'the Christ.'"[54]

But why is an anointing with the Spirit helpful to the Word in the singular, cooperative work of bringing about the Kingdom of God? While it is certainly true that Jesus' mission was to proclaim the Kingdom of God, it is also true that Jesus identifies his very self with the Kingdom of God. At the level of simple exegesis, the Jesus of the synoptic Gospels describes a kingdom that is "already mysteriously present" in his work and words.[55] Jesus, in introducing himself to the people of Judea, is able to announce that the Kingdom of God is "at hand": Precisely because Jesus is Emmanuel, God "is with us" (Mt 1:23, 18:20, 28:20).[56] If the Kingdom of God is where the Spirit of God acts, then the Kingdom of God is present first in the person of Jesus insofar as it is Jesus upon whom that Messianic Spirit rests at the baptism (cf. Lk 17:21).[57] The Spirit is the power of the kingdom, entrusted to the Anointed, the Messiah, the Christ (cf. Lk 11:20).[58] This is the mean-

---

53. Kilian McDonnell, OSB, *The Baptism of Jesus in the Jordan* (Collegeville, Minn.: Liturgical Press, 1996), 112.

54. McDonnell, *The Baptism of Jesus,* 117.

55. *ABD* IV.57.

56. *ABD* IV.58. It concludes, "the Kingdom of Heaven in Matthew is the message of Jesus … but also the message about Jesus."

57. In the words of Roch Kereszty, OCist., "The Kingdom of God is thus the hidden but powerful presence of God in Jesus restoring wholeness and life to all those who accept him in faith," *Jesus Christ: Fundamentals of Christology* (New York: Alba House, 2002), 113.

58. The phrase "finger of God" is understood (e.g., by Augustine) as referring to the Spirit of God. Cf. *De spir. et litt.* 27.15.

ing of the words spoken by the Voice at the moment of the Baptism: "This is my Son, whom I love; with him I am well pleased" (Mt 3:17). Its opening words ("This is my Son") point the reader to an enthronement psalm, proclaiming Jesus to be the Davidic figure establishing the kingdom through the iron rod of harsh judgment and harkening to Christ's chosen eschatological identity as the Son of Man (cf. Ps 2:7); its conclusion ("in whom I am well-pleased") points us to Isaiah's "Servant Song," in which the faithful servant establishes universal justice with such gentle mercy that "a bruised reed he will not break, and a dimly burning wick he will not quench," typical of Jesus' ministry of healing and forgiveness in the interim (Is 42, esp. 1–3).[59]

In his own exegesis of the baptism, Raniero Cantalemessa describes two ways in which Christ's baptismal anointing with the Spirit might be understood. Taken in an active sense, the anointing is something Jesus does, invoking the Spirit "to attest Christ's dignity" before the crowds. This interpretation of the baptism makes sense if we have a Christology in which Jesus possesses and exercises all of the divine prerogatives of the Eternal Word in his human nature: Since such a Jesus needs no help from the Spirit for his mission, what else could the event be but a testimony to his divinity? A hard division between the work or economy of Jesus and of the Spirit would seem to suggest a similar confidence that Jesus possessed the power to complete his mission; to say that Jesus might have achieved the work of redemption—or even a major part of that work—by his own solitary power, human or divine, is surely a precondition of Christomonism. Or, suggests Cantalemessa, we might think about the baptism as a passive event, because in it, Jesus receives in his humanity and from the Spirit the strength he needs for the work of establishing the kingdom: "The Holy Spirit comes to anoint Jesus with the powers necessary for his mission, which is not simply the mission of saving the human race but of saving it in a particular way... the way of self-abasement, willing obedience, and expiatory sacrifice. To skip this moment in Jesus' life would mean putting off his redemptive 'fiat' until the night in Gethsemane."[60] This passive interpretation of the Baptism makes Jesus dependent upon the power of the Holy Spirit for the accomplishment of his work—not because he is not the omnipotent Word

59. Kereszty, *Jesus Christ*, 99–103.
60. Cantalemessa, *The Holy Spirit in the Life of Jesus*, 11.

of God from all eternity (he is) but because "though he was in the form of God, he did not regard equality with God something to be grasped" and "emptied himself," even "becoming obedient to death" (Phil 2:5–8).[61] Such a claim not only fits with the biblical data—"After the baptism that John preached ... God anointed"—christed—"Jesus of Nazareth with the Holy Spirit and power. He went about doing good and healing all those oppressed by the devil" (Acts 10:37ff)—but it also renders Jesus the ultimate model of our own relationship with the Holy Spirit, who is to guide and strengthen us as well (cf. Heb 12:2).[62] Christ himself is the kingdom, humanity empowered by Spirit.[63]

It may seem that integrating the work of Word and Spirit in Christ's ministry could itself end in another kind of Christomonism. Commenting on a similar move by Barth, Guretzki asked, "how can Barth so closely identify the work of Christ and the work of the Spirit without being opened to the charge of making the Spirit's role in the economy of salvation superfluous?"[64] For Irenaeus, however, the mutual reliance of Spirit on Jesus and Jesus on Spirit does not end in an identity; as McDonnell comments, Irenaeus avoids a reduction of Jesus' divinity to the Spirit which descended upon him at the Baptism because he separates the question of Jesus' divinity (Jesus as the incarnation of the Logos) from this anointing with the Spirit of God. As a result, the Spirit does not become a constituent part of the person of the Redeemer; the Spirit continues to *act upon Jesus Christ*, never acting *as Jesus Christ*.[65] Cooperation does not destroy distinction.[66]

61. This emptying, or *kenosis,* is the basis of "kenotic Christology," which, while not denying that Jesus knew that God was his true Father and had sent him on a saving mission, and without denying that Jesus is the fully divine Word, holds that the Word's omniscience and omnipotence are not fully expressed in the earthly life of his human nature. Cf. the International Theological Commission's 1985 document, "The Consciousness of Christ Concerning Himself and His Mission," http://www.vatican.va/roman_curia/congregations/cfaith/cti_documents/rc_cti_1985_coscienza-gesu_en.html.

62. McDonnell sees this verse as a reference to Christ's baptism (*The Baptism of Jesus*, 11).

63. Cf. Imbelli, "Dwelling Place for God in the Spirit," 186–88 and 195–96.

64. Guretzki, *Karl Barth*, 142. Barth's answer to this is that the Spirit is the Teacher of the Word (cf. CD 1/2, 244). Though that fits well with Barth's doctrine of revelation, the biblical texts speak of the Spirit as empowering Christ. Hence, Cantalamessa asserts that the Spirit need not teach words to the Word, but gives power to his words (cf. Cantalamessa, *The Holy Spirit in the Life of Jesus*, 39).

65. McDonnell, *The Baptism of Jesus*, 116–23.

66. On the importance of the conjoint working of Christ and the Spirit, and the Spirit's extension of the work to believers, see Imbelli, "Christ, the Giver of the Spirit," 132.

Anointed for Mission (but Not Only Mission)

Here, we can speak of our participation in this second anointing, the one by which the Spirit empowers Jesus for the proclamation of the kingdom. As McDonnell—continuing his commentary on Irenaeus—notes,

The participation of believers in the anointing of Jesus at the Jordan is central.... The Spirit descends on Jesus so that the Spirit "might get accustomed to dwell in the human race, to repose on men, to reside within the word God has modeled, working the Father's will in them and renewing them from oldness to newness in Christ." All of this is the work of the Spirit descending on Jesus at the Jordan.... "We ourselves received from the superabundance of this anointing, and thus we are saved."[67]

Already in Luke, we see the disciples of Jesus sharing in his messianic anointing to reverse the effects of sin and specifically to assist in establishing the Kingdom of God (Lk 10:9).[68]

Recalling that Isaiah described the Davidic Messiah as anointed with the Spirit of God for the mission of establishing the kingdom, we turn to a different prophecy in Isaiah 11:2, in which that Spirit is described in detail: "The spirit of the LORD shall rest upon him: a spirit of wisdom and of understanding, A spirit of counsel and of strength, a spirit of knowledge and of fear of the LORD, and his delight shall be the fear of the LORD" (Is 11:2). It was precisely in picking up the scroll of Isaiah at Nazareth and identifying himself as the one upon whom this Spirit rested that Jesus staked his claim to be the Messiah (Lk 4:18–21). The Roman collect for confirmation, first found in Hippolytus' *Apostolic Tradition* and used consistently in the Latin tradition, reads:

Almighty and eternal God, who in your kindness gave to this servant a new birth through water and the Holy Spirit, and granted to him remission of all his sins; send forth from heaven upon him your sevenfold Spirit, the Holy Consoler. The Spirit of wisdom and understanding. The Spirit of counsel and fortitude. The Spirit of knowledge and piety. Mercifully fill him with the Spirit of your fear, and

---

67. McDonnell, *The Baptism of Jesus*, 119–20.

68. Cantalamessa, quoting Vatican II's assertion that the Lord Jesus "has made his Mystical Body share in the anointing by the Spirit with which he himself has been anointed," comments that the Church is "brought about by sharing in Christ's anointing," particularly through sacramental anointing (*The Holy Spirit in the Life of Jesus*, 13, 16–17).

seal him with the sign of the cross of Christ, that he may obtain everlasting life. Through Christ our Lord.

For as much effort as we expend teaching children the seven gifts of the Holy Spirit, the real importance of these seven gifts is that they point to the one kingdom-establishing Spirit in whose anointing of Jesus they will share by the chrismatic anointing of confirmation. It is precisely by reason of this anointing, Augustine writes, that the anointed are called Christians, sharing in Christ's anointing and becoming "other Christs."[69] Within the Ethiopian tradition, the connection between chrismation/confirmation and the establishment of the Kingdom of God is clearer. The chrismating priest, invoking the Holy Spirit over the chrism, asks, "May it be a dwelling place for justice, a seal of life, and assurance for your servants." In anointing the newly baptized, he prays, "I anoint you with the holy anointing of our God, the Messiah, and with the indelible seal," and again, "I anoint you with the downpayment [arrha] of the kingdom of heaven," and "I anoint you with the anointing of the Holy Spirit, the fulfillment of grace through faith and justice."[70] If our anointing with the Spirit makes us *alter Christus*, confessing Jesus "the Christ" is clearly as much a pneumatological as a Christological confession.

The above discussion of Christ's two anointings — the Son's eternal anointing with the Spirit and its earthly manifestation by which Jesus is anointed with the Spirit of power and which is extended to his followers — has sought to remind us that Jesus is anointed with the power of the Spirit for a specific purpose: the extension of the Kingdom of God, through the establishment of justice, the destruction of the ways in which creation falls short of God's will for it, and the reversal of the effects of sin.[71] This sketch of the mission of Jesus, however, is only partial, lacking as yet Jesus' final purpose of the proclamation of the Kingdom of God. We do not share in Christ's annoiting only for the purpose of sharing his mission.

69. For example, *en. Ps.* 26.2. Engaging this theme, Imbelli writes, "the Link between Christ and Church is precisely the Spirit who anoints Jesus as the Christ and who, through Jesus, now anoints believers as Christians, anointed ones" (Imbelli, "Christ, the Giver of the Spirit," 131).

70. Cf. Emmanuel Fritsch, "Mēron et chrismation dans la liturgie éthiopienne modern," in *Chrismation et confirmation: Questions autour d'un rite post-baptismal*, ed. Carlo Braga (Roma: Edizioni Liturgiche, 2009), 253–64. My translation.

71. On the realization of creation's end in Christ "now extended by the Spirit to the whole mankind," see Imbelli, "Dwelling Place for God in the Spirit," 195.

What has been omitted can only be filled in through a brief look at a third, final anointing: the anointing of the Lord's feet by the sinful woman (cf. Lk 7:36–38). Her liberation was in the service not of an individualized will to power but rather in the service of a will to communion, in service of her relation with Jesus (and by extension, but only by extension, his disciples). Christ's anointing as Israel's redeemer is also Christ's anointing as Israel's spouse: It is an anointing with the Spirit that is also the Spirit of Love and communion between Father and Son, and it calls forth the return anointing made by the woman who, because she was liberated from many sins, had therefore "shown great love" (Lk 7:47). Imbelli speaks of our redemption as "personation," the idea that "we are ourselves are not yet persons but are through Christ and the Spirit in the process of becoming persons." This is exemplified by Dante's transformation through the course of the *Divine Comedy,* an "individual becoming person through the transformation of his relations and thus rendered integral and apt to enter into the relational community of the Trinity." Personhood, he concludes, "is less a given than a gift: the grace of relation to the three-personed God."[72] To share in Christ's anointing with the Spirit and with the sinful woman to return to Christ the anointing of our own love allows us to enter the communion of love which is the kingdom, realizing the ancient promise of Yahweh's espousal of Israel.

Conclusion

Fr. Imbelli's Christocentricism is strident; as he once wrote, "One cannot stress enough that the only grounds Christians have for speaking of a God who is Trinity is Jesus Christ."[73] It is not Christomonism. He sees this Christocentric experience as moving dynamically toward the experience (and thus the doctrine) of the Trinity. Fr. Imbelli found Walter Kaspar's description of Trinitarian doctrine as "the grammar of doxology," as the basic pattern that a Christian's praise of God takes, "a stimulating suggestion"; in what may be most characteristic of his own theological thought, however, he encourages us to transcend the merely textual implications of "grammar": "The 'grammar' is, of course, indispensable; but the hymnody, the prayer,

72. Imbelli, "For my shield," 136. Cf. "The New Adam and Life-Giving Spirit," 249.

73. Imbelli, "For my shield," 134. For an elaboration on the relationship between personhood and mission, see chapter 14 by Angela Franks in this volume, "The Mission and Person of Christ and the Christian in Hans Urs von Balthasar."

and the poetry remain the privileged expression of our praise and thanksgiving. Doxology is the soil where the doctrine takes root and becomes life-giving." In his frequent turns to iconography and Dante, in the course which ended in a shared supper and liturgy, in his familiar notes that he remembers his friends in prayer through the year, Fr. Imbelli has pointed us all to the rich experience in which theology takes root.[74] His concern about the "Christological deficit" is perhaps motivated precisely by the need to account for the ways in which the Gospel message is fundamentally about the proclamation *of the Kingdom of God*, for the establishment of this kingdom is also fundamentally Trinitarian, promising as it does the Spirit as our advocate for the kingdom. We are closer to recapturing a Christocentric proclamation of the Gospel when we realize that the kingdom exists, in seed, within Christ himself, as Christ himself, and that the kingdom is advanced when we are united to Christ, who gives us the Spirit by which we are conformed to the Jesus who is the kingdom in miniature. Properly understood, one cannot even say "Jesus Christ"—or "Christocentricism"!—without speaking of the Father who anoints him Christ with the power of the Spirit, for the establishment of the kingdom. By appreciating that the Christ's redemptive work is done by Christ through the Spirit which anoints him, that the work of Son and Spirit are not parallel but deeply integrated, and that this anointing is in the service of our betrothal to the Lord, we see more clearly that to call Jesus "the Christ" contains the full Trinitarian faith of the Gospel. But our incorporation into the kingdom through the extension of Christ's anointing with the Spirit brings with it a powerful imperative to evangelize. However correct the Scholastic claim that the Spirit's defining characteristic within the Trinity is to be passively "spirated" by the Father and Son might be, the Spirit is far from passive: in fact, the Spirit's "personal being and agency *is koinonia*"—the Spirit bursts into the economy with love's own restless drive to draw all to the Beloved.[75]

---

74. He himself would name the doxological "moment" of the liturgy, especially of baptism and confirmation, as the privileged context for the development of any doctrine of the Holy Spirit. See Robert Imbelli. "The Holy Spirit," *The New Dictionary of Theology*, ed. Joseph A. Komonchak, Mary Collins, and Dermat Lane (Wilmington, Del.: Glazier, 1987), 474.

75. Imbelli, "The New Adam and Life-Giving Spirit," 252.

14

The Mission and Person of Christ and the Christian in Hans Urs von Balthasar

ANGELA FRANKS

Fr. Robert Imbelli has repeatedly returned to the "Christic center" of Catholic faith and life, as exemplified by the "New Evangelization."[1] He summarizes this evangelical movement as "the call to renewed conversion to Jesus Christ and the passionate desire to share his Good News with others that they 'may have life and have it to the full.'"[2] Hand in hand with this Christocentric vision of evangelization is Imbelli's emphasis on the Christian's transformation, which is a kind of "Christification."[3] Transformation is ultimately a matter of being made a new creation "in Christ," Imbelli

Thanks are due to Adrian Walker, Jeremy Wilkins, and participants at the 2017 Symposium on Advancing the New Evangelization at Benedictine College, all of whom provided comments on earlier drafts of this essay.

1. The Christic center is developed in, *inter alia*, Robert P. Imbelli, *Rekindling the Christic Imagination: Theological Meditations for the New Evangelization* (Collegeville, Minn.: Liturgical Press, 2014), 1–18. The theme of the New Evangelization ties together the whole book but is developed, in particular, on pages 91–101.

2. Imbelli, *Rekindling the Christic Imagination*, xix.

3. Imbelli, *Rekindling the Christic Imagination*, 5–6. Imbelli cites Paul Evdokimov's development of this theme as a variation of *theosis*, in particular, in the latter's *Orthodoxy*, trans. Jeremy Hummerstone (Hyde Park, N.Y.: New City Press, 2011).

notes, citing 2 Corinthians 5:17.[4] This happens primarily through the Eucharist, in and by means of which we become "eucharistic selves."[5] The transubstantiation of the bread and wine is a model for the transformation of ourselves into the Incarnate Son, a transformation that does not despise the material but rather elevates it to be truly revelatory of God. This is possible because, as the Colossians hymn audaciously declares, it first happened in Jesus Christ: "in the all too human face of this executed criminal we can glimpse the very image of the invisible God."[6]

In this essay, I will develop the resonances of Fr. Imbelli's thought with that of Hans Urs von Balthasar, in particular, as it concerns the questions of trinitarian Christology, identity, and mission. Balthasar argues that the identity of the Incarnate Son is simply his mission as the "One sent." This identity-in-mission is the temporal extension of his eternal procession from the Father. His divine person is this subsisting relation of filiation, and, as incarnate, this relation is transposed into mission. Further, what is simply true of Jesus Christ can be analogously true of the Christian who participates in Christ's universal and unique mission. This participation-in-mission is the reception of theological personhood, and it is an essential element in the New Evangelization.[7]

In this brief summary, many themes dear to Fr. Imbelli's heart are sketched. Indeed, Imbelli's engagement with Balthasar's theology has been receptive, yet not uncritical. In particular, he has judged Balthasar's insistence that personhood is a properly theological and not philosophical category to be, perhaps, excessive.[8] At the close of this essay, I will try to do justice to his concerns while explicating Balthasar's own. In this way, I will continue a conversation with Robert Imbelli begun many years ago. My hope is that this essay might be one expression of "being *in Christ*," name-

---

4. Imbelli, *Rekindling the Christic Imagination*, 52.

5. Imbelli, *Rekindling the Christic Imagination*, 53.

6. Imbelli, *Rekindling the Christic Imagination*, 5.

7. For different, although complementary, treatments of Balthasar in relation to the New Evangelization, see Peter Henrici, SJ, "Von der Auslegung zu den Denkanstössen: Zur Wirkungsgeschichte Balthasars im Blick auf die Neue Evangelisierung," in Hans Urs von Balthasar-Stiftung, *Eine Theologie für das 21. Jahrhundert: Zur Wirkungsgeschichte Hans Urs von Balthasars*, Symposium zu seinem 25. Todestag (Einsiedeln: Johannes Verlag, 2013), 12–25; Angelo Cardinal Scola, "L'Apporto della theologia di Hans Urs von Balthasar alla Nuova Evangelizzazione," in the same volume, 150–74.

8. Although he cites the distinction approvingly in *Rekindling the Christic Imagination*, 42.

ly, a moment of "communication and communion" of friends seeking the life-giving truth of Christ together.[9]

The Identity Crisis of the Mission Field

The New Evangelization attempts to bring the Gospel into the post-Christian mission field of the developed world.[10] The work of sociologist Zygmunt Bauman displays a snapshot of this world. He names it a "liquid modernity," which privileges flexibility, flow, ever more choices, and ever fewer limits or "solids."[11] It is, as Ratzinger puts it, "the primacy of the 'makable' over the 'made,'" of the synthetic over the given, of potential matter over actual form.[12] Liquid modernity glorifies what Servais Pinckaers calls the "freedom of indifference," a freedom that relies upon numerous options, rather than the "freedom for excellence," the freedom that is oriented toward the good.[13] The slogan for liquid freedom of indifference could be "I choose choice."[14]

In the liquid mission field, the primary focus becomes the effort, as T. S. Eliot writes, "to prepare a face to meet the faces that you meet."[15] This is the endless project of personal identity-construction; yet, given the unquestioned presupposition of the freedom of indifference, this project must be pursued apart from questions about ultimate goods. Such goods hamper the

---

9. As Fr. Imbelli summarizes this life *en Christoi* in *Rekindling the Christic Imagination*, 75.

10. See, for example, John Paul II, Encyclical Letter on the Permanent Validity of the Church's Missionary Mandate, *Redemptoris missio* (December 7, 1990) at the Holy See, http://w2.vatican.va/content/john-paul-ii/en/encyclicals/documents/hf_jp-ii_enc_07121990_redemptoris-missio.html, especially §33; Congregation for the Doctrine of the Faith, *Doctrinal Note on Some Aspects of Evangelization*, October 6, 2007, at the Holy See, http://www.vatican.va/roman_curia/congregations/cfaith/documents/rc_con_cfaith_doc_20071203_nota-evangelizzazione_en.html. The magisterial teaching on the New Evangelization is usefully summarized by Perry J. Cahall, "The Nucleus of the New Evangelization," *Nova et Vetera* (English edition) 11, no. 1 (2013): 39–56.

11. In particular, see Zygmunt Bauman, *Liquid Modernity* (Cambridge: Polity Press, 2000), and *Does Ethics Have a Chance in a World of Consumers?* Institute for Human Sciences Vienna Lecture Series 3 (Cambridge, Mass.: Harvard University Press, 2009).

12. Joseph Ratzinger, *Introduction to Christianity*, 2nd ed., trans. J. R. Foster and Michael J. Miller (San Francisco: Ignatius Press, 2004), 65.

13. Servais Pinckaers, OP, *The Sources of Christian Ethics*, 3rd ed., trans. Sr. Mary Thomas Noble, OP (Washington, D.C.: The Catholic University of America Press, 1995), 327–78.

14. A slogan on a sign held by a prochoice protester.

15. T. S. Eliot, *The Love Song of J. Alfred Prufrock* (1920), line 27.

freedom of indifference by channeling it: if something is truly good, I might be pressured by its very goodness into accepting it. And once my will is so pressured, I cannot be free. As a result, our liquid pursuit of identity does not — cannot — concern itself with what is truly good but rather with how to appear good.

Liquid modernity is fascinated with appearances, which are privileged over reality. We try to *look* good rather than to *be* good. We immerse ourselves in activity. But there is no natural telos to the trajectory of appearances. If the goal is not the positive "good" but rather the comparative "better," there is no place to rest, because one can always look better. As Baumann says, everyone is enrolled into the exhausting and endless labor of identity-formation from scratch.[16] The futile *technē* of self-creation *ex nihilo* is the contemporary crisis of identity. It is a dispersion of the self into ephemeral appearances.

To meet this crisis requires understanding who I am beyond what I do or how I appear. To reframe the problem using philosophical terminology: the answer to the question "who am I" cannot be found in a list of metaphysical accidents. A further problem is that neither can a satisfying answer be found in substance, insofar as a human being is an individual substance of a rational nature. This definition is true, of course, and a necessary foundation. But it is not sufficient to provide personal identity. What makes me different from all the other subsisting individuals with a rational nature? We see this even more clearly when thinking about why we love a particular person. The answer is surely not because she is an individual rational substance.

Hans Urs von Balthasar suggests a solution to this quandary in his *Theo-Drama* when he traces the development, within Christian thought, of the distinction between rational individuals and persons. He offers a way out of the impasse by moving from philosophy to theology, from subsisting individuals to the personalizing mission given to each human being by God. This theme was no afterthought for Balthasar's theology; his nephew, the philosopher Peter Henrici, noted that "mission" (*Sendung*) was Balthasar's "favorite word."[17] The reason why is found in Balthasar's own experience of

16. Bauman, *Liquid Modernity*, 22–28.

17. Henrici proposes that this *Lieblingswort* was replaced by task (*Auftrag*) in Balthasar's later writings. Peter Henrici, "Die Weltauftrag des Christen," in *Vermittlung als Auftrag*, ed. Hans Urs von Balthasar-Stiftung, Symposium zum 90. Geburtstag von Hans Urs von Balthasar 27–29 September 1995 (Einsiedeln: Johannes Verlag, 1995), 136, quoted in Hans-Peter Göbbeler, *Existenz als*

being called to the priesthood, which was, as he later expressed it, an experience of hearing God declare, *You have nothing to choose. You are called.* This call impressed him with a conviction that God had a unique, unrepeatable mission prepared for him.[18] Perhaps this early conviction helped to direct his thought toward Trinitarian theology, which reveals that mission implicates not only human existence but the very Persons of God.

Mission Is—and Is from—the Trinity

In his exploration of personal mission, Balthasar relies explicitly on the theology of Trinitarian missions developed by Thomas Aquinas in question 43 of the *Prima Pars* of the *Summa Theologica*, a *locus classicus* of Trinitarian theology of mission.[19] This question depends heavily, however, on what comes before, in particular Thomas's development in questions 27 through 29 concerning the processions, relations, and Persons of God. Question 27 develops the processions of the Son and the Spirit by drawing upon question 3, which demonstrates that God must be simple. In order not to vi-

---

Sendung: Zum Verständnis der Nachfolge Christi in der Theologie Hans Urs von Balthasars (St. Ottilien: EOS-Verlag, 1997), 22. There is some truth to this statement, but the heavy use of *Sendung* in the *Theo-Drama* (a later work), as I will show, undercuts this argument somewhat.

18. In Hans Urs von Balthasar, "Por qué me hice Sacerdote," in *Por qué me hice Sacerdote,* ed. Jorge y Ramón María Vala (Salamanca: Sígueme, 1959), reprinted in Elio Guerriero, *Hans Urs von Balthasar* (Milan: Edizioni Paoline, 1991), 369; the Guerriero translation into Italian omits "you have nothing to choose." The version used here (also attested to in other sources) is found in Peter Henrici, SJ, "Hans Urs von Balthasar: A Sketch of His Life," in *Hans Urs von Balthasar: His Life and Work,* ed. David L. Schindler (San Francisco: Ignatius Press/Communio Books, 1991), 11. The Spanish-language original is out of print and very difficult to find.

19. Cited at, *inter alia,* Hans Urs von Balthasar, *Theology of History* (San Francisco: Ignatius Press, 1994), 31 (hereafter, *TH*); Hans Urs von Balthasar, *Theo-Drama,* vol. 3, *The Dramatis Personae: The Person in Christ,* trans. Graham Harrison (San Francisco: Ignatius Press, 1992), 201 (hereafter, *TD* 3). Hans-Peter Göbbeler provides an insightful exegesis of Balthasar's treatment of mission, but neglects the importance of the Thomistic formula, in *Existenz als Sendung.* A similar judgment applies to Carolyn A. Chau, *Solidarity with the World: Charles Taylor and Hans Urs von Balthasar on Faith, Modernity, and Catholic Mission,* Theopolitical Visions 19 (Eugene, Ore.: Cascade Books, 2016). Michele M. Schumacher, on the other hand, grasps and appreciates the Thomistic Trinitarian theology behind Balthasar's theology of mission, summarized at *A Trinitarian Anthropology: Adrienne von Speyr and Hans Urs von Balthasar in Dialogue with Thomas Aquinas* (Washington, D.C.: The Catholic University of America Press, 2014), 326. Similarly, but more briefly, see the treatment in Aidan Nichols, OP, *Balthasar for Thomists* (San Francisco: Ignatius Press, 2020), 66, 83–85.

olate divine simplicity, the Son can proceed from the Father—and the Spirit proceed from the Father and the Son—only as internal, not external, processions.[20] Thus, the processions *are* the Persons of the Son and the Spirit, because anything that is in God *is* God: hence, Thomas's declaration that the Trinitarian persons are subsistent relations.[21]

"Paternity" is a relation that nowhere subsists as a creature; we cannot travel somewhere to gaze upon or interact with "paternity" existing as a substance (as subsisting). We gaze upon persons who are fathers, upon substances who have the accidental relation of paternity.[22] Only in the Trinity are things otherwise. Because of divine simplicity, God is not a substance who has accidents.[23] God does not *have* relations, or indeed any other accident. Again, if anything is in God, it is God. Unlike in us, therefore, the relation of paternity in God subsists, as Thomas develops in question 29. God the Father *is* the subsisting relation of paternity.

This theoretical breakthrough is the foundation of Thomas's rich theology of the Trinitarian missions.[24] In question 43, Thomas explains that

20. Hence the importance of the Augustinian insight into the spiritual processions of knowing and loving as the only adequate analogy to the processions in God, at least if one's goal is to maintain divine simplicity. All other processions in our experience involve either material or temporal separation or else division into parts.

21. Thomas Aquinas, *Summa Theologica*, Ia, q. 29, a. 4 (hereafter, *ST*). All translations from the *Summa Theologica* come from the English Dominican translation (1920), accessible at www .newadvent.org/summa. I here assume the substantial identity of the notional act of generation with the Person of the Father, although they can be rationally distinguished: "The notional acts differ from the relations of the persons only in their mode of signification; and in reality are altogether the same" (*ST* Ia, q. 41, a. 1, ad 2). See also Gilles Emery, OP: "In truth, the person of the Father is simple: In the Father, there is no real difference between *what* he is (God), *who* he is (the Father), and *that through which* he is the Father (paternity)." "The Purpose of Trinitarian Theology in St. Thomas Aquinas," trans. Sr. Mary Thomas Noble, OP, in *Trinity, Church, and the Human Person: Thomistic Essays* (Naples, Fla.: Sapientia Press of Ave Maria University, 2007), 27–28.

22. Obviously, in this metaphysical formulation, "accident" does not have any negative valence.

23. From the *respondeo* of *ST*, Ia, q. 28, a. 2: "Now whatever has an accidental existence in creatures, when considered as transferred to God, has a substantial existence; for there is no accident in God; since all in Him is His essence."

24. For the importance of question 43 to the drafting of Vatican II document *Ad Gentes*, see Andrew Meszaros, "The Thomistic Underpinnings of *Ad Gentes*," *Nova et Vetera* (English edition) 13 (2015): 875–901. For a lucid Thomistic exploration of the divine missions, with a critique of Karl Rahner's *Grundaxiom* postulating the equivalence of the "immanent" and "economic Trinity," see Gilles Emery, OP, "*Theologia* and *Dispensatio*: The Centrality of the Divine Missions in St. Thomas's Trinitarian Theology," *The Thomist* 74 (2010): 515–61. A harmonious approach is in Jeremy D.

the missions of the Son and the Spirit are extensions of their Persons: the internal procession that the Son *is* now has a new, external term in the economy.[25] The Person of the incarnate Son does not change in completing his mission, because he *is* his mission, as he is the procession from the Father. *Missio* is *processio* extended into time.[26] In other words, the eternal processions of the immanent Trinity are the principles of the temporal missions within the economy. Hence, the Son's mission into the world is identical with himself; his mission is he himself as incarnate.

Balthasar develops this equation of mission and person by proposing that the attitude of Jesus is the historical translation of his eternal, hypostatic stance before the Father.[27] The incarnate Son "exists in no other way than in this double movement" proceeding from the Father toward the world in mission.[28] This identity bound up in mission is the economic translation of the Son's "heavenly form of existence," which is his divine filiation.[29] This filiation is the eternal being-begotten by the Father, "the uninterrupted reception of everything that he is, of his very self, from the Father."[30] The sub-

Wilkins, "Why Two Divine Missions? Development in Augustine, Aquinas, and Lonergan," *Irish Theological Quarterly* 77, no. 1 (2012): 37–66, and "Trinitarian Missions and the Order of Grace," in *Philosophy and Theology in the Long Middle Ages: Essays in Honor of Professor Stephen Brown*, ed. Kent Emery, Russel L. Friedman, and Andreas Speer (Leiden: E. J. Brill, 2011), 689–708.

25. "Mission signifies not only procession from the principle, but also determines the temporal term of the procession. Hence mission is only temporal. Or we may say that it includes the eternal procession, with the addition of a temporal effect" (*ST*, Ia, q. 43, a. 2, ad 3).

26. "This mission ... is nothing but the 'timeward' side of his eternal procession from the Father. This is the express teaching of Saint Thomas," citing the Commentary on the Sentences, I, d. 14, q. 1, a. 1 sol, in Hans Urs von Balthasar, "The Serenity of the Surrendered Self: Three Variations on a Theme," in *Explorations in Theology*, vol. 5, *Man Is Created*, trans. Adrian Walker (San Francisco: Ignatius Press, 2014), 43.

27. See Hans Urs von Balthasar, *The Christian State of Life*, trans. Sr. Mary Frances McCarthy (San Francisco: Ignatius Press, 1977), 183–200. An insufficient grasp of the hypostatic center in Thomas's category of mission leads R. Jared Staudt to confuse divine missions with appropriations in his critique of Balthasar's Trinitarian Christology in "For the Holy Trinity: The Mission of Christ and the Order of His Human Soul," *Angelicum* 91, no. 3 (2014): 569–606.

28. Hans Urs von Balthasar, *Christian Meditation*, trans. Sister Mary Theresilde Skerry (San Francisco: Ignatius Press, 1989), 52–53.

29. *TH*, 31. It is worth noting again that in *TD* 3, he frequently repeats (sometimes referencing Thomas) that the Son's mission is the economic modality of his eternal procession. See, for example, 201.

30. *TH*, 30. In *Christian Meditation*, Balthasar describes the triune subsistent relations as "an interminable flowing of the Divine Persons from one another to one another and in one another — an ever actual self-giving" (95).

sistent relation that *is* the Son is a relation of receiving from the Father. This receptivity will become economic obedience in his temporal mission.[31]

The vectors of this mission into the world reach to the furthest possible extent, to the Cross and to the descent into hell. In this way, the comprehensive nature of the mission aligns with its divine template, in which the Father's generation of the Son conveys the entirety of the divine nature to the latter, with no remainder. As the Father fully expresses his divinity in the generation of the Word, so the extension of that procession into time in the Son's universal mission will fully express the extent of the triune God's will to save.

Mission: The Becoming and Being of Christ

Given that the mission of Christ is his eternal procession with a temporal term, the question of Christ's experience of time immediately arises. It is in the nature of the mission itself to exist within the tension between eternity and time. Balthasar introduces this tension in a section of *Theo-Drama*, volume 3, entitled "Mission: Being and Becoming." Christologically, the tension is translated in this way: Jesus exhibits, and theological reflection confirms, a "paradoxical unity" of being and becoming.[32] On the one hand, Jesus is the Son eternally proceeding from the Father. On the other hand, his mission sends him into the world of time. The temporal entry is no mere divine tourism but rather a thorough-going commitment to entering temporality. The hypostatic union entails the assumption of a human nature, one

31. Contra Staudt, who argues against Balthasar that the Son is not sent "from the Father alone" but rather from the entire Trinity ("For the Trinity," 595). One may argue that, *in a certain sense*, the whole Trinity sends the Son, because of convertibility of Person and nature in God (Ia, q. 39, a. 1) and because of the unity of the divine will. But it is contrary to the intent of Thomas's equation of *processio* and *missio* to assert that the Son *is not sent* by the Father alone (given that the Son proceeds from the Father alone). Question 43, a. 8, addresses this issue directly by noting that one can say both that the Son is sent by the Father alone and also that the whole Trinity sends the Son. ("If the sender be designated as the principle of the person sent, in this sense not each person sends, but that person only Who is the principle of that person who is sent; and thus the Son is sent only by the Father; and the Holy Ghost by the Father and the Son. If, however, the person sending is understood as the principle of the effect implied in the mission, in that sense the whole Trinity sends the person sent.")

32. *TD* 3, 157. The section runs from 154–163, but it serves as the introduction to the following two sections, which together cover more than sixty pages. These questions are at the heart of Balthasar's Christology.

that is marked by temporal becoming, and Jesus does not shed this nature like a used-up skin when he ascends to his Father. But how can "becoming" apply to the eternal Son?

Balthasar will hint at a resolution to the tension between being and becoming in volume 3 of the *Theo-Drama* and only fully unpack it in his treatment of Trinitarian eschatology in volume 5 ("The Last Act").[33] In volume 3, he argues that when the existence of Jesus transposes into time the eternal being of the triune God, this transposition includes the translation of God's eternal act of being into the changing streams of time. Hence, "both *being* and *becoming* in the Incarnate One express a single *being*, which, while we may not call it *becoming*, is the streaming-forth of eternal life [*strömendes ewiges Leben*], superevent [*(Über-)Ereignis*]."[34] Theo-drama is found first and foremost not in the world but in the "superevent" of the triune God himself.[35]

In *TD* 3, however, Balthasar's primary concern is not yet this "superevent" but rather the delineation of Christ's mission as the point of intersection of his being and becoming. "Mission" is the category that will hold together these poles of being and becoming, of eternity and time.[36] Balthasar begins with "becoming" by exploring the content of Christ's consciousness as his awareness of being the One Sent by the Father.[37] We see elements of this consciousness in Jesus's human knowledge, in his freedom, and in his prayer.[38]

---

33. In the German original, these are volumes 2 (part 2) and 4, respectively. Due to constraints of space, this essay will not develop Balthasar's solution in *TD* 5.

34. *TD* 3, 159, italics in the original.

35. "The dramatic dimension that is part of the definition of the person of Jesus does not belong exclusively to the worldly side of his being; its ultimate presuppositions lie in the divine life itself" (*TD* 3, 159).

36. "The concept of 'mission' contains two elements. First there is the relationship to the one who sends, who is present in the mission itself but is not identical with the one who is sent. Second, there is the mission's future prospect" (*TD* 3, 168).

37. Balthasar's mission-Christology is closely paralleled in the mission-Christology of Joseph Ratzinger, as expressed especially in the latter's *Introduction to Christianity*, 184–228, *Behold the Pierced One: An Approach to a Spiritual Christology*, trans. Graham Harrison (San Francisco: Ignatius Press, 1986), 13–46, and "On the Essence of the Priesthood," in *Called to Communion: Understanding the Church Today*, trans. Adrian Walker (San Francisco: Ignatius Press, 1996), 105–131.

38. Summarized in Mark L. Yenson, *Existence as Prayer: The Consciousness of Christ in the Theology of Hans Urs von Balthasar*, American University Studies, Series VII: Theology and Religion, vol. 330 (New York: Peter Lang, 2014), 107–57.

Balthasar builds his treatment of Jesus's human knowledge not from *a priori* theological commitments to what is fitting for the incarnate Son in his humanity. Instead, he argues consistently that the motive for the Incarnation is God's plan of salvation *pro nobis*.[39] In this reading, the human, temporal experience of the incarnate Son is governed not by what is fitting for his divinity but rather by what is necessary for his salvific mission. Thus, Christ's human knowledge is measured by his mission; if it is not needed for his mission, he "does not know" it (e.g., the Hour, the end of time).[40] "The knowledge is not itself the measure, but that which is measured; whereas his mission is the measure that measures all else."[41]

Indeed, because Jesus's mission is identical with his person, both of which are received from the Father, his identity can never be in doubt, nor does his awareness of it begin at a particular moment in time. "Jesus Christ dedicates his whole self to his mission; he is entirely one with it. He is the 'One sent.'"[42] Since Jesus always is the Son of the Father, as man he is always aware, in a developmentally appropriate manner, of this identity and of his mission to save. This mission-consciousness is grounded in his ontology as the relation of filiation proceeding eternally from the Father. It is this unity of identity and mission that will inspire Balthasar to formulate personhood in theological rather than philosophical, terms, as we will see in the concluding section.

The process of the Son's historical reception of mission-knowledge, as

39. In the following paragraphs, I will not attempt a comprehensive account of Balthasar's theology of Christ's knowledge. Rather, my goal will be to understand the connection between Christ's knowledge and mission in order to see what that implies for our own mission and identity. For a sympathetic treatment of Christ's knowledge that attempts to provide more explanatory categories for the Balthasarian position, see Randall S. Rosenberg, "Christ's Human Knowledge: A Conversation with Lonergan and Balthasar," *Theological Studies* 71 (2010): 817–45. For a comparison with Thomistic Christology, see Nichols, *Balthasar for Thomists*, 85–86.

40. "Jesus undergoes an historical learning process ... but essentially this is paralleled by an inward learning whereby he is *initiated more and more deeply* into the meaning and scope of his mission" (*TD* 3, 179).

41. *TH*, 38. Further, Christ's *visio immediata* of the Father is constituted by his intuitive mission-consciousness; the Son beholds his Father constantly only *in* the mission the Father gives him (*TD* 3, 166–68). Balthasar returns to and summarizes this theme at 191–196. Rosenberg rightly notes, however, that this theme is "fluid" in Balthasar, in that Balthasar sometimes appears to allow for beatific knowledge by Christ (Rosenberg, "Christ's Human Knowledge," 828–29). Cf. Yenson, *Existence as Prayer*, 130–33.

42. *TD* 3, 166.

unveiled by the Gospel of John, translates into time the Son's eternal reception of his being from the Father. The eternal Word spoken by the Father is simply the Son himself; so too, the temporal receiving of his mission from the Father constitutes Christ's identity in time. "[H]e understands the Word he hears from God to be identical with himself. He receives *himself* from the Father—both once for all and in an eternal *and* temporally ever-new 'now.'"[43] In John, this eternal-reception-in-time is expressed by the present or the perfect tense: "The Father shows the Son all that he himself is doing" (Jn 5:20). "I speak of what I have seen with my Father" (8:38). Within time, Jesus experiences the vectors of coming from and returning to the Father as eternal.[44] Concretely, this means that "it is possible," as Balthasar says, to argue that Jesus's understanding of his hour was not filled out with content—what precisely his hour would entail—until his public life and its disappointments revealed the full extent of what his mission would entail.[45]

This excursus on Christ's human knowledge underscores that the mission is received from the Father (because the Father sends the Son—the *missio* reflects the eternal *processio*), and it completely forms Jesus's consciousness of himself.[46] Yet its givenness does not mean that Christ lacks human freedom in carrying it out. In fact, the Son is given free scope in carrying out his mission.[47] The mission is both truly the Son's and completely a gift from the Father. Balthasar here gives the example of the inspired artist. "The artist is never more free than when, no longer hesitating between artistic possibilities, he is, as it were, 'possessed' by the true 'idea' that presents itself to him in finite form and follows its sovereign commands. And, if the inspiration is genuine, the work will bear the utterly personal stamp of the artist in absolute clarity."[48] Thus, one might say that a mission is "slumbering with-

---

43. *TD* 3, 180.

44. *TD* 3, 180: "And, in his *temporal* consciousness, he experiences this gift of himself (from the Father's hand) as *timeless* (as the absolute 'I am' utterances make plain)."

45. *TD* 3, 181.

46. *TD* 3, 166: his self-consciousness has its "source and measure" in his mission.

47. "Jesus wields this totality in complete freedom" (*TD* 3, 167).

48. He continues: "Sublime inspiration awakens in the person inspired a deeper freedom than that involved in arbitrary choice; for that very reason, it stamps the work with the character of personal uniqueness and necessity" (*TD* 3, 198). Thus, freedom for excellence is not opposed to the choice found in the freedom of indifference but rather catches it up and integrates it into a greater context.

in him like a child in its mother's womb, pressing to be delivered — out of the womb of his most personal freedom."[49]

This is why Jesus must pray, not simply as an example to us but also to stay close to the source of his mission, the Father. Balthasar argues that prayer is essential to Jesus, the One sent, because the mission is not something that is "open to his gaze in its entirety; it is to be implemented step by step according to the Father's instructions (in the Holy Spirit)."[50] This existence is one of faith and obedience. Jesus is called to watch and pray, without anticipation of the hour of his mission; for this reason, Balthasar calls patience a more central Christian virtue than even humility.[51]

This understanding of Jesus's mission-structured consciousness and activity provides a particular economic role for the Holy Spirit, expressed by Balthasar as "Trinitarian inversion."[52] In the eternal Trinity, there exists an *ordo naturae* among the Persons, which is an "order according to origin, without priority."[53] Within that order, the Son is, with the Father, related to the Spirit in a relation of "active spiration" (spirating), while the Spirit is related to the Father and the Son in a relation of "passive spiration" (being spirated). In the economy, Balthasar argues, the eternal activity of the Son and the eternal "passivity" of the Spirit are inverted, such that the Spirit is "active" over the obedient, incarnate Son. Christ "is conceived and born, is

49. *TD* 3, 198. He continues, speaking of Christ (and analogously of us): "he will not be able to say that his mission existed (in some eternal time) *prior* to his having affirmed and grasped it; for it is always his. Nor is it his in the sense that it lies ready, prefabricated, so that he only needs to assemble it. No, he must fashion it out of himself in utter freedom and responsibility; indeed, in a sense, he even has to invent it."

50. "The decisive final stage is not within the Son's power at all. The full universality of his task would be unattainable without his total self-abandonment in Passion and death. That is why it is so important for him to keep in step with his mission, not anticipating anything, least of all the 'hour.' The 'food' by which Jesus lives (Jn 4:34), that is, doing his Father's will, is not given once for all; the 'word' by which a man lives comes forth ever-new 'from the mouth of God' (Dt 8:3 = Mt 4:4)" (*TD* 3, 170).

51. On patience, see *TH*, 37. On the faith of Christ, see also Hans Urs von Balthasar, "*Fides Christi*: An Essay on the Consciousness of Christ," in *Explorations in Theology*, vol. 2, *Spouse of the Word*, trans. Edward T. Oakes, SJ (San Francisco: Ignatius Press, 1991), 43–80; *TH*, 40–50. In *TD* 3, Balthasar distinguishes his understanding of Christ's faith from the typically Protestant one in which Jesus's faith, while exemplary, "is not qualitatively different" from the faith of Christians (171, footnote 11).

52. Developed in *TD* 3, 183–91, and revisited in Hans Urs von Balthasar, *Theo-Logic*, vol. 3, *The Spirit of Truth*, trans. Graham Harrison (San Francisco: Ignatius Press, 2005), 177–84, 291–97.

53. *ST*, Ia, q. 42, a. 3.

at others' disposal and submits to events—which is expressed grammatically by a passive form."[54] The Son's refusal to anticipate the Father's will "is identical with assent to the Holy Spirit, by whom, moment by moment, the will of the Father is mediated."[55] Such complete obedience is seen from the very first moment of the Incarnation, when the Son is made incarnate *de Spiritu Sancto*, as the Apostles' Creed renders it (based on Lk 1:35). It continues in the anointing of the Spirit upon him in his baptism (cf. Is 61:1; Lk 4:18) and in driving him out into the desert (Lk 4:1).

Trinitarian inversion does not disrupt the *ordo naturae* of the eternal triune relations because it expresses economically the eternal, dual aspect of the Spirit, as detailed in the third volume of the *Theo-Logic*. On the one hand, the Holy Spirit is the fruit that proceeds from the love of the Father and Son; this is the more "objective" aspect. On the other hand, he is that love itself, as the bond of love of the Father and Son; this is the more "subjective" aspect.[56] Trinitarian inversion is possible without violating the order of the processions in the economy, because it is the mission-transposition of the eternal aspect of the Holy Spirit as the unity of Father and Son.[57] This is the "subjective" aspect of the Spirit, but the "objective" face is also present in the economy, when the Spirit acts more like an external law operating over and above Christ.[58] This dual experience of the Spirit by the incarnate Son is reflected in the diverse language Jesus uses about his mission: it is sometimes "my mission," sometimes the mission of the Father who sends him by means of the Spirit: "I have come to do, not my own will, but the will of him who sent me" (Jn 6:38).

All of these aspects of Christ's consciousness and activity—the element of "becoming" found in his knowledge, freedom, and prayer—shed light on

54. *TD* 3, 184. For how the language of "passivity" can be applied to the eternal God, see *ST*, Ia, q. 41, a. 1, ad 2.

55. *TH*, 39.

56. Summarized in Balthasar, *Theo-Logic*, vol. 3, 307, and developed in 307–411. The Spirit as the bond (*nexus*) of love between Father and Son is treated also at *ST*, Ia, q. 37, a. 1, ad 3, and q. 37, a. 2. See the history of the theological debates up to the time of Thomas and the latter's resolution in Gilles Emery, *The Trinitarian Theology of Saint Thomas Aquinas*, trans. Francesca Aran Murphy (Oxford: Oxford University Press, 2007), 233–45.

57. *TD* 3, 187. "What hovers between Jesus and the Father as the mediation of mission is the economic form of the eternal unanimity between Father and Son" (*TD* 3, 511).

58. "An infinite variety of possibilities is available to the Spirit.... Accordingly, the Son experiences his mission on earth, now as something more personal, now as something more impersonal" (*TD* 3, 522).

Jesus's "being." The mission of Jesus is unique precisely because of its ontological identity with his person: "His mission (*Sendung*) alone is identical with the 'I' who is thus sent (*gesendet*)."[59] Only in Christ do role and person perfectly coincide, because only in him is a human nature united to a divine personal relation extended into time.[60] Balthasar expresses this in metaphysical language by naming Jesus the "concrete *analogia entis*": distinct from God as man, and yet the divine Son.[61] Historically, this expresses itself in the reality that "his whole being is in motion" from and toward the Father who sent him.[62] Let us turn to a deeper exploration of the temporal matrix in which this must happen.

Christ's Time, Our Time

Given the origin of the Son's mission in his eternal procession, the template for the Son's experience of time must be rooted in his eternal receptivity of his being from the Father (his divine filiation). "Now it is his receptivity to everything that comes to him from the Father that is the basis of *time* and *temporality* as these terms apply to the Son in his creaturely form of existence."[63] This receptivity concretely manifests itself in Jesus' human obedience, his refusal to anticipate, as we have seen.

59. *TD* 3, 231. This ever-greater difference between Christ and ourselves is repeated frequently. See, for example, 150: Christ's "role" "cannot be exchanged for any other role, since it is a 'mission' that has ultimately fused with the person and become identical with him."

60. "The point of identity [between role and person] is his mission from God (*missio*), which is identical with the Person *in* God and *as* God (*processio*): this is the main conclusion of the present volume" (*TD* 3, 533, emphasis in the original).

61. Expressed at footnote 5, *TH*, 69–70, inter alia. Further, Christ reveals that the analogy of creatures with God is possible only because of the prior, eternal, and infinite distinction and unity of the triune God (*TD* 3, 228); see also Angela Franks, "Trinitarian *Analogia Entis* in Hans Urs von Balthasar," *The Thomist* 62, no. 4 (October 1998): 533–59, doi 10.1353/tho.1998.0002. In a lengthy and ultimately frustrating footnote at *TD* 3, 228–30 (note 68), Balthasar toys with the implication of this concrete *analogia entis* as it concerns Jesus's being as a creature: is there a proper secondary being [*esse secundarium*] that can be attributed to him? He does not satisfactorily resolve the question here or elsewhere. See Angela Franks, "The Epiphany of Being: Trinitarian *Analogia Entis* and the Transcendentals in Hans Urs von Balthasar," PhD diss. (Boston College, 2007), 209–16 and Appendix 1, 354–58.

62. *TD* 3, 153.

63. *TH*, 33. The passage continues: "This receptivity is the very constitution of his being [as *processio*], by which it is perpetually open to receive his mission from the Father. This temporal constitution is so far from contradicting his eternal being as Son that it is what directly, intelligibly

But what is Christ's time? Is it the time of paradise? Is it the experience of fallen time? Is it aeveternity? Rather than delineating Christ's time in terms of our human experiences, Balthasar appropriates an Augustinian sense of the analogous nature of time, one that is marked by personal presence rather than existing as an impersonal matrix or container within which history flows forward.[64] What is Christ's presence to himself within time?

Balthasar argues that Christ's time transcends all historical modalities of time, including the above-mentioned ones, because he himself is the measure of time. Thus, his experience of time is measured by his reception of his mission, and it is unique because his mission is unique. Nevertheless, this reception occurs within an economy governed by man's rejection of his divine origin.[65] In contrast to the Son, whose identity is structured by the Trinitarian relations of coming from and returning to the Father, and by the breathing forth of the Spirit, the human *imago Dei* rejected this Trinitarian pattern of existence. Sinful man insists he has no divine origin or destiny. His life is not governed by Trinitarian vectors.

This reality helps to explain the discontinuity so often evident between Jesus and those around him. His disciples and the crowds wish him to act, and quickly, while instead he sleeps on a boat (Mt 8:23–27) or dallies while people are dying (Lk 8:40–56; Jn 11:6). It is not as though Jesus floats above time in some kind of Docetist superhistory. Instead, he reads the urgency of time differently; the one thing necessary is the will of his Father (his mission).[66] Christ's time, as the translation of his eternal receptivity to the Father, exists in a kind of temporal "now" structured by obedient openness

---

and appropriately reveals that eternal being in this world. It is precisely *because* the Son is eternal that he assumes temporality as his form of expression when he appears in the world, elevating it so as to make of it a precise, suitable, perfectly fitting utterance of his eternal being as Son" (*TH*, 34).

64. See Hans Urs von Balthasar, *Das Ganze im Fragment: Aspekte der Geschichtstheologie* (Einsiedeln: Johannes Verlag, 1990), translated idiosyncratically as *A Theological Anthropology* (New York: Sheed and Ward, 1967); Hans Urs von Balthasar, "Finite Time within Eternal Time: On the Christian Vision of Man," *Explorations* 5, 47–65.

65. "Insofar as he knows he is the Only Son of the Eternal Father, he has his own particular time (even as man), measured by his acceptance of the Father's will concerning his particular, all-embracing mission. But insofar as he genuinely becomes man, his existence is subject not only to general human and historical time but also to that modality of time that is marked by universal sin ('subject to futility')" (*TD* 3, 15). Cf. *TH*, 40–43.

66. "Jesus is from the beginning beyond 'care' … and in the care-lessness of one who may leave everything once and for all to the providential care of the Father." Hans Urs von Balthasar, *Wer Ist ein Christ?* Herder-Bücherei, vol. 335 (Einsiedeln: Benziger Verlag, 1965), 66–67, my

to the Father's will. Jesus's mission-consciousness requires that his sense of time center around two poles: the awaiting of the imminent arrival of the kingdom in his "hour" and the "calm security of someone who lives entirely for his mission."[67] In his consciousness, future and present meet; the light (Jn 12:35–36) is "always just rising *now*, always shining *just for this present time*."[68] With the resurrection, the temporal mission of the Son is definitively caught up into the eternity of the Lamb who was slain before the foundation of the world.[69]

With the resurrection, which enables the mystical body of Christ to take on the universal dimensions of its Head's mission, the Church can also have some participation in Christ's time. Man need not remain trapped in sinful and disobedient self-enclosure. The time of the Church is structured not by our own plans but only by Christ's; it is purely the time of mission: "the time of the Church has no momentum of its own, but is in its entirety determined by the momentum of the time of Christ."[70]

Just as time becomes Christologically charged, so too does space. The forty days after the resurrection manifests a new order of time, one marked not by death but rather a kind of "blessed spaciousness [*seliges Raumhaben*]" over which the risen Christ has sovereignty.[71] In the time of the Church, which is our time of mission, the dramatic stage is a space that is both open

---

translation; rendered differently in the English translation: *Who Is a Christian?* trans. John Cumming (New York: Newman Press, 1965), 61.

67. *TD* 3, 92.

68. *TH*, 74, emphasis in the original.

69. "So the mission of Jesus always has the same here-and-now significance; he remains the 'Lamb slain before the foundation of the world' on God's throne (Rev 13:8)" (*TD* 3, 513).

70. Hans Urs von Balthasar, *Glory of the Lord*, vol. 7, trans. Brian McNeil, ed. John Riches (San Francisco: Ignatius Press, 1989), 175, and developed in 175–88. Due to the limits of space, I cannot explicate how mission-christology extends into mission-ecclesiology, which is treated in most of what remains in *TD* 3. He summarizes at *TD* 3, 271: "[W]e are to assimilate our own 'I' more and more completely to our God-given mission and to discover in this mission our own identity, which is both personal and social." The universal mission of the Church, embodying Christ's universal mission to save, is the precondition for the particular mission of each Christian. The communion of saints is rooted in the communion of mission-persons within Christ's universal mission (*TD* 3, 349). See also Göbbeler, *Existenz als Sendung*, 67–116, which also treats the question of how the priesthood and marriage could be viewed as ecclesial missions. The personal-social nature of ecclesial mission is personified in Mary, treated in *TD* 3, 283–360.

71. *TH*, 86. This mode of time is the "foundation for every other mode of his presence in time, in the Church, and in the world" (*TH*, 87).

and empty: empty because Jesus has departed, but the stage is open because it is simultaneously charged with his presence. In fact, Jesus himself is the stage upon which we can play out our mission; hence, the acting area is "not static" but "a perduring event."[72] In imitation of Christ, the Christian himself can become the acting space for the Father's will: as Christ the God-man provides the "space" for the Father's will and the "space" for us to live in faith, so the Christian can provide the Father with "as much space ... as God wants to demand."[73] This availability becomes the basic structure of Christian existence. Ultimately, the "space" of Christian existence, "the definitive space in which we are at home," is "the space of the fulfilled mission of the Son, who has returned home to the eternity of the Trinity with all his earthly experiences."[74] It is the "space" of the distinction between the Trinitarian Persons, which exists as filled with loving communion and in which the human being can participate.[75] *"The 'where' of the Son is the Father,"* while "the 'where' of the Christian is in Christ himself."[76]

This spaciousness is an especially pregnant revelation of the fullness of eternity, in which the fullness of the divine nature is handed over to the Son in his generation by the Father. This mode of time is shared with the Church, who will then enable Christians to enter Christ's time through the liturgy, the sacraments, and the missions of Christians.[77] We have seen that those who accept their missions *en Christoi* participate analogously in Christ's temporal existence. The Christian is the one who shares in Christ's "universally saving, obedient Yes to God," which marks Christ's time.[78] In this way, the liquid flow of time is not destroyed but redeemed in the obedient receptivity of Christian discipleship to the grace of the present moment.

72. *TD* 3, 54, and explicated in *TD* 3, 41–56. See also *TD* 3, 249: the "acting area" that is Christ "is a personal and personalizing area."

73. Balthasar, *Who Is a Christian?* 62, translation modified.

74. Balthasar, *Christian Meditation*, 48.

75. Hans Urs von Balthasar, *Theo-Drama: Theological Dramatic Theory*, vol. 5, *The Last Act*, trans. Graham Harrison (San Francisco: Ignatius Press, 1998), 91–95; Balthasar, "Finite Time within Eternal Time," 53: "God the Father grants the Son the 'space' in which he, too, can be the same one God, while both grant this same 'space' to the Holy Spirit." Cf. *TD* 3, 22: "In Christological terms, the creature's obedient distance from his Creator and Master becomes transparent, revealing that 'distance' within the Godhead, in the Spirit, between the Son and the Father."

76. Balthasar, *Christian State of Life*, 185, 212, emphasis in the original.

77. *TH*, 86, 94–111.

78. Balthasar, *Who Is a Christian?* 60, translation modified slightly (in German: *Wer Ist ein Christ?* 65).

"The mode of existence he requires of his followers, that is, 'watching and praying,' the readiness that *does not anticipate*, is patterned on his own."[79]

Yet the Church cannot experience Christ's time simply as he himself experienced it. The relationship between time and eternity within the body of Christ is structured by analogy, a similarity with a greater dissimilarity.[80] This dissimilarity is clear: because of the equation of *processio* and *missio* in the divine Son, "Jesus always has and *is* his mission," such that eternity and time meet hypostatically in him, whereas we receive our mission in faith in a moment in time.[81] The similarity remains, however, as a kind of solidarity in mission, a "coworking and cosuffering with those who are estranged from God ... opens up an area of Christian mission in which the latter, *en Christoi*, can be given a share in his salvific work and suffering for the world."[82] Let us turn now to this dynamic of solidarity in mission.

Mission and Identitiy

We can now ask if this connection between mission and person in Christ leads us any closer to an answer to the vexing question of our own personhood: what do we mean when we ask, "Who am I?"[83] Jesus answers this question through his mission-consciousness: he is the One sent. Whereas Jesus simply is his mission, however, we are not capable of that kind of unity of being and life. We are fragmented, both naturally and morally. We are finite creatures, made up of parts, but our dissimilarity from the One Sent goes still deeper. As Balthasar argues, "man is, in himself, something indef

---

79. *TD* 3, 111.

80. "As far as the Church was concerned, there could be no more precise discipleship than that attained through analogous transposition" (*TD* 3, 142).

81. *TD* 3, 171. In "Finite Time within Infinite Time," Balthasar construes the reception of mission (in the Ignatian moment of *electio*) in temporal terms: "Reaching backward into the past and forward into the future, I take hold of my entire transitory temporality and place it undivided within God's eternal time" (64).

82. *TD* 3, 241.

83. The first volume of the *Theo-Drama*, the "Prolegomena," addresses this topic by means of a tour through dramatic theory, climaxing in the question of the relation of role to mission, in *Theo-Drama: Theological Dramatic Theory*, vol. 1, trans. Graham Harrison (San Francisco: Ignatius Press, 1988), 481–648. Cf. the treatment in Alois M. Haas, "Zeigen — Geben — Sagen: Hans Urs von Balthasars Entwurf einer theologischen Phänomenologie," in *Eine Theologie für das 21. Jahrhundert*, 26–57, especially 46–50.

inite."[84] On his own, man exists as an individual conscious subject, but that very definition lacks any concrete content, as the next section will explore further.

Further, because of original sin, we have forsaken the original unity that held our parts together in harmony in favor of the dispersion of our powers. We succumb to liquid flow. As we have seen, the identity crisis within the mission field entails flowing from one constructed self to another. It is a life of *divertissement*, as T. S. Eliot saw when he spoke of our "strained time-ridden faces / Distracted from distraction by distraction."[85] But this liquidity is not wholly unlike Jesus's experience, as we have seen: "his whole being is in motion" from and toward the Father.[86] Further, Christ tastes our state of sinful dispersion during the Paschal Mystery, without actually being fractured by sin. On Holy Saturday, Balthasar argues, Jesus experiences "the hell of those who have lost both God and every personal name (that is, the personal consciousness that comes from possessing a mission)."[87] Without himself becoming a sinner, he sits at the table of sinners to feel the loss of meaning and identity that comes with sin.[88]

But this solidarity extends through the resurrection to a solidarity within the body of Christ. Within the Church, Christ exists in a mission-solidarity with his followers. The subtitle of the third volume (in English translation) of the *Theo-Drama* is "Persons in Christ." The precise nature of this "in Christ," the Pauline *en Christoi*, is the focus of the book.[89] Existence *en Christoi* is

84. *TH*, 73.

85. T. S. Eliot, *Burnt Norton*, first of *The Four Quartets*, III, lines 103–4.

86. *TD* 3, 153.

87. *TD* 3, 162, which continues: "In this way, in this collapse and rebirth [of descent and exaltation], he maintains his identity; and so, as the matrix of all possible dramas, he embodies the absolute drama in his own person, in his personal mission. Here it becomes clear that this person, in order to preserve his identity, must be Trinitarian: in order to be himself, he needs the Father and the Spirit." See the similar approach by Ratzinger, summarized in Edward Oakes, SJ, *Infinity Dwindled into Infancy: A Catholic and Evangelical Christology* (Grand Rapids, Mich.: William B. Eerdmans, 2011), 372–91. For an alternative reading, see Alyssa Lyra Pitstick, *Light in Darkness: Hans Urs von Balthasar and the Catholic Doctrine of Christ's Descent into Hell* (Grand Rapids, Mich.: William B. Eerdmans, 2007), and *Christ's Descent into Hell: John Paul II, Joseph Ratzinger, and Hans Urs von Balthasar on the Theology of Holy Saturday* (Grand Rapids, Mich.: William B. Eerdmans, 2016).

88. As did St. Therese of Lisieux, when she sat at the table of sinners. See *Story of a Soul: The Autobiography of St. Therese of Lisieux*, 3rd ed., trans. John Clarke, OCD (Washington, D.C.: ICS Publications, 1996), 211.

89. The phrase *en Christoi* is introduced at *TD* 3, 27; he compares it with the Johannine

explained by analogy to the dramatic stage, as we have seen. Once more: Christ himself is this stage, the arena in which other persons can carry out finite missions through the instrumentality of the Church.

Let us explore more closely the implications of this for the individual and his identity. The incarnate Son "makes room within himself, that is, an acting area for dramas of theological moment, involving other, created persons." Balthasar emphasizes that, "while the personal mission of Jesus is unique, it is also capable of 'imitation' by those who are called, in him, to participate in his drama."[90] This Christian existence is "existence as mission."[91]

This means that, as Christ's person is his mission, so too analogously for us can we asymptotically approach our identity through our share in his mission.[92] "Thus, in the very discipleship in which the Christian 'loses his soul,' he can attain his true identity."[93] This occurs through the reception of a personal and personalizing charism that calls the Christian to salvation by means of a particular "task and mission that belong to him and to no one else."[94] Such a mission is the unique crystallization of the Church in

"inclusion" formulas ("He who abides in me." [Jn 15:51]). It is exegeted with particular reference to Paul at *TD* 3, 245–50. The aesthetic equivalent of living *en Christoi* is what Balthasar calls "Christian attunement" [*Stimmung*] to Christ's form. See *The Glory of the Lord: A Theological Aesthetics*, vol. 1, *Seeing the Form*, trans. Erasmo Leiva-Merikakis, ed. Joseph Fessio, SJ, and John Riches (San Francisco: Ignatius Press, 1989), 241–57. Cf. *The Grain of Wheat: Aphorisms*: "When our strings are well tuned, God can spontaneously play on our soul. And we should aim at nothing more than this: to stretch out and be attuned to God" (trans. Erasmo Leiva-Merikakis [San Francisco: Ignatius Press, 1995], 43); the theme is also treated in Hans Urs von Balthasar, "What Is Distinctively Christian in the Experience of God?" in *Explorations in Theology*, vol. 4, *Spirit and Institution*, trans. Edward T. Oakes, SJ (San Francisco: Ignatius Press, 2013), 29–40.

90. TD 3, 162. Balthasar develops this on the basis of the analogy of being that exists between the Christian and the risen Christ. "The Christian's required identification with his Christian mission (for which he is 'chosen before the foundation of the world') stands in an analogy to the identity that characterizes Jesus Christ" (162). Analogy is the necessary metaphysical structure that enables the Christian to be baptized *en Christoi*.

91. Göbbeler argues this is the best formulation for Balthasar's understanding of Christian existence in *Existenz als Sendung*, 24, citing Hans Urs von Balthasar, "Existenz als Sendung: Christus und seine Nachfolge," *Christliche Innerlichkeit* 18 (1984): 274–78. In *Who Is a Christian?* Balthasar dedicates a section to "Existenz aus der Sendung" (in German: *Wer ist ein Christ?* 90–95; rendered "The Mission Gives Life" in the English translation, 86–91).

92. Cf. the treatment of mission and person in Schumacher, *A Trinitarian Anthropology*, 99–123.

93. *TD* 3, 162.

94. Hans Urs von Balthasar, "Charis and Charisma," in *Explorations*, vol. 2, 303. Cf. Hans Urs von Balthasar, *Prayer*, trans. Graham Harrison (San Francisco: Ignatius Press, 1986), 58–60.

a particular individual—in service of the Church as a whole, to be sure, but not for that reason reduced to a mere functionality. Missions have their own relative beauty and reality within the greater universality of the Church.[95] Accepting one's unique mission from God enables one to grasp "that most intimate idea of his own self—which otherwise would remain undiscoverable."[96]

In Christ, therefore, "each individual is given a personal commission; he is entrusted both with something unique to do and with the freedom to do it. Bound up with this commission is his own, inalienable, personal name; here—and only here—role and person coincide."[97] Only in my mission from Christ do I receive my name. Only here do my doing and my being finally coalesce. As with Christ, so too for us obedience to mission is not heteronomy but the true fulfillment of ourselves.[98] As we have seen, mission in Christ is like a work of art, "slumbering within him like a child in its mother's womb, pressing to be delivered—out of the womb of his most personal freedom."[99]

Recall the pattern of Christian time, a time that refuses to anticipate, which suffuses Christian existence: "The mode of existence he requires of his followers, that is, 'watching and praying,' the readiness that *does not anticipate*, is patterned on his own."[100] Note that here Balthasar emphasizes that discipleship is a "mode of existence," that is, a way of *being*, before it is a course of *action*.[101] Such a mode does not concern *what* a person is—his na-

---

95. Balthasar, "Charis and Charisma," 312.

96. *TD* 3, 263. For Balthasar, uniqueness is a good that reflects the Trinitarian particularity. "It is exceedingly good and in every respect positive that an otherness exists in God himself, by virtue of which God is first of all an infinite inner life of self-giving." See *Christian Meditation*, 61, echoing succinctly the longer exposition in *TD* 5, 81–85, *inter alia*. I treat the positivity of otherness in Franks, "Trinitarian *Analogia Entis* in Hans Urs von Balthasar," 546–59.

97. *TD* 3, 51.

98. The self-dispossession of mission is not a destruction but an enrichment, as we see in Mary, who is "enriched" by Christ "in proportion to her self-expenditure" (Balthasar, *Christian Meditation*, 63).

99. *TD* 3, 198. See note 49 above.

100. *TD* 3, 111.

101. This language echoes the language used by Maximus the Confessor and other Fathers to distinguish the personal existence of the Trinitarian hypostases, namely, *tropos tēs hyparxeōs*. It is discussed in *Theo-Logic*, vol. 3, 117–21; Hans Urs von Balthasar, *Cosmic Liturgy: The Universe According to Maximus the Confessor*, trans. Brian E. Daley, SJ (San Francisco: Communio Books/Ignatius Press, 2003), 221.

ture—but rather *who* he is. It concerns, that is, the person and her mission. Further, as with the case in Jesus' earthly life under the conditions of Trinitarian inversion, so too for the Christian will obedience and "the refusal to anticipate" constitute the spirituality of Christian mission.

This insight connecting mission with existence is stated in a definitive way by Balthasar, but he is not the only one to speak of the primacy of being over doing (*agere sequitur esse*) in mission. In fact, the Church's documents on mission ground evangelization in identity, prior to programs and action. For example, Karol Wojtyła's commentary on Vatican II, *Sources of Renewal*, emphasizes that the Christian in faith shares in the divine Son's state of being-mission, and that this participation is always personally unique: "Thus [the Christian] takes part in the 'state of mission' in which all the Church continually finds itself; and each individual is a unique, unrepeatable embodiment of the salvific 'state.'"[102]

In other words, as *Ad Gentes* 2 explains, the Church is missionary by *nature*, in her being, prior to her activities. Mission is *who* the Church is more than what she does, just as the missions of the Son and Holy Spirit are *who* they are, the temporal extensions of their Persons, and not simply roles taken on *ad extra*.[103] Pope Paul VI forcefully reiterates this truth in *Evangelium nuntiandi*: "evangelization is the grace and vocation proper to the Church, her deepest identity. She exists in order to evangelize."[104] John Paul II echoes him in *Redemptoris missio*: "We are missionaries above all because of *what we are* as a Church whose innermost life is unity in love, even before we become missionaries *in word or deed*."[105] Hence, mission-identity is always a matter of being before doing, of holiness before apostolate. This reality is based on

102. Karol Wojtyła, *Sources of Renewal: The Implementation of the Second Vatican Council*, trans. P. S. Falla (San Francisco: Harper and Row, 1980), 207. As Michael Waldstein summarizes Wojtyła's teaching, "Mission is thus not in the first place an attitude of moral commitment in response to a moral duty, but a way of *being* that is rooted in the person of Jesus as the Son of God." See the Introduction in John Paul II, *Man and Woman He Created Them*, trans. Michael Waldstein (Boston: Pauline Books and Media, 2006), 93, emphasis mine.

103. Cf. Balthasar, from *Christian State of Life*: "The Church as a whole is a missionary Church because the head, whose body it is, is totally the *missio* of the Father" (346).

104. Paul VI, Apostolic Exhortation *Evangelii nuntiandi* (December 8,1975), §14, at the Holy See, http://w2.vatican.va/content/paul-vi/en/apost_exhortations/documents/hf_p-vi_exh_19751208_evangelii-nuntiandi.html.

105. John Paul II, *Redemptoris missio*, §23, emphasis in the original.

the Trinitarian presuppositions of the Son's mission as an extension of his person.

Here, in an analogously distant way, the Christian's mission echoes the mission of the Son, which in turn reveals his mode of existence as the proceeding Son. In Christ, we experience *Mit-Sohnschaft*, our adoptive sonship in the Son. Balthasar argues this *Mit-Sonschaft* is a participation in the being-begotten by God (1 Jn 2:29, etc.), as 1 John describes as a kind of "abiding" (2:6, 17; 2:24–29, etc.). Thus, Christian life shares in Trinitarian rhythms. Christian prayer is, at its core, an abiding, a participation in the triune life of love, in beholding the Father through the eyes of the incarnate Son in the union of the Holy Spirit.[106] This is why Balthasar is skeptical of techniques for prayer, because union with God cannot be extracted from the divine by means of a spiritual technology. Union with God can only be a gift of a state of being, which Balthasar identifies as the fundamental Christian state (*Christlicher Stand*) that underlies all the manifold states of life within the Church. This "stance" is a participation in Christ's own stance vis-à-vis the Father, "the taking of a stand eternally 'with the Father' as the original Word in whom the Father creates and sustains all things (Jn 1:1; Heb 1:3)."[107] Yet because this state of union does not extract the Christian from the world but instead sends him back into it, the "stance" of the Christian is always simultaneously a movement of mission to the world.[108]

Conclusion: Theological and Philosophical Personhood

What are the implications of this exposition of the mission-identity of Christ and, analogously, Christians? Balthasar argues that through bestowing a share of his mission, Christ bestows true personhood on human beings. This personalization through mission constitutes "the deepest, theological sense" of personhood.[109] Yet such an equation of personhood with

---

106. In Balthasar, *Prayer*, 177–97.

107. Balthasar, *The Christian State of Life*, 184–85.

108. Balthasar, *The Christian State of Life*, 183, 212.

109. Balthasar, "The Serenity of the Surrendered Self," 41. "Serenity of the surrendered self" is the translation given for the German word *Gelassenheit*, which Balthasar here brings into play with the theme of Ignatian indifference. Göbbeler calls attention to the Ignatian background behind Balthasar's sense of the center of Christian existence: God chooses, and we choose what God chooses. Cf. the work by Werner Löser, SJ, in particular, "The Ignatian *Exercises* in the Work of

theological mission raises the question: is personhood only a theological category? What happened to philosophical personhood?[110]

Balthasar defends his position by sketching a history of how the word "person" developed. The evidence clearly indicates that *persona* was drafted into service in order to meet theological exigencies concerning the persons of Christ and of the triune God.[111] Until the revelation of the Incarnation, philosophy did not have need to treat of "person" beyond what was already achieved in thinking about an individual conscious subject. Balthasar argues that the conceptual development of *persona* since the patristic era has not advanced significantly beyond this point, encapsulated by the Boethian definition of a person as an individual substance of a rational nature.[112]

Balthasar's insight is that "person" requires theological content in order to fill out the formal structure of Boethius's definition with material content.[113] The Boethian approach adequately describes the class of individuals who count as persons, but it remains an impersonal approach to personhood, in that it cannot explain what distinguishes one person from another. It does not get at what is personal about personhood.

Balthasar notes two historical responses to this challenge: articulating personhood, either by means of distinguishing qualities, or else through the individual act of being of a person.[114] The former way is exemplified by

---

Hans Urs von Balthasar," in *Hans Urs von Balthasar: His Life and Work*, 103–20, and Mark A. McIntosh, especially *Christology from Within: Spirituality and the Incarnation in Hans Urs von Balthasar*, Studies in Spirituality and Theology 3 (Notre Dame. University of Notre Dame Press, 2000).

110. See also the treatment in Nichols, *Balthasar for Thomists*, 131–35.

111. *TD* 3, 208–20. This topic is revisited by Balthasar in his "On the Concept of the Person," originally published in 1986 and then expanded for inclusion in *Explorations*, vol. 5, 114–25; cf. the analysis in *Theo-Logic*, vol. 3, 131–41, with an eye to the personhood of the Spirit.

112. Boethius, *De Duabus Naturis*, c. 3; summarized in *TD* 3, 217–18. For this reason, it is inaccurate to call Balthasar a personalist philosopher. He is a personalist theologian, as I will show. Boethius comes in for harsher criticism in Balthasar, "On the Concept of the Person," 118–21.

113. In a similar way, I argue that Balthasar's approach to personhood provides material content to the formal structures of knowing the embodied self as found in Karol Wojtyła, in Angela Franks, "Thinking the Embodied Person with Karol Wojtyła," *Nova et Vetera* (English edition) 16, no. 1 (2018): 141–71.

114. In fact, Balthasar notes three paths, without counting them as such. On *TD* 3, 204–5, he describes two approaches: the delineation of empirical characteristics and the relationality of a person to other persons. I have folded both approaches into the first response, that is, the utilization of accidents as a means of describing individual personhood. The second way I list above, the existential approach, is treated later, on 216–19.

Gregory of Nyssa, while some Church fathers and Thomistic schools will take the latter option. Gregory's approach lines up with common sense: I am distinct from that person because of my appearance, my gifts, my relationships, and so forth, all the concrete qualities that here-and-now go into who I am. But ethical landmines lie underneath. If my qualities change, do I lose my personhood?[115] If I lose certain socially valued qualities—such as my earning potential or attractiveness—am I less than a person? This way of thinking can lead to a utilitarian forgetting of personal dignity, replaced by liquid identities and personal achievement.

The latter approach avoids these pitfalls by privileging being over doing. In Thomas's treatment of *persona* in the *Summa Theologica*'s treatise on the Trinity, he subtly changes the Boethian definition to "a subsisting individual of a rational nature" (Ia, q. 29, a. 3). This change has the benefit of avoiding the ambiguous term "substance," but it also introduces, in *subsistens*, the aspect of being that is missing from Boethius. This existential note was picked up and developed by some Thomists, to fruitful effect.[116] Certainly such an approach is ethically safer, since in this context, personhood, and hence personal dignity, is not a matter of measuring up to a qualitative threshold; rather, it is grounded in one's very existence. But what has happened to personal uniqueness? Certainly, my act of being is not yours, but is there noth-

---

115. Conversely, if I am defined by my relationships, do I have the agency to change them? Some poststructuralist gender theory proposes an anthropology so wedded to relational forces as to embed human agency completely within these forces. See Angela Franks, "A Wojtylian Reading of Performativity and the Self in Judith Butler," *Christian Bioethics: Non-Ecumenical Studies in Medical Morality* 26, no. 3 (2020): 221–42. Melissa Moschella highlights the ethical implications from a feminist perspective: "If we are really a product of our social relations, how can a woman raised in a patriarchal environment transcend that environment in order to criticize it and form an identity in opposition to it?" See "Personal Identity and Gender: A Revised Aristotelian Approach," in *Gender Identities in a Globalized World*, ed. Ana Marta González and Victor J. Seidler (New York: Humanity Books, 2008), 75–108. Connecting these questions to a reading of Balthasar's theory of women is Aristotle Papanikolaou, "Person, Kenosis and Abuse: Hans Urs von Balthasar and Feminist Theologies in Conversation," *Modern Theology* 19 (2003): 41–65, who does an able job of defending Balthasar from feminist critiques; cf. Carolyn A. Chau, "'What Could Possibly Be Given?': Towards an Exploration of Kenosis as Forgiveness — Continuing the Conversation between Coakley, Hampson, and Papanikolaou," *Modern Theology* 28 (2012): 1–24.

116. Balthasar does not advert to it here, but this move has echoes both in his own *Theology of History*, 12, fn. 1, as well as in Maximus the Confessor's development of *tropos tēs hyparxeōs*. See the treatment in Jörg Disse, *Metaphysik der Singularität: Eine Hinführung am Leitfaden der Philosophie Hans Urs von Balthasars*, Philosophische Theologie, vol. 7 (Vienna: Passagen Verlag, 1996).

ing more to say about personal differentiation? What about my situation as a unique individual within history? This approach is impersonal and abstract.

While Balthasar does not say it in so many words, his approach unites both ways by speaking to how the unique qualities of a person (the first way) might bear upon the enduring being—and hence dignity—of the person (the second way). He was convinced that philosophy, on its own, does not have the resources to move the question forward. The purely philosophical approach to personhood has reached an impasse. A theological understanding of personhood as rooted in mission, however, shows that the distinctive characteristics of a person unfold within the existence of a historical life ordered to her God-given mission.[117] This call suffuses an individual life with concrete content, bending all its accidental qualities toward an organizing purpose bestowed "from above" (Eph 4:10ff). The call orders all the attributes of a conscious subject into a meaningful goal, like iron filings to a magnet.[118]

Mission is, however, primarily a matter of being before action, as we have seen; in this way, the second personalizing element—the concrete act of existence—reemerges. Personal missions are analogously dependent on the Son's mission that is the extension of his person, of his subsistent being-Son. In a person's mission, being has concrete, historical content. It is the being of holiness before it is the doing of apostolate.

This resolution depends on returning to the theological inspiration for *persona*, a term expressing the subsisting relations that each of the triune hypostases is. Within the triune God, because of God's simplicity, the divine persons are distinguished only by these relations of origin.[119] As I have argued, such an approach cannot directly apply to finite persons, because we are not simply constituted by our relations, or by any accident, as important as these may be for us. But what the Trinitarian analogate reveals is that personhood is established by a relation of origin to God.

117. "Only as an individual can a Christian be called to the service of the Church, and as a member of the Church be called to the service of the world." Hans Urs von Balthasar, *The Moment of Christian Witness*, trans. Richard Beckley (San Francisco: Ignatius Press, 1994), 33.

118. See *TD* 3, 248. For the magnet and filings image, see Balthasar, *Christian State of Life*, 74. Cf. Ratzinger: "Meaning that is self-made is in the last analysis no meaning. Meaning, that is, the ground on which our existence as a totality can stand and live, cannot be made but only received" (Ratzinger, *Introduction to Christianity*, 73).

119. *ST*, Ia, q. 30, especially aa. 1–2; cf. *Catechism of the Catholic Church*, §254.

In other words, just as the Trinitarian Persons are constituted by their re-lational vectors, so too analogously is our personhood constituted by divine-ly instituted vectors: our coming from and returning to God.[120] Our person-hood is not primarily a matter of our qualities or of our existence; these are important but secondary realities, following the primary one. The essential content of a person's identity resides in her "definition" by God, in the name that she receives from him and toward which she must strive to order her life, if it is to make any sense. Within this mission-context, our experience of liquid time can be inserted and redeemed within the eternal "movement" of the subsistent triune relations. The flow of human mission, received from God, moving out into the world, and back to God, is in this way an image of the "flowing eternal life" of the unchanging God.[121] As the Son's eternal "stance" is simultaneously his proceeding from and returning to the Father in love, so too analogously can we take up our "stance" in this eternal "super-event." This Trinitiarian stance that is simultaneously movement is in fact the deep structure of our created reality, which comes from and returns to the triune Creator. When embraced by rational freedom through grace, this fluid stance gives an *imago*-directionality to our otherwise aimless flow. By standing within the Son, as adoptive sons, human persons bend their innate fluidity into the channels carved out by the triune processions.

In this way, the incarnate Son provides the model and the prime analo-gate for the reality of finite personhood. Ontologically, human beings are individually existing rational substances. This ontological individuality, which is correctly grasped in philosophy, is in potency to the fullness of finite theological personhood, because only such a substance is capable of receiving and carrying out a mission in full knowledge and freedom.[122] Unlike the on-tological substratum, theological personhood is not automatic. It involves a dramatic choice to embrace one's identity *en Christoi*, or else to continue the postlapsarian, titanic project of carving out an identity in which nothing is

---

120. Cf. the development of this idea in Ratzinger, *Introduction to Christology*, 184–90. Ratzinger's own historical assessment, which closely matches Balthasar's, is found in Joseph Ratzinger, "On the Understanding of 'Person' in Theology," trans. Michael J. Miller, in *Dogma and Preaching* (San Francisco: Ignatius Press, 2011), 181–96. Balthasar cites this essay in "On the Concept of the Person," 119, footnote 10.

121. Balthasar, "Charis and Charisma," 301, 308.

122. Cf. *TD* 3, 270.

received from nor ordered to one's divine origin. No one can make the decision for him.[123]

Archetypal Christian missions show us how finite human beings can make this dramatic choice in favor of mission-identity. When the bright light knocked Saul off the well-worn path, he found the mission he was being given had a name. That name was "Paul." As Balthasar says, Christ "*expropriated* him in order to *personalize* him."[124] The case of Paul underscores that "man is not what he thinks himself to be but what God appoints him to be."[125]

This exposition of Christ's mission-identity indicates that Robert Imbelli's use of the term "Christification" would have been entirely intelligible to Balthasar, for this one term summarizes the whole dynamic of life *en Christoi*. Mission-identity is, paradoxically, an identity in which the center of gravity has been relocated outside of the self.[126] As Imbelli argues, Christian existence entails transformation from self-centeredness into a "Eucharistic self."[127] Christian missions form "a single loaf of bread which everyone should share."[128] This sharing in Christ's Eucharistic mission is the New Evangelization, and Robert Imbelli's theology both testifies to and enacts it.

---

123. Balthasar, *The Moment of Christian Witness*, 33.

124. *TD* 3, 247, emphasis in the original. Cf. "The Serenity of the Surrendered Self," 41: "Take Paul or Augustine or Francis or Ignatius as an example. What God saw as disorder had to be burned out of their lives so that, laying hold of their task, they could become the unique persons, the unique shapers of history, whom we recognize them to be centuries later."

125. *TD* 3, 267. Cf. a poem by Karol Wojtyła that locates the source of identity in Christ: "Whoever enters Him keeps his own self. / He who does not / has no full part in the business of this world / despite all appearances." Karol Wojtyła, "Participation," in *The Quarry*, from *Collected Poems*, trans. Jerzy Peterkiewicz (London: Hutchinson, 1981), 86.

126. "The Christian has to learn an always deeper expropriation.... The better he learns to pray, the more the heart of the praying man is expropriated" (Balthasar, *Wer Ist ein Christ?* 124, 125, my translation, found in another rendition in *Who Is a Christian?* 119, 120). Cf. Balthasar, *Glory of the Lord*, vol. 7, 399–415.

127. Imbelli, *Rekindling the Christic Imagination*, 53.

128. Balthasar, *Who Is a Christian?* 121.

15

The Creed of the Council of Chalcedon
and the New Evangelization

THOMAS G. WEINANDY, OFM, CAP

I am very pleased to have been asked to contribute to this volume of essays honoring Fr. Robert Imbelli. I consider him a wise counselor, a devoted priest, a committed teacher, a holy man, and a trustworthy friend. He is also gentle of heart and humble of mind—probably in contrast to me. I would like to think that what binds us together, as fellow Catholics, is our mutual love for Jesus and for his Church.

With the above in mind, I would like to address what may appear a very unlikely topic—that of the relationship between the Creed of the Council of Chalcedon (AD 451) and what is termed the New Evangelization. How could a creed that is so overtly theological and, some would attest, philosophically impenetrable, be of any immediate relevance and consequence for the nitty gritty pastoral work of evangelizing unbelievers, twenty-first-century secular men and women who have little or no clue of the simple and unadorned gospel proclamation, and thus have only a slight understanding of a first-century man from Nazareth? This unique juxtaposition of topics, nonetheless, came to me when I read and pondered Robert's short but compelling book *Rekindling the Christic Imagination: Theological*

Meditations for the New Evangelization.[1] This book is a gem, for it gathers together, in a most creative fashion, theology, liturgy, literature, and art and in so doing provides a compelling way forward in the Church's renewed efforts to preach the Gospel to all nations. To conjoin Chalcedon with Imbelli's desire to promote effectively the New Evangelization, I will first examine the Council's creed, and then attempt to show that the faith the Council professes lies at the very heart of Imbelli's evangelistic stratagem. I want to demonstrate that so many of the most crucial aspects of the New Evangelization, from the proclamation of salvation in Christ, to the Eucharist as the source and summit of Christian life, are unintelligible without the Christological dogma encapsulated in the Creed of Chalcedon. Indeed, Chalcedon is a *sine qua non* of the New Evangelization: without it, evangelization is not only impoverished but impossible.

The Creed of the Council of Chalcedon

Imbelli speaks of "the Christic imagination." There is no early Christian creed that more embodies this Christic mind than Chalcedon's, for it provides a magisterial articulation of the ontology of the Incarnation—the metaphysics of who Jesus *is*. Is it not, however, this very ontology (who talks about metaphysics today?) that is not only inappropriate when attempting to engender faith but also off-putting? "Just give them the simple gospel message." I think Imbelli would, with a composed smile, raise his eyebrows at such a negative and uninformed reaction. He recognizes that if one does not know who Jesus *is*, one does not know the gospel, and to be ignorant of the gospel, even if one says that he or she believes, means one does not personally know Jesus as one's Lord and Savior. So what does Chalcedon profess concerning the glorious ontological constitution of Jesus? What is the amazing metaphysics of the Incarnation?

Chalcedon declares that the Lord Jesus Christ is "one and the same Son." This same Son is

perfect in divinity and perfect in humanity, the same truly God and truly man composed of rational soul and body, the same one in being (*homoousion*/consubstantial) with the Father as to the divinity and one in being (*homoousion*/consub-

---

1. Robert Imbelli, *Rekindling the Christic Imagination: Theological Meditations for the New Evangelism* (Collegeville, Minn.: Liturgical Press, 2014).

stantial) with us as to the humanity, like unto us in all things but sin. The same was begotten from the Father before the ages as to the divinity and in the latter days for us and our salvation was born as to his humanity from Mary the Virgin Mother of God (*Theotokos*).[2]

This *is* who Jesus *is*! Jesus is "one and the same Son" and thus one and the same person or subject. He possesses one identity, one "who." Who Jesus is, his identity, is that of being the Father's Son. Moreover, being the Father's Son demands that Jesus be perfectly divine as his Father, "truly God," and so he is of one and the same divine nature with his Father. He is "consubstantial (*homoousion*)" with his Father, for both are constitutive of the one being of God. What the one God is is the Father begetting his Son. (Obviously, the Holy Spirit is also one in being [*homoousion*] with the Father and the Son, but that is a different topic than the one we are presently considering.) Thus, all who deny that Jesus, as the Father's Son, is not as fully divine as his Father is divine, such as Arius and his followers down to this day, are heretics. They propose a different metaphysical understanding of who Jesus ontologically "is"—one that repudiates scripture and the now conciliar magisterial tradition.

Now, the marvelous incarnational truth is that Jesus, who is the Father's perfect divine Son, is the one and the same Son who is also perfect in his humanity, "truly man," and so of the same nature (consubstantial/*homoousion*) with us who are human beings. This genuine historical man named Jesus possesses the same identity as man as he does as God—that of being the Father's Son. The Son of God, then, exists in two distinct ontological orders. The Son metaphysically exists as God and as man—complete in both manners of existence. As those who deny the full divinity of the Son are in error, so those who reject his authentic humanity, such as Apollinarius who disallowed Jesus possessing a "rational soul," are equally mistaken. For Chalcedon, the Son who is eternally "begotten from the Father" is one and the same Son who "in the latter days for us and our salvation was born as to his humanity from Mary the Virgin Mother of God." Here Chalcedon makes evident the soteriological significance of Jesus being the Son of God Incar-

---

2. All quotations from the Council of Chalcedon are taken from Heinrich Denzinger, *Compendium of Creeds, Definitions, and Declarations on Matters of Faith and Morals*, ed. P. Hünerman, English edition eds. R. Fastiggi and A. Englund Nash, 43rd edition (San Francisco: Ignatius Press, 2012), paragraphs 301 and 302.

nate. Humankind would not be saved if Jesus was not truly the Son of God, for only God is able to save us. Nor would humankind be saved if Jesus was not fully man, for only as man can the Son of God save us. Thus, the Son of God *came to exist* as man for our salvation.

When the Gospel of John in 1:14 declares that "the Word became flesh," that incarnational "*becoming*" of the Word must terminate in the Word *actually existing* as man. Nestorius did not grasp the significance of this incarnational becoming but rather perceived the two natures only as closely aligned with one another, which meant that the Son did not actually *exist* as man. There is, therefore, a threefold truth that must be acknowledged for a proper conception and articulation of the Incarnation. It must *truly be the divine Son of God* who is man (contra Arius). The Son of God *must truly be man* (contra Apollinarius). And the Son of God must *truly be* man (contra Nestorius). For our salvation, Jesus must be *truly the Son of God* who *truly exists* as *truly man*. The ontology of the Incarnation, the metaphysics of who Jesus is, utterly governs the efficaciousness of our salvation.

Because all of the above defines who Jesus ontologically is, Chalcedon declares that it must be acknowledged that one and the same Son exists "in two natures," and these natures are neither confused, changed, nor divided or separated. The manner of the "natures's" existence is not confused or changed because the incarnational "becoming" is not the compositional merging of natures, whereby they form a third kind of being—a being that is neither truly God nor truly man—but one that is an amalgamation of both, a hybrid fusion of divinity and humanity. Thus, in becoming man, neither the Son's divinity nor his humanity is confused so as to alter them. Nor, then, are they changed. The Son of God remains truly God, and his humanity remains authentically human. Although the incarnational "becoming" is not the compositional union of "natures," which would demand change or mutation of both, the incarnational "becoming" is the coming to be of humanity with its simultaneous ontological union with the "person" of the Son such that the person of the Son exists not only as God but also now exists as man. Thus, while the natures are not confused or changed by way of alteration, they are nonetheless not separated or divided, because it is one and the same Son who now exists as God and as man. The incarnational "becoming" is the ontological uniting of the humanity to the person of the Son such that the person of the Son actually comes to exist as man. This is why the incarnational union is termed a hypostatic union—an ontological union whereby one and the same person exists in two manners—as God and as man. Of course, we cannot fully comprehend or fully articulate this hypostatic mystery, but we do know what the mystery is. This is why someone like Athanasius or Cyril of Alexandria could argue for the truth of the mystery and yet pronounce the mystery "ineffable" and beyond human understanding.[3]

It must be emphasized that while we cannot fully grasp the mystery of the Incarnation, we do actually know what the mystery is. This known mystery, a mystery known and believed from apostolic times, is central to the New Evangelization, for it embodies the central truth of the Christian faith—our salvation is Jesus Christ, true God and true man.

At this juncture, we can now turn to Imbelli's "Christic imagination" for "the New Evangelization," for it is Chalcedon's creed that underwrites his proposal, and it is Chalcedon that will make his counsel successful.

The Centrality of Jesus and the New Evangelization

The Singularity of the Incarnate Son

At the very onset of his book, Imbelli endorses Pope Benedict's declaration that possessing a personal relationship with Jesus is of the utmost evangelistic importance and so of paramount salvific significance. "In some theological circles," what has taken hold, however, is "an odd aversion to affirmations of the uniqueness and universality of Jesus Christ,"[4] Such detestation is often founded upon the presence of religious pluralism—the notion that there could be or are many "saviors" within a variety of religious beliefs. Thus, Jesus is but one "savior" among other viable alternatives. The underlying foundation for Imbelli's refutation of such notions, as well as his insistence upon the need to have a personal relationship with Jesus as the singular Lord and universal Savior, lies within Chalcedon's creed. The possibility of having a personal union between the believer and Jesus resides in truth that

---

3. I have addressed the theological significance of the Chalcedon Creed on a number of occasions. See, for example, *Does God Change?: The Word's Becoming in the Incarnation* (Still River, Mass.: St. Bede's Publications, 1985), 32–66; *Jesus the Christ* (Huntington, Ind.: Our Sunday Visitor Press, 2003, reprinted by Ex Fontibus Company, 2017), 65–79; *Jesus: Essays in Christology* (Ave Maria, Fla.: Sapientia Press, 2014), 119–45, 302–16; "The Doctrinal Significance of the Councils of Nicaea, Ephesus, and Chalcedon," in *The Oxford Handbook of Christology,* ed. Francesca Aran Murphy (Oxford: Oxford University Press, 2015), 549–67.

4. Imbelli, *Rekindling the Christic Imagination*, xvi.

the Son of God actually became man. In doing so, all human beings are able to relate to the Son of God on a human level, and this human relationship is enhanced by the fact that the Son of God now exists as a risen man. To believe in the risen Incarnate Jesus is to be united to him and so be in communion with who he truly is—the Father's Son. Jesus' singularity as the supreme Lord of all and his uniqueness as the universal Savior of all of humankind resides within his very ontological constitution as the Son of God existing as man.

Likewise, Jesus establishes himself as the distinct supreme Lord of all and the unique universal Savior of humankind by performing, as the Father's Son, those saving acts that are truly efficacious—the forgiveness of sins and the offering of eternal life in the Holy Spirit. Moreover, unlike other proffered saviors, Jesus is, then, the only one with whom it is possible to have a personal saving relationship. Other "saviors" only offer what is considered to be saving guidance, and their importance ceases once the saving instruction is given, whereas one obtains Jesus' saving benefits only if one is personally united to him, for he, literally, embodies within himself the saving benefits. For example, Buddha merely offers spiritual guidance, and Mohammed, as a prophet, simply informs his adherents what they are to do in order to please God and so achieve a blissful life after death. Once Buddha or Mohammed convey their particular "salvific knowledge," their importance ceases, for their "message" and not "themselves" are what "saves." Within Christianity, however, Jesus, as the Incarnate Son of God, never loses his saving contemporary significance. To be personally united to the risen Incarnate Jesus is to partake of his purifying and sanctifying divine life as the Father's Son. Chalcedon's creed, in conformity with scripture, highlights this singularity of Jesus as the Father's Incarnate Son, and in so doing, establishes why he alone is the universal Lord and Savior—for Chalcedon, there is no other.[5] This inherent Chalcedonian conviction allows Imbelli to assert: "A theology in the service of the New Evangelization must be one in which the uniqueness and originality of Jesus is probed with creativity and imagination" for there is an "inexhaustible newness of Jesus."[6]

In the light of the doctrinal centrality of Jesus, Imbelli also maintains

---

5. For an examination of the difference between Christianity and Islam see my "*Dei Verbum*: The Centrality of Jesus and Islam," in *Jesus: Essays in Christology*, 317–22.

6. Imbelli, *Rekindling the Christic Imagination*, 16.

"that Christianity cannot be reduced to moralism." Rather, it "opens upon an apprehension of transcendent reality."[7] Yes, Christians are to live morally good lives, but such holiness of life is lived only by abiding within the transcendent reality—only by living within Jesus, for in him alone can the faithful be transformed by the Holy Spirit into righteous children of the all-holy Father. Thus, Christian ethics is not simply a this-worldly affair but a life that replicates and is lived within the transcendent divine life of the holy Trinity. Imbelli progressively deepens this understanding of the necessity of being united to Jesus.

Because Jesus is the Son of God existing as man, he is the new high priest who lovingly offers himself to his Father on behalf of humankind. Here, the incarnational existence of the Son is critical. Who offers himself as high priest to the Father is the Son, but the manner in which he offers himself is as man, and it is thus the incarnational totality of the priesthood and the sacrificial offering that is salvific—the human Jesus as the Father's Son. Thus, for Imbelli, the Incarnate Son Jesus is in himself the new Adam, as well as becoming the new Adam by recreating humankind through his death and resurrection. "Christ is the eschatological Adam, the human intended by God from all eternity. The new eschatological age has dawned with the resurrection of Jesus from the dead, the first born of many brothers and sisters" (6). Christ, therefore, embodies within himself the concrete expression of universal salvation, and so is himself the universal Savior.

Eucharistic Imagination

Imbelli beautifully perceives that within his implicit Chalcedonian understanding of the Incarnation rests a Eucharistic communion. "If we were to characterize the imagination of Jesus, we could speak of it, then, as a 'eucharistic imagination' impelled by his *passion for communion*."[8] The Son of God came to exist as man precisely to have eternal communion with man, and within that communion humankind would be subsumed into the saving newness of Jesus' own divine life. Jesus, as his name YHWH-Saves designates, is himself salvation. "Salvation, at its core, is not something Jesus brings, but *who Jesus is*," for the salvation is not extrinsic to him. Salvation

---

7. Imbelli, *Rekindling the Christic Imagination*, xxiii.
8. Imbelli, *Rekindling the Christic Imagination*, 10.

"is a new self being transformed into the likeness of Christ. To be saved is to enter into the body of Christ as a living member."[9]

This Christic communion, then, as intimated already, involves the whole of the Trinity. To be in Christ is to be within the primordial mystery—the source of all divine mysteries, the communion of the Father, the Son, and the Holy Spirit.[10] While the communion of persons within the Trinity is spiritual, our communal life within the Trinity is incarnational, that is, we, who are bodily, only live within the Trinity's communion of life and love by being subsumed into the humanity of the Son. By living within the body of the Son, thus being transformed into his likeness by the Holy Spirit, we are taken up into the very source of all life and love, that of the Father. For Imbelli, in keeping with Chalcedon, all forms of Gnosticism are thus expelled. Materiality is not jettisoned as unworthy of divine communion, but in being assumed by Word who created it good and re-created it anew, human beings, in the wholeness of who they are, are able now to be incorporated into the divine personal communion of the Trinity. The Son of God *existing* as man, this ontological incarnational oneness, is then the *sine qua non* for the possibility of human beings being united to the Son's humanity and so being united to the divine Son himself. Only if one is in communion with the Son's humanity is one also simultaneously taken up into the Trinitarian communion of the Father in the love of the Holy Spirit. Here, in this incarnational communion, Imbelli sees the heart of the New Evangelization.

At our deepest level, human beings yearn for truth and love, for communion. This yearning for communion is the fertile soil in which seeds of the New Evangelization can be planted. The baptismal water poured in the name of the triune God will allow the young plants to grow to the maturity God desires.[11]

Eucharistic Communion

Founded upon the incarnational union between believers and the risen Incarnate Son, Imbelli advances his inquiry to that of the Eucharist. He first notes that "the Ascension is not postscript but recapitulation: taking up the whole history of Christ into eternal life."[12] In the taking up all that per-

9. Imbelli, *Rekindling the Christic Imagination*, 17.

10. Imbelli, *Rekindling the Christic Imagination*, 21–43.

11. Imbelli, *Rekindling the Christic Imagination*, 43.

12. Imbelli, *Rekindling the Christic Imagination*, 48.

tains to Jesus and his salvific work, there is also the recapitulation of all that is human into Christ. This taking up of all into Christ is most fully enacted, in accordance with Catholic theology, within the Eucharistic celebration. "This is why, though there are many Eucharistic celebrations throughout the world, in all the rich diversity of languages, there is only one Eucharist eternally offered by the ascended Christ to the Father in the Holy Spirit."[13] Within the Eucharistic liturgy, those who live in Christ are conjoined to his once-and-for-all sacrifice and so reap the saving benefits that accrue to that one sacrifice—forgiveness of sins and reconciliation with the Father in the Holy Spirit. Moreover, in receiving the risen Lord Jesus Christ in communion, the faithful become one with him, and in communion with him enter into communion with his Father in the love of the Spirit. Thus, the Eucharist most fully enacts and expresses here on earth the eschatological heavenly communion that is yet to come. Before treating the eschatological nature of the Eucharist, we must first pause to unveil the Chalcedonian underpinning of this Eucharistic communion.

Again, only if it is *truly* the Son of God who *truly* exists as *truly* man, now in a risen and glorious manner, can there truly be a Eucharistic communion. Jesus, the risen Incarnate Son, gives himself completely in the Eucharist. He gives himself in the entire manner in which he now exists—the whole of his risen humanity as the Son of God. Because the Son of God *exists* as man, to receive Jesus' risen body and blood in the Eucharist is to partake of the undivided risen Incarnate Word. Without this ontological unity of the divinity and the humanity in the one person of the Father's Son, we would not, in receiving his risen humanity, also partake of his divinity. Only if the humanity is metaphysically one with the person of the divine Son, are we, in receiving Jesus in the Eucharist, taken up into the entire saving mystery that is the Incarnation—the Son of God existing as man. As Imbelli states: "The risen Christ is present as he who comes to recapitulate all things in himself, bringing the story of each and the stories of all to judgment and salvation. He is present as *viaticum*: food for the journey."[14]

This Chalcedonian understanding of the Incarnation, likewise, underlines and gives expression to the very eschatological nature of the Eucharist. As Imbelli declares: "The liturgy is eschatologically charged! Our Eucha-

---

13. Imbelli, *Rekindling the Christic Imagination*, 49.
14. Imbelli, *Rekindling the Christic Imagination*, 64.

ristic celebration of the Lord's Day, the Eighth Day of the new creation, is not the satisfying of an obligation or the enjoyment of a social gathering, but the burning desire to meet the Lord who comes that we might and all of the world may have life and have it to the full."[15] In the sacrifice of the Mass and in the Eucharist, we partake of the Eschaton here on earth—the Eschaton that is Jesus himself. It is necessary for Imbelli, therefore, that the New Evangelization "accent this eschatological dimension of the Eucharist far more than in the past. It must strive to broaden believers' horizon beyond the one-dimensionality of a secularism that fails to do justice even to the secular. We must learn anew to long ardently for the fulfillment of our ultimate hope: the transfiguration of all in Christ."[16]

Ecclesial Communion

As he proceeds to examine the ecclesial communion that exists within the Church, Imbelli speaks to the heart of what I am proposing here. What is distinctive to Christianity is its "Christological ontology."[17] This Christic ontology is a Chalcedonian ontology—Jesus is one and the same Son who exists perfectly as God and perfectly as man. Moreover, this Christological ontology focuses on Jesus' glorified humanity for it reveals not only that he is the Father's Son but also makes possible humankind's communion with him. For Imbelli, to be "*in Christ*, then, is to be immersed in a field of new, life-bestowing communication and communion," and this entails that we "live *from Christ*," for to live in Christ is to be nurtured on his life—the Father's divine life of the Holy Spirit.[18] This is what it means to be and to grow into one mature man or person in Christ.[19] As Imbelli will emphasize later, in accordance with Vatican II, Jesus as the Incarnate Son reveals to man what man was meant to be. Jesus is our exemplar, our cause, and our end, for only as we live in, with, and through him do we become fully human, formed in his likeness, and so fully alive to the glory of God the Father.[20]

Imbelli's "Christological ontology" allows him further to accentuate that, within Catholic ecclesiology, the Church is not only spiritual but also

---

15. Imbelli, *Rekindling the Christic Imagination*, 65.
16. Imbelli, *Rekindling the Christic Imagination*, 65–66.
17. Imbelli, *Rekindling the Christic Imagination*, 74.
18. Imbelli, *Rekindling the Christic Imagination*, 75.
19. Imbelli, *Rekindling the Christic Imagination*, 76.
20. Imbelli, *Rekindling the Christic Imagination*, 86–87.

visible, and that visibility is again founded upon the Chalcedonian truth that the Son assumed our humanity—visible flesh. "Catholic ecclesiology affirms both the visible and invisible dimensions of the church: both the institutional and the charismatic. But the institutional exists for the sake of the charismatic; its purpose is to serve the building up of the body of Christ in the Spirit."[21] Jesus, as the Son of God, achieved our salvation through his fleshly life, a Spirit-filled human life that he offered in love to the Father out of love for us. Jesus, then, as the messianic Incarnate Son of God, is the Father's primordial sacrament of our salvation. In keeping with this incarnational Chalcedonian principle, the Church, in accordance with Vatican II, is also a sacrament for it to effect what it symbolizes—it efficaciously makes present the saving deeds of Christ, or Christ makes present his efficacious saving deeds through the actions of the Church—by word and sacraments. Since the Church is a sacrament, "it both embodies the reality it signifies and bears witness to it. It is both communion and mission. Its joy is not complete until it is universally shared."[22] Thus, while Vatican II is for Imbelli an "ecclesiological council," its ecclesiology is "Christologically saturated."[23]

Recovering What the Incarnation Means

Imbelli concludes by emphasizing what he is attempting to do—recover the full theological meaning and implications of the Incarnation. Only if the New Evangelization is thoroughly Christic will it succeed in bringing the gospel to all in a manner that is compelling and believable. Only this Christic imagination can "animate, impel, and sustain an evangelical commitment."[24] Imbelli states:

The present book argues that the full meaning of the incarnation only truly appears when seen radiating from its source in the very life of the triune God. The incarnation of Jesus realizes its continuing presence in the sacrament of the Eucharist, and patiently works its ultimate purpose: to fill up the body of Christ—the body of redeemed humanity.[25]

21. Imbelli, *Rekindling the Christic Imagination*, 78.
22. Imbelli, *Rekindling the Christic Imagination*, 84.
23. Imbelli, *Rekindling the Christic Imagination*, 79.
24. Imbelli, *Rekindling the Christic Imagination*, 92.
25. Imbelli, *Rekindling the Christic Imagination*, 92.

Thus, the New Evangelization is a "Christification"—a conforming of the world and all of humankind into the likeness of Christ, for only then is all made new in him.

≪

I have not attempted in this chapter to offer a full reading of Imbelli's marvelous book. There is so much beauty and truth in it that I have passed over. Rather, I wanted, as stated at the beginning, to feature Chalcedon's Creed as the Christological premise upon which Imbelli constructs his study of the Christic imagination and the New Evangelization. Nor does my essay imply that Imbelli was not himself instinctively aware of Chalcedon's presence within his study. He could only conceive and articulate all that he Christically proposes for the success of the New Evangelization from within a Chalcedonian ontology—by already knowing in faith the metaphysics of the Incarnation, of who Jesus *is* as the Spirit-filled Incarnate Son of the Father. The primary purpose of this chapter is to alert the reader to a truth that, while obvious, may have nonetheless been overlooked. For Robert, the Council of Chalcedon does not profess a lifeless and sterile doctrine but rather proclaims the heart of the gospel. Only from within this life-giving Christic doctrine can the Christic imagination be rekindled and the New Evangelization so flourish.

BIBLIOGRAPHY

Selected Works by Robert P. Imbelli
Books

Rekindling the Christic Imagination: Theological Meditations for the New Evangelization. Collegeville, Minn.: Liturgical Press, 2014.

Handing on the Faith: The Church's Mission and Challenge. Edited with an introduction by Robert P. Imbelli. New York: Herder and Herder, 2006.

"Man's Quest for Salvation in the Thought of Josiah Royce." PhD diss., Yale University, 1973.

Articles and Chapters

"No Decapitated Body: Remembering and Misremembering Vatican II." *Nova et Vetera,* English edition, 18, no. 3 (2020): 757–75.

"'He Is the Head of the Body, the Church' (Col 1:18): Salvation as Incorporation into Christ." *Communio: International Catholic Review* 46 (Summer 2019): 288–309.

"*Sursum Corda:* Ascension Theology and Spirituality." In *"Sufficit Gratia Mea." Miscellanea di studi offerti a Sua Em. Il Card. Angelo Amato in occasione del sua 80° genetliaco,* edited by Manlio Sodi, 359–68. Pontificia Academia Theologica Itineraria 14. Città del Vaticano: Libreria Editrice Vaticana, 2019.

"Jesus Christ the Way and the Goal: Accompaniment and Discernment in Christ." *Fellowship of Catholic Scholars Quarterly* 40 (Fall/Winter 2017): 29–35.

"Benedict and Francis." In *Go into the Streets! The Welcoming Church of Pope Francis,* edited by Thomas P. Rausch and Richard R. Gaillardetz, 11–27. New York: Paulist Press, 2016.

"The Christocentric Mystagogy of Joseph Ratzinger." *Communio: International Catholic Review* 42 (Spring 2015): 119–43.

"The Identity and Ministry of the Priest in Light of Vatican II: The Promise and Challenge of *Presbyterorum Ordinis.*" *Josephinum Journal of Theology* 22, nos. 1–2 (2015): 23–43.

"Christ brings all Newness: The Irenaean Vision of Evangelii Gaudium." *PATH—Periodicum Internationale editum a Pontificia Academia Theologiae* 13, no. 2 (2014): 367–76.

C21 Resources. Exploring the Catholic Intellectual Tradition (Spring 2013). Editor. https://issuu.com/church21c/docs/c21resourcesspring2013?mode=window.

"The Heart has its Reasons." *C21 Resources. Exploring the Catholic Intellectual Tradition* (Spring 2013): 3–6.

"Receiving Vatican II: Renewing the Christic Center." *Lonergan Workshop* 26 (2012): 187–209.

"The Reaffirmation of the Christic Center." In *Sic et Non: Encountering* Dominus Iesus, edited by Stephen J. Pope and Charles Hefling, 96–106. Maryknoll, N.Y.: Orbis, 2002.

"The New Adam and Life-Giving Spirit: The Paschal Pattern of Spirit Christology." *Communio: International Catholic Review* 25, no. 2 (Summer 1998): 233–52.

"The Holy Spirit." In *The New Dictionary of Theology*, edited by Joseph Komonchak et al., 474–89. Wilmington, Del.: Glazier, 1987.

"Dwelling Place for God in the Spirit." *Dunwoodie Review* 6, no. 2 (1966):175–206.

Columns in Periodicals

"Newman and Dulles: Two Witnesses to Christ." *The Catholic Thing*, September 28. 2019. https://www.thecatholicthing.org/2019/09/28/newman-and-dulles-two-witnesses-to-christ/.

"Tintoretto's Enlightenment." *The Catholic Thing*, June 2, 2019. https://www.thecatholicthing.org/2019/06/02/tintorettos-enlightenment/.

"The Glory of the Transfigured Crucified." *The Catholic Thing*, March 17, 2019. https://www.thecatholicthing.org/2019/03/17/the-glory-of-the-transfigured-crucified/.

"God's Tower." *The Catholic Thing*, February 17, 2019. https://www.thecatholicthing.org/2019/02/17/gods-tower/.

"For me to live is Christ!" *The Catholic Thing*, December 9, 2018. https://www.thecatholicthing.org/2018/12/09/for-me-to-live-is-christ/.

"Commentary. At the Name of Jesus." *First Things*, October 19, 2018. https://www.firstthings.com/web-exclusives/2018/10/letters-from-the-synod-2018–13.

"Second Peter: From Periphery to Center." *The Catholic Thing*, June 10, 2018. https://www.thecatholicthing.org/2018/06/10/second-peter-from-periphery-to-center/.

"Eucharist and New Creation." *The Catholic Thing*, March 29, 2018. https://www.thecatholicthing.org/2018/03/29/eucharist-and-new-creation/.

"At the Name of Jesus." *The Catholic Thing*, January 21, 2018. https://www.thecatholicthing.org/2018/01/21/at-the-name-of-jesus/.

"On Being Truly Dogmatic." *First Things*, January 9, 2018. https://www.firstthings.com/web-exclusives/2018/01/on-being-truly-dogmatic.

"The King Whom God Gives." *The Catholic Thing*, November 26, 2017. https://www.thecatholicthing.org/2017/11/26/the-king-whom-god-gives/.

"The Principled Ambivalence of Pope Francis." *First Things*, November 7, 2017. https://www.firstthings.com/web-exclusives/2017/11/the-principled-ambivalence-of-pope-francis.

"The Transfiguration of Humanity (Homage to Paul VI)." *The Catholic Thing*, August 6, 2017. https://www.thecatholicthing.org/2017/08/06/the-transfiguration-of-humanity-homage-to-paul-vi/.

"Faith, Belief, and the Trinity." *The Catholic Thing*, June 11, 2017. https://www.thecatholic
thing.org/2017/06/11/faith-belief-and-the-trinity/.

"Benedict XVI at 90: Why His Theology Still Matters." *Crux*, April 16, 2017. https://
cruxnow.com/commentary/2017/04/benedict-xvi-90-theology-still-matters/.

"The Obedience of Faith." *The Catholic Thing*, December 18, 2016. https://www
.thecatholicthing.org/2016/12/18/the-obedience-of-faith/.

""Mercy and 'Metanoia.'" *The Catholic Thing*, September 11, 2016. https://www
.thecatholicthing.org/2016/09/11/mercy-and-metanoia/.

"A Pure Distillation of 1970's Catholicism." *The Catholic Thing*, August 28, 2016. https://
www.thecatholicthing.org/2016/08/28/a-pure-distillation-of-1970s-catholicism/.

"Karl Rahner: An Appreciation and Critique." *First Things*, July 11, 2016. https://www
.firstthings.com/web-exclusives/2016/07/karl-rahner-an-appreciation-and-critique.

"Christ Brings All Newness." *The Catholic Thing*, December 13, 2015. https://www
.thecatholicthing.org/2015/12/13/christ-brings-all-newness/.

"Do This in Memory of Me." *America*, April 22, 2013, 18–20.

"History, Hope and Iphones. Continuing the Conversation." *Commonweal*, October 7,
2011, 7–8."Continue the Conversation: Suggestions for Theologians and Bishops in
Search of Common Ground." *America*, May 30, 2011. https://www.americamagazine
.org/issue/778/article/continue-conversation.

"Refashioning Catholic Imagination: Newman's Writings Offer a Framework for a New
Way of Thinking." *America*, September 27, 2010. https://www.americamagazine.org/
issue/748/article/refashioning-catholic-imagination.

"Model of the Church: Cardinal Avery Dulles (1918–2008)." *Commonweal*, January 12,
2009. https://www.commonwealmagazine.org/model-church.

"For my shield this day a mighty power." *Priests and People* (April 1999): 133–37.

"Rome and Relativism: *'Dominus Iesus' and the CDF.*" *Commonweal*, October 20, 2000,
12–15.

"Christ, the Giver of the Spirit." *Priests and People* 10, no. 4 (April 1996): 129–33.

"Catholic Identity after Vatican II: The Theology of Frans Jozef van Beeck." *Commonweal*, March 11, 1994, 12–16.

"'Dual Loyalties in Catholic Theology': An Exchange of Views." *Commonweal*, April 24,
1992, 212–23.

Other Works

Achard of St. Victor. *Achard of Saint Victor: Works*. Translated by Hugh Feiss. Cistercian
Studies 165. Kalamazoo, Mich.: Cistercian Publications, 2001.

Althaus, Paul. *Die Christliche Wahrheit*. 7th ed. Glütersloh: Glütersloher Verlaghaus, 1966.

Anatolios, Khaled. *Athanasius: The Coherence of his Thought*. London: Routledge, 1998.

Anderson, Floyd, ed. *Council Daybook* (Sessions 1 and 2). Washington, D.C.: NCWC,
1965.

Anselm of Canterbury. *Prayers and Meditations of St Anselm*. Translated by Benedicta
Ward. London: Penguin Books, 1973.

Aristotle. *The Complete Works of Aristotle*. Revised Oxford Translation. Edited by Jonathan
Barnes. 2 vols. Princeton, N.J.: Princeton University Press, 1984.

Ashley, Benedict. *The Dominicans*. Wilmington, Del.: Michael Glazier Inc., 1991.

Atwan, R., and L. Wieder, eds. *Chapters into Verse: Poetry in English Inspired by the Bible.* New York: Oxford University Press, 1993.

Augustine. *Confessions.* Translated by Henry Chadwick. Oxford: Oxford University Press, 1991.

———. *Enchiridion on Faith, Hope, and Love.* Introduction by Thomas S. Hibbs. Translated by J. B. Shaw. Washington, D.C.: Regnery Publishing, 1996.

———. *Instructing Beginners in Faith.* Translated by Raymond Canning. Hyde Park, N.Y.: New City Press, 2006.

———. *Teaching Christianity.* Translated by Edmund Hill. Hyde Park, N.Y.: New City Press, 1996.

———. *The Works of Saint Augustine.* Edited by John E. Rotelle. 49 vols. Hyde Park, N.Y.: New City Press, 1990–present.

Aulén, Gustave. *Christus Victor: An Historical Study of the Three Main Types of Idea of Atonement.* London: SPCK, 1931.

Balthasar, Hans Urs von. *Karl Barth. Darstellung und Deutung seiner Theologie.* Köln: Jakob Hegner, 1951.

———. "God Has Spoken in Human Language." In *The Liturgy and the Word of God*, edited by A. G. Martimort et al., 33–52. Collegeville, Minn.: Liturgical Press, 1959.

———. *Wer ist ein Christ?* Herder-Bücherei 335. Einsiedeln: Benziger Verlag, 1965. English translation: *Who Is a Christian?* Translated by John Cumming. New York: Newman Press, 1965.

———. *The Christian State of Life.* Translated by Mary Frances McCarthy. San Francisco: Ignatius Press, 1977.

———. "Existenz als Sendung: Christus und seine Nachfolge." *Christliche Innerlichkeit* 18 (1984): 2742-78.

———. *Prayer.* Translated by Graham Harrison. San Francisco: Ignatius Press, 1986.

———. *Christian Meditation.* Translated by Mary Theresilde Skerry. San Francisco: Ignatius Press, 1989.

———. *Explorations in Theology.* 5 vols. San Francisco: Ignatius Press, 1989–2014.

———. *Das Ganze im Fragment: Aspekte der Geschichtstheologie.* Einsiedeln: Johannes Verlag, 1990. English translation: *A Theological Anthropology.* New York: Sheed and Ward, 1967.

———. *The Glory of the Lord: A Theological Aesthetics.* Translated by Erasmo Leivà-Merikakis, Andrew Louth, Brian McNeil et al. 7 vols. San Francisco: Ignatius Press, 1982–1989.

———. *Theo-Drama: Theological Dramatic Theory.* Translated by Graham Harrison. 5 vols. San Francisco, CA: Ignatius Press, 1988–1998.

———. "The Council of the Holy Spirit." *Communio: International Catholic Review* 17, vol. 4 (1990): 595–611.

———. *A Theology of History.* San Francisco: Ignatius Press/Communio Books, 1994.

———. *The Moment of Christian Witness.* Translated by Richard Beckley. San Francisco: Ignatius Press, 1994.

———. *Cosmic Liturgy: The Universe according to Maximus the Confessor.* Translated by Brian E. Daley. San Francisco: Ignatius Press/Communio Books, 2003.

———. *Theo-Logic: Theological Logical Theory*. Translated by Adrian J. Walker. 3 vols. San Francisco, CA: Ignatius Press, 2004–2005.

Baltzer, Klaus. *Deutero-Isaiah*. Translated by Margaret Kohl. Minneapolis, Minn.: Fortress Press, 2001.

Barclay, William. *New Testament Words*. Louisville, Ky.: Westminster John Knox, 1974.

Barth, Karl. *The Word of God and the Word of Man*. Translated by Douglas Horton. New York: Harper and Row, 1957.

———. *The Humanity of God*. Louisville, Ky.: Westminster John Knox Press, 1960.

Basil the Great. *On the Holy Spirit*. Translated by Stephen Hildebrand. Yonkers, N.Y.: St. Vladimir's Seminary Press, 2011.

Bauman, Zygmunt. *Liquid Modernity*. Cambridge: Polity Press, 2000.

———. *Does Ethics Have a Chance in a World of Consumers?* Institute for Human Sciences Vienna Lecture Series 3. Cambridge, Mass.: Harvard University Press, 2009.

Begbie, Jeremy S., and Steven R. Guthrie, eds. *Resonant Witness: Conversations between Music and Theology*. Grand Rapids, Mich.: Eerdmans, 2011.

Bellinger, William H., and William R. Farmer, eds. *Jesus and the Suffering Servant: Isaiah 53 and Christian Origins*. Harrisburg, Pa.: Trinity Press International, 1998.

Bennett, Thomas A. *Labor of God: The Agony of the Cross as the Birth of the Church*. Waco, Tex.: Baylor University Press, 2017.

Bernard of Clairvaux. *Sermons on the Song of Songs*. Translated by Kilian Walsh and Irene M. Edmonds. 4 vols. Kalamazoo, Mich.: Cistercian Publications, 1971–1980.

Bertone, Tarcisio. *The Last Secret of Fatima*. Translated by Adrian J. Walker. New York: Doubleday, 2008.

Beumer, Johannes. "Mariologie und Ekklesiologie bei Isaak von Stella." *Münchener Theologische Zeitschrift* V (1954): 48–61.

Bobik, Joseph. "Aquinas on *Communicatio*, the Foundation of Friendship and *Caritas*." *The Modern Schoolman* 64, no.1 (1986): 1–18.

Boethius. *De Duabus Naturis [Contra Eutychen]*. In *Theological Tractates. The Consolation of Philosophy*. Translated by H. F. Stewart et al. Loeb Classical Library. Vol. 74. Cambridge, Mass.: Harvard University Press, 1973, 72–129.

Bonaventure. *The Reduction of the Arts to Theology*. Latin-English edition. Edited by Zachary Hayes. St. Bonaventure, N.Y.: Franciscan Institute, 1996.

Bouyer, Louis. *The Cistercian Heritage*. Translated by Elizabeth A. Livingstone. Westminster, Md.: The Newman Press, 1958.

Bovon, François. *A Commentary on the Gospel of Luke*. Translated by James E. Crouch. 3 vols. Minneapolis, Minn.: Fortress Press, 2002–2013.

Bradley, Denis. *Aquinas on the Twofold Human Good*. Washington, D.C.: The Catholic University of America Press, 1997.

Brague, Rémi. "From What Is Left Over." *First Things*, August/September 2017, 39–44.

Brennan, Robert Edward. *The Seven Horns of the Lamb: A Study of the Gifts Based on Saint Thomas Aquinas*. Milwaukee, Wis.: Bruce, 1966.

de Broglie, Guy. "La vraie Notion thomiste des 'praeambula fidei." *Gregorianum* 34, no. 3 (1953): 345–89.

Brown, Raymond E. *The Death of the Messiah: From Gethsemane to the Grave*. 2 vols. New York: Doubleday, 1994.

Burnham, Frederick P., ed. *Postmodern Theology. Christian Faith in a Pluralist World*. San Francisco: Harper and Row, 1989.

Buttrick, G. A., ed. *The Interpreter's Dictionary of the Bible*. 5 vols. New York: Abingdon, 1962–1976.

Bychkov, Oleg V., and James Fodor, eds. *Theological Aesthetics after von Balthasar*. Burlington, Vt.: Ashgate, 2008.

Bynum, Caroline Walker. *Jesus as Mother: Studies in the Spirituality of the High Middle Ages*. Berkeley: University of California, 1982.

Byrne, Brendan. *Life Abounding: A Reading of John's Gospel*. Collegeville, Minn.: Liturgical Press, 2014.

Cahall, Perry J. "The Nucleus of the New Evangelization." *Nova et Vetera*, English edition, 11, no. 1 (2013): 39–56.

Cahill, Brendan. *The Renewal of Revelation Theology (1960–1962)*. Tesi Gregoriana, Serie Teologia 51. Rome: Editrice Pontificia. Università Gregoriana, 1999.

Calvin, John. *Institutes of the Christian Religion*. Translated by Henry Beveridge. Grand Rapids, Mich.: Eerdmans, 1989.

———. *A Harmony of the Gospels Matthew, Mark, and Luke* [Calvin's Commentary on the Bible]. https://www.studylight.org/commentaries/cal.html.

Cantalamessa, Raniero. *The Holy Spirit in the Life of Jesus: The Mystery of Christ's Baptism*. Translated by Alan Neame. Collegeville, Minn.: Liturgical Press, 1994.

Casey, Thomas. *Life and Soul: New Light on a Sublime Mystery*. Springfield, Ill.: Templegate, 2005.

Castelli, E., ed. *L'Hermeneutique de la liberté religieuse*. Paris: Aubier, 1968.

Cessario, Romanus. *Introduction to Moral Theology*. Washington, D.C.: The Catholic University of America Press, 2001.

———. "On the Place of Servais Pinckaers († 7 April 2008) in the Renewal of Catholic Theology." *The Thomist* 73, no. 1 (2009): 1–27.

Charue, André-Marie. *Carnets conciliaires de l'évêque de Namur A.-M. Charue*. Edited by Leo Declerck and Claude Soetens. Louvain-la-Neuve: Faculté de Théologie, 2000.

Chau, Carolyn A. "'What Could Possibly Be Given?': Towards an Exploration of Kenosis as Forgiveness – Continuing the Conversation between Coakley, Hampson, and Papanikolaou." *Modern Theology* 28, no. 1 (2012): 1–24.

———. *Solidarity with the World: Charles Taylor and Hans Urs von Balthasar on Faith, Modernity, and Catholic Mission*. Theopolitical Visions 19. Eugene, Ore.: Cascade Books, 2016.

Congar, Yves. *La Foi et la Théologie*. Le Mystère Chrétien, Théologie Dogmatique 1. Paris: Desclée, 1962.

———. *Situation et tâches présentes de la théologie*. Paris: Cerf, 1967.

———. *Jean Puyo interroge le Pére Congar*. Paris: Le Centurion, 1975.

———. "Erinnerungen an eine Episode auf dem II. Vatikanischen Konzil." In *Glaube im Prozess. Christsein nach dem II. Vatikanum*, edited by E. Klinger and K. Wittstadt, 22–32. Freiburg: Herder, 1984.

———. *My Journal of the Council*. Translated by Mary John Ronayne and Mary Cecily Boulding. Translation editor, D. Minns. Collegeville, Minn.: Liturgical Press, 2012.

Constable, Giles. *The Reformation of the Twelfth Century*. Cambridge: Cambridge University Press, 1998.

Coolman, Boyd Taylor. "Hugh of St. Victor on 'Jesus Wept': Making Christological Sense of Jesus' Tears and Conceiving Ideal *Humanitas* in the Twelfth Century." *Theological Studies* 69, no. 3 (2008): 528–56.

Cummings, Andrew McLean. *The Servant and the Ladder: Cooperation with Evil in the Twenty-First Century*. Leominster: Gracewing, 2014.

Dante Alighieri. *The Divine Comedy*. Translated by C. H. Sisson. Oxford: Oxford University Press, 2008.

Davies, W. D., and Dale C. Allison Jr., eds. *A Critical and Exegetical Commentary on the Gospel according to Saint Matthew*. 3 vols. London: T. and T. Clark International, 2004.

Deines, Roland. "The Holy Spirit in Matthew's Gospel." In *The Earliest Perceptions of Jesus in Context: Essays in Honour of John Nolland on His 70th Birthday*, edited by Aaron White, David Wenham, and Craig A. Evans, 213–35. Edinburgh: T. and T. Clark, 2018.

Deman, Thomas. "Probabilisme." In *Dictionnaire de théologie catholique*, cols. 417–619. Paris: Letouzey et Ane, 1936.

Disse, Jörg. *Metaphysik der Singularität: Eine Hinführung am Leitfaden der Philosophie Hans Urs von Balthasars*. Philosophische Theologie 7. Vienna: Passagen Verlag, 1996.

Dulles, Avery. *The Splendor of Faith: The Theological Vision of Pope John Paul II*. New York: Crossroad Publishing Company, 2003.

———. *Church and Society*. New York: Fordham University Press, 2008.

Dupuis, Jacques. "Western Christocentrism and Eastern Pneumatology." *Clergy Monthly* 35, no. 5 (1971): 190–98.

———. *Toward a Christian Theology of Religious Pluralism*. Maryknoll, N.Y.: Orbis, 1997.

Eiesland, Nancy L. *The Disabled God: Towards a Liberatory Theology of Disability*. Nashville, Tenn.: Abingdon, 1994.

Emery, Gilles. *The Trinitarian Theology of Saint Thomas Aquinas*. Translated by Francesca Aran Murphy. Oxford: Oxford University Press, 2007.

———. *Trinity, Church, and the Human Person: Thomistic Essays*. Ave Maria, Fla.: Sapientia Press, 2007.

———. "*Theologia* and *Dispensatio*: The Centrality of the Divine Missions in St. Thomas's Trinitarian Theology." *The Thomist* 74, no. 4 (2010): 515–61.

——— and Matthew Levering, eds. *The Oxford Handbook of the Trinity*. Oxford: Oxford University Press, 2011.

Evdokimov, Paul. *Orthodoxy*. Translated by Jeremy Hummerstone. Hyde Park, N.Y.: New City Press, 2011.

Fee, Gordon D. *God's Empowering Presence: The Holy Spirit in the Letters of Paul*. Peabody, Mass.: Hendrickson, 1994.

———. *Pauline Christology: An Exegetical-Theological Study*. Peabody, Mass.: Hendrickson, 2007.

Feingold, Lawrence. *The Natural Desire to See God in St. Thomas Aquinas and His Interpreters*. Ave Maria, Fla.: Sapientia Press, 2010.

Fitzmeyer, Joseph A. *The Gospel according to Luke X–XXIV*. New York: Doubleday, 1985.

Franks, Angela. "Trinitarian *Analogia Entis* in Hans Urs von Balthasar." *The Thomist* 62, no. 4 (1998): 533–59.

———. "The Epiphany of Being: Trinitarian *Analogia Entis* and the Transcendentals in Hans Urs von Balthasar." PhD diss., Boston College, 2007.

———. "Thinking the Embodied Person with Karol Wojtyła." *Nova et Vetera*, English edition, 16, no. 1 (2018): 141–71.

———. "A Wojtyłian Reading of Performativity and the Self in Judith Butler." *Christian Bioethics: Non-Ecumenical Studies in Medical Morality* 26, no. 3 (2020): 221–42.

Frazier, William. "The Incredible Christian Capacity for Missing the Christian Point." *America* 167, no. 16 (November 21, 1992).

Freedman, D. N., ed. *The Anchor Bible Dictionary.* 6 vols. New York: Doubleday, 1992.

Fries, Heinrich, ed. *Handbuch theologischer Grundbegriffe.* 2 vols. Munich: Kösel, 1962.

Fritsch, Emmanuel. "Mēron et chrismation dans la liturgie éthiopienne modern." In *Christmation et confirmation: Questions autour d'un rite post-baptismal,* edited by Carlo Braga, 253–64. Roma: Edizioni liturgiche, 2009.

Fulton, Rachel. *From Judgment to Passion: Devotion to Christ and the Virgin Mary, 800–1200.* New York: Columbia University, 2002.

Gaggero, Leonard. "Isaac of Stella and the Theology of Redemption." *Collectanea Cisterciensia* 22 (1965): 21–36.

Gaillardetz, Richard. *An Unfinished Council.* Collegeville, Minn.: Liturgical Press, 2015.

Garrison, James D. *Pietas from Vergil to Dryden.* University Park: Pennsylvania State University Press, 1992.

Gathercole, Simon J. *The Pre-Existent Son: Recovering the Christologies of Matthew, Mark and Luke.* Grand Rapids, Mich.: Eerdmans, 2006.

Gaventa, Beverly Roberts. *Our Mother Saint Paul.* Louisville, Ky.: Westminster John Knox, 2007.

Gilbert of Hoyland, *Sermons on the Song of Songs I–IV.* Translated by Lawrence C. Braceland. 3 vols. Cistercian Fathers Series 20. Kalamazoo, Mich.: Cistercian Publications, 1978–1981.

Gillon, Louis B. *Christ and Moral Theology.* Translated by Cornelius Williams. Staten Island, N.Y.: Alba House, 1967.

Girard, René. *Things Hidden since the Foundation of the World.* Research undertaken in collaboration with Jean Michel Oughourlian and Guy Lefort. Translated by Stephen Bann and Michael Metteer. Stanford, Calif.: Stanford University Press, 1987.

———. *I See Satan Fall Like Lightning.* Translated by James G. Williams. Maryknoll, N.Y.: Orbis Books, 2002.

Gleason, Robert W., ed. *A Theology Reader.* New York: Macmillan, 1966.

Göbbeler, Hans-Peter. *Existenz als Sendung: Zum Verständnis der Nachfolge Christi in der Theologie Hans Urs von Balthasars.* St. Ottilien: EOS-Verlag, 1997.

Gondreau, Paul. *The Passions of Christ's Soul in the Theology of St. Thomas Aquinas.* Beiträge zur Geschichte der Philosophie und Theologie des Mittelalters, Neue Folge 61. Münster: Aschendorff Verlag, 2002.

Gregory the Great. *Homélies sur l'Évangile.* Vol. 2. In Sources Chrétiennes 522. Translated by R. Étaix and G. Blanc. Paris: Cerf, 2008.

———. *Regula Pastoralis.* In *Opere Di Gregorio Magno* 7. Edited by Floribert Rommel.

Rome: Citta nuova, 2008. English translation: *The Book of Pastoral Rule*. Translated by George E. Demacopoulos. Popular Patristics Series 34. Crestwood, N.Y.: St. Vladimir's Seminary Press, 2007.

Guarino, Thomas. "*'Essentia et non Gradu Tantum Differant'*: A Note on the Priesthood and Analogical Predication." *The Thomist* 77, no. 4 (2013): 559–76.

———. "Analogy and Vatican II: An Overlooked Dimension of the Council?" *Josephinum Journal of Theology* 22, nos. 1–2 (2015): 44–58.

———. *The Disputed Teachings of Vatican II: Continuity and Reversal in Catholic Doctrine*. Grand Rapids, Mich.: Eerdmans, 2018.

Guerriero, Elio. *Hans Urs von Balthasar*. Milan: Edizioni Paoline, 1991.

Guretzki, David. *Karl Barth on the Filioque*. New York: Routledge, 2009.

Gustafson, James. *Can Ethics Be Christian?* Chicago, Ill.: University of Chicago, 1975.

Hans Urs von Balthasar-Stiftung, ed. *Vermittlung als Auftrag*. Symposium zum 90. Geburtstag von Hans Urs von Balthasar, 27.–29 September 1995. Einsiedeln: Johannes Verlag, 1995.

———, ed. *Eine Theologie für das 21. Jahrhundert: Zur Wirkungsgeschichte Hans Urs von Balthasars*. Symposium zu seinem 25. Todestag. Einsiedeln: Johannes Verlag, 2014.

Harries, Richard. *The Passion in Art*. Hants, England: Ashgate, 2004.

Harrison, Carol. *Beauty and Revelation in the Thought of Saint Augustine*. Oxford: Clarendon Press, 1992.

Hefling, Charles C. "Revelation and/as Insight." In *The Importance of Insight: Essays in Honour of Michael Vertin*, edited by John J. Liptay, Jr. and David S. Liptay, 97–115. Toronto: University of Toronto Press, 2007.

Hengel, Martin. *Crucifixion*. Translated by John Bowden. London: SCM Press, 1977.

Henrici, Peter. "Hans Urs von Balthasar: A Sketch of His Life." In *Hans Urs von Balthasar: His Life and Work*, edited by David L. Schindler, 7–43. San Francisco: Ignatius Press/ Communio Books, 1991.

Hercsik, Donath. *Jesus Christus als Mitte der Theologie von Henri de Lubac*. Frankfurter Theologische Studien 61. Frankfurt: Knecht, 2001.

Herdt, Jennifer A. "The Endless Construction of Charity: On Milbank's Critique of Political Economy." *Journal of Religious Ethics* 32, no. 2 (2004): 301–24.

von Hildebrand, Dietrich. *The Heart: An Analysis of Human and Divine Affectivity*. South Bend, Ind.: St Augustine's Press, 2007.

Hill, Edmund. "*De Doctrina Christiana*: A Suggestion." *Studia Patristica* 6 (1962): 443–46.

Hill, Wesley. *Paul and the Trinity: Persons, Relations, and the Pauline Letters*. Grand Rapids, Mich.: Eerdmans, 2015.

Hodge, Joel. "Recovering the Liturgical Background to Christian Atonement: The Approach of James Alison and Joseph Ratzinger." *Irish Theological Quarterly* 81, no. 3 (2016): 284–305.

Hugh of St. Victor. *Six opuscules spirituels*. In Sources Chrétiennes 155. Edited and translated with introduction and notes by Roger Baron. Paris: Éditions du Cerf, 1969.

———. *L'œuvre de Hugues de Saint-Victor, I: De institutione novitiorum; De virtute orandi; De laude caritatis; De arrha anime*. Edited and translated by H. B. Feiss, P. Sicard, D. Poirel, and H. Rochais (Sous la Règle de Saint Augustin). Turnhout: Brepols, 1997.

Irenaeus of Lyon. *Adversus Haereses*. In Sources Chrétiennes 100, 153, 211, 264, 294. Edited by Adelin Rousseau et al. Paris: Les Éditions du Cerf, 1965–1982.

Isaac of Stella. *The Selected Works of Isaac of Stella: A Cistercian Voice from the Twelfth Century*. Edited by Dániel Deme. Burlington, Vt.: Ashgate, 2007.

———. *Sermons*. In Sources Chrétiennes 130, 207, 339. Edited by Anselm Hoste and Gaetano Raciti. Translated by Gaston Salet. Vols. 1–3. Paris: Les Éditions du Cerf, 1967, 1974, and 1987.

———. *Sermons on the Christian Year*. Translated by Hugh McCaffery. Kalamazoo, Mich.: Cistercian Publications, 1979.

Javelet, Robert. *Image et ressemblance au douzième siècle: de Saint Anselme à Alain de Lille*. Vol. 1. Paris: Éditions Letouzey & Ané, 1967.

Jenson, Robert W. "You Wonder Where the Spirit Went." *Pro Ecclesia* 2, no. 3 (1993): 296–304.

Jerome. *Commentary on Matthew*. Translated by Thomas P. Scheck. Washington, D.C.: The Catholic University of America Press, 2008.

John Chrysostom. *Homilies on the Gospel of St. Matthew*. Translated by George Prevost and M. B. Riddle. Nicene and Post-Nicene Fathers, First Series, 10. Edited by Philip Schaff. Peabody, Mass.: Hendrickson, 1995.

John Paul II. [Karol Wojtyła.] *Sources of Renewal: The Implementation of the Second Vatican Council*. Translated by P. S. Falla. San Francisco: Harper and Row, 1980.

———. [Karol Wojtyła.] *Collected Poems*. Translated by Jerzy Peterkiewicz. London: Hutchinson, 1981.

———. "Address to Professors and Students of the Augustinian Patristics Institute (*Sono Lieto*)." May 8, 1982, *AAS* 74 (1982): 794–800.

———. *Man and Woman He Created Them*. Translated with an introduction by Michael Waldstein. Boston: Pauline Books and Media, 2006.

Jone, Heribert. *Moral Theology*. Translated by Urban Adelman. Westminster, Md.: The Newman Bookshop, 1951.

Jungmann, Joseph. *The Mass of the Roman Rite: Its Origin and Development (Missarum Sollemnia)*. Translated by Francis Brunner. Vol. 1. New York: Benziger, 1951.

Kaczor, Christopher. *Proportionalism and the Natural Law Tradition*. Washington, D.C.: The Catholic University of America Press, 2002.

Kereszty, Roch. *Jesus Christ: Fundamentals of Christology*. New York: Alba House, 2002.

Kittel, Gerhard, and Gerhard Friedrich, eds. *Theological Dictionary of the New Testament*. Translated by Geoffrey W. Bromiley. 10 vols. Grand Rapids, Mich.: William B. Eerdmans, 1964–1976.

Knitter, Paul. "Christomonism in Karl Barth's Evaluation of Non-Christian Religions." *Neue Zeitschrift für systematische Theologie une Religionsphilosophie* 13, no. 1 (1971): 99–121.

Labourdette, Michel. *Cours de théologie morale*. 2 vols. Paris: Parole et Silence, 2010–2012.

Legge, Dominic. *The Trinitarian Christology of St Thomas Aquinas*. Oxford: Oxford University Press, 2017.

Leithart, Peter J. *The Gospel of Matthew through New Eyes*. 2 vols. Monroe, La.: Athanasius Press, 2017–2019.

Leo the Great. *Sermons III* (38–64). Sources Chrétiennes 74. Translated by R. Dolle. Paris: Cerf, 2004.

Levering, Matthew. "The Holy Spirit and the Old Testament." *The Thomist* 79, no. 3 (2015): 345–81.

Lewis, C. S. *Broadcast Talks*. London: Geoffrey Bles, 1942.

Lincoln, Andrew T. *The Gospel according to St John*. London: Continuum, 2005.

Lombardo, Nicholas E. *The Logic of Desire*. Washington, D.C.: The Catholic University of America Press, 2011.

Lonergan, Bernard. *De Verbo Incarnato*. Rome: Universitas Pontificia Gregoriana, 1964.

———. *Method in Theology*. New York: Herder, 1972.

———. *A Third Collection: Papers by Bernard J. F. Lonergan*. Edited by Frederick E. Crowe. Mahwah, N.J.: Paulist Press, 1984.

———. *Collection*. Vol. 4 of *Collected Works of Bernard Lonergan*. Edited by Frederick E. Crowe and Robert Doran. Toronto: University of Toronto Press, 1993.

———. *Understanding and Being*. Vol. 5 of *Collected Works of Bernard Lonergan*. Edited by Elizabeth A. Morelli and Mark D. Morelli. Toronto: Toronto University Press, 2000.

———. *Philosophical and Theological Papers 1965–1980*. Vol. 17 of *Collected Works of Bernard Lonergan*. Edited by Robert C. Croken and Robert M. Doran. Toronto: University of Toronto Press, 2004.

———. *The Triune God: Systematics*. Vol. 12 of *Collected Works of Bernard Lonergan*. Translated by Michael G. Shields. Edited by Robert M. Doran and H. Daniel Monsour. Toronto: University of Toronto Press, 2007.

———. *A Second Collection*. Vol. 13 of *Collected Works of Bernard Lonergan*. Edited by Robert M. Doran and John D. Dadosky. Toronto: University of Toronto Press, 2016.

———. *The Incarnate Word*. Vol. 8 of *Collected Works of Bernard Lonergan*. Translated by Charles C. Hefling. Edited by Robert M. Doran and Jeremy D. Wilkins. Toronto: University of Toronto Press, 2016.

Long, Steven A. *Natura Pura: A Rediscovery of Nature in the Doctrine of Grace*. New York: Fordham University Press, 2010.

de Lubac, Henri. *Surnaturel: etudes historiques*. Paris: F. Aubier, 1946.

———. "Commentaire du préambule et du chapitre I." In *La Révélation divine, Unam Sanctam 70a*, edited by B.-D. Dupuy, 157–302. Paris: Cerf, 1968.

———. *Theology in History*. San Francisco: Ignatius Press, 1996.

———. *The Splendor of the Church*. San Francisco: Ignatius Press, 1999.

———. *Corpus Mysticum: The Eucharist and the Church in the Middle Ages: A Historical Survey*. Translated by Gemma Simmonds et al. Notre Dame, Ind.: University of Notre Dame Press, 2007.

Luz, Ulrich. *Matthew 21–28. A Commentary*. Translated by James E. Crouch. Edited by Helmut Koester. Minneapolis, Minn.: Fortress Press, 2005.

———. *Matthew 1–7: A Commentary*. Translated by James E. Crouch. Edited by Helmut Koester. Minneapolis, Minn.: Fortress Press, 2007.

Marcus, Joel. *Mark 8–16*. New Haven, Conn.: Yale University Press, 2009.

Marrou, Henri-Irénée. *Saint Augustin et la fin de la culture antique*. 4th ed. Paris: E. de Boccard, 1958.

Marty, Martin. "What Went Wrong?" *The Critic* 34 (Fall 1975): 49–53.

Matera, Frank J. *New Testament Theology: Exploring Diversity and Unity.* Louisville, Ky.: Westminster John Knox, 2007.

McCabe, Herbert. *God Matters.* London: Geoffrey Chapman, 1987.

———. *Exploring the Catholic Faith: A Guide through the Basics.* Boston: Pauline Books and Media, 2008.

McDonnell, Kilian. *The Baptism of Jesus in the Jordan.* Collegeville, Minn.: Liturgical Press, 1996.

McGill, V. J. "Scheler's Theory of Sympathy and Love." *Philosophy and Phenomenological Research* 2, no. 3 (March 1942): 273–91.

McIntosh, Mark A. *Christology from Within: Spirituality and the Incarnation in Hans Urs von Balthasar.* Studies in Spirituality and Theology 3. Notre Dame, Ind.: University of Notre Dame Press, 2000.

McKnight, Scot. *Jesus and His Death.* Waco, Tex.: Baylor University Press, 2005.

Meier, John P. *A Marginal Jew.* 2 vols. New York: Doubleday, 1991–1994.

Merrigan, Terrence. "The Imagination in the Life and Thought of John Henry Newman." *Cahiers victoriens et édouardiens* 70 (Autumn 2009): 187–217.

Mersch, Émile. *La Théologie du corps mystique.* 2 vols. Paris: Desclée de Brouwer, 1944.

Meszaros, Andrew. "The Thomistic Underpinnings of *Ad Gentes.*" *Nova et Vetera*, English edition, 13, no. 3 (2015): 875–901.

Meyendorff, John. *Christ in Eastern Christian Thought.* Washington, D.C.: Corpus Books, 1969.

Migne, J.-P., ed. Patrologia cursus completus. Series Latina. 221 vols. Paris: 1844–1864. http://patristica.net/latina/.

———. Series Graeca. 161 vols. Paris: 1857–1866. http://patristica.net/graeca/.

Milbank, John. *The Suspended Middle: Henri de Lubac and the Debate concerning the Supernatural.* Grand Rapids, Mich.: Eerdmans, 2005.

Miner, Robert. *Thomas Aquinas on the Passions: A Study of Summa Theologiae, 1a2ae 22–48.* Cambridge: Cambridge University Press, 2009.

Morrison, Karl F. *I Am You: The Hermeneutics of Empathy in Western Literature.* Princeton, N.J.: Princeton University Press, 1988.

Moschella, Melissa. "Personal Identity and Gender: A Revised Aristotelian Approach." In *Gender Identities in a Globalized World*, edited by Ana Marta González and Victor J. Seidler, 75–108. New York: Humanity Books, 2008.

Murphy, Francesca Aran, ed. *The Oxford Handbook of Christology.* Oxford: Oxford University Press, 2015.

Mutschler, Bernard. *Irenäus als johanneischer Theologe.* Studien und Texte zu Antike und Christentum 21. Tübingen: Mohr Siebeck, 2004.

Newman, John Henry. *An Essay in Aid of a Grammar of Assent.* London: Longmans, Green, and Co., 1903.

———. *Fifteen Sermons Preached before the University of Oxford.* London: Longmans, Green, and Co., 1909.

Niebuhr, H. Richard. *The Kingdom of God in America.* Harper and Row, 1937.

Nolland, John. *The Gospel of Matthew.* Grand Rapids, Mich.: Eerdmans, 2005.

Nouwen, Henri J. M. *Behold the Beauty of the Lord: Praying with Icons.* South Bend, Ind.: Ave Maria Press, 1987.

Oakes, Edward. *Infinity Dwindled into Infancy: A Catholic and Evangelical Christology.* Grand Rapids, Mich.: William B. Eerdmans, 2011.

O'Collins, Gerald. "Crucifixion." In *Anchor Bible Dictionary*, edited by David N. Freedman et al., 1207–10. Vol. 1. New York: Doubleday, 1992.

O'Malley, John W. *What Happened at Vatican II.* Cambridge, Mass.: The Belknap Press of Harvard University, 2008.

Papanikolaou, Aristotle. "Person, Kenosis and Abuse: Hans Urs von Balthasar and Feminist Theologies in Conversation." *Modern Theology* 19, no. 1 (2003): 41–65.

Pennington, Jonathan T. *Heaven and Earth in the Gospel of Matthew.* Grand Rapids, Mich.: Baker Academic, 2009.

Peterson, Brandon. "Critical Voices: The Reactions of Rahner and Ratzinger to 'Schema XIII' (*Gaudium et Spes*)." *Modern Theology* 31, no. 1 (2015): 1–26.

Philips, Gérard. *L'Église et son Mystère au IIe Concile du Vatican.* 2 vols. Paris: Desclée, 1967–1968.

———. *Primauté et Collégialité: Le dossier de Gérard Philips sur la Nota Explicativa Praevia (Lumen gentium, chap. III).* Edited by Jan Grootaers. Leuven: Leuven University Press, 1986.

———. *Carnets conciliaires de Mgr Gérard Philips, secrétaire adjoint de la commission doctrinale.* Edited by K. Schelkens. Leuven: Peeters, 2006.

Pinckaers, Servais. *The Sources of Christian Ethics.* Translated by Mary Thomas Noble. Washington, D.C.: The Catholic University of America Press, 1995.

———. *Passions and Virtue.* Translated by Benedict M. Guevin. Washington, D.C.: The Catholic University of America Press, 2015.

Piolanti, Antonio. "La nostra soledarità soprannaturale nel pensiero di Isacco della Stella." *Palestro del Claro* VII (1956): 1–18.

Pitstick, Alyssa Lyra. *Light in Darkness: Hans Urs von Balthasar and the Catholic Doctrine of Christ's Descent into Hell.* Grand Rapids, Mich.: William B. Eerdmans, 2007.

———. *Christ's Descent into Hell: John Paul II, Joseph Ratzinger, and Hans Urs von Balthasar on the Theology of Holy Saturday.* Grand Rapids, Mich.: William B. Eerdmans, 2016.

Pizzutto, Pietro. *La teologia della rivelazione di Jean Daniélou. Influsso su Dei Verbum e valore attuale.* Rome: Gregorian University Press, 2003.

Plato. *Plato. Complete Works.* Edited by John M. Cooper. Indianapolis, Ind.: Hackett Publishing Co., 1997.

Pope, Stephen, ed. *The Ethics of Thomas Aquinas.* Washington, D.C.: Georgetown University Press, 2002.

Porter, Lawrence B. *The Assault on Priesthood.* Eugene, Ore.: Wipf and Stock, 2012.

Purcell, Jim. "Focus on Preaching the Kingdom is key to ending clericalism." *National Catholic Reporter*, August 20, 2016. https://www.ncronline.org/news/spirituality/focus-preaching-kingdom-key-ending-clericalism.

Quintilian. *Institutio Oratoria.* Edited by Michael Winterbottom. Oxford: Clarendon Press, 1970.

Raciti, Gaetano. "Isaac de l'Étoile." In *Dictionnaire de Spiritualité.* Vol. 7, cols. 2011–38. Paris: Beauchesne, 1971.

Rahner, Karl. *Theological Investigations.* 23 vols. London: Crossroad, 1961–1992.

———. *Foundations of Christian Faith.* Translated by William Dych. New York: Crossroad, 2002.

————. *Sämtliche Werke*. Vol. 21, *Das Zweite Vatikanum. Beiträge zum Konzil und seiner Interpretation*, edited by Gunther Wassilowsky. Freiburg: Benzinger–Herder, 2013.

Rasimus, Tuomas, ed. *The Legacy of John: Second-Century Reception of the Fourth Gospel.* Leiden: Brill, 2010.

Ratzinger, Joseph. "Kein Heil außerhalb der Kirche?" In *Das neue Volk Gottes: Entwürfe zur Ekklesiologie*, 339–61. Düsseldorf: Patmos, 1969.

————. with Vittorio Messori. *The Ratzinger Report: An Exclusive Interview on the State of the Church*. Translated by Salvator Attanasio and Graham Harrison. San Francisco: Ignatius Press, 1985.

————. *Behold the Pierced One: An Approach to a Spiritual Christology*. Translated by Graham Harrison. San Francisco: Ignatius Press, 1986.

————. *The Feast of Faith: Approaches to a Theology of the Liturgy*. Translated by Graham Harrison. San Francisco: Ignatius Press, 1986.

————. *Principles of Catholic Theology*. Translated by Mary Frances McCarthy. San Francisco: Ignatius Press, 1987.

————. *The Meaning of Christian Brotherhood*. San Francisco: Ignatius Press, 1993.

————. *"In the Beginning…": A Catholic Understanding of the Story of Creation and the Fall*. Translated by Boniface Ramsey and Helen A. Saward. Grand Rapids, Mich.: Eerdmans, 1995.

————. *A New Song for the Lord: Faith in Christ and Liturgy Today*. Translated by Martha M. Matesich. New York: Crossroad, 1996.

————. *Called to Communion: Understanding the Church Today*. Translated by Adrian Walker. San Francisco: Ignatius Press, 1996.

————. *Salt of the Earth. The Church at the End of the Millenium*. San Francisco: Ignatius Press, 1997.

————. *Milestones. Memoirs 1927–1977*. Translated by Erasmo Leiva-Merikakis. San Francisco: Ignatius Press, 1998.

————. *The Spirit of the Liturgy*. Translated by John Saward. San Francisco: Ignatius Press, 2000.

————. *Introduction to Christianity*. Translated by J. R. Foster and Michael J. Miller. San Francisco: Ignatius Press, 2004.

————. *Homily for the Fortieth Anniversary of "Gaudium et Spes."* March 18, 2005. http://www.vatican.va/roman_curia/congregations/cfaith/documents/rc_con_cfaith_doc_20050318_ratzinger-gaudium-spes_en.html.

————. "Eucharist: Setting Transformations in Motion." *Origins* 35 (September 1, 2005): 202–4.

————. *What It Means to Be a Christian*. San Francisco: Ignatius Press, 2006.

————. *Jesus of Nazareth: From the Baptism in the Jordan to the Transfiguration*. Vol. 1. Translated by Adrian J. Walker. New York: Doubleday, 2007.

————. *Jesus of Nazareth: Holy Week: From the Entrance into Jerusalem to the Resurrection*. Vol. 2. Translated by Philip J. Whitmore. San Francisco: Ignatius Press, 2011.

————. "France Visit: Address on Culture." *Origins* 38 (September 25, 2008): 248–53.

————. *Faith and the Future*. San Francisco: Ignatius Press, 2009.

————. *Gesammelte Schriften*. Edited by Gerhard Ludwig Müller. Vol. 2, *Offenbarungsverständnis und Geschichtstheologie Bonaventuras*. Freiburg: Herder, 2009.

————. *Gesammelte Schriften*. Edited by Gerhard Ludwig Müller. Vol. 7, *Zur Lehre des Zweiten Vatikansichen Konzils*. Freiburg: Herder, 2012.

————. *Dogma and Preaching: Applying Christian Doctrine to Daily Life*. San Francisco: Ignatius Press, 2011.

————. "Germany Visit: Meeting with Catholics Active in Church and Society." *Origins* 41 (October 13, 2011): 305–7.

————. "Speech on the Interpretation of the Second Vatican Council." *Origins* 42 (February 28, 2013): 601–8.

————. *Theology of the Liturgy: The Sacramental Foundation of Christian Existence*. Vol. 11 of *Joseph Ratzinger: Collected Works*. Edited by Michael J. Miller. Translated by John Saward, Kenneth Baker, Henry Taylor et al. San Francisco: Ignatius Press, 2014.

Rodríguez, Rafael. *Structuring Early Christian Memory: Jesus in Tradition, Performance, and Text*. London: T and T Clark, 2010.

Rosenberg, Randall S. "Christ's Human Knowledge: A Conversation with Lonergan and Balthasar." *Theological Studies* 71, no. 4 (2010): 817–45.

Ross, Ellen M. *The Grief of God: Images of the Suffering Jesus in Late Medieval England*. New York: Oxford University Press, 1997.

Roukema, Riemer. *Jesus, Gnosis and Dogma*. New York: T and T Clark, 2010.

Ruddy, Christopher. "'For the Many': The Vicarious-Representative Heart of Joseph Ratzinger's Theology." *Theological Studies* 75, no. 3 (2014): 564–84.

————. "'Smaller but Purer'? Joseph Ratzinger on the 'Little Flock' and Vicarious Representation." *Nova et Vetera*, English edition, 13, no. 3 (2015): 713–41.

Sauer, Hanjo. "Von den 'Quellen der Offenbarung' zur 'Offenbarung selbst.'" In *Glaube im Prozess: Christsein nach dem II. Vatikanum*, edited by E. Klinger and K. Wittstadt, 514–45. Freiburg: Herder, 1984.

————. *Erfahrung und Glaube: Die Begründung des pastoralen Prinzips durch die Offenbarungskonstitution des II. Vatikanischen Konzils*. Frankfurt am Main: Peter Lang, 1993.

Schaefer, Mary. "Twelfth Century Latin Commentaries on the Mass: Christological and Ecclesiological Dimensions." PhD dissertation, University of Notre Dame, 1983.

Schenk, Richard. "*Officium signa temporum perscrutandi:* New Encounters of Gospel and Culture in the Context of the New Evangelization." In *Scrutinizing the Signs of the Times in the Light of the Gospel*, edited by J. Verstraeten, 167–203. Bibliotheca Ephemeridum Theologicarum Lovaniensium 208. Leuven: Peeters, 2007.

Schumacher, Michele M. *A Trinitarian Anthropology: Adrienne von Speyr and Hans Urs von Balthasar in Dialogue with Thomas Aquinas*. Washington, D.C.: The Catholic University of America Press, 2014.

Schnackenburg, Rudolph. *Gottes Herrschaft und Reich*. Freiburg: Herder, 1958. English translation: *God's Rule and Kingdom*. Translated by John Murray. New York: Herder and Herder, 1965.

————. *The Gospel of Matthew*. Translated by Robert R. Barr. Grand Rapids, Mich.: Eerdmans, 2002.

Schwager, Raymund. *Jesus in the Drama of Salvation: Toward a Biblical Doctrine of Redemption*. Translated by James G. Williams. New York: Crossroads, 1999.

Senior, Donald. *Matthew*. Nashville, Tenn.: Abingdon Press, 1998.

Sherwin, Michael. "Eulogie pour le P. Servais Pinckaers, o.p." *Nova et Vetera*, 84, no. 2 (2009): 133–36.

Slater, Thomas. *A Manual of Moral Theology for English Speaking Countries*. Vol. 1. New York: Benzinger Brothers, 1925.

Southern, R. W. *The Making of the Middle Ages*. New Haven, Conn.: Yale University, 1953.

Staudt, R. Jared. "For the Holy Trinity: The Mission of Christ and the Order of His Human Soul." *Angelicum* 91, no. 3 (2014): 569–606.

Suenens, Léon-Josef. "Aux origines du Concile Vatican II." *Nouvelle revue théologique* 107 (1985): 3–21.

Testaferri, Francesco. "Lo 'Schema Rahner-Ratzinger': *De revelatione Dei et hominis in Jesu Christo facta* e la discussione sul *De fontibus* all'inizio del Concilio Vaticano II." *Lateranum* 80 (2012): 29–60.

Theresa of Liseux. *Story of a Soul: The Autobiography of St. Therese of Lisieux*. 3rd ed. Translated by John Clarke. Washington, D.C.: ICS Publications, 1996.

Thomas Aquinas. *Summa Theologica*. Translated by English Dominican Province. New York: Benzinger Brothers, 1947.

———. *Commentary on the Gospel of St. Matthew*. Translated by Paul M. Kimball. Camillus, N.Y.: Dolorosa Press, 2012.

Torrell, Jean-Pierre. *Christ and Spirituality in St. Thomas Aquinas*. Translated by Bernhard Blankenhorn. Washington, D.C.: The Catholic University of America Press.

Trippen, Norbert. *Joseph Kardinal Frings (1887–1978)*. 2 vols. Paderborn: Ferdinand Schöningh, 2003–2005.

Vacant, A. et al., eds. *Dictionnaire de théologie catholique*. 15 vols., plus indexes. Paris. Letouzey et Ané, 1902–1972.

Valls, Carmen Aparicio and Dotolo Carmelo and Gianluigi Pasquale, eds. *Sapere teologico e unità della fede: Studi in onore del Prof. Jared Wicks*. Roma: Editrice Pontificia Università Gregoriana, 2004.

Vanstone, W. H. *The Stature of Waiting*. New York: Morehouse, 1982.

Viller, Marcel, and Charles Baumgartner, et al., eds. *Dictionnaire de Spiritualité: ascétique et mystique, doctrine et histoire*. 17 vols. Paris: G. Beauchesne, 1932–1995.

Voegelin, Eric. *Glaubhaft ist Nur Liebe*. Einsiedeln: Johannes Verlag, 1963.

———. *Heart of the World*. San Francisco: Ignatius Press, 1979.

———. *Dare We Hope "That All Men Be Saved?" with a short discourse on Hell*. Translated by David Kipp and Lothar Krauth. San Francisco: Ignatius Press, 1988.

———. *Published Essays, 1966–1985*. Vol. 12 of *The Collected Works of Eric Voegelin*. Edited by Ellis Sandoz. Baton Rouge: Louisiana State University Press, 1990.

Vorgrimler, Herbert, ed. *Commentary on the Documents of Vatican II*. 5 vols. New York: Herder and Herder, 1967–1969.

Vos, Geerhardus. *The Teaching of Jesus concerning the Kingdom of God*. New York: American Tract Society, 1903.

Wales, Jordan Joseph. "Contemplative Compassion: Gregory the Great's Development of Augustine's Views on Love of Neighbor and Likeness to God." *Augustinian Studies* 49, no. 2 (2018): 199–219.

Wassilowsky, Günther. *Universales Heilssakrament Kirche: Karl Rahners Beitrag zur Ekklesiologie des II. Vatikanums*. Innsbruck-Vienna: Tyrolia, 2001.

Wawrykow, Joseph. "Jesus in the Moral Theology of Thomas Aquinas." *Journal of Medieval and Early Modern Studies* 42, no. 1 (2012): 13–33.

Weinandy, Thomas. *Does God Change? The Word's Becoming in the Incarnation.* Still River, Mass.: St. Bede's Publications, 1985.

———. *Jesus the Christ.* Huntington, Ind.: Our Sunday Visitor Press, 2003. Reprinted by Ex Fontibus Company, 2017.

———. *Jesus: Essays in Christology.* Ave Maria, Fla.: Sapientia Press, 2014.

Westerholm, Stephen, ed. *The Blackwell Companion to Paul.* Oxford: Blackwell, 2011.

Wicks, Jared. "Peter Smulders and Dei Verbum: 1. A Consultation on the Eve of Vatican II." *Gregorianum* 82, no. 2 (2001): 241–97.

———. "Six Texts by Prof. Joseph Ratzinger as *peritus* before and during Vatican Council II." *Gregorianum* 89, no. 2 (2008): 233–311.

———. "Vicarious Representation." *Letter and Spirit* 7 (2011): 209–20.

———. *Investigating Vatican II: Its Theologians, Ecumenical Turn, and Biblical Commitment.* Washington, D.C.: The Catholic University of America Press, 2018.

Wilkins, Jeremy D. "Trinitarian Missions and the Order of Grace." In *Philosophy and Theology in the Long Middle Ages: Essays in Honor of Professor Stephen Brown,* edited by Kent Emery, Russel L. Friedman, and Andreas Speer, 689–708. Leiden: E. J. Brill, 2011.

———. "Why Two Divine Missions? Development in Augustine, Aquinas, and Lonergan." *International Theological Quarterly* 77, no. 1 (2012): 37–66.

Williams, George H. "Mercy in the Grounding of a Non-Elitist Ecological Ethic." In *Festschrift in Honor of Charles Speel,* edited by Thomas J. Sienkewicz and James E. Betts, 24–51. Monmouth, Ill.: Monmouth College, 1997.

Winter, Gibson. *Elements for a Social Ethic.* New York: Macmillan, 1968.

Wright, G. Ernest. *God Who Acts: Biblical Theology as Recital.* London: SCM, 1952.

Yenson, Mark L. *Existence as Prayer: The Consciousness of Christ in the Theology of Hans Urs von Balthasar.* American University Studies, Series VII: Theology and Religion, Vol. 330. New York: Peter Lang, 2014.

Zizioulas, John. "Truth and Communion." In *Being as Communion,* 67–122. Crestwood, N.Y.: St. Vladimir's Seminary Press, 1985.

Magisterial and Ecclesiastical Documents

Acta apostolicae sedis. Rome: Typis Polyglottis Vaticanis, 1909 to present.

Acta synodalia sacrosancti concilii Vaticani secundi. 5 vols. Vatican City: Typis polyglottis Vaticanis, 1970–1978.

Benedict XVI. "The Regensburg Address." September 12, 2006. *Acta Apostolicae Sedis* 98 (2006): 728–39. Also available at https://w2.vatican.va/content/benedict-xvi/en/speeches/2006/september/documents/ hf_ben-xvi_spe_20060912_university-regensburg.html.

———. *Anglicanorum coetibus.* Apostolic Constitution. November 4, 2009. http://www.vatican.va/content/benedict-xvi/en/apost_constitutions/documents/hf_ben-xvi_apc_20091104_anglicanorum-coetibus.html.

———. *Address to Parish Priests and Clergy of Rome.* February 14, 2013. https://w2.vatican.va/content/benedict-xvi/en/speeches/2013/february/documents/hf_ben-xvi_spe_20130214_clero-roma.html.

Catechism of the Catholic Church: With Modifications from the Editio Typica. New York: Doubleday, 1995.

Congregation for Catholic Education. "Instruction on the Study of the Fathers of the Church in the Formation of Priests." *Origins* 19, no. 34 (1990): 550–61.

Congregation for the Doctrine of the Faith. *Dominus Iesus.* Declaration. August 6, 2000. http://www.vatican.va/roman_curia/congregations/cfaith/documents/rc_con_cfaith_doc_20000806_dominus-iesus_en.html.

———. Doctrinal Note. *On Some Aspects of Evangelization.* October 6, 2007. http://www.vatican.va/roman_curia/congregations/cfaith/documents/rc_con_cfaith_doc_20071203_nota-evangelizzazione_en.html.

Decrees of the Ecumenical Councils. Edited by Norman Tanner. 2 vols. London: Sheed and Ward and Georgetown University Press, 1990.

Denzinger, Heinrich, ed. *Compendium of Creeds, Definitions, and Declarations on Matters of Faith and Morals.* Edited by P. Hünerman. Edited for the English edition by R. Fastiggi and A. Englund Nash. 43rd ed. San Francisco: Ignatius Press, 2012.

International Theological Commission. "The Consciousness of Christ Concerning Himself and His Mission." 1985. http://www.vatican.va/roman_curia/congregations/cfaith/cti_documents/rc_cti_1985_coscienza-gesu_en.html.

John Paul II. *Redemptoris missio.* Encyclical Letter. December 7, 1990. http://w2.vatican.va/content/john-paul-ii/en/encyclicals/documents/hf_jp-ii_enc_07121990_redemptoris-missio.html.

———. *Veritatis splendor.* Encyclical Letter. August 6, 1993. http://www.vatican.va/content/john-paul-ii/en/encyclicals/documents/hf_jp-ii_enc_06081993_veritatis-splendor.html.

Paul VI. *Evangelii nuntiandi.* Apostolic Exhortation. December 8, 1975. http://www.vatican.va/content/paul-vi/en/apost_exhortations/documents/hf_p-vi_exh_19751208_evangelii-nuntiandi.html.

CONTRIBUTORS

KHALED ANATOLIOS is a priest of the Melkite Greek Catholic Church and professor of theology at the University of Notre Dame, and has taught at Boston College. He specializes in the Christological and Trinitarian theology of the patristic period. He is author of *Retrieving Nicaea: The Development and Meaning of Trinitarian Doctrine* (2011); and *Athanasius* (2004).

RYAN CONNORS is a priest of the Diocese of Providence. He is professor of moral theology at St. John's Seminary, Brighton, and completed a doctorate at the Pontifical University of St. Thomas Aquinas in 2018. His areas of research include the history of moral theology, St. Thomas Aquinas's treatment of the virtues, and moral cooperation with evil.

BOYD TAYLOR COOLMAN is professor of theology at Boston College specializing in medieval theology and, in particular, Victorine theology. He is author of *The Theology of Hugh of St. Victor: An Interpretation* (2013); and, most recently, *Knowledge, Love, and Ecstasy in the Theology of Thomas Gallus* (2017).

BRIAN E. DALEY, SJ, is a Jesuit priest and Catherine F. Huisking Professor of Theology at the University of Notre Dame. He specializes in the study of the early church, particularly the development of Christian doctrine from the fourth to the eighth centuries. He is author of *Gregory of Nazianzus* (2006); *Light on the Mountain: Greek Patristic and Byzantine Homilies on the Transfiguration of the Lord* (2013); and, most recently, *God Visible: Patristic Christology Reconsidered* (2018). He was awarded the Ratzinger Prize in 2013.

ANGELA FRANKS is professor of theology at St. John's Seminary, Boston. She completed her doctorate at Boston College. She specializes in the theology of the body, the New Evangelization, Trinity, Christology, and the thought of John Paul II and Hans Urs von Balthasar. She is author of *Contraception and Catholicism: What the Church Teaches and Why* (2013).

THOMAS G. GUARINO is a priest of the Archdiocese of Newark and professor of systematic theology at Seton Hall University and Immaculate Conception Seminary School of Theology. He is author of *Foundations of Systematic Theology* (2005); *Vattimo and Theology* (2009); and, more recently, *Vincent of Lérins and the Development of Christian Doctrine* (2013).

FREDERICK LAWRENCE is professor of theology at Boston College and a leading specialist in the thought of Bernard Lonergan and the philosophy of hermeneutics. His collection of essays has been published as *The Fragility of Consciousness: Faith, Reason, and the Human Good* (2017).

MATTHEW LEVERING holds the James N. and Mary D. Perry, Jr., Chair of Theology at the University of Saint Mary of the Lake, Mundelein, Illinois. He completed his doctorate at Boston College and is author of monographs including *Scripture and Metaphysics: Aquinas and the Renewal of Trinitarian Theology* (2004); and *Predestination: Biblical and Theological Paths* (2011). He is also editor of numerous books and serves as coeditor for *Nova et Vetera* and the *International Journal of Systematic Theology*.

ANDREW MESZAROS is lecturer in systematic theology at the Pontifical University, St. Patrick's College, Maynooth, Ireland. A graduate of Boston College, he is author of *The Prophetic Church: History and Doctrinal Development in John Henry Newman and Yves Congar* (2016).

GERALD O'COLLINS, SJ, is a Jesuit priest and theologian. He taught fundamental and systematic theology at the Pontifical Gregorian University (1973–2006), where he was also dean of the theology faculty from 1985 to 1991. He is currently an adjunct professor at the Australian Catholic University and a research fellow of the University of Divinity, Melbourne. He has authored or coauthored innumerable articles and seventy-six books, most recently including a trilogy published by Oxford University Press: *Revelation: Towards a Christian Interpretation of God's Self-Revelation in Jesus Christ* (2016); *Inspiration: Towards a Christian Interpretation of Biblical Inspiration* (2018); and *Tradition: Understanding Christian Tradition* (2018).

NATHANIEL PETERS is director of the Morningside Institute and a lecturer at Columbia University. He completed his doctorate at Boston College and is currently working on an English translation of letters of William of Saint-Thierry.

CHRISTOPHER RUDDY is associate professor of historical and systematic theology at the Catholic University of America. He is author of *The Local Church: Tillard and the Future of Catholic Ecclesiology* (2006); and *Tested in Every Way: The Catholic Priesthood in Today's Church* (2006). He has also taught at the University of St. Thomas (St. Paul), St. John's University (Collegeville), and the College of St. Benedict (St. Joseph), all in Minnesota.

ANDREW SALZMANN is associate professor at Benedictine College in Atchison, Kansas. He completed his doctorate at Boston College. His research focuses on Augustine and his reception in the twelfth and twentieth centuries, with special attention to anthropology and pneumatology.

THOMAS WEINANDY, OFM, CAP, is a member of the Congregation for the Doctrine of the Faith's International Theological Commission. A prolific author, he has written or edited seventeen books, including *Does God Suffer?* (2000); *The Father's Spirit of Sonship: Reconceiving the Trinity* (2011); *Jesus: Essays in Christology* (2014); and *Jesus Becoming Jesus: A Theological Interpretation of the Synoptic Gospels* (2018). He has taught at a number of colleges and universities, including Greyfriars Hall, Oxford; the Dominican House of Studies, Washington, D.C.; and the Gregorian University, Rome. Pope Francis conferred upon him the Pro Ecclesia et Pontificae Award in 2013.

JARED WICKS, SJ, is a Jesuit priest and theologian. He taught fundamental theology at the Gregorian University, Rome (1979–2004), serving as dean of the theology faculty from 1991 to 1997, and later was scholar in residence at the Pontifical College Josephinum in Columbus, Ohio (2011–2017). He was a member of Lutheran-Catholic ecumenical commissions for dialogues internationally (1986–2006) and in the United States (2005–2019). His books include *Luther and His Spiritual Legacy* (1983; reprint, 2016); *Luther's Reform: Studies on Conversion and the Church* (1992; reprint, 2019); *Doing Theology* (2009); and, most recently, *Investigating Vatican II: Its Theologians, Ecumenical Turn, and Biblical Commitment* (2018).

INDEX

Abraham, 39, 43, 44, 48, 121n25, 131, 143

Adam, 39–40, 72, 156; new or second, 72, 127, 182, 262, 306

adoration. *See* worship

Aelred of Rievaulx, 213

affectivity, 20, 85, 154–58, 170, 202, 205–28

aggiornamento, 3, 55

Amoris Laetitia, 23

analogy, 55, 60–63, 73, 76, 77, 95–108, 154–56, 169–170, 273, 277n20, 289, 291, 294, 297–98; *analogia entis*, 54, 81, 285–89, 291

anointing, 59, 188, 262–71, 284

anthropology, 44, 153, 156, 169, 175, 182–83, 257, 296n115

Apollonarius, 302–3

Apostle/apostolic, 15, 24, 30, 37–40, 50, 83, 121, 127, 196, 208, 212, 227n127, 237, 268, 284, 304

Aquinas, Thomas, 37, 53, 55, 65, 73, 76, 95, 96–99, 105–6, 113, 130, 134, 136, 139, 146–49, 191–92, 194n19, 196–201, 214n80, 218n98, 276–96

Aristotle, 55, 73, 87, 93

Arius, 302–3

Arrupe, Pedro, 6

Athanasius, 87n11, 304

atonement, 133, 158, 256–61

Augustine, 42, 59, 62, 68, 71–72, 93n31, 111–17, 122–29, 149, 231–51, 256, 269, 277n20

Aurelius, 234–36

Balthasar, Hans Urs von, 53–54, 60, 64–65, 67n40, 74–75, 129n46, 131, 253, 255, 270n73, 272–99

baptism: Christ's, 90–93, 133–34, 138–40, 264–67; the Christian's, 24, 133, 162, 165, 170, 200; with fire, 134–40

Barth, Karl, 53–55, 64, 253–54, 267

beatific vision or knowledge, 55–58, 281n41

beatitudes, 199

beauty, 22, 39, 43, 111–29, 187–88, 292

Benedict XVI, 9n27, 19n55, 29–51, 77–78, 92, 102n23, 103n27, 173–88, 208n61, 274, 280n37, 290n87, 297n118, 298n120, 304

Bernard of Clairvaux, 212

Bible. *See* Scripture

blasphemy, 84, 147–50

Boethius, 295–96

Bonaventure, 37, 46

Calvin, John, 130–39, 148–49

Cantalamessa, Raniero, 262n46, 266, 268

caritas. See love

casuistry, 191–203

Chalcedon, 54n5, 300–311

Christomonism, 253–54, 262–70

Church: birthed by Christ, 126–27; as bride, 10; as Christ's body, 40, 50, 75–76, 83, 100–101, 104, 153–71, 187–88, 239, 246, 256, 262n45, 268n68, 287, 289, 290, 293n103, 306–7, 310; and liturgy, 174, 184, 187–88; and mission, 290–94; as People, 43, 143, 239, 246; as presented at Vatican II, 100–106; and proclamation, 38–40; in relation to Gnosticism, 83–84, 91, 94; in relation to the Son and the Spirit, 255–56, 268, 269n69; in relation to theology, 11–15; as temple, 187; time of, 287–89

335

communion: ecclesial, 78, 83–84, 179, 309–10; eucharistic, 114, 116–17, 167, 306–9; in and with God, 29, 45, 49, 54, 93, 157, 167–68, 170, 180, 270, 274, 288

compassion, 120, 205–28

Congar, Yves, 31–34, 41–45, 59, 95, 98, 100n15, 105–7

congratulation, 205–28

courage. *See* fortitude

covenant, 17, 113–17, 141n35, 152n65, 188

creation, 4, 30, 38–46, 51, 53, 55n7, 57, 59n13, 63, 69, 78–94, 99, 103, 126, 136n20, 142, 154–57, 161, 180, 182–83, 221–24, 239–41, 254, 269, 277, 285, 288n75, 289; new, 70, 178, 255, 261, 272, 308

Cyril of Alexandria, 304

Daniélou, Jean, 31, 45

Dei Verbum, 3, 4, 8, 15, 17–18, 45, 55, 103–4, 255

deification, 12, 103, 159, 168, 178

discernment, 22–24, 66, 81, 89

discipleship, 17–20, 23–24, 54, 98, 138, 181, 195, 200, 209, 250, 268, 270, 288–89, 291–92

divinization. *See* deification

dogma, 7, 10, 16–18, 65, 190, 253, 301

Dominus Iesus, 7–10, 104, 107–8, 189–91, 255

Dupuis, Jacques, 9n27, 253–56

ecumenism, 36n20, 107

eschatology, 38, 39–42, 48, 54–55, 58, 101, 116, 138, 140, 145, 149, 152, 159, 162, 266, 280–81, 306–309

Eucharist. *See* sacraments

evil, 62, 67–72, 123, 136, 140, 175, 194, 213–14, 218n98, 221, 226

Father: Church's dependency on, 187; reconciliation with, 41n27, 46, 67, 250, 268; relation to the Son and the Spirit, 18, 38–39, 45, 58–59, 63, 72–75, 85–94, 124, 131–33, 146–47, 151–52, 154–58, 162–65, 167–70, 174–75, 180–84, 188, 208, 252–55, 267n61, 270–71, 273, 277–98, 302–8; who raises his Son, 73, 101

forgiveness, 48, 72–75, 114, 115, 118–21, 127, 140, 147–51, 157–60, 165, 169, 210, 226n124, 239, 250, 259, 266, 305, 308

fortitude, 113, 117, 158, 193–94, 203, 212–13, 268

freedom, 46–47, 62, 65, 71–76, 144, 147, 152, 156, 166, 168, 182n40, 183, 192, 203, 231, 274–75, 280, 282–84, 292, 298

friendship, 17, 18, 53, 61, 73, 157–58, 180, 195, 247

Gaudium et Spes, 4, 45, 100–102, 183, 194, 255

gift: divine, 38, 40, 42n30, 47, 49, 54–55, 57–58, 60, 62, 65–66, 84, 113, 117, 123, 155, 163, 167, 179, 182, 184, 223, 239, 270, 282, 294; of Holy Spirit, 67, 75, 125, 135, 139–40, 156–57, 164, 199–202, 269

Girard, René, 71, 75

Gnosticism, 37, 78–94

grace, 11, 13, 23, 39–49, 54n5, 57–58, 66, 71–72, 76, 90, 98, 148–49, 155, 159, 161, 186, 192–201, 226, 231, 254, 269–70, 298

Gregory of Nyssa, 296

Gregory the Great, 127, 226n124

Haight, Roger, 253n2, 254

healing, 6, 118–19, 121, 127, 239, 266–67

holiness, 1, 18, 58, 72, 100, 103, 121, 130, 139, 143, 148, 182, 187, 198, 256, 260, 294, 297, 305–6

Hugh of St. Victor, 205–28

hypostatic union, 38, 48–49, 159, 280, 303–4

imagination, 2, 13, 16–25, 30, 56, 203, 253, 305–6, 310–11

Imbelli, Robert, 1–25, 100–108, 151, 187–88, 189–91, 203–4, 253–71, 272–73, 299, 300–301, 304–11

Irenaeus of Lyon, 6n15, 17, 48n42, 77–94, 176, 250, 265–68

Isaac of Stella, 153–70

Israel, 38, 41, 43n32, 49, 143, 156, 176–80, 186, 250, 263, 270

Jerome, 134–35, 145–48, 216n93

John Chrysostom, 134–35, 138–40, 144–46

John Paul II, 10, 183, 189–204, 274n10, 293–96, 299

judgment: divine (last), 75, 101, 136, 158, 247, 308; epistemic, 52, 61–66, 68–69, 73, 202, 248, 257–59

Kingdom, 163, 201, 260–62; as eschatological, 30, 38–43, 48, 51; as God's presence, 140–45, 152; in relation to Christ and the Spirit, 263–71; in relation to Christ's death, 115–18

koinonia. See communion

Last Supper, 113–18, 124–25, 127, 129, 163, 181

laxism (moral), 192–93

Leo the Great, 127

liturgy, 4n12, 13–14, 17, 22, 36n20, 93, 103, 112, 166–67, 173–88, 232, 249, 251, 253, 271, 288, 301, 308

Lonergan, Bernard, 52–76

love, 6n15, 155–57, 169, 177–79, 181–82, 202, 222–24, 239–40, 246–50, 260–61, 270; *caritas*, 53, 226–27; divine, 12, 13, 38–43, 47–48, 53–76, 82–84, 125, 128, 146, 154, 169–70, 184, 284, 294, 298, 307; of self, 20, 68

de Lubac, Henri, 3, 17–18, 47, 161n31, 197n32

Lumen Gentium, 3–4, 14, 96–99, 104, 106, 127n41

magnanimity, 222

marriage, 13, 61, 158, 194, 201 287n70; nuptial fused with maternal, 227; wedding feast, 30, 38, 49–50, 159

Mary, 13, 39, 44, 48, 98–100, 103, 127, 165, 182, 287n70, 292n98, 302

McCabe, Herbert, 53, 55, 57, 59, 76, 180n30, 181n31

McDonnell, Kilian, 265, 267, 268

mediation, 13, 16, 20, 64, 67, 74–75, 257; Christ as mediator, 3, 14, 45n36, 46, 55–58, 100, 130, 158, 183, 259, 261; Holy Spirit as mediator, 284; Mary as mediatrix, 97–100; vicarious representation, 49n43, 177–79

mercy, 49n43, 149–50, 166, 188, 206–8, 215–19, 247–48, 266

mission. *See* Trinity

Montini, G. B. *See* Paul VI

Moses, 57, 123, 126, 131, 143, 145–46, 166, 180, 237, 251

natural law, 194, 201

Nestorius, 303

Newman, John Henry, 2, 16, 19–21, 24n71, 60

obedience, 23–24, 40, 43, 54, 107, 288, 292–93; Christ's, 138–40, 266–67, 179, 283–86

Optatam totius, 191, 193

orthodoxy, 90, 177, 179, 184, 186

paschal mystery, 60, 72–75, 103, 119, 126n39, 135, 149, 151, 154, 159, 169–70, 204, 206, 251, 253, 255n8, 283n50, 290, 306; ascension, 14, 126n39, 161, 162, 164, 168–69, 280, 307–8; passion and death, 48, 54, 56, 111–29, 151, 163–64, 166, 168, 181, 210, 246, 262, 267, 283n50; resurrection, 56, 73, 75, 116, 121, 187, 191, 239, 247, 287, 290

Paul, 23–24, 41, 58–59, 70, 73, 103n25, 112, 114–15, 127, 130–33, 151, 164, 183, 205–12, 226–27, 237, 241, 243–44, 250, 256, 290, 299

Paul VI, 3, 32, 98n10, 100n15, 101n20, 103n27, 293

personhood, 42n29, 262, 270, 272–99

Philips, Gérard, 96–100

Plato, 87; neoplatonic, 154

pneumatology, 8n23, 161, 252–71

prayer, 37, 43n32, 66, 120–21, 143, 163, 174–75, 180–82, 220, 250, 252, 270–71, 280, 283–84, 289, 292, 294, 299n126

predestination, 148

Presbyterorum Ordinis, 105–6

pride, 222–24, 247

priesthood, 147, 234–35, 269, 276, 287n70; Christ's, 163–64, 168–69, 177n14, 306; participation in Christ's, 96–100, 105–6, 166–67, 187–88

Rahner, Karl, 30–36, 42n29, 44–45, 50n47, 60, 98, 101n18, 264n50, 277n24

Ratzinger, Joseph. *See* Benedict XVI

recapitulation, 39, 44, 54, 67, 116, 141n35, 169, 307–8

reconciliation. *See* forgiveness

ressourcement, 10–16, 78, 103

resurrection. *See* paschal mystery

revelation, 3–4, 8–18, 75, 83, 88–90, 102, 131, 144, 154, 194, 255, 295; as communication and communion, 52–59, 64–67, 76, 250; in relation to catechesis, 241–43; Vatican II's doctrine of, 29–51, 102–7, 254–55

rigorism (moral), 192

Royce, Josiah, 256–63; on community, 259; on interpretation, 257; as theologian, 263; on will, 258; on work of Christ, 260-61; on work of Holy Spirit, 260

sacraments: in general, 11, 13–14, 22, 48, 103, 125, 160–61, 164, 184, 188, 288, 310; of baptism, 165; of confirmation/chrismation, 268–71; of the Eucharist, 22, 113–17, 153–70, 178, 186, 188, 235, 251, 273, 299, 301, 306–10; of reconciliation: 74, 159

sacrifice: Christ's death as, 47, 113–17, 164–69; Eucharist as, 164–69; as love, 177–78

Sacrosanctum Concilium, 3, 175–76, 249, 255

saints: as witness and exemplars, 187, 203; communion of, 99–100, 287n70

salvation, 14–15, 23, 64, 71, 91, 132, 140, 179, 184, 221, 235, 247, 281, 291, 293; in Christ, 2–12, 23, 29, 37–44, 46–48, 50, 104, 116–18, 123, 126, 132, 154, 166, 190, 204, 249, 262, 289, 301–11; history, 44, 178, 191, 256; in the Spirit, 58–60, 132, 148, 157, 162, 164, 262

sanctity. *See* holiness

Scripture: as containing Christ, 188; as containing true knowledge, 83–85; as enlightening, 49; interpretation of, 234–43, 249–251; as source in tradition/theology, 15–16, 33, 36–37, 50n47, 231–51; and spiritual life, 20

Second Vatican Council, 1, 9, 15, 127, 174, 190, 255, 293, 309–10; Christocentric vision of, 3–5, 18, 254–55; participation and analogy at, 95–108; Ratzinger and, 29–51, 175, 183. *See also Council documents by name*

sin: Christ's victory over and forgiveness of, 38–42, 48, 72, 154, 217, 239, 268, 287; in general, 45, 47, 67–72, 74, 182, 188, 286–90; the unpardonable, 148–50

Spirit: animating the Church, 37–38, 40, 161–70; descent of, 121; as love, 63; mission of, 203, 276–86; in relation to the Son, 9, 18, 89, 125, 130–52, 191, 253–71, 293–94, 302, 305–11; role in salvation, 55–60, 67, 75, 156–58, 200–202; and Scripture, 243; sin against, 147–50; of truth, 48, 91 93, 194

suffering: according to the Gnostics, 85; Christ's, 56, 72–75, 111–29, 262n45; our response to or co-suffering, 205–28; relation to sin, 69, 264, 289

testimony: as criterion for rationality, 80–94; to the Gospel, 15, 37, 40, 42, 50, 131, 187–88, 249, 310.

Transfiguration, 134, 190, 264, 309

transformation, 12, 17, 23–25, 47, 58, 74–75, 128, 178–81, 187, 192, 195–204

Trinity, 7–8, 12, 93, 130–31, 238–39, 252–54, 270–71; analogy for, 62–65, economic, 46, 90–92, 264, 278, 283, 286, 288, 293–98, 306–7; procession and mission, 276–79; in relation to Christology, 130–52, 273; in relation to the Church, 153–70; trinitarian notions (filiation, generation, paternity, spiration), 63, 93, 271, 273, 277–79, 281, 283, 285, 288; Word/logos, 4–5, 38–51, 53, 57–60, 63, 76, 78, 89–91, 93, 131, 139, 154–56, 159, 161, 183, 194, 239, 249, 261, 264–68, 282, 294, 303, 307

Vatican II. *See* Second Vatican Council

Veritatis splendor, 189–204

virtues: in moral theology, 191–202

witness. *See* testimony

Wojtyła, Karol. *See* John Paul II

Word (eternal logos). *See* Trinity

worship, 13, 66, 93, 137–40, 143, 173–88